Microsoft
Visual Basic 5
The Cram Sheet

This Cram Sheet contains the distilled, key facts about Microsoft Visual Basic 5. Review this information last thing before you enter the test room, paying special attention to those areas where you feel you need the most review. You can transfer any of these facts from your head onto a blank sheet of paper before beginning the exam.

VARIABLES AND PROCEDURES

1. Know the data types and important attributes.

2. **Erase** initializes fixed-size arrays, reclaims memory from dynamic arrays. **Array (arg1, arg2)** creates array of variants.

3. Know how to declare variable and procedure scope and lifetime. Know that **Friend** procedures are in class modules only and are visible to all modules but not to the controlling class.

4. Know this about procedure arguments: **ByVal** arguments passed by value, **ByRef** arguments passed by address; use **Any** instead of data type to suppress type checking; **ParamArray**—last argument to a procedure—creates optional array of variants.

5. Know the meaning and use of these special values:

   - **Null** Value of **Variant** containing no valid data (use **IsNull** to test for **Null**)
   - **Empty** Value of uninitialized **Variant**
   - **Nothing** Value of an object variable not referencing an object
   - **vbNullString** Use to pass a zero value string to an external module

CLASSES AND OBJECTS

6. **For Each** iterates through properties of an object and enumerates items in a collection.

7. Early binding resolves objects at compile time; late binding resolves objects at runtime.

8. Define events with **Event** statement; use **RaiseEvent** to invoke custom events.

9. Expose properties via **Property Let**, **Property Get**, and **Property Set**.

10. Container classes obtain all public properties and procedures of child classes via **Implements**.

11. The methods of collections are: **Add**, **Item**, and **Remove**. The property of collections is **Count**. VB has built-in collections such as **Forms** and **Controls**.

39. Know the following about the InternetTransfer control, which implements HTTP and FTP:

- Important methods: **OpenURL** (asynchronous) and **Execute** (synchronous) open or retrieve files (with **OpenURL**, specify a URL address and whether to receive the file as a string or as an array of type **Byte**). See Tables 12.1 and 12.2 on page 310 for supported commands of the two methods.

HELP

40. What's This Help is implemented by setting the **WhatsThisHelp** property of a form to **True**. Set the **WhatsThisHelpID** property of controls to a Help context ID.

41. Use the StatusBar control and its **Panel** objects to display short help, date, time, and so on.

42. Use the CommonDialog control for flexible help display. Use the **HelpContext, HelpCommand, HelpKey**, and **HelpFile** properties with the **ShowHelp** method.

TESTING

43. Know these tools: Watch window: monitor specified variables or expressions, cause execution to break on specific conditions, alter the value of variables; Locals window: monitor all variables currently in scope; Immediate window: execute statements or capture debugging output; Call Stack window: view procedure calls started but not completed.

44. Use the **Debug** object's **Print** method to send output to the Immediate window and **Assert** method to evaluate conditions (breaks if condition is false). **Debug** statements are removed at compilation.

COMPILING AND DISTRIBUTING

45. VB5 programs are 32-bit only. Know this about compiling:

- Valid targets: Standard EXE; ActiveX EXE; ActiveX DLL; ActiveX control.
- Compile to p-code (pseudo-code) or native code (machine language).
- Compile optimization options: Fast code, small code, or no optimization.
- Programs consist of one or more projects. Multiple projects are saved as groups. A program can have only one **Sub Main**.

46. Use the Setup Wizard to create a distribution setup program or Internet download setup.

47. Install directories are done via macros such as $(WinSysPath) and $(AppPath).

48. Internet downloads are created in CAB files. The primary CAB file contains an ActiveX component and an INF file. You can link to Microsoft for secondary CAB files containing other needed components. Microsoft digitally signs these files and certifies them as safe.

49. As part of the setup process for ActiveX components, you are required to certify them as safe.

50. Specify "Require License" for ActiveX controls on the Project Properties.mization.

- Programs consist of one or more projects. Multiple projects are saved as groups. A program can have only one **Sub Main**.

ertification
nsider™ Press

31. There are five types of **Recordset** objects:
    - **Table-type** All columns in a single table, updateable
    - **Dynamic-type** One or more columns from multiple tables from a query, updateable
    - **Dynaset-type** One or more columns from multiple tables, forward/backward scrolling, updateable
    - **Snapshot-type** Normally not updateable, most useful for reporting
    - **Forward-only-type** Same as snapshot, but can scroll forward only

32. Scroll through a recordset with **MoveFirst**, **MoveLast**, **MoveNext**, and **MovePrior**. Determine record count by **MoveLast** and use **RecordCount**. **AbsolutePosition** is record number. **AddNew** method adds a new record. **Delete** removes a record. **Edit** edits current record. **Update** saves changes.

33. Know this about the **QueryDef** object, which is a query of the database:
    - Use **Execute** method to run the query, **Cancel** method to halt a running asynchronous query.
    - **RecordsAffected** contains number of records altered. **MaxRecords** restricts number of rows.

34. Data controls represent a recordset. The **DataSource** property of data aware controls associates the control with the Data control. Bind to a column in the recordset with the **DataField** property.

35. Use **Validate** event to edit changes to a record. Use **DataChanged** property of data bound controls to determine what data was changed. Use **Error** event to test for database errors.

ACTIVEX

36. Know this about ActiveX technology:
    - COM stands for Component Object Model; DCOM stands for Distributed Component Object Model.
    - In-process server runs in the same memory space as the application using it (example: ActiveX DLL). Out-of-process server runs in its own memory space (example: ActiveX EXE). Out-of-process servers are invoked asynchronously.
    - ActiveX documents are programs that run inside of a browser.
    - When a UserControl is placed on a Form, PictureBox, or Frame, it derives some of its properties from the container via the **Extender** object (not available during the **Initialize** event). All VB controls have a **Container** property referencing the container upon which the control is placed.
    - Save and read settings via the **ReadProperties** and **WriteProperties** methods of the **PropertyBag** object.
    - Expose UserControl properties with **PropertyPage** object.
    - The **Instancing** property determines whether an ActiveX EXE's or ActiveX DLL's publicly available class can be utilized outside of the current project as well as how it can be utilized.
    - To test an ActiveX EXE, run it in the development environment, and then start another instance of Visual Basic and run a project that uses the ActiveX EXE. To test an ActiveX Document EXE, compile it, and then load the resulting VBD file into Internet Explorer and run it from there. Use the **Hyperlink** object's **NavigateTo** method to load other documents.
    - To test an ActiveX DLL, add another project into the same instance of the VB file.

37. **CreateObject** creates an **Automation** object such as a Microsoft Word document. **GetObject** obtains reference to existing object. **SourceDoc** specifies an OLE document and **SourceItem** specifies data with an OLE document.

INTERNET

38. You should know the following about the Winsock control:
    - Important protocals are: **Protocol**, **RemoteHost**, **RemotePort**, and **LocalPort**.
    - Important methods are: **Connect**, **Bind**, **Listen**, **GetData**, and **Close**.
    - Important events are: **SendProgress** and **DataArrival**.

12. Only one MDIForm per project. Forms with **MDIChild** property set to **True** close with MDIForm.

13. **Me** always returns a reference to the form.

14. Form's **Initialize** event occurs before **Load** event. Use **CloseQuery** to intercept an **UnLoad**.

15. Assigning objects to variables: **New** creates a new instance; **Set** assigns object reference.

16. **TypeOf** returns type of object in an **If** statement only.

17. **Screen** object is the entire Windows desktop. Know these key properties: **ActiveControl**; **ActiveForm**; **Fonts** (array indexed by **FontCont**); **MousePointer**; **MouseIcon**; **Height** and **Width**.

18. Key **App** object properties: **EXEName**, **HelpFile**, and **hInstance**.

CONTROLS

19. Key properties of most controls: **TabIndex**, **Index**, and **KeyPreview** (forms only).

20. Key events of most controls: **KeyUp**, **KeyDown**, **KeyPress**; **GotFocus** and **LostFocus**.

21. Key methods of most controls: **ZOrder** and **SetFocus**. Also see Table 8.1 on page 187.

22. Know the usage of these ActiveX controls:
    - **CommonDialog** Displays various dialogs such as File Save
    - **MSFlexGrid** Displays data in tabular format
    - **ImageList** Maintains collection of **ListImage** objects
    - **ListView** Displays items similar to Windows Explorer
    - **Slider** Sets and displays discrete values
    - **TabStrip** Contains multiple **Tab** objects
    - **ToolBar** Contains **Button** objects associated with an application

- **TreeView** Lists **Node** objects in hierarchical order
- **UpDown** Displays and sets values when associated with another buddy control

EXTERNAL MODULES/WINDOWS API

23. Use **Alias** in a **Declare** statement if external name is illegal.

24. All objects have a handle returned by the **hWnd** property. Forms have **hDC** property to return graphical device context. Use **AddressOf** to pass procedure address.

25. To access the Registry, use **GetSetting**, **GetAllSettings**, **DeleteSetting**, and **SaveSetting**.

ERROR HANDLING

26. Know the properties of the **Err** object (**Number**, **Description**, **HelpContext**, **HelpContextID**, **LastDLLError**, and **Source**) and the **Err** object's methods (**Clear** and **Raise**).

27. Know how to turn on error handling: **On Error GoTo** *linelabel* or **On Error Resume Next**. To turn off: **On Error GoTo 0**. Handle errors and then use **Resume**, **Resume Next**, or **Resume** *linelabel*.

DATA HANDLING

28. The **DBEngine** object contains the **Errors** collection to record multiple errors.

29. There are two types of **Workspace** objects: Microsoft Jet and ODBCDirect.

30. Know this about transactions:
    - **BeginTrans** method of the **Workspace** object starts a transaction. Transactions are ended by the **CommitTrans** or **Rollback** methods. Transactions can be nested. Rolling back outer transactions will "undo" commits of inner transactions.
    - Optimistic locking means that rows aren't locked until updated. Pessimistic locking means rows are locked as soon as they are accessed.

Are You Certifiable?

That's the question that's probably on your mind. The answer is: You bet! But if you've tried and failed or you've been frustrated by the complexity of the MCSD and MCSE programs and the maze of study materials available, you've come to the right place. We've created our new publishing and training program, *Certification Insider Press*, to help you accomplish one important goal: to ace an MCSD or MCSE exam without having to spend the rest of your life studying for it.

The book you have in your hands is part of our *Exam Cram* series. Each book is especially designed not only to help you study for an exam but also to help you understand what the exam is all about. Inside these covers you'll find hundreds of test-taking tips, insights, and strategies that simply cannot be found anyplace else. In creating our guides, we've assembled the very best team of certified trainers, MCSD and MCSE professionals, and networking course developers.

Our commitment is to ensure that the *Exam Cram* guides offer proven training and active-learning techniques not found in other study guides. We provide unique study tips and techniques, memory joggers, custom quizzes, insights about trick questions, a sample test, and much more. In a nutshell, each *Exam Cram* guide is closely organized like the exam it is tied to.

To help us continue to provide the very best certification study materials, we'd like to hear from you. Write or email us (craminfo@coriolis.com) and let us know how our *Exam Cram* guides have helped you study, or tell us about new features you'd like us to add. If you send us a story about how an *Exam Cram* guide has helped you ace an exam and we use it in one of our guides, we'll send you an official *Exam Cram* shirt for your efforts.

Good luck with your certification exam, and thanks for allowing us to help you achieve your goals.

Keith Weiskamp

Keith Weiskamp
Publisher, Certification Insider Press

Microsoft
Visual Basic 5

Michael MacDonald

Certification
Insider™ Press

An imprint of

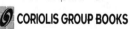 **CORIOLIS GROUP BOOKS**

an International Thomson Publishing company I(T)P®

Albany, NY • Belmont, CA • Bonn • Boston • Cincinnati • Detroit • Johannesburg • London
Madrid • Melbourne • Mexico City • New York • Paris • Singapore • Tokyo • Toronto • Washington

Microsoft Visual Basic Exam Cram

Limits of Liability and Disclaimer of Warranty

Trademarks

The Coriolis Group, Inc.
An International Thomson Publishing Company
14455 N. Hayden Road, Suite 220
Scottsdale, Arizona 85260

602/483-0192
FAX 602/483-0193
http://www.coriolis.com

Library of Congress Cataloging-in-Publication Data
MacDonald, Michael D.
    MCSD Microsoft Visual Basic 5 exam cram / by Michael D. MacDonald.
        p.   cm.
    Includes index.
    ISBN 1-57610-236-X
    1. Electronic data processing personnel--Certification.
2. Microsoft software--Examinations--Study guides.   3. Microsoft Visual
BASIC   I. Title.
QA76.3.M32   1998
005.26'8--dc21   98-47337
                                                        CIP

Printed in the United States of America
10 9 8 7 6 5 4 3 2 1

Publisher
Keith Weiskamp

Acquisitions
Shari Jo Hehr

Project Editor
Jeff Kellum

Production Coordinator
Kim Eoff

Cover Design
Anthony Stock

Layout Design
April Nielsen

About The Author

Michael MacDonald is a client/server consultant and instructor (teaching database, Visual Basic, and PowerBuilder) for Worcester Polytechnic Institute in Worcester, MA. After beginning his career as an accountant (and eventually managing the accounting operations for a major government contractor), Michael moved into data processing. He now has more than 15 years experience on nearly all hardware platforms. His experience with Visual Basic dates back to the early 1980s with C-Basic (on the CP/M platform) to QuickBasic and Microsoft Professional Basic and all versions of Visual Basic.

Experienced in numerous languages, from Fortran and Cobol to Visual Basic and C++, Michael, who still wears a shirt saying "Give Me CP/M Or Give Me Death," has been a leading client/server developer for years. He has received several industry awards, and has frequently been sought after as a speaker at a number of conventions.

Michael has authored 5 books and nearly 50 magazine articles on topics ranging from relational database design to client/server development to social implications of computing. Michael is also author of a number of successful shareware packages in file encryption and MIDI arranging.

A married father of two, Michael is active in child advocacy groups, and has tutored literacy skills to patients leaving state hospitals.

Acknowledgments

I would like to thank several very fine editors at the Coriolis Group. First is my acquisitions editor, Shari Jo Hehr, who offered advice and encouragement. Second is my project editor, Jeff Kellum, who worked tirelessly in offering constructive criticisms, who coached me on any number of areas related to the production of this book, and who kept telling me, "No, Mike, you can't write an 1,100-page book." Also, I'd like to thank the copy editor, Scott Calamar, who constantly reminded me that in English, every sentence has a verb and forms a complete thought. Jeff and Scott also challenged any number of statements that I made, forcing me to rethink both presentation and comment to achieve what I hope is a fine book.

I'd also like to thank and dedicate this book to a wonderful family: my wife Patricia, my daughter Amanda, and my son Peter. Each was patient and supportive as I worked the long hours necessary to research and write this book. They are my inspiration.

Contents

. . . .

Introduction

Welcome to *Microsoft Visual Basic 5 Exam Cram*! This book aims to help you get ready to take—and pass—the Microsoft certification test numbered "Exam 70-165," entitled "Designing Applications with Microsoft Visual Basic 5." This introduction explains Microsoft's certification programs in general and talks about how the *Exam Cram* series can help you prepare for Microsoft's certification exams.

Exam Cram books help you understand and appreciate the subjects and materials you need to pass Microsoft certification exams. *Exam Cram* books are aimed strictly at test preparation and review. They do not teach you everything you need to know about a topic. Instead, I present and dissect the questions and problems that I've found that you're likely to encounter on a test. I've worked from Microsoft's own training materials, preparation guides, and tests, and from a battery of third-party test preparation tools. My aim is to bring together as much information as possible about Microsoft certification exams.

Nevertheless, to completely prepare yourself for any Microsoft test, you should begin your studies with some classroom training, or pick up and read one of the many study guides available from Microsoft and third-party vendors. I also strongly recommend that you install, configure, and fool around with the software or environment that you'll be tested on, because nothing beats hands-on experience and familiarity when it comes to understanding the questions you're likely to encounter on a certification test. Book learning is essential, but hands-on experience is the best teacher of all!

The Microsoft Certified Professional (MCP) Program

The MCP Program currently includes four separate tracks, each of which boasts its own special acronym (as a would-be certificant, you need to have a high tolerance for alphabet soup of all kinds):

➤ **MCPS (Microsoft Certified Product Specialist)** This is the least prestigious of all the certification tracks from Microsoft. Attaining MCPS status requires an individual to pass at least one core operating system exam. Passing any of the major Microsoft operating system exams—including those for Windows 95, Windows NT Workstation, or Windows NT Server—qualifies an individual for MCPS credentials. Individuals can demonstrate proficiency with additional Microsoft products by passing additional certification exams.

➤ **MCSE (Microsoft Certified Systems Engineer)** Anyone who possesses a current MCSE is warranted to possess a high level of expertise with Windows NT (either version 3.51 or 4) and other Microsoft operating systems and products. This credential is designed to prepare individuals to plan, implement, maintain, and support information systems and networks built around Microsoft Windows NT and its BackOffice family of products.

To obtain an MCSE, an individual must pass four core operating system exams plus two elective exams. The operating system exams require individuals to demonstrate competence with desktop and server operating systems and with networking components.

At least two Windows NT-related exams must be passed to obtain an MCSE: Implementing and Supporting Windows NT Server (version 3.51 or 4) and Implementing and Supporting Windows NT Server in the Enterprise (version 3.51 or 4). These tests are intended to indicate an individual's knowledge of Windows NT in smaller, simpler networks and in larger, more complex, and heterogeneous networks, respectively.

Two more tests must be passed: networking and desktop operating system related. At present, the networking requirement can be satisfied only by passing the Networking Essentials test. The desktop operating system test can be satisfied by passing a Windows 3.1, Windows for Workgroups 3.11, Windows NT Workstation (the version must match whichever core curriculum is pursued), or Windows 95 test.

The two remaining exams are elective exams. The elective exams can be in any number of subject or product areas, primarily BackOffice components. These include tests on SQL Server, SNA Server, Exchange, Systems Management Server, and the like. But it is also possible to test out on electives by taking advanced networking topics like Internetworking with Microsoft TCP/IP (here again, the version of Windows NT involved must match the version for the core requirements taken).

➤ **MCSD (Microsoft Certified Solution Developer)** This track is aimed primarily at developers and is the one in which most Visual Basic developers will be interested. This credential indicates that individuals who pass it are able to design and implement custom business solutions around particular Microsoft development tools, technologies, and operating systems. To obtain an MCSD, an individual must demonstrate the ability to analyze and interpret user requirements; select and integrate products, platforms, tools, and technologies; design and implement code and customize applications; and perform necessary software tests and quality assurance operations.

To become an MCSD, an individual must pass a total of four exams: two core exams plus two elective exams. For the two core exams, you must pass exam 70-150 or 70-160, which are Microsoft Windows Operating Systems and Services Architecture I and Microsoft Windows Architecture II, respectively. For the second core exam, you have to take and pass either test 70-151 or 70-161 (Microsoft Windows Operating Systems and Services Architecture II and Microsoft Windows Architecture II, respectively. Be aware that tests 70-150 and 70-151 are being phased out and may have been retired by the time you read this.

Additionally, you have to take and pass two elective exams from subjects such as MS SQL Server, Visual Basic, Access, Excel, Visual Fox Pro, or Implementing OLE in MFC Applications.

Whatever mix of tests is completed toward MCSD certification, individuals must pass four tests to meet the MCSD requirements. It's not uncommon for the entire process to take 6 to 12 months, and many individuals find that they must take a test more than once to pass. The primary goal of the *Exam Cram* series is to make it possible, given proper study and preparation, to pass all of the MCSD tests on the first try.

Finally, certification is an ongoing activity. Once a Microsoft product becomes obsolete, MCSDs (and other MCPs) typically have a 12-to 18-month time frame in which they can become recertified on current product versions (if individuals do not get recertified within the specified time period, their certification is no longer valid). Because technology keeps changing and new products continually supplant old ones, this should come as no surprise.

➤ **MCT (Microsoft Certified Trainer)** Microsoft Certified Trainers are individuals who are deemed capable of delivering elements of the official Microsoft training curriculum, based on technical knowledge and instructional ability. Thus, it is necessary for an individual seeking MCT credentials (which are granted on a course-by-course basis) to pass the related certification exam for a course and successfully complete the official Microsoft training in the subject area, as well as demonstrate an ability to teach.

This latter criterion may be satisfied by showing a Cross-Industry Training Certificate from Novell or Banyan or by taking a Microsoft-sanctioned workshop on instruction. Microsoft makes it clear that MCTs are an important cog in the Microsoft training channels. Instructors must be MCTs to teach in any of Microsoft's official training channels, including its affiliated Authorized Technical Education Centers (ATECs), Authorized Academic Training Programs (AATPs), and the Microsoft Online Institute (MOLI).

The best place to keep tabs on the MCP Program and its various certifications is on the Microsoft Web site. The current root URL for the MCP program is entitled "Certification Online" at www.microsoft.com/Train_Cert/mcp/default.htm. Microsoft's Web site changes frequently, so if this URL doesn't work, try using the Search tool on Microsoft's site with either "MCP" or the quoted phrase "Microsoft Certified Professional Program" as the search string. This will help you find the latest and most accurate information about the company's certification programs. You can also obtain a special CD that contains a copy of the Microsoft Education And Certification Roadmap. The Roadmap covers much of the same information as the Web site, and it is updated quarterly. To obtain your copy of the CD, call Microsoft at 1-800-636-7544, Monday through Friday, 6:30 AM through 7:30 PM Pacific Time.

Taking A Certification Exam

Alas, testing is not free. You'll be charged $100 for each test you take, whether you pass or fail. (When you recertify on an exam, the charge is 50 percent of the then current fee.) In the United States and Canada, tests are administered by Sylvan Prometric. Sylvan Prometric can be reached at 1-800-755-3926 or 1-800-755-EXAM, any time from 7:00 AM to 6:00 PM, Central Time, Monday through Friday. If this number doesn't work, try 612-896-7000 or 612- 820-5707.

To schedule an exam, call at least one day in advance. To cancel or reschedule an exam, you must call before 6:00 PM Central Time the day before the test (or you may be charged regardless). When calling Sylvan Prometric, please have the following information ready for the telesales staffer who handles your call:

➤ Your name, organization, and mailing address.

➤ Your Microsoft Test ID. (For most U.S. citizens, this is your social security number. Citizens of other nations can use their taxpayer IDs or make other arrangements with the order-taker.)

➤ The name and number of the exam you wish to take. (For this book, the exam number is 70-165, and the exam name is "Developing Applications with Microsoft Visual Basic 5.")

➤ A method of payment must be arranged. (The most convenient approach is to supply a valid credit card number with sufficient available credit. Otherwise, payments by check, money order, or purchase order must be received before a test can be scheduled. If the latter methods are required, ask you order-taker for more details.)

When you show up to take a test, try to arrive at least 15 minutes before the scheduled time slot. You must bring and supply two forms of identification, one of which must be a photo ID.

All exams are completely closed-book. In fact, you will not be permitted to take anything with you into the testing area, but you will be furnished with a blank sheet of paper and a pen. I suggest that you immediately write down the most critical information about the test you're taking on the sheet of paper. *Exam Cram* books provide a brief reference—The Cram Sheet, located in the front of the book—that lists the essential information from the book in distilled form. You will have some time to compose yourself, to record this information, and even to take a sample orientation exam before you must begin the real thing. I suggest you take the orientation test before taking your first exam; because they're all more or less identical in layout, behavior, and controls, you probably won't need to do this more than once.

When you complete a Microsoft certification exam, the software will tell you whether you've passed or failed. All tests are scored on a basis of 1,000 points, and results are broken into several topical areas. Even if you fail, I suggest you ask for—and keep—the detailed report that the test administrator should print for you. You can use the report to help prepare for another go-round, if needed. If you need to retake an exam, you'll have to call Sylvan Prometric, schedule a new test date, and pay another $100.

Tracking MCP Status

As soon as you pass any Microsoft operating system exam, you'll attain Product Specialist (MCPS) status. Microsoft also generates transcripts that indicate the exams you have passed and your corresponding test scores. You can order a transcript by email at any time by sending an email addressed to mcp@msprograms.com. You can also obtain a copy of your transcript by downloading the latest version of the MCT Guide from the Web site and consulting the section entitled "Key Contacts" for a list of telephone numbers and related contacts.

Once you pass the necessary set of four exams, you'll be certified as an MCSD. Official certification normally takes anywhere from four to six weeks, so don't expect to get your credentials overnight. When the package arrives, it will include a Welcome Kit that contains a number of elements, including:

➤ An MCSD certificate, suitable for framing, along with an MCSD Professional Program membership card and lapel pin.

➤ A license to use the MCP logo, thereby allowing you to use the logo in advertisements, promotions, and documents, and on letterhead, business cards, and so on. Along with the license comes an MCP logo sheet, which includes camera-ready artwork. (Note: before using any of the artwork, individuals must sign and return a licensing agreement that indicates they'll abide by its terms and conditions.)

➤ A subscription to *Certification Update*, which is a bimonthly newsletter from the MCP program that keeps you apprised of changes in the program.

➤ A subscription to *Microsoft Certified Professional* magazine, which provides ongoing data about testing and certification activities, requirements, and changes to the program.

➤ A free Priority Comprehensive 10-pack with Microsoft Product Support, and a 25 percent discount on additional Priority Comprehensive 10-packs. This lets you place up to 10 free calls to Microsoft's technical support operation at a higher-than-normal priority level.

➤ A one-year subscription to the Microsoft Beta Evaluation program. This subscription will get you all beta products from Microsoft for the next year. (This does not include developer products. You must join the MSDN program or become an MCSD to qualify for developer beta products.)

Many people believe that the benefits of MCSD certification go well beyond the perks that Microsoft provides to newly—anointed members of this elite group. I'm starting to see more job listings that request or require applicants to have a Microsoft certification in Visual Basic or an MCSD, and many individuals who complete the program can qualify for increases in pay or responsibility. As an official recognition of hard work and broad knowledge, MCSD certification is indeed a badge of honor in many IT organizations.

How To Prepare For An Exam

At a minimum, preparing for the Visual Basic 5 test requires that you obtain and study the following materials:

➤ The Microsoft Visual Basic manuals (or online documentation and help files, which ship on the CD with the product and also appear on the TechNet CDs).

➤ The exam prep materials, practice tests, and self-assessment exams on the Microsoft Training And Certification Download page (www.microsoft.com/Train_Cert/download/downld.htm). Find the materials, download them, and use them!

➤ This *Exam Cram* book! It's the first and last thing you should read before taking the exam.

In addition, you'll probably find any or all of the following materials useful in your quest for Visual Basic expertise:

➤ **Microsoft Training Kits** Although there's no training kit currently available from Microsoft Press for VB5, many other topics have such kits. It's worthwhile to check to see if Microsoft has come out with anything by the time you need the information.

➤ **Study Guides** I recommend Exam Preps from The Coriolis Group's Certification Insider Press. These comprehensive study guides feature highly interactive, real-world exercises and projects to reinforce important topical discussions. The companion CD-ROM includes two complete interactive practice exams.

➤ **Other Publications** You'll find direct references to other publications and resources in this book, but there's no shortage of materials available about Visual Basic. To help you sift through some of the publications out there, I end each chapter with a "Need To Know More?" section that provides pointers to more complete and exhaustive resources covering the chapter's information. This should give you an idea of where I think you should look for further discussion. A title that I particularly like is *Hardcore Visual Basic 5.0* by Bruce McKinney (Microsoft Press, Redmond, Washington, 1997, ISBN 1-57231-422-2).

➤ **The TechNet CD** TechNet is a monthly CD subscription available from Microsoft. TechNet includes all the Windows NT BackOffice Resource Kits and their product documentation. In addition, TechNet provides the contents of the Microsoft Knowledge Base and many kinds of software, white papers, training materials, and other good stuff. TechNet also contains all service packs, interim release patches, and supplemental driver software released since the last major version for most Microsoft programs and all Microsoft operating systems. A one-year subscription costs $299—worth every penny, even if only for the download time it saves.

By far, this set of required and recommend materials represents a nonpareil collection of sources and resources for Visual Basic topics and software. I anticipate that you'll find this book belongs in this company. In the section that follows, I explain how this book works, and I give you some good reasons why this book counts as a member of the required and recommended materials list.

About This Book

Each topical *Exam Cram* chapter follows a regular structure, along with graphical cues about especially important or useful material. Here's the structure of a typical chapter:

➤ **Opening Hotlists** Each chapter begins with lists of the terms, tools, and techniques that you must learn and understand before you can be fully conversant with the chapter's subject matter. I follow the hotlists with one or two introductory paragraphs to set the stage for the rest of the chapter. Here, you'll find an estimate of the number of questions related to the chapter's topic likely to appear on any given certification test.

➤ **Topical Coverage** After the opening hotlists, each chapter covers a series of at least four topics related to the chapter's subject title. Throughout this section, I highlight material most likely to appear on a test using a special Exam Alert layout, like this:

 This is what an Exam Alert looks like. Normally, an Exam Alert stresses concepts, terms, software, or activities that will most probably appear in one or more certification test questions. For that reason, I think any information found offset in Exam Alert format is worthy of unusual attentiveness on your part. Indeed, most of the facts appearing in The Cram Sheet (in the front of this book) appear as Exam Alerts within the text.

Even if material isn't flagged as an Exam Alert, *all* the contents of this book are at least tangential to something test-related. To focus on quick test preparation, this book is lean; you'll find that what appears in the meat of each chapter is critical knowledge.

I have also provided tips that will help build a better foundation of VB-based knowledge. Although the information may not be on the exam, it is highly relevant and will help you become a better test-taker.

 This is how tips are formatted. Keep your eyes open for these, and you'll become a Visual Basic test guru in no time! Even better, I like to think that you will become a VB application development guru even quicker!

➤ **Exam Prep Questions** This section presents a series of mock test questions and explanations of both correct and incorrect answers. I also try to point out especially tricky questions by using a special icon, like this:

Ordinarily, this icon flags the presence of an especially devious question, if not an outright trick question. Trick questions are calculated to "trap" you if you don't read them more than once, and carefully, at that. Although they're not ubiquitous, such questions make regular appearances in the Microsoft exams. That's why I say exam questions are as much about reading comprehension as they are about knowing Visual Basic material inside out and backwards.

➤ **Details And Resources** Every chapter ends with a section entitled "Need To Know More?". This section provides direct pointers to Microsoft and third-party resources that offer further details on the chapter's subject. In addition, this section tries to rate the quality and thoroughness of the topic's coverage by each resource. If you find a resource you like in this collection, use it, but don't feel compelled to use all the resources. On the other hand, I only recommend resources I use on a regular basis, so none of my recommendations will be a waste of your time or money.

The bulk of the book follows this chapter structure slavishly. But, there are a few other elements that I'd like to point out: a sample test along with an answer key, as well as a detailed glossary. Finally, look for The Cram Sheet, which appears in the front of this *Exam Cram* book. It is a very valuable tool that represents a condensed and compiled collection of facts, figures, and tips that I think you should memorize before taking the test. Because you can dump this information out of your head onto a piece of paper before answering any exam questions, you can master this information by brute force—you only need to remember it long enough to write it down when you walk into the test room. You might even want to look at it in the car or in the lobby of the testing center just before you walk in to take the test.

How To Use This Book

If you're prepping for a first-time test, I've structured the topics in this book to build on one another. Therefore, some topics in later chapters make more sense after you've read earlier chapters. That's why I suggest you read this book from front to back for your initial test preparation. If you need to brush up on a topic or you have to bone up for a second try, use the index or table of contents to go straight to the topics and questions that you need to study. Beyond the tests, I think you'll find this book useful as a tightly focused reference to some of the most important aspects of Visual Basic.

Given all the book's elements and its specialized focus, I've tried to create a tool that you can use to prepare for—and pass—Microsoft Certification Exam 70-165, "Designing Applications with Microsoft Visual Basic 5." Please share your feedback on the book with me, especially if you have ideas about how I can improve it for future test-takers. I will consider everything you say carefully, and will respond to all suggestions. You can reach me via email at mikemacd@tiac.net. Please remember to include the title of the book in your message. For up-to-date information on certification, online discussions forums, sample tests, content updates, and more, visit the Certification Insider Press Web site at www.examcram.com.

Thanks, and enjoy the book!

Microsoft Certification Tests

Terms you'll need to understand:

√ Radio button

√ Checkbox

√ Exhibit

√ Multiple-choice question formats

√ Careful reading

√ Process of elimination

Techniques you'll need to master:

√ Preparing to take a certification exam

√ Practicing—to make perfect

√ Making the best use of the testing software

√ Budgeting your time

√ Saving the hardest questions until last

√ Guessing (as a last resort)

As experiences go, test-taking is not something that most people anticipate eagerly, no matter how well they're prepared. In most cases, familiarity with the material being tested helps ameliorate test anxiety. In plain English, this means you probably won't be as nervous when you take your fourth or fifth Microsoft certification exam as you will be when you take your first one.

But whether it's your first test or your tenth, understanding the exam-taking particulars (how much time to spend on questions, the setting you'll be in, and so on) and the testing software will help you concentrate on the material, rather than on the environment. Likewise, mastering a few basic test-taking skills should help you recognize—and perhaps even outfox—some of the tricks and gotchas you're bound to find in some of the Microsoft test questions.

In this chapter, I'll explain the testing environment and software, and describe some proven test-taking strategies that you should be able to use to your advantage. I have compiled this information for you from actual live testing, comparing notes with others who have taken the exam, sources with Microsoft, and experience back to Visual Basic version 1.

The Testing Situation

When you arrive at the Sylvan Prometric Testing Center, where you scheduled your test, you'll need to sign in with a test coordinator. He or she will ask you to produce two forms of identification, one of which must be a photo ID. Once you've signed in and it's time to take the test, you'll be asked to deposit any books, bags, or other items you brought with you, and you'll be escorted into a closed room. Typically, that room will be furnished with anywhere from one to a half dozen computers, with dividers separating the workstations.

You'll be supplied with a pen or pencil and a blank sheet of paper, or in some cases, an erasable plastic sheet and an erasable felt-tip pen. You're allowed to write down any information you want and you can write on both sides of the page. I suggest that you memorize as much as possible of the material that appears on The Cram Sheet (which is located at the very front of the book), and then write that information down on the blank sheet as soon as you sit down in front of the test machine. You can refer to it any time you like during the test, but you'll have to surrender the sheet when you leave the room.

Most test rooms feature a wall with a large picture window. This is to permit the test coordinator to monitor the room, to prevent test-takers from talking to one another, and to observe anything out of the ordinary. You may have to sign a sheet of paper attesting that you understand this. The test coordinator will have preloaded the Microsoft certification test you've signed up for—for this book, that's Exam 70-165—and you'll be permitted to start as soon as you're seated in front of the machine.

All Microsoft certification exams permit you to take up to a certain maximum amount of time to complete the test (the test itself will tell you; it maintains an ongoing on-screen counter/clock so you can check the time remaining any time you like). Exam 70-165 consists of 60 questions, randomly selected from a pool of questions. You're permitted to take up to 75 minutes to complete the exam.

The questions for Exam 70-165 are focused in four broad areas: design issues, coding issues, debugging issues, and distribution issues. My impression was that coding issues make up about 60 percent of the test. Debugging seemed to be about 10 percent of the test with the remainder split about evenly between Design and Distribution.

All Microsoft certification exams are computer generated and use a multiple-choice format. Although this may sound quite simple, the questions are constructed not just to check your mastery of basic facts and figures about Visual Basic 5; they also require you to evaluate one or more sets of circumstances or requirements. Often, you'll be asked to give more than one answer to a question; likewise, you may be asked to select the best or most effective solution to a problem from a range of choices, all of which technically are correct. It's quite an adventure, and involves real thinking, but this book will show you what to expect, and how to handle the problems, puzzles, and predicaments you're likely to find on the test. Of the "multichoice" questions (those where you have to select more than one response), most require you to select two answers. Some may require three. Because the questions are randomly generated, your experience may be slightly different.

Test Layout And Design

A typical test question is depicted here. It's a multiple choice question (taken from Chapter 2 of this book) that requires you to select a single correct answer. I've reproduced the entire text of this question, and follow it with some further explanation and discussion. The questions in each chapter are based on material covered in that particular chapter. The answers and explanations immediately follow each question. Chapter 16 provides an additional test consisting of 60 questions, and the answers and explanatory text follow in Chapter 17.

Question 1

> What is the data type of variable **a** below?
>
> ```
> Dim a, b, c As Integer
> ```
>
> ○ a. Integer
> ○ b. Variant
> ○ c. User defined
> ○ d. None of the above

The correct answer is b. When more than one variable is being declared on a single line, each must be explicitly defined as to its type. In this case, only the third variable is an **Integer**. Variable a defaults to a **Variant**.

The sample question here corresponds closely to those questions you'll see on Microsoft certification tests. To select the correct answer, position the cursor over the radio button next to answer b, and click the mouse to select that particular choice. In this case, knowing which answer to pick depends on understanding how variables are declared and also understanding Visual Basic's defaults.

Next, we'll examine a question that requires choosing multiple answers. The question was taken from Chapter 3. This type of question provides checkboxes, rather than the radio buttons, for marking all appropriate selections.

Question 2

> Which of the following are true of a function? [Check all correct answers]
>
> ❏ a. Another type of module
> ❏ b. A procedure
> ❏ c. Different from a sub in that it must return a value
> ❏ d. Different from a sub in that it allows arguments or parameters

The correct answers are b and c. Both subs and functions are procedures. Functions require return values. A function is not a module; it is a part of a module.

For this type of question, one or more choices must be selected to get full credit for the question. Although Microsoft won't comment, it appears that at least for the Visual Basic 5 exam, you can get partial credit for a question.

Although there are many f,orms in which these two basic types of questions can appear, they constitute the foundation upon which all the Microsoft certification exam questions rest. More complex questions may include so-called "exhibits," which are usually screen shots of some Visual Basic dialog or, more often, a small snippet of code. There will be a button marked "Exhibit" that opens a smaller window. You'll be expected to use the information displayed therein to guide your answer to the question. Familiarity with both Visual Basic as a programming language and as a development environment is the key to passing the test. Be prepared to toggle between the code and the question as you work. The question and/or code snippets are often complex enough that you can't remember them in their entirety.

Using Microsoft's Test Software Effectively

A well-known principle when taking tests is to first read over the entire test from start to finish, but to answer only those questions that you feel absolutely sure of on the first pass. On subsequent passes, you can dive into the complex questions more deeply, knowing how many such questions you have to deal with.

Fortunately, Microsoft test software makes this approach easy to implement. At the bottom of each question, you'll find a checkbox that permits you to mark that question for a later visit. As you read each question, if you answer only those you're sure of, and mark for review those that you're not, you can keep going through a decreasing list of open questions as you knock the trickier ones off in order.

Another strategy to consider would be to read the entire question and take a guess and also mark the question for later review. Sometimes, the question is so complex that you don't have time to completely reread it a second time, and a guess is better than a blank answer. This way, if you don't have time to go back and reread the question, at least you have an answer. You may want to use both strategies. When you get to the end of the test, a screen will show you those questions that you marked for review and those that are incomplete. An incomplete question is one that you didn't answer at all or, in the case of multichoice questions, did not provide the correct number of responses.

There's at least one potential benefit to reading the test over completely before answering the trickier questions: Sometimes, you find information in later questions that shed more light on earlier ones. Other times, information you read on later questions may jog your memory about Visual Basic that also will help with earlier questions. Either way, you'll come out ahead if you defer those questions about which you're not absolutely sure of the answer(s). As an example, there was a question in a test I took in which two of the choices were **KeyPress** and **KeyDown**. Both are valid keywords but, for the circumstances given, **KeyPress** was the correct response. I incorrectly chose **KeyDown** because that is the keyword used in another language for the given situation. Later in the test, a question made mention of the **KeyPress** event. I went back and changed my answer to **KeyPress** and am quite sure I scored a couple of points higher than I otherwise would have.

Keep working on the questions until you are absolutely sure of all your answers or until you know you'll run out of time. If there are still unanswered questions, you'll want to zip through them and guess. Leaving a question unanswered guarantees you will receive no credit for that question, but a guess has at least a chance of being correct. This strategy only works because Microsoft doesn't penalize for incorrect answers (that is, it treats incorrect answers and no answer as equally wrong).

At the very end of your test period, you're better off guessing than leaving questions blank or unanswered.

When guessing, use the process of elimination to improve your odds. If you can eliminate one choice out of four, you have improved your odds of guessing correctly from 25 percent to 33 percent. Sometimes, even when you didn't "know" the answer, you can eliminate all but the correct choice(s). This is then called a *very* educated guess!

Taking Testing Seriously

The most important advice I can give you about taking any Microsoft test is: Read each question carefully! Some questions are deliberately ambiguous; some use double negatives; others use terminology in incredibly precise ways. I have taken numerous practice tests and real tests, and in almost every test, I am sure that I have missed at least one question because I didn't read it closely or carefully enough. Especially watch out for superlatives such as "always" or "never" in the question. These are often designed to focus on how thoroughly you understand Visual Basic but may have the effect of making you nervous. For instance, a statement such as "When not explicitly declared, Visual Basic always defaults to the **Variant** data type" will throw anyone for a loop and start one wondering if there is some little "trick" in Visual Basic hidden in some obscure document. Look at these questions carefully but don't start doubting what you already know. In this case, Visual Basic *does* always default to the **Variant** data type. But, how about this statement: "Visual Basic always warns of syntax errors when the Check For Syntax Errors option is turned on." In this case, this is an untrue statement; unfortunately, Visual Basic misses many syntax errors. As an example, if you mistype a keyword, VB will assume that you are referencing a procedure and you will receive a "sub or function not found" error at compile time. Finally, how about a variation: "Visual Basic checks for syntax errors when the Check For Syntax Errors option is turned on." Here, the answer is yes, VB checks for syntax errors when the Check For Syntax Errors option is turned on. Of course, "checking" for syntax errors is not always the same as "finding" syntax errors.

Here are some suggestions on how to temper the tendency to jump to an answer too quickly:

➤ Make sure you read every word in the question. If you find yourself jumping ahead impatiently, go back and start over.

➤ As you read, try to restate the question in your own terms. If you can do this, you should be able to pick the correct answer(s) much more easily.

➤ When returning to a question after your initial read-through, reread every word—otherwise, your mind falls quickly into a rut. Sometimes, seeing a question afresh after turning your attention elsewhere lets you notice something you missed before, but the strong tendency is to see what you've seen before. Try to avoid that tendency at all costs.

➤ If you return to a question more than twice, try to articulate to yourself what you don't understand about the question, why the answers don't appear to make sense, or what appears to be missing. If you chew on the subject for a while, your subconscious may provide the details that are lacking, or you may notice a "trick" that will point to the correct answer.

➤ As mentioned earlier, you can often help yourself by using the process of elimination. By removing from consideration answers that are patently incorrect, you will have less to consider from the remaining choices. If nothing else, you will improve your odds if you end up having to guess.

Above all, try to deal with each question by thinking through what you know about the Visual Basic language, as well as the development environment's characteristics and behaviors. If you have developed in other languages, but are not sure how a particular problem is solved in Visual Basic, you can often apply what you know about the other languages. Most programming languages tend to be alike in capabilities and how things are done. By reviewing what you know (and what you've written down on your information sheet), you will often recall or understand things sufficiently to determine the answer to the question.

Question-Handling Strategies

Based on the tests I've taken, a couple of interesting trends have become apparent in the answers. For those questions that take only a single answer, usually two or three of the answers will be obviously incorrect, and two of the answers will be plausible. This was true, for instance, of the question with the **KeyPress** and **KeyDown** choices that I mentioned earlier. But, of course, only one can be correct. Unless the answer leaps out at you (and if it does, reread the question to look for a trick; sometimes, those are the ones you're most likely to get wrong), begin the process of answering by eliminating those answers that are most obviously wrong.

Things to look for in the "obviously wrong" category include spurious menu choices, keywords, and compiler directives that don't exist, and terminology you've never seen before. If you've done your homework for a test, no valid information should be completely new to you. In that case, unfamiliar or bizarre terminology probably indicates an incorrect answer. As long as you're sure what's right, it's easy to eliminate what's wrong. And if you are sure of what is wrong, you can often work yourself towards what is correct.

Numerous questions assume that the Visual Basic defaults (such as the default data type) are in effect. It's essential, therefore, to understand that (for example), a variable declared **Public** in Visual Basic is visible to all modules unless you have set the **Option Private Module** option. If you know the defaults, and understand what they mean, this knowledge will help you cut through many Gordian knots.

Likewise, when considering questions with multiple answers, it is essential that you understand all aspects of the subject being queried, as well as the default behavior of Visual Basic. Look at the following question and pick which answers are correct.

Question 3

What is the Data control used for? [Check all correct answers]

- ❏ a. Any file opened for Random or Binary
- ❏ b. Any dynaset-type **RecordSet**
- ❏ c. Any forward-only-type **RecordSet**
- ❏ d. Any snapshot-type **RecordSet**
- ❏ e. Any valid DAO or RDO object.

Answers b and d are correct. Answer b is correct because you can open a dynaset with the Data control. Answer d is correct because you can open a snapshot with the Data control. Answer a is incorrect because you cannot use a Data control for files opened in Random or Binary mode. Answer c is incorrect because the Data control does not support the forward-only type **RecordSet**. Answer e is incorrect because the Data control does not support all DAO objects (for instance, the **TableDef** object) and it does not support any RDO objects.

As you work your way through the test, another counter that Microsoft thankfully provides will come in handy—the number of questions completed and questions outstanding, as well as a clock that shows the time remaining. Budget your time by making sure that you've completed one-fourth of the questions one-quarter of the way through the test period (or about 15 questions in the first 18 or 19 minutes). Check again three-quarters of the way through (about 45 questions in the first 55 to 60 minutes). If you're not done when 70 minutes have elapsed, use the last 5 minutes to guess your way through the remaining questions. Remember, guesses are more valuable than blank answers. If you haven't a clue about any of the remaining questions, pick answers at random, or choose all a's, b's, and so on. The important thing is to submit a test that has some answer for every question.

Mastering The Inner Game

In the final analysis, knowledge breeds confidence, and confidence breeds success. If you study the materials in this book carefully, and review all of the "Exam Prep Questions" section at the end of each chapter, you should be aware of those areas where additional learning and study are required.

Next, follow up by reading some or all of the materials recommended in the "Need To Know More?" section at the end of each chapter. The idea is to become familiar enough with the concepts and situations that you find in the sample questions to be able to reason your way through similar situations on a real test. If you know the material, you have every right to be confident that you can pass the test.

Once you've worked your way through the book, take the practice test in Chapter 16. This will provide a reality check, and will help you identify areas you need to study further. Make sure you follow up and review materials related to the questions you miss before scheduling a real test. Take the real test only when you've covered all the ground, and feel comfortable.

If you take our practice test and don't score at least 75 percent correct, you'll want to practice further. At a minimum, download the Personal Exam Prep (PEP) tests and the self-assessment tests from the Microsoft Certification And Training Web site's download page (its location appears in the next section).

If you're more ambitious, or better funded, you might want to purchase a practice test from one of the third-party vendors that offers them. I have looked at materials from Self Test Software and they appear to be well done. I have talked to people and heard good things about the software from Transcender Corporation. D.O.C. software is a third vendor of Microsoft certification test preparation software, and I have had very good luck with it. Its tests take a different tack than do other vendors in that the software does not attempt to emulate "testing conditions." Instead, the software allows you to take a test timed or untimed, or to take a test concentrating only in one area (of your choosing, of course). See the next section in this chapter for contact information.

Unfortunately, at the time of this writing, neither D.O.C. nor Self Test had a VB5 test prepared. Self Test told me that it had made no decision whether to release a VB5 version to replace its VB4 test. The president of D.O.C. told me that it was still weighing the financial feasibility of a VB5 test after disappointing sales of its VB4 version.

Armed with the information in this book, and with the determination to augment your knowledge, you should be able to pass the certification exam. But if you don't work at it, you'll spend the test fee more than once before you finally do pass. If you prepare seriously, the execution should go flawlessly. Good luck!

Details And Resources

By far, the best source of information about Microsoft certification tests comes from Microsoft itself. Because its products and technologies—and the tests that go with them—change frequently, the best place to go for exam-related information is online.

If you haven't already visited the Microsoft Training And Certification pages, do so right now. As I am writing this chapter, the Training And Certification home page resides at www.microsoft.com/train_cert/default.htm (see Figure 1.1).

> *Note: The home page may not be at that location by the time you read this, or it may have been replaced by something new and different, because things change regularly on the Microsoft site. Should this happen, please read the sidebar titled "Coping With Change On The Web."*

The menu options in the left-hand column of the home page point to the most important sources of information in the Training And Certification pages. Here's what to check out:

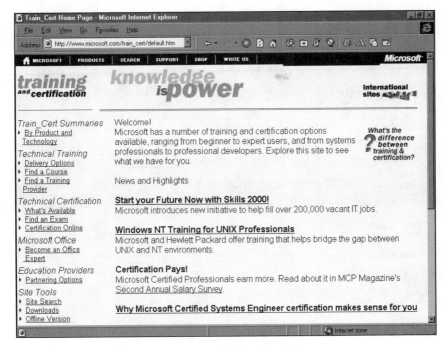

Figure 1.1   The Training And Certification home page.

➤ **Train_Cert Summaries/By Product and Technology** Use this to jump to summaries of all classroom education, training materials, study guides, and other information for specific products. Under the heading of Microsoft Visual Tools/Visual Basic, you'll find an entire page of information about Visual Basic training and certification. This tells you a lot about your training and preparation options, and mentions all the tests that relate to Visual Basic.

➤ **Technical Certification/Find an Exam** Pulls up a search tool that lets you list all Microsoft exams, and locate all exams pertinent to any Microsoft certification (MCSD, MCSE, MCPS, and so on), or those exams that cover a particular product. This tool is quite useful not only to examine the options, but also to obtain specific test preparation information, because each exam has its own associated preparation guide. For this test, be sure to grab the one for 70-165. See Figure 1.2 for the ways you can search.

➤ **Site Tools/Downloads** Here, you'll find a list of the files and practice tests that Microsoft makes available to the public. These include several items worth downloading, especially the Certification Update, the

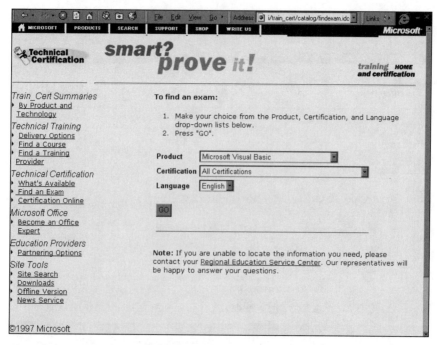

Figure 1.2 The Microsoft Exam Search Page at www.microsoft.com/ isapi/train_cert/catalog/findexam.idc.

Personal Exam Prep (PEP) tests, various assessment exams, and a general Exam Study Guide. Try to make time to peruse these materials before taking your first test. As this book was going to press, a VB5 version of self-assessment test and just become available. I recommend using both the VB4 and VB5 versions. Figure 1.3 shows the process of selecting a test.

Coping With Change On The Web

Sooner or later, all the specifics I've shared with you about the Microsoft Training And Certification pages, and all the other Web-based resources I mention throughout the rest of this book, will go stale or be replaced by newer information. In some cases, the URLs you find here might lead you to their replacements; in other cases, the URLs will go nowhere, leaving you with the dreaded "404 File not found" error message.

When that happens, please don't give up! There's always a way to find what you want on the Web, if you're willing to invest some time and energy. To begin with, most large or complex Web sites—and Microsoft's qualifies on both counts—offer a search engine. Looking back at Figure 1.1, you'll see that a Search button appears along the top edge of the page. As long as you can get to the site itself (and I'm pretty sure that it will stay at www.microsoft.com for a long while yet), you can use this tool to help you find what you need.

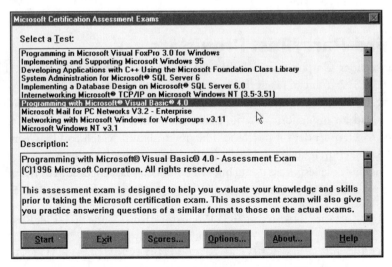

Figure 1.3   The menu for the practice Microsoft certification tests.

The more particular or focused you can make a search request, the more likely it is that the results will include information you can use. For instance, you can search the string

```
"training and certification"
```

to produce a lot of data about the subject in general, but if you're looking for the Preparation Guide for Exam 70-165, Developing Applications With Microsoft Visual Basic 5.0, you'll be more likely to get there quickly if you use a search string such as this:

```
"Exam 70-063 AND preparation guide"
```

Likewise, if you want to find the Training and Certification downloads, try a search string such as this one:

```
"training and certification AND download page"
```

Finally, don't be afraid to use general search tools such as www.search.com, www.altavista.digital.com, or www.excite.com to search for related information. Even though Microsoft offers the best information about its certification exams online, there are plenty of third-party sources of information, training, and assistance in this area that do not have to follow the Microsoft party line. The bottom line is: If you can't find something where the book says it lives, start looking around. If worse comes to worst, you can always email me! I just might have a clue.

Third-Party Test Providers

Transcender Corporation is located at 242 Louise Avenue, Nashville, TN, 37203-1812. You can reach the company by phone at 1-615-726-8779, or by fax at 1-615-320-6594. Trancender's URL is www.transcender.com; you can download an order form for the materials online, but it must be mailed or faxed to Transcender for purchase. The practice tests, which cost between $89 and $179 if purchased individually (with discounts available for packages containing multiple tests), are useful but pricey. When I last checked, Transcender's VB5 practice test was not yet available. The VB4 test had been priced at $129.

Self Test Software is located at 4651 Woodstock Road, Suite 203-384, Roswell, GA, 30075. The company can be reached by phone at 1-770-641-9719 or 1-800-200-6446, and by fax at 1-770-641-1489. Visit the Web site at www.stsware.com; you can even order the wares online. STS's tests are cheaper than Transcender's—$69 when purchased individually, $59 each when two or more are purchased simultaneously—but otherwise quite comparable, which makes them a good value. Unfortunately, when I talked with Self Test, it did not have plans to release a VB5 test.

D.O.C. Software is located at 27 Glendale Drive, Danbury, CT, 06811. The company can be reached by phone at 1-203-790-1769 and by fax at 1-203-778-5093. Visit the Web site at www.docsoftware.com/. Like Transcender, the Visual Basic 5 practice exam was not ready at the time of this writing, The price for the Visual Basic 4 exam was $49.95, which is very reasonable. I have used other D.O.C. products and found them well done. As noted earlier, D.O.C. does not attempt to simulate test conditions in that you are given 5-minute tests consisting of 15 random questions. However, you are allowed to specify that questions be in any area that you may find troublesome (such as "Object Linking and Embedding").

Visual Basic Data Types

Terms you'll need to understand:

- √ Objects
- √ Variables
- √ Variable scope, precision, accuracy
- √ Visual Basic data types
- √ Order of operations
- √ Number types
- √ Visual Basic variable defaults
- √ Arrays
- √ Variant arrays
- √ Dynamic arrays
- √ Dim and ReDim
- √ Public, Private, and Static
- √ Friend

Techniques you'll need to master:

- √ Correctly identifying those data types that slow down an application
- √ Coding an application to avoid mathematical errors
- √ Converting one data type to another
- √ Understanding the difference between explicit and implicit variable declaration
- √ Understanding the limitations of Option Explicit
- √ Declaring variables with different scopes and lifetimes
- √ Declaring procedures with different scopes
- √ Declaring and manipulating static and dynamic arrays

In this chapter, we will begin our trek towards Visual Basic certification with the very basic essentials. We will explore the VB data types, both in terms of what is available and in terms of how they impact your application. My main focus will be on the intrinsic data types—the **Integer**, **String**, and so on. Although I will touch upon the **Object** data type, this is discussed more extensively in Chapters 3 and 4. The **Variant** data type is a special case and figures prominently in this chapter as well as Chapters 3 and 4. Of course, **Variant**s also play a major factor in the certification exam.

We will also take a look at what a well-coded application is and branch quickly into how your choice of data types impacts the application's performance and accuracy. Then, we'll examine each of the data types before finally delving into the more specialized topics of **Variant**s, arrays, and so on.

What Is A Well-Coded Application?

A well-done application, first and foremost, works. Not far behind that requirement is that it work as efficiently as possible within the constraints of clear, concise code and user friendliness. As an example, consider the following two snippets of code

```
If iCtr Then
    ' do something
```

and:

```
If iCtr = True Then
    ' do something
```

Both are functionally the same. If **iCtr** is any non-zero value, the expression evaluates to **True** and the next line of code is executed. However, although the intent may be clear to you, the soon-to-be Microsoft Certified Solutions Developer, it may be less clear to someone else who needs to modify the program. The actual coding style of the first snippet is an old-timer's trick to save a processing cycle or two. As such, it actually is more efficient, but clarity of coding usually takes precedence over any cutesy tricks and, even more, today's highly optimized compilers often negate the cost savings.

A well-designed and well-coded program will choose the proper events to place code. For instance, assume you have a form on which you have placed a command button called Save. You also have a Save item in the menu. Many programmers will place identical code in both places because the two objects perform the same function. This is poor practice because any changes that are made later will need to be done twice. It is also a violation of the object-oriented goal of code reuse and encapsulation of functionality (see Chapter 4). A better solution is to create a form module procedure and call it from both the command button and the menu.

Today's client/server programs spend most of their time either "idling," waiting for user input, or writing or reading from the database. Therefore, your programs will perform best if you concentrate your efforts in those areas.

Even so, common sense can often realize significant efficiencies. Consider a **For...Next** construct that loops through an array of 500 elements. We could code **For iCtr = 1 to UBound (array)**, calculating the upper bound 500 times. It is more efficient to assign the calculated value to a variable

```
iTop = UBound (array)
```

and then use that variable in the loop:

```
For iCtr = 1 To iTop
```

 The prior two methods for achieving the same result lead us to one of the more devilish aspects of the Microsoft certification exams. You'll often be asked for the "best" solution—not simply the "correct" solution.

Another key area of good programming is user friendliness. This involves a well-thought-out graphical user interface (GUI), as well as choosing the proper event in which to place code that reacts to user interaction. The design of a proper GUI is a science unto itself and is beyond the scope of this book. There are, however, many fine articles, including some on the Microsoft Web site (www.microsoft.com), that address this issue.

Using the correct data type is an important element of program performance and a crucial element of program accuracy. Let's consider each concept in turn.

Data Types And Program Performance

Visual Basic data types range in size anywhere from 1 to 12 bytes. All else being equal, a shorter data type can be moved, evaluated, and operated on more quickly than a longer data type. This is implicitly obvious. However, "all else" is not always equal.

Consider Table 2.1. I wrote a simple program to compare the times it took to perform simple assignment logic using each of the Visual Basic intrinsic data types. In the table, I show the efficiency of each data type relative to the **Byte** data type. For example, after compiling the program to unoptimized pseudo-code (p-code), the **Boolean** data type took 69.81 percent as long to perform the assignment logic, as did the **Byte** data type. I used **Byte** because, at one byte in length, it is the simplest data type. Figures 2.1 and 2.2 show times (for 9 million assignments) displayed in the program. Some of the results are astounding in their relative inefficiencies.

There are two morals to be gleaned from our little test. One is that, all else being equal, shorter data types *do* process more efficiently than longer data types. The other is that the purpose of the data type plays a large role in efficiency. A floating-point number (**Single** and **Double**) will take a little longer than equivalent-length integers (**Integer** and **Long**) because the FPU (floating-point unit) does not need to be invoked. In other words, 1 is a more simple number than 1.01 for the computer to handle. The greater moral is to use integers where you can (anywhere that the numbers are guaranteed to be whole, such as loop counters). Note that the **Decimal** data type is new to Visual Basic

Table 2.1	Processing times expressed as a percentage of the time it took to perform 9-million byte operations.		
Data Type	**Length**	**P-Code**	**Native**
Boolean	16-bit	69.81%	114.14%
Byte	8-bit	100.00%	100.00%
Currency	64-bit	101.32%	341.41%
Date	64-bit	26,006.06%	381,818.18%
Decimal	96-bit	652.86%	4,843.43%
Double	64-bit	89.16%	84.84%
Integer	16-bit	66.33%	69.69%
Long	32-bit	75.08%	82.82%
Single	32-bit	88.00%	84.84%
String	8-bit *	293.80%	3,041.41%
* The string used was one byte long but can be of varying length.			

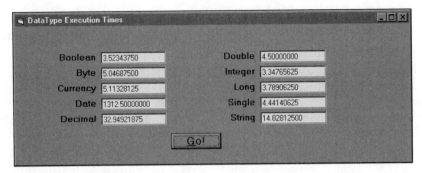

Figure 2.1   Measuring the execution efficiency of Visual Basic data types. The test was done compiling to p-code.

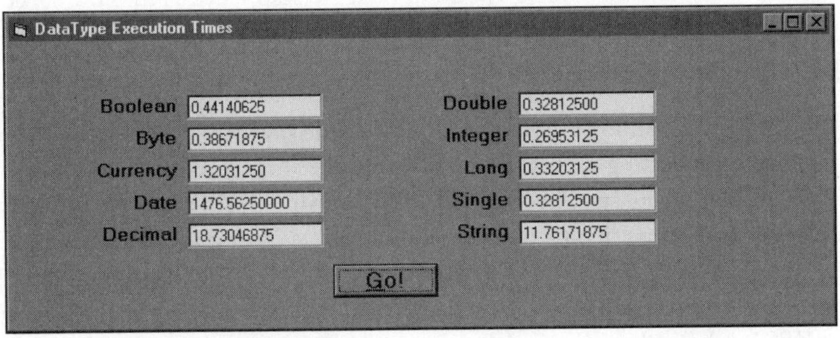

Figure 2.2   Another look at data type efficiency, this time after compiling to native code.

and is not full supported. It is implemented as the underlying data type of a **Variant** and must be assigned using the **CDec** function:

```
decSalary = CDec (10150.52)
```

Data Types And Program Accuracy

Computers are far from the most accurate number-crunchers in the world. The five pounds or so of gray matter inside your head is far more accurate. The old adage that computers can make mistakes much faster than any human is very true.

The problem lies in the inherent limitation that all computers store numbers in digital (as opposed to analog) format. Consider an 8-bit data type. Any one bit can be one of two possible values: zero or one. Therefore, 8 bits can represent at most 2^8 (or 256) possible values. The **Single** data type is 32 bits long and so can store up to 2^{32} (or 4,294,967,296) possible values. Admittedly, this is a large number, but consider all of the possible numbers between 1 and 2 (1.01, 1.02, and so on). The number is infinite. Therefore, the best a computer can do is to approximate the number.

Most experienced developers have been "burned" at some time by unexpected rounding errors and *overflows* (numbers too big or too small to be contained in the variable's data type). Try coding an application where you have a **Single** data type to which you have assigned the value 123456789. Now, perform 16 divisions followed by 16 multiplications of the value by number 1012. The result is a rounding error of 152. If the application performed 17 divisions, it would have created an "overflow" error. What has happened is that the successive divisions created a number too small for the **Single** data type to store so that Visual Basic begins losing digits.

If the same program logic used the **Double** data type (which is larger), Visual Basic has no rounding errors. Still, if the number of iterations is increased to 106, rounding errors start occurring with the **Double** data type. At 106 iterations, the error is less than .1. At 108 iterations, the error is more than 3 and by 110 iterations, the error is in the thousands! At 111 iterations, the result is zero—the computations have exceeded Visual Basic's storage range. Although the VB developer is unlikely to encounter such severe situations, he or she should still consider the potential of computation errors when choosing data types and balance that concern against the time it takes to perform those computations (as outlined in Table 2.1).

Data Types Explored

Visual Basic is rich in the data types you may choose for your variables. These can be thought of in terms of *simple*, *complex*, and *object* data types. Simple data types, such as **Integer** and **String**, are those that Visual Basic supplies for you. Complex data types encompass user-defined data types, as well as more advanced implementations, such as arrays. Simple and complex data types are referred to as *intrinsic* data types. Finally, **Object** data types are actual Visual Basic objects, such as forms and command buttons, as well as objects that you create yourself. I will discuss each in turn.

Number And Character Types

Integers are whole numbers (e.g., no decimal or fraction) and, as such, are most useful for pointers, handles, counters, and so on. Their advantages are speed of operation and minimal storage requirements. Visual Basic provides two *signed* integers with the **Integer** and **Long** data types. A signed number can be either negative or positive and reserves one bit for the *mantissa*. The mantissa is a fancy term for the sign of a number. Additionally, the **Byte** data type can be used for any small (1 to 255) unsigned (positive) value. Moving a fractional number into an integer (**Integer** or **Long** VB data types) results in the decimal portion being dropped. For instance, 3.14 becomes 3 and 15.2 becomes 15.

Scaled integers are data types that look like real numbers (see the next paragraph) but are actually integers. Visual Basic implements the **Currency** and **Decimal** data types this way: When you set **currAmount = 1.14**, Visual Basic actually stores it as 11400 (the **Currency** data type supports up to four pseudo decimal points). The **Decimal** data type works similarly except that Visual Basic scales it by storing a power of 10, which specifies the number of digits to the right of the decimal point. The advantage is that you get the speed of integer operations and avoid the rounding errors inherent in floating-point operations. The disadvantage is that true floating-point operations are not possible.

Real numbers are those that can be represented with a fixed number of decimal places. The numbers 14 and 1 $\frac{1}{2}$ (1.5) are real numbers, but 1 $\frac{1}{3}$ isn't, because it cannot be represented in a fixed number of decimal places. Visual Basic does not have a real data type per se; it uses *floating-point numbers* instead.

Floating-point numbers approximate non-real numbers by storing them in exponential format—often called scientific format—where the exponent signifies where the decimal point should be. For instance, 1.14E-7 means the decimal point should be moved seven positions to the left (0.000000114) whereas 1.14E+7 means the decimal point should be moved seven places to the right (11400000). This represents a compact way to store very large and very small numbers.

The **String** data type is used to store character data. Unlike other languages, the VB **String** is not "null-terminated" (which means that the end of the **String** is indicated by a null character). Instead, VB maintains an internal table of **Strings**. VB allows variable-length **Strings** (which can be of any length from empty to approximately 2 billion characters) and fixed-length **Strings**, which, as the name implies, are always of the same length. If the data is not long enough to fill the **String**, the remainder is filled with spaces.

Table 2.2 lists each Visual Basic data type, along with its length, range, conversion functions, and usage notes. Note that all numerical data types default to

Table 2.2   Visual Basic data types.

Type	Length	Min Value	Max Value	Conv	Notes
Boolean	16 bits	False	True	CBool	Use for "truth" statements.
Byte	8 bits	0	255	CByte	Equivalent to C's char data type.
Currency	64 bits	-9 trillion	+ 9 trillion	CCurr	Use for monetary calculations.
Date	64 bits	1 Jan 100	31 Dec 9999	CDate	Use for date and time calculations.
Decimal	96 bits	See note 1	See note 1	CDec	Use for huge real numbers.
Double	64 bits	See note 2	See note 2	CDbl	Use for floating-point calculations.
Integer	16 bits	-32,768	+32,767	CInt	Use for most integer operations.
Long	32 bits	-2 billion	+2 billion	CLng	Use for large integer operations.
Single	32 bits	See note 3	See note 3	CSng	Use for moderate size floating-point operations.
String	Varies	0 chars	2^{31} chars	CStr	Can be fixed or variable length.

Note 1: The **Decimal** data type can hold a number of +/- 79,228,162,514,264,337,593,543,950,335 if no decimal positions are used. The number of decimal positions can be from 0 to 28.

Note 2: The **Double** data type can hold numbers from -1.79769313486232E308 to -4.94065645841247E-324 for negative values and +4.94065645841247E-324 to +1.79769313486232E308 for positive values.

Note 3: The **Single** data type can hold numbers from -3.402823E38 to -1.401298E-45 for negative values and +1.401298E-45 to +3.402823E38 for positive values.

zero when first declared. **Boolean** defaults to **False**, **Date** defaults to midnight, 30 Dec 1899. **String** defaults to empty.

Variant Data Type

The **Variant** data type is a source of confusion to many VB developers. It is a 16-bit pointer to the underlying data; *it does not actually store the value assigned to it*. However, it *is* a data type unto itself. It is capable of storing any valid

Visual Basic data type, including **Object**. Though its underlying data type might be **String** or **Integer**, its own data type remains **Variant**. When declared but not initialized (prior to having data assigned to it), it has a value of **Empty** (*not* **Null**). Only if the underlying data is **Null** will a **Variant** have a value of **Null**.

The **Variant** data type is inefficient. When a value is assigned to it, the **Variant** takes its type from the data and will use the "smallest" appropriate data type. Thus, **vNum = 1** will create an **Integer** data type while **vNum = 18.2** will create a **Single**. If the number becomes too large, Visual Basic will "promote" it (e.g., from **Integer** to **Long**). **Variant** is Visual Basic's default data type. If you subsequently assign an incompatible value (such as assigning a **String** to a **Variant** that had been storing an **Integer**), the **Variant**'s underlying data type changes to accommodate. The **Variant** cannot be used for fixed-length **String** data types.

To convert a value to a **Variant**, use the **CVar** function.

 To force a **Variant** to recognize a date, use the pound sign modifier:

```
vValue = #1-July-1998#
```

To determine the type of variable within the **Variant**, use the **VarType** function, which returns a number from zero to 17, or the value 8192. As an example

```
If VarType (vVar) = vbLong
```

returns true if the underlying data type of **vVar** is **Long**. These numbers, which can be evaluated as Visual Basic constants, are enumerated in Table 2.3.

You can perform some trickery with the **Variant** data type to perform mathematical operations on seemingly non-numeric data. Assume you have a value of "$10,654.15" stored in a **Variant**. Visual Basic compares the value to the Regional Setting in the Windows Control Panel. If it is a valid format for that country (in this case, with a dollar sign, a comma for the thousands separator, and a period for the decimal point), it can have mathematical operations performed on it as seen in the following snippet of code:

```
' demonstrate math on strings
Dim vNumber1 As Variant, vNumber2 As Variant
vNumber1 = "$12,100.14"
vNumber2 = "8,016,.32"
' Displays 4083.82
MsgBox vNumber1 - vNumber2
```

Table 2.3	Visual Basic constants to determine data type.	
Constant	**Value**	**Meaning**
vbEmpty	0	Empty
vbNull	1	Null
vbInteger	2	Integer
vbLong	3	Long integer
vbSingle	4	Single-precision floating-point number
vbDouble	5	Double-precision floating-point number
vbCurrency	6	Currency value
vbDate	7	Date value
vbString	8	String
vbObject	9	Object
vbError	10	Error value
vbBoolean	11	Boolean value
vbVariant	12	Variant (used only with arrays of **Variant**s)
vbDataObject	13	A data access object
vbDecimal	14	Decimal value
vbByte	17	Byte value
vbArray	8192	Array

This raises some interesting issues of ambiguity (in this case, ambiguous to the compiler) when strings are stored as **Variants**. Suppose we wanted to concatenate two **Variants** whose underlying data type is **String**. **vString1** has a value of "1000" while **vString2** has a value of "is a number". You might code it as:

```
vString3 = vString1 + vString2
```

You would not get the expected result ("1000 is a number"). Instead, you would get a type mismatch error. Visual Basic evaluates the first variable (**vString1**) to determine if it is a number and, if so, assumes the plus operator (+) indicates an arithmetic operation, which is clearly wrong. I will discuss concatenation (and other operators) in the next chapter, but this provides a good example of why you will want to use the ampersand (&) instead of the plus sign to indicate concatenation.

Object Data Type

Object is a special Visual Basic data type that stores a 32-bit reference to a Visual Basic object such as a form or class. (This is discussed extensively in Chapters 3 and 4.) When initialized, an **Object** variable has a value of **Nothing** (not **Null**).

You can use one or more variables to refer to a Visual Basic object. Unlike other Visual Basic data types, you must use the **Set** keyword to make any assignments. To reinitialize the variable, you need to set it to **Nothing**. Memory is not freed until all variables pointing to an object are reinitialized, even if you think you have destroyed the object. For instance, if you **Load** a form and then reference it with a variable of type **Object**, the memory occupied by the form is not released until you both **UnLoad** the form *and* reinitialize the variable.

The **Is** Functions

Visual Basic has a number of functions to determine the type of a variable. They are most useful in determining the underlying data type of a **Variant**. The **Is** functions are as follows:

➤ **IsNumeric** Returns **True** for all data types except for **String** and **Object**. Note that VB considers **Date, Boolean,** and **Byte** to be numeric. VB returns **True** for the **Variant** data type if the underlying data type is any VB numeric data type.

➤ **IsDate** Returns **True** for **Date** and for **Variant** if the underlying data type is **Date**.

➤ **IsEmpty** Returns **True** only for a **Variant** that has not been initialized.

➤ **IsObject** Returns **True** for the **Object** data type and for **Variant** if the underlying data type is **Object**.

➤ **IsNull** Returns **True** if a variable's value is **Null**. The nature of **Null** is discussed at the end of Chapter 3.

 Always use the **IsNull** function to determine whether a **Variant** is **Null**. Because the two expressions **If MyVar = Null** and **If MyVar <> Null** are both **Null** themselves, they always return **False**.

User-Defined Data Type

The Visual Basic user-defined data type isn't a data type per se. It's a mechanism using the **Type...End Type** construct that allows the VB developer to create his or her own data type. It is used to create "collections" of data, similar to what is called a record in COBOL and a structure in many other languages. The individual members of the **Type** can be of any data type themselves including arrays. When *instantiated* (created) in a program, it can be declared as an array of the **Type** itself. For instance, if a **Type SignOnRec** were declared (via **Type…End Type**), it might be created in the application as an array **Dim strRecIn (14) As SignOnRec**. User-defined data types are public by default. You can override this using the **Private** keyword. However, in a class module, user-defined data types can only be private.

Visual Basic Defaults

Visual Basic does not require that you declare any variables. If you do not code **Option Explicit** (which requires all variables in the module in which it occurs to be explicitly declared before they can be used) into your program, you may declare a variable at any time merely by using that variable.

Early releases of Visual Basic, and this is true for most implementations of Basic since it was introduced in 1964, had a default data type of **Single**. Therefore, if you did not declare a data type, it defaulted to **Single**. Since the introduction of Visual Basic 4, the default has changed to **Variant**, where Visual Basic infers the data type from its context. In other words, the statement

```
my_variable = "CAT"
```

creates a **Variant** whose underlying data type is **String**.

Default behavior can be overridden with the mostly archaic **Def***datatype* statement, where *datatype* might be **Int** (**DefInt**) for **Integer** or **Dbl** (**DefDbl**) for **Double**. For instance, you can cause all variables in your program to default to the **Boolean** data type with the statement: **DefBool A – Z**. This says that any variable beginning with a letter from A to Z (case-insensitive) will default to the **Boolean** data type.

 Unlike the C language, Visual Basic is completely case-insensitive in terms of variable naming, procedure naming, and so on.

Another way to override default behavior is by appending a *data type designator* to the variable. The percentage sign (%), for instance, tells Visual Basic that the data type is an **Integer**, as seen in this statement:

Table 2.4	Type declaration characters.
Type	**Character**
Byte	None
Boolean	None
Currency	@
Data	None
Decimal	None
Double	#
Integer	%
Long	&
Object	None
Single	!
String	$
Variant	None

```
myInt% = 14
```

These special characters are no longer fully supported, probably because Visual Basic has more data types than there are special characters. These type declaration characters are summarized in Table 2.4.

Letting Visual Basic assign your data type is normally a bad programming practice because, at best, you cannot be sure VB will choose the most efficient data type. (In fact, because it defaults to the inefficient **Variant**, you can be pretty sure that VB will almost always choose the least efficient one.) Worse, this can sometimes result in subtle, hard-to-find errors.

Allowing Visual Basic to create variables on the fly is an even worse habit. The mistyping of a previously used variable results in very difficult-to-find bugs, which is a notorious weakness in the Basic language. This can be surmounted, however, by the explicit declaration of all variables, which can be done through the **Dim**, **ReDim**, **Static**, **Private**, and **Public** keywords. I will explore this in a moment.

 Relying on VB to create the variables for you is called *implicit declaration*. Using **Dim**, **ReDim**, and so on, to declare variables is called *explicit declaration*.

Explicit Variable Declaration In Visual Basic

You can enforce explicit declarations (in other words, you can make sure that all variables are declared before they are used) by using the **Option Explicit** statement. This is done at either the module level or the project level. To enforce it at the project level, select Tools|Options from the menu and select the Editor tag. Click on Require Variable Declaration. This places **Option Explicit** at the top of all modules (in the Declarations section).

There are two schools of thought on where to declare variables (setting aside matters of scope, which will be discussed later in this chapter). The first is to declare all variables at the top of the procedure or module. The second is to declare variables right before using them. Visual Basic supports either convention.

Variable Declaration

The five keywords used to declare a variable are **Dim**, **ReDim**, **Static**, **Public**, and **Private**. The syntax of each is as follows:

➤ **Dim** [With Events] *varname* [(subscripts)] [As [New] *vartype*] [, ...]

➤ **ReDim** [Preserve] *varname* [(subscripts)] [As *vartype*] [, ...]

➤ **Static** *varname* [(subscripts)] [As [New] *vartype*] [, ...]

➤ **Public** [With Events] *varname* [(subscripts)] [As [New] *vartype*] [, ...]

➤ **Private** [With Events] *varname* [(subscripts)] [As [New] *vartype*] [, ...]

Dim

Most variables will be declared with the **Dim** keyword. Variables declared with **Dim** at the module level are *visible* to all procedures within the module, whereas variables declared with **Dim** at the *procedure* level are only visible within that procedure.

The **With Events** clause creates an object that can respond to an ActiveX control. (This will be discussed more fully in Chapters 4 and 8.) It can only be used within class modules. The *varname* is the name you assign to the variable. Subscripts declare that the variable is an array (see "Visual Basic Arrays" later in the chapter). The *vartype* declares that the variable will be a certain data type. **New** is used to implicitly create an object the first time it is referenced (the object will not exist until **New** is first used, whereas omitting it causes the object to be created and storage allocated immediately). Therefore, the variable is not created until it is actually assigned a value. **New** cannot be used with intrinsic data types, nor can it be used in conjunction with the **With Events** clause. **Preserve** will be discussed, along with dynamic arrays, in a few pages.

ReDim

ReDim is mostly used to resize arrays previously declared as dynamic (see the section titled "Dynamic Arrays" later in this chapter). The **Preserve** keyword is used only in conjunction with **ReDim**. Otherwise, its syntax is the same as **Dim**.

ReDim can also be used to declare a variable not previously declared, even if you've used **Option Explicit**. This can lead to hard-to-find bugs, so it should not be used.

Static

Static is used to declare a variable at the procedure level. The variable retains its value as long as your program is running. It is otherwise identical to **Dim** except that the **With Events** clause is not supported. **Static** can also be used to declare an entire procedure as being **Static** (for example: **Static Sub mySub**), in which case all variables within the procedure are also automatically **Static**.

Be careful of the context of the **Static** keyword. A procedure that is declared as **Static [Static Function calcTotal (iX As Integer, iY As Integer)]** causes all locally declared variables within that procedure to be static (to retain their values between executions of the procedure). A variable that is declared **Static** within a non-static procedure (a procedure that has not been declared as **Static**) retains its value between executions, but other locally declared variables do not. This is prime fodder for the exam to trip you up.

Public

Public variables are declared at the module levels. By default, they are then available to *all* modules being executed (even those outside of your project). If **Option Private Module** has been declared, then the variable is only visible to the current project.

You cannot use **Public** to declare a fixed-length string in a class module.

Private

Private is used to declare variables at the module level. It makes these variables visible to all procedures within that module, but they cannot be seen by procedures outside of that module. Otherwise, it is identical in use to **Public** and **Dim**.

Variable Scope And Lifetime

When you refer to a variable scope, you refer to its visibility—that is, who can "see" it and who can change it. When we discuss variables in this context, the same rules apply to object data types and intrinsic data types. This is a confusing topic for many developers. I have attempted to summarize visibility rules as succinctly as possible in the next paragraph.

As noted, a variable declared as **Public** can be "seen" by all modules running on your system. If you have the **Option Private Module** clause in effect, variables are only visible within the current project. Thus, if a variable is declared as **Public**, a standard module can read and change the variables declared in another standard module. If the variable is declared as **Private**, however, it can only be accessed by procedures within the module in which it is declared. When **Dim** is used to declare a variable at the procedure level, the variable is *local* in scope, meaning that it cannot be seen or changed by any other procedure in any module. When the procedure is exited, the variable is destroyed. **Static** can also be used to declare variables at the procedure level (and not at the module level); in that case, it is functionally equivalent to **Dim**, except that the variable is not destroyed and retains its value between calls to the procedure.

 When you declare a variable at the procedure level, you can reuse the variable's name in other procedures with no conflict *unless* the variable has been declared as **Static**.

As a final note, Visual Basic once sported the **Global** keyword to declare variables as global in scope. It has been retained for backward compatibility, but it is no longer documented and is reported to cause inconsistent results.

 It cannot be stressed enough that by declaring a procedure (sub or function) as **Static**, you are effectively causing all variables within the procedure to be static. On the other hand, if you do not declare a procedure as **Static**, you are free to declare any variables within the procedure as **Static**.

Procedure Scope

Procedures also have scope. When you place a command button on a form and then double-click it, Visual Basic opens the program editor and creates a procedure **Sub command_button_click**. Because procedures default to global visibility, all modules in all projects can access that procedure. (When you create an event procedure by double-clicking on a control, VB inserts **Private**, which overrides the default behavior.)

Procedure scope can be altered with the **Private, Public,** and **Friend** keywords. If the **Option Private** (not to be confused with the **Option Private Module** variable visibility modifier) option is used, **Public** procedures are visible only within the current project. Procedures declared as **Private** are visible only within the module in which they are defined.

The **Friend** keyword is used to declare procedures, but only within class modules. These procedures are visible to all modules within the project, but not to a class that instantiated the class with the **Friend** procedure (if class A instantiates class B, the procedures within class B declared with **Friend** are not available to class A nor do they appear in the type library of class A). It is a strange implementation. **Friend** is a concept used in other languages, but those languages typically allow you to say whom you will be "friendly" with (in other words, what other classes can access the procedure). Its purpose is to expose a **Private** variable within the class under control of the class. (Essentially, this means that though the variable may be visible outside of the class, only the class itself can change it. This is a process called *encapsulation*, which is defined in Chapter 3. I will expand upon the definition and use of classes in Chapter 4.)

Visual Basic Arrays

An array is a collection of *logically related* data. The data elements stored in the array do not need to have any physical relationship with each other; they can be grouped together merely for the convenience of the developer.

Arrays may have any Visual Basic data type, including any Visual Basic object. When you copy an existing control on a form and select Paste, you are implicitly creating an array of that control. Thus, if you have a command button named **cmdProcess** and copy and paste it, you have created an array of type **cmdProcess**.

 Each element in an array of controls is always the same "type" as the base element and, thus, inherits all of its properties from that base element. This is as close as Visual Basic gets to "inheritance" in the object-oriented sense (discussed in Chapter 3).

Each item in an array is an *element* and is referenced by its *subscript*, often called its *index*. When you create an array of command buttons, for instance,

Visual Basic automatically increments the array's subscript so that each command button can be individually referenced.

To declare an array, simply follow the variable name with the number of elements, enclosed in parentheses:

```
Dim myArray (21) As Integer
```

 There is a key difference between arrays of controls and arrays of other variable types. For arrays of controls, the elements do not need to be numbered contiguously. For instance, you can have an array of five command buttons with the **Index** properties set to 2, 4, 6, 8, and 10. To change the index number of each control, use the control's property page and alter its **Index** property.

With the control exception noted, when you create an array of a certain number of elements, Visual Basic reserves space for every item in that array, regardless of whether you actually use them. Avoid making an array larger than you require, as this wastes memory and can slow your program. To calculate the storage requirements of an array, multiply the number of elements by the variable size. To that, add 20 bytes, plus 4 bytes for each dimension in the array.

Array Subscripts

Arrays always begin with element number zero unless explicitly declared otherwise. You can use **Option Base 1** to override this behavior and force all arrays to begin with element 1. The beginning of the array (the lowest element number) is referred to as its *lower bound*. The highest element number is referred to as its *upper bound*. The Visual Basic **LBound** and **UBound** functions return the lower and upper bounds of an array respectively (i.e. **LBound (array)**. You can use the **To** keyword to modify the numbering:

```
Dim sVar (3 To 8) As String
```

The subscripts may be any valid Visual Basic **Long**, and thus, may range as low as -2,147,483,648 and as high as 2,147,483,647. The subscripts may be numeric *literals* (a literal is any specific value, rather than a value stored in a variable) or any variable previously declared as a constant (**Const**). You cannot use a non-constant variable, or any function returning a numeric result, to size an array, except with the **ReDim** statement (see the section titled "Dynamic Arrays"). If the number is fractional, it is rounded (1.49 becomes 1 and 1.5 becomes 2).

Array Scope

The same rules about visibility with non-subscripted objects also apply to arrays. To make an array visible throughout a project, use the **Public** keyword when declaring the array. To limit its scope to the current module, use the **Private** keyword.

Multidimensional Arrays

By default, arrays have one dimension. The number of dimensions is indicated by the number of subscripts. A three-dimension array might look like this:

```
Dim iTotals (2 To 4, 1 To 2, -18 To 57)
```

Dynamic Arrays

You can dynamically resize an array so that it can grow or shrink as needed. To declare a dynamic array, omit the number of elements in the **Dim** (or **Public**, **Private**, or **Static**) statement:

```
Dim iDynamic ( ) As Integer
```

When you determine the number of elements required, you allocate the storage with the **ReDim** keyword. You can repeatedly use **ReDim** to alter the number of elements in an array, and the subscript may be specified as a literal (as with **Dim**), a variable, or the result of a function returning a numeric result. Redimensioning the array destroys all of the data contained in the array (effectively reinitializing it) unless you use the **Preserve** keyword. If you increase the number of elements in an array and use **Preserve**, all of the data in the array is preserved and the new elements are initialized. If you shrink the size of the array, only that data in the remaining elements is retained.

Technically, you do not need to specify the data type of an array when redimensioning the array; it retains its original data type. However, it is good practice to do so because it serves as one more check so that you do not inadvertently create a new variable by using **ReDim** in its declarative mode. For instance, the last line in this code resizes **iArray** to two elements (0 and 1). If you left off the data type and made a typing mistake, such as **ReDim iAray (1)**, you will have created a new array of **Variant**s.

When you use the **Preserve** keyword, only the upper bound of the last dimension can be modified. You can, however, change the number of dimensions if you are not using **Preserve**, as seen in the following code:

```
' Declare a dynamic array
Dim sArray () As String
' Redimension the array
ReDim sArray (2, 4) As String
' Redimension last element
ReDim Preserve sArray (2,8) As String
' This causes a runtime error
ReDim Preserve sArray (3, 8) as String
' This also causes a runtime error
ReDim Preserve sArray (4) As String
' Without Preserve, you can change both the
' upper and lower bounds
ReDim sArray (3 To 5, 2 To 10)
```

 Use **Erase** to clear the contents of an array (**Erase myArray**). If the array is fixed, all values are initialized. If the array is dynamic, all memory is reclaimed. To use the array again, you will have to **ReDim** it. Erasing a fixed array does NOT mean you can now **ReDim** it!

Variant Arrays

You can never change the data type of an array unless that data type is part of a **Variant** array (and even with an array of **Variant**s, you can only change the underlying data type). However, each element in a **Variant** array can hold a *different* underlying data type. Further, if a **Variant** is equal to an array, you *can* change the data type of that array.

You can dynamically create an array of **Variant**s with the **Array** function. Each element can be of any data type. The following code creates a one-dimensional array of three items and then displays them. The data types are **Integer**, **Date**, and **String** respectively:

```
Dim vArray As Variant
vArray = Array(3, #1/19/98#, "cat")
MsgBox vArray(0)
MsgBox vArray(1)
MsgBox vArray(2)
```

Arrays Of Arrays

You can create arrays of arrays by employing an array of **Variant**s. These can be nested as deeply as you need. Assume, for instance, that you have two arrays of type **String**:

```
Dim sNames (10) As String
```

Assume also that you have two arrays of **Variant**s:

```
Dim vArray1 (10) As Variant, vArray2 (10) As Variant
```

You can then set any element of the first **Variant** array equal to the entire contents of the **String** array:

```
vArray1 (1) = sNames
```

You can then nest array references by setting an element of the second **Variant** array equal to the first **Variant** array

```
vArray2 (1) = vArray1
```

To reference an item in the **String** array nested in the second **Variant** array, you append the appropriate subscripts such as:

```
MsgBox vArray2 (1) (1) (3)
```

In this example, the message box will display the contents of the first element of **vArray2**, which contains **vArray1**. A further reference is made to the first element of **vArray1**, which contains the **String** array **sNames**. Finally, a reference is made to the third element of **SNames**. If **sNames (3)** is equal to "Visual Basic," then that is what will display in the message box.

Constants

Visual Basic constants are very powerful—they can make a program very readable. They can, and usually do, yield significant performance gains because Visual Basic resolves their values at compilation, instead of at runtime. The trade-off is that once a variable has been designated as a constant, it cannot be changed at runtime (hence the term constant).

Visual Basic 5 has added many new built-in constants that are enumerated in the Help file (search on the term "Constant"). Typical Visual Basic constants are **vbNormal** (a file attribute), **vbSaturday** (day of week), and **vbCalGreg** (indicates the Gregorian calendar is being used). You will not be asked to memorize them all on the exam, but you will be expected to use them and to understand that they are *not* reserved words. Table 2.3 listed some VB constants to denote a data type, including **vbSingle** with a compiler assigned value of 4. You can, however, define a constant **vbSingle** with a different value (**Const vbSingle = 10189**). This does not generate an error—instead, the value you assign overrides that which Visual Basic normally would have assigned.

You can also create your own constants using the following syntax:

[**Public|Private**] **Const** *varname* **As** data type = value

Constants default to **Private**. You can specify **Public** or **Private** when constants are defined at the module level, but not when they are defined at the procedure level.

Exam Prep Questions

Question 1

What is the data type of "a" below?

```
DIM a, b, c As Integer
```

○ a. **Integer**

○ b. **Variant**

○ c. User-defined

○ d. None of the above

The correct answer is b. Each variable needs to be declared explicitly or it defaults to type *Variant*. Only "c" is defined as type **Integer**. Because "a" is not explicitly declared, answers a, c, and d are incorrect. The trick is not to make the (easy to do) mistake in looking at the declaration and jumping to the conclusion that all three variables are of type **Integer**.

Question 2

What is the data type of "a" below?

```
DefInt A - Z
a = 1
B = 2
```

○ a. **Integer**

○ b. **Variant**

○ c. User-defined

○ d. None of the above

Answer a is correct because of the *DefInt* statement, which causes all variables beginning with the letters A through Z to be *Integer* data types. Do not let the question throw you with the mixture of upper- and lowercase. Testing is a stressful situation and we can easily look for things that aren't there. Visual Basic is not case-sensitive. Answer b is incorrect because variables default to **Variant** only when not explicitly declared otherwise. Answer c is incorrect because the variable is not a user-defined data type. Answer d is incorrect because the correct choice is given.

Question 3

> If you run the following code in the development environment, will it run correctly?
>
> ```
> Dim iCtr As Integer
> For iCtr = 1 To 35000
> Next
> ```
>
> ○ a. Yes
>
> ○ b. No, you will get an overflow error
>
> ○ c. No, because the **Next** statement is invalid
>
> ○ d. Yes, but only if **DefPos** is used to make all variables positive

Answer b is correct because the loop goes to 35,000 and integers can only go up to 32,767. Answer a is wrong because the code, in fact, will terminate in an error. Answer c is wrong because the **Next** statement is valid—you do not have to provide an argument to the **Next** statement. Answer d is wrong because there is no such thing as a **DefPos** statement.

Question 4

> What is the visibility and lifetime of **lCount** in the following code found inside of a standard module?
>
> ```
> Static Sub Calculate ( arg1, arg2)
> Public lCount As long
> lCount = arg1 + arg2
> End Sub
> ```
>
> ○ a. Global and permanent
>
> ○ b. Global and lifetime of the module only
>
> ○ c. Local and permanent
>
> ○ d. None of the above

Answer d is the correct choice. You cannot have a *Public* statement inside of a sub or function; they are only declared at the module level. Answer a would have been correct if the variable had been declared **Public** at the module level. Answer b is a bit ambiguous and should have given a tip-off to the correct answer. Once a standard module is loaded, it does not "go away" until the application is ended, thus making answer b essentially the same as answer a.. Answer c would have been correct had the variable been declared with **Dim**.

Question 5

Calculate the memory taken up by the following array:

```
Dim iArray (10, 10) As Integer
```

○ a. 0 bytes

○ b. 200 bytes

○ c. 220 bytes

○ d. 228 bytes

Answer d is correct. The amount of memory needed for an array is equal to the space taken up by the data itself, plus 20 bytes of overhead per array, plus 4 bytes per dimension of each array: (100 integers x 2 bytes each = 200 bytes) + 20 bytes + (2 dimensions x 4 bytes per dimension = 8 bytes) = 200 + 20 + 8 = 228. The trick here is that you have to stop yourself from going for the "obvious" answer (b, which is incorrect). Answer a is incorrect because a static array always takes up memory. Answer b and c are incorrect because they fail to take into account the overhead for an array.

Question 6

> Which line of code will execute?
>
> ```
> Dim iVar As Integer
> iVar = 118
> If iVar Then
>     ' line 1
> else
>     ' line 2
> End If
> ```
>
> ○ a. Line 1
>
> ○ b. Line 2
>
> ○ c. Neither, because the **If** statement is invalid
>
> ○ d. Neither, because **iVar** is not a **Boolean**

Answer a is correct because Visual Basic treats any non-zero value as being *True*. If iVar had been equal to zero, line 2 would have executed. Therefore, answer b is incorrect. Answer c is incorrect because Visual Basic treats any **If** statement as a test of truth (**True** or **False**); it defaults to examining the zero or non-zero value of the variable if no explicit test is provided. Answer d is wrong because you do not need to use a **Boolean** unless you are explicitly testing for **True** or **False**.

Question 7

What will be displayed in the message box?

```
Dim iArray (5) As Integer
Dim sArray(5) As String
Dim myVar1, myVar2 As Integer
iArray (1) = 3
sArray (1) = "Visual Basic"
myVar1 = Array (iArray)
ReDim Preserve myVar1 (20)
myVar1 (7) = sArray
myVar1 (6) = myVar1
MsgBox myVar1 (6) (7) (1)
```

- ○ a. 3
- ○ b. Visual Basic
- ○ c. Nothing, because that value has not been initialized
- ○ d. A runtime error, because you cannot store an array within itself

Answer b is correct. As odd as it may sound, an array can be nested within itself. Element 6 points back to the *myVar* array. Element 7 stores the array of strings, and element 1 of the array of strings is equal to "Visual Basic." Answer a is wrong because it is not the value stored in the element being displayed (though at first glance, it appears that it is). Answer c is wrong because arrays don't need to be initialized before they are used (**Dim**ming or **ReDim**ming an array is an implicit initialization). Answer d is wrong because you can, in fact, store an array within itself.

Question 8

What will the message box display?

```
Const vbSingle = 5
Const vbDouble = 4
Dim sString As String
Dim sngVar As Single
If VarType(sngVar) = vbSingle Then
    sString = "single "
End If
If VarType(sngVar) = vbDouble Then
    sString = sString & "double"
End If
MsgBox sString
```

○ a. **Single**

○ b. **Double**

○ c. You will get a runtime error because **vbSingle** and **vbDouble** are Visual Basic constants

○ d. Empty string

Answer b is correct. Visual Basic allows you to override the built-in constants. *VarType (Single)* returns a 4, which was used to assign *vbDouble.* A little trickery here, because the test plays off our insecurities. Few of us have ever attempted to change a Visual Basic-supplied constant (because we have no reason to do so) and so we elevate them to the status of sainthood. But, they (VB-supplied constants) are no different than any others. Don't let the test-writers trick you into suspecting that what you know to be right isn't. Answer a is wrong for the reasons just mentioned. The first **If VarType** statement evaluates to **False** and so the message box is not displayed. Answer c is wrong because VB does allow you to change the values of Visual Basic constants. Answer d is wrong because there is no way for the code to create an empty string.

Question 9

What is the data type of the following:

```
Dim vValue
```

☐ a. **Integer**
☐ b. **Variant**
☐ c. **Empty**
☐ d. There is no data type until a value is assigned

Answer b is correct. This question is merely designed to make you doubt what you probably already know: *Variant* **is a data type.** Answer a is wrong because no assignment of type **Integer** has been made. Answer c is wrong because **Empty** is a value and not a data type. Answer d is wrong because **Variant** is a data type, although the underlying data type is not determined until an assignment is made.

Question 10

You have a class module in which the following is coded:

```
Public Type EmpRec
  EmpID As String * 5
  EmpName As String * 30
End Type
```

You later instantiate **EmpRec** in the following code:

```
Dim strEmpRec As EmpRec
strEnpRec.EmpID = "123456"
MsgBox strEmpRec.EmpID
```

What is displayed?

○ a. 12345
○ b. 23456
○ c. Nothing—the string is too big
○ d. None of the above

Answer d is the correct answer because the code will not run. You cannot de-clare a user-defined data type *Public* **in a class module.** The trick here is to look at what the answer choices actually mean and to ignore the extraneous detail. Answer d seems to imply that what will be displayed is actually something else. When taking the Microsoft exam, look at the code sample very carefully, with an eye towards whether it will even run at all! Answers a, b, and c are all incor-rect for the same reason that answer d is correct. If the user-defined data type had been declared **Private**, then answer a would have been correct. When an assignment of a literal that is too long is made to a fixed-length string, the string is truncated at the right side. Answer b would have been wrong (had the type been declared **Private**) because strings are not left-truncated. Answer c would have been incorrect because Visual Basic truncates when a string that is too long is assigned to a fixed-length string variable.

Need To Know More?

 Aitken, Peter: *Visual Basic5 Programming EXplorer*. Coriolis Group Books, Scottsdale, AZ, 1997. ISBN 1-57610-065-0. In Chapter 4, Peter provides a well-done and concise introduction to VB data types.

 Harrington, John, Mark Spenik, Heidi Brumbaugh, and Cliff Diamond: *Visual Basic 5 Interactive Course*. Waite Group Press, Corte Madera, CA, 1997. ISBN 1-57169-077-8. Chapter 3 is devoted to the subject of data types and their associated functions (such as conversion functions).

 Jamsa, Kris Ph.D. and Lars Klander: *1001 Visual Basic Programmer's Tips*. Jamsa Press, Las Vegas, NV, 1997. ISBN 1-884133-56-8. This well-done book is not broken into chapters, but rather into "tips." Tips 65 through 114 provide a well-documented discussion of all of the VB data types and extend the discussion into areas outside of the scope of this book, such as Tip 92, which discusses VB and "pointers." Tips 162 through 183 and 189 through 202 delve into the **String** data type, while Tips 292 through 330 provide a thorough discussion of arrays.

 McKinney, Bruce: *Hardcore Visual Basic*, Second Edition (which covers version 5). Microsoft Press, Redmond, WA, 1997. ISBN 1-57231-422-2. In Chapter 1, Bruce provides an interesting history of VB data types and a discussion of when to use which and the impact of data types on program performance.

 Search the online books on the VB CD for "Introduction to Variables, Constants and Data Types," which reviews all of the VB data types and has an excellent discussion on the vagaries of the **Variant** data type. Also discussed in this section are arrays and dynamic arrays.

 Microsoft places the most current Knowledge Base online at www.microsoft.com/support/. Enter search terms such as "array," "Variant," "data type," and so on, to view articles detailing tips (and sometimes fixes) revolving around the issues discussed in this chapter.

There are a number of Web sites devoted to the subject of Visual Basic. Use a search engine such as Yahoo! (www.yahoo.com) or Hotbot (www.hotbot.com) with a search term such as "Visual Basic 5" (be sure to place the search term in quotes so that only pages containing the entire term as one string are returned). A well-done site with tips and sample code that I liked was the VB Palace at home.computer.net/~mheller/. Another site that was under "reconstruction" when I visited was a site hosted by Temple University at thunder.ocis.temple.edu/~shariq/vb/index.html.

Visual Basic Coding

Terms you'll need to understand:

√ Object Browser

√ Instantiation

√ Expose

√ Reuse and Inheritance

√ Event-driven programming

√ Classes

√ Encapsulation

√ Polymorphism

√ Subs and functions

√ Form, standard, and class modules

√ Early and late binding

√ Null, Empty, and Nothing

√ MDI, SDI

√ Screen object

√ Variable promotion

√ Visual Basic operators

Techniques you'll need to master:

√ Using the Object Browser

√ Exploring and manipulating attached object libraries

√ Using RegSrv32 to register ActiveX EXEs and DLLs

√ Adding components to your project

√ Discovering and utilizing an object's name and class

√ Declaring a sub or function with appropriate scope

√ Using ParamArray in a sub or function declaration

√ Changing a project's startup module

√ Creating an MDI application

√ Manipulating and using the properties of the Screen object

In this chapter, I review the art and science of Visual Basic coding. I will focus on the background needed to maximize your productivity with Visual Basic; this can be broken into a number of broad areas, beginning with productive use of the editing environment and concluding with such advanced topics as object-oriented programming. As always, we will keep an eye to the certification exam.

Visual Basic Scripting

The Visual Basic MSCD exam is not out to measure how well you program—that is not possible with this type of examination (especially because it is computer graded). It does, however, intend to measure how well you can use the Visual Basic language and environment to develop your applications. The environment (the *IDE* or Integrated Development Environment) offers many aids to help in the development of the Visual Basic application. You are not likely to find many questions concerning how well you remember the menu structure in the program editor. Questions instead are targeted toward evaluating your ability to *use* that environment. (However, watch out for questions that list nonexistent menu choices.) I urge you to fire up Visual Basic and follow along.

 It may seem a bit trivial, but remember that the left mouse button is the "chooser" while the right button is the "explainer." Put in exam-ese, the right button exposes an object's properties through context menus. The left button implements those choices.

Mousing Around

Right-click anywhere in the editor and a pop-up or context menu appears. Most of the options in these menus are also available on the main menu, but placed here for added convenience. Not all options are implemented in the same way, though. For instance, when you select Bookmark under the Edit menu, a *cascading menu* appears. A cascading menu is one that leads to another pop-up menu. This Bookmark menu leads to a series of choices that allow you to move rapidly to the next or prior bookmark, as well as to toggle a bookmark. Under the context menu, however, Bookmark is a subchoice that cascades from the Toggle selection. Click on Toggle and you can select Bookmark, which merely toggles a bookmark on or off on the current line. From the Toggle menu, you can also set breakpoints in your code.

 When you use the Menu Editor to create a menu for your VB application, you indent one level to create a submenu. Indenting further creates cascading menus. Visual Basic automatically adds a right-arrow symbol on the "parent" menu item to indicate that selecting that menu item leads to a cascading menu.

Also available on the context menu are a number of program aids. Right-click on any variable and select Quick Info to obtain a summary of the variable's scope and type. Right-click within the parentheses of any function and select Parameter Info to obtain a summary of the function's arguments and return type. Right-click on any variable and select Definition, and Visual Basic moves the cursor to where the variable was first defined. Do the same on a Visual Basic keyword and click on Definition, and the Object Browser opens and moves to the definition of that keyword. (I will discuss the Object Browser in more detail in the "Object Browser" section later in this chapter.)

Interestingly, right-clicking on an object in your project and Visual Basic returns an error message stating that it "cannot jump to *objectname* because it is hidden." This clearly seems to be a bug.

Right-click while coding and select List Properties And Methods, and you are brought to a scrolling dialog box that lists essentially anything that could be typed in, given the current context. Use the arrow keys, if desired, to scroll to your choice, and then press the Tab key and Visual Basic will finish the typing for you.

Note: Though it is listed as a separate option, the Complete Word context menu choice (obtained by pressing Ctrl+spacebar) is functionally equivalent to the List Properties And Methods option.

You can highlight a block of code and right-click to cut, copy, or paste it. Holding down the left mouse button on a highlighted block of code allows you to drag it to a different location (if you've enabled the Cut And Paste option on the Editor tab in the dialog available under Tools|Options). Unfortunately, you cannot right-click and drag a block of code to get the Copy or Move dialog, as implemented in the Windows Explorer.

In the Object View mode of development, right-clicking on a control on your form also brings up a context menu that includes Properties. Some third-party controls have their own property pages, which are displayed in this manner.

Right-click on the Properties dialog and you get three choices. *Dockable* allows you to dock the dialog anywhere that is convenient. *Description*, when checked, displays a short summary of each property at the bottom of the dialog. *Hide* closes the dialog (use F4 to reopen it).

The right-mouse button offers another convenient shortcut: right-click on a form and you are presented with easy access to the Menu Editor. (Otherwise, the Menu Editor is only available from the Tools menu, although everything else is available in the active window.)

Keying Around

Well-crafted code, whatever the language, should be indented to reflect program logic and nesting. As an example, all program statements between **For** and **Next** should be indented to indicate that the code only executes in the context of that loop. You can set the indentation level (which defaults to four characters) and also auto indentation by selecting Tools|Options from the menu and choosing the Editor tab (see Figure 3.1). (Note that "tab" is essentially a user term, whereas technically it is known as a property page—I use the terms synonymously.) Auto indentation keeps your cursor at the same indent level when you press the Enter key, which is a convenience.

I discuss most of these options in Chapter 6 in the section titled "Other Error Prevention Strategies."

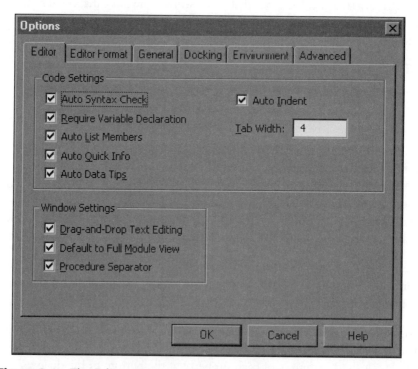

Figure 3.1   The Editor Options property page dialog.

Object Browser

A tool that you will want to become intimately familiar with is Visual Basic's Object Browser. This tool, available from the View menu or by pressing F2, allows examination of your project and, indeed, the entire Visual Basic environment in an object-oriented manner. Open the Object Browser and examine the left-hand column (see Figure 3.2).

 My only beef with the Object Browser is that it does not support a hierarchical view of classes to show the relations between them. Nevertheless, this is a window that you will want to resize and keep open, tucked in a corner somewhere, as you develop your application.

In the left pane of the Object Browser, you'll see a list of all of the available classes that can be included in your code. Objects may be part of another EXE, a DLL, an object library (.OLB), a table library (.TLB), or (most commonly) an ActiveX (.OCX) control. The DLLs listed are known as ActiveX DLLs; this means that they have special "entry points" for registering and unregistering their services with Windows. In general, the Object Browser is said to be a *table library browser.*

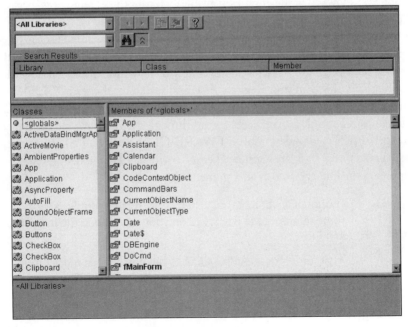

Figure 3.2   The Visual Basic Object Browser.

Anywhere that you see the word ActiveX, stand up and take notice! The exam is riddled with questions about ActiveX components and documents. I delve deeply into ActiveX in Chapter 9. Running a close second are questions related to data access, but that will have to wait until Chapter 10.

The standard controls that come with Visual Basic (labels, checkboxes, and so on) are embedded in an object library. Like an OCX, the objects *expose* (make visible and available to be used) their methods (functions) and properties. If you examine VB5.OLB, you'll see the standard Visual Basic controls. A type library carries this one step further by embedding one or more object libraries.

DLLs expose certain functions and procedures by *exporting* (essentially synonymous with exposing) them. If you right-click on CommCtrl.DLL, you will see one of the "non-resident" exported functions is **Create-PropertySheetPage**. (A property sheet is also known as a tabbed dialog—each page or tab is a property sheet page.) ActiveX DLLs can also contain objects that expose their methods and functions to Visual Basic. VBA5.DLL is an example (it contains the Visual Basic language).

You can add and delete from this list of *references* by right-clicking in the classes pane of the Object Browser, as mentioned earlier. You will be presented with a dialog that shows all of the libraries available (VB calls these "references" because the libraries are referenced when compiling), as seen in Figure 3.3. The references checked are already part of your project. Those that are not in use are listed alphabetically following those that are in use. To add additional libraries, use the Browse button. To get a fascinating overview of how these pieces fall together, run RegEdit (back up your Registry first) and search for the term "OLE (Part" (include the left parenthesis) in the Data section. Microsoft implements OLE and ActiveX controls as five pieces spread through the Registry; the main piece is called HKEY_CLASSES\SOFTWARE\CLASSES\TYPELIB. Services available to Visual Basic are registered here. To manually add them, run RegSrv32, supplying the library name as an argument.

Though it is not a part of Visual Basic, you are highly likely to see some references to RegSrv32 on your exam. Keep the following in mind:

➤ In order for an ActiveX EXE to be registered, it must support the **/RegServer** and **/UnRegServer** command line arguments. ActiveX DLLs must have DLLRegisterServer and DLLUnRegisterServer entry points.

➤ When installing Visual Basic, the Setup program will halt if it finds an ActiveX EXE or DLL that does not appear to be able to be registered. It then offers you the option to register it or not. VB depends on the presence of the **OLESelfRegister** keyword in the object's version information to make this determination. Unless you are certain that the EXE or DLL is capable of self-registration, choose No.

➤ The source of the object, usually a third-party vendor, can tell you if the object can be registered.

➤ To manually register the object, select Run from the Start button in Windows. Type in "RegSrv32 *filename.*" Alternatively, you can add a shortcut to RegSrv32.EXE in your SendTo folder. Then, right-click on the file to be registered, choose Send To, and select RegSrv32.

You should include only those objects that you actually require in your project. Note that you can't remove VBA (Visual Basic for Applications) or Visual

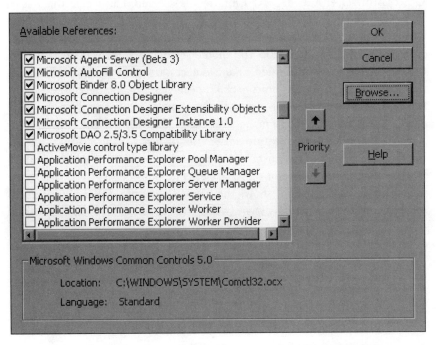

Figure 3.3   The References dialog allows you to add and delete objects, perhaps from another application or third-party library, to and from your Visual Basic project.

Basic objects and procedures. VBA is the Visual Basic language itself and the objects and procedures are the runtime controls. You do not need the other Visual Basic objects listed unless you want to launch Visual Basic itself as a server from your program. Including unneeded objects in your project will only slow down compile times as Visual Basic searches through this list, attempting to resolve calls in your program. Use the arrow keys to change the search order. Bringing an object closer to the top forces Visual Basic to search through it before searching other object libraries. This can be important if there are naming conflicts—for instance, if you load two libraries that both contain a **MidiPlayer** object.

The Object Browser is a veritable treasure trove of information, revealing all about your project and about the attached objects. Use the second text box (in Figure 3.2, it is the text box immediately left of the binoculars icon) to type in a search term and click on the "binoculars" icon. The results are shown in the middle pane. As a test, make sure that the Microsoft Windows Common Controls library is checked in the References dialog. Now, in the top text box in the Object Browser, ensure that <All Libraries> is selected. This means that Visual Basic will search all attached libraries. Notice that you can also choose any number of libraries, including the project on which you are currently working. Now, search for the term "tab." You should see many "hits" in the middle part of the browser. Resize this middle pane as necessary and scroll down. The left-hand side shows in which library each hit occurred. The middle column shows the class, such as a **TabStrip**. Some will also show a member on the right-hand side if a search happened to make a hit there. You see that **DataBindings** or **TabFixedHeight** is a member (property, in this context) of **TabStrip**. Try searching for "Caption." You see a list of all of the classes (objects) of which **Caption** is a member. Click on one of these classes. The bottom display scrolls to the appropriate line. Figure 3.4 shows the menu classes of the VB library. You'll see that **Caption** is a member (type **String**) of **Menu** as well as an explanation of how the property is used.

 There is a reason that I go to some length about Visual Basic's Object Browser. It encapsulates much of Microsoft's efforts to migrate Visual Basic to an object-oriented environment, including the all-important (at least as far as the exam is concerned) terminology.

Programming—1990s Style

In the following pages, I will guide you through the concepts of *event-driven* and *object-oriented* development. The concepts that I cover in the next few sections are crucial to the understanding of topics that will be covered on the

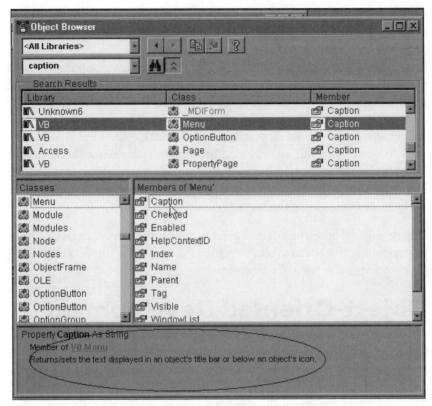

Figure 3.4   Search results of the Object Browser.

exam. In either case, your skills as a VB developer can only be enhanced by an understanding and appreciation of object-oriented concepts.

Event-Driven Vs. Object-Oriented

Event-driven programming was born in the graphical interface of the Macintosh, Windows, and so on. Object-oriented development is really a separate concept, pioneered in Smalltalk and C++.

A graphical user interface (GUI) sports an array of controls, which the user interacts with. The user dictates program flow rather than the other way around. For instance, the user clicks on a command button, and Windows adds the **Click** event to its *event queue*. Code is written to react to that event, thus the term *event-driven programming*. This is a significant break from the procedural model of the 1970s and 1980s, embodied in most third-generation languages (3GLs) such as COBOL and Basic. However, bear in mind that the event-driven model is more a function of the GUI than of the underlying language.

Event-driven programming poses some challenging problems to the uninitiated. Code is broken into small, seemingly unrelated chunks attached to objects. The user has near total control over program flow. The developer needs to be especially astute as to what is happening, both in the application itself and in the system as a whole. For instance, consider a situation where you are performing a lengthy operation (perhaps a sort): If you do not change the mouse pointer to an hourglass, the user may think the machine has locked up, and he or she may reboot. If you don't put the **DoEvents()** function in your sort's loop, the user will be unable to use any other programs (because your program will tie up the CPU). If you don't disable the Sort button (assuming that is how the user invoked the sort routine), the user could inadvertently start a second instance of the sort with undesirable results.

Object-oriented development is an entirely different concept than event-driven programming. It seeks to maximize reuse of previously written code. It introduces concepts that we will now review.

Object-Oriented Development

Anyone who has programmed for a living for any length of time will tell you that he or she has seldom completed a project without looking back at how he or she might have done it better. Such is also true in the world of object-oriented development. You will almost certainly never achieve object-oriented nirvana. Instead, the goal is to strive for continued improvement, while realizing that none of us will ever actually be perfect.

The benefits of object-oriented development aren't always easy to describe to the uninitiated. In fact, object-oriented development usually requires an up-front cost whose payback may not be realized for months or, sometimes, years. And yet, even the naysayers are employing object-oriented development each time they fire up any modern 4GL. Each time you draw a command button on a form, you are employing one of the pillars of object-oriented development: *reuse*. Somebody (in this case, the Visual Basic development team at Microsoft and the writers of the Windows API) has pre-written an object that you can use over and over again, changing only those behaviors (such as caption and event scripts) that need to be customized. In the meantime, you are working with the sure knowledge that the "code" behind the control has been thoroughly debugged. If you "rolled-your-own" command button on every form, you and I both know that your productivity would go down just as surely as the number of bugs would soar.

So, let's explore what "object-oriented development" means. I will discuss later how it is implemented in Visual Basic. In order to understand the concepts of object-oriented development, one must master the terms. You will see these on your Microsoft certification exam.

 The term *object-oriented development* is fairly new and is essentially synonymous with the more traditional term *object-oriented programming*. It symbolizes the move away from the term *programming*, which is more indicative of a third-generation language, towards *software engineering* and *application development*. The new terminology better describes the lifecycle of creating an application, from the design of the GUI and the database, to integrating the various components into the finished application.

Objects

An *object* is a "thing" that encompasses both data and behaviors. The data are not necessarily records from a database. Data may simply be variables used to calculate screen size or some other custodial function. Behaviors are the object's manifestations; how it appears (if it has a graphical representation at all), and its properties and methods. Every object has four items in common:

➤ **Properties** What is it about the object that defines it? Examples include **Caption, Visible,** and **Sorted.**

➤ **Methods** What can the object do? Methods are services that an object provides. Examples include **Print, Retrieve,** and **Show.**

➤ **Events** What types of things can happen to the object? Examples include **Click, Scroll,** and **Load.**

➤ **Attributes** Everything there is to know about the object. Properties, methods, and events are really a subset of attributes.

 In terms of methods and properties, allow me to offer a simple distinction: If it is a verb (***Word.Document*.Print**), then it is a method. If it is a noun (***Word.Document.FileName* = "C:\MyFile.Doc"**), then it is a property.

The term *instantiate* refers to the process of creating an object from a class. If you design a form named **frmMain** in the development environment, it is a *class* of type **frmMain.** It does not become an object until it is instantiated, which happens when you **Load** it. If you have several copies of **frmMain** in memory, each is called an *instance* of the class **frmMain.**

Manipulating Object Properties

Visual Basic provides a few different methods for interacting with the attributes of an object. The brute force method is something like:

```
cmdGo.Caption = "Go!"
cmdGo.Enabled = True
cmdGo.Default = True
cmdGo.Visiuble = True
```

You can make your code somewhat more readable and efficient using the **With...End With** construct, where the object being operated on is the argument to **With**:

```
With cmdGo
    cmdGo.Caption = "Go!"
    cmdGo.Enabled = True
    cmdGo.Default = True
    cmdGo.Visiuble = True
End With
```

Additionally, Visual Basic controls have default attributes. Thus, if you are setting that default property, you don't need to reference it in your assignment. The default property of the TextBox control is **Text**; you can set the control's **Text** property simply by coding:

```
txtResult  = "Successful!"
```

Likewise, VB controls have default events. If you double-click on a command button while in design mode, the **Click** event is "assumed" by VB. Default properties and events of many common VB controls and objects are listed in Table 3.1.

If you assign a control to a variable of type **Variant**, the variable can be treated as though it had properties. Assuming you defined a **Variant** as type **Object**, you can use the **Set** keyword to make the variable equal to any valid VB control:

```
Set vObjecty = txtResult
```

Then, you can access the control's **Text** property:

```
vObject.text = "Successful"
```

Table 3.1   Default properties and events of common Visual Basic controls and objects.

Control	Attribute	Type	Event
App	N/A	N/A	N/A
Check Box	**Value**	Property	**Click**
Collection	**Item**	Method	N/A
Combo Box	**Text**	Property	**Change**
Command Button	**Caption**	Property	**Click**
ContainedControls	**Item**	Property	N/A
Container (DAO)	**QueryDefs**	Property	N/A
Data	**Caption**	Property	**Validate**
DataBinding	**DataField**	Property	N/A
DataBindings	**Item**	Property	N/A
DataObjectFiles	**Item**	Property	N/A
DirListBox	**Path**	Property	**Click**
DriveListBox	**Path**	Property	**Click**
Err	**Number**	Property	N/A
Error	**Description**	Property	N/A
Field	**Value**	Property	N/A
FileListBox	**FileName**	Property	**Click**
Form	**Controls**	Property	**Load**
Frame	**Caption**	Property	**DragDrop**
HScrollBar	**Value**	Property	**Change**
Image	**Picture**	Property	**Click**
Label	**Caption**	Property	**Click**
Line	**Visible**	Property	N/A
ListBox	**Text**	Property	**Click**
MDIForm	**Controls**	Property	**Load**
Menu	**Enabled**	Property	**Click**
OLE	**Action**	Property	**Updated**
Option Button	**Value**	Property	**Click**
ParentContols	**Item**	Property	N/A

(continued)

Table 3.1	Default properties and events of common Visual Basic controls and objects *(continued)*.		
Control	**Attribute**	**Type**	**Event**
PictureBox	**Picture**	Property	**Click**
RecordSet	**Field**	Property	N/A
RichTextBox	**TextRTF**	Property	**Change**
Shape	**Shape**	Property	N/A
TextBox	**Text**	Property	**Change**
Timer	**Enabled**	Property	**Timer**
UserControl	N/A *	N/A *	**GotFocus**
VScrollBar	**Value**	Property	**Change**
WebBrowser	**Name**	Property	**StatusTextChange**

*For the UserControl, default action is that of the embedded intrinsic control(s).

However, if instead you code

```
vObject = "Success"
```

you would not get the expected results (which would be to set the **Text** property). Instead, you would change the underlying data type of **vObject** from **textResult** to **String** with the assignment. This underscores the lesson you learned in Chapter 2—that a **Variant** is of data type **Variant** and it is *not* whatever the underlying variable type is. Therefore, it is not of type **Object**.

 As this example showed all too clearly, you need to pay *very* close attention to **Variant**s, both in your code (where unexpected things can happen) and on your certification exam (where very unpleasant things can happen). Follow the life of a **Variant** line by line and watch out for the ones that change their nature by becoming a new data type.

Examining The Identity Of An Object

Sometimes you need to know the identity of the object you are dealing with. You do so by examining the **Name** property. Every Visual Basic object has a **Name** property, which is not to be confused with the **Caption** or **Text** properties. If you create a form, its **Name** property might be **frmMath** (as in the example in Chapter 2). Although you can change the **Name** of an object at design time, it is generally read-only at runtime.

The **Me** keyword returns a *reference* to the current form, and the **ActiveControl** keyword returns a reference to whatever object currently has focus, which can be seen in Figure 3.5. In the figure, the left text box has been set equal to the value of **Me.Name**, which is the **Name** property of the form. The right text box has been set equal to **ActiveControl.Name**, which is the **Name** property of the control that has focus.

At design time, you can only have one control for any **Name** property. In other words, you cannot give two different controls the same name. You can, of course, create an array of controls differentiated by their subscripts.

At runtime, you can create new instances of a control, each sharing the same name, by using the **New** keyword:

```
Dim frmNew As New frmMath
```

This line of code creates a new instance of **frmMath**. Each has the same name. So, how do you differentiate between the two? Put in object-oriented development terms, how do you obtain a *reference* to the one that you want to deal with? I will discuss this in Chapter 4, in the section titled "Collections."

Examining The Nature Of An Object

The **TypeOf** keyword helps us to look at an object and evaluate from what class it is derived. When using **TypeOf**, you use the **Is** keyword as a comparison operator instead of the equals sign (=). Any comparison must be done in an **If** statement:

```
If TypeOf myControl Is CommandButton Then ...
```

You cannot assign an object reference to another variable using **TypeOf**.

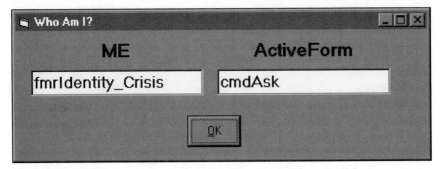

Figure 3.5 Discovering the identity of Visual Basic controls.

Communicating With An Object

One cannot end the discussion of objects without delving into *messages*. Windows is full of them. A joke on the Microsoft Web site goes something like this: "How many OOP programmers does it take to change a light bulb? None, a properly OOP-designed light bulb would accept a ChangeBulb message."

Messages are what makes Windows tick. When you modify the background color of a form (*form*.**BackColor** = **vbRed**), the compiler actually sends the form a message, via the Windows API, that tells the Form to change its **BackColor** property. I review this in more detail in Chapter 7 in the section titled "Messages." For now, understand that almost any attribute of a form maps directly to a Windows message.

Classes

A class is an *abstraction* of an object. An abstraction, in turn, is the definition of an object that is similar to others of the same type.

There are many excellent books that delve deeply into object-oriented concepts. Although I will discuss those issues critical to the Visual Basic certification exam, you may wish to refer to some of the titles listed in the "Need To Know More?" section at the end of this chapter.

As an example of a class, examine Visual Basic's **Form** object. It has certain properties such as **Visible** and **Caption**. When you create a **Form** in the development environment and then customize it (changing the **Caption**, adding controls, and so on), you are doing what is known as *subclassing*—customizing a class definition to create a new class. When your application **Show**s the **Form**, you are instantiating the class to create an object. If the **Form**'s **Name** property is **frmMath**, you are instantiating an object of type **frmMath**.

There are three pillars of object orientation (reuse, encapsulation, and polymorphism) that I will discuss briefly. The Visual Basic certification exam will not ask questions about the definition of object-oriented development per se. Instead, the exam will frame questions about Visual Basic with the assumption that you have a general understanding of object-oriented concepts.

Reuse

The holy mantra of object-oriented development is *reuse*. The goal of reuse is obvious: to reduce development time by reusing previously written code. Effective reuse goes beyond merely reusing some Accounts Receivable aging algorithm. You seek to reuse objects and all of their associated attributes. Doing so means that you can, for instance, save time or increase productivity by adding a previously written module of Accounts Receivable routines to projects, as needed. You further gain by the knowledge that the routines have been pre-tested and debugged. Also, you have security knowing that one program will process past due balances the same as the next. Finally, if there is a need to modify a routine, you have only one place to change it, and then, by recompiling all programs in which that routine appears, the change *propagates* (flows down to) through all of those programs.

Object-oriented development purists will tell you that the terms *reuse* and *inheritance* are one in the same. Inheritance is the best way to *implement* reuse, but the two terms are not the same. Inheritance is simply one method to accomplish the goal of reuse. Recall that at the beginning of this section, I stated that every time you draw a command button on a form you are implementing reuse. You are doing that without the use of inheritance. Instead, you are instantiating an object of the class (type) command button.

Unfortunately, Visual Basic does not support inheritance. There are other methods to achieve reuse. You can "sort of" simulate the best of inheritance through the use of "containment" in a process known as *delegation*. In Chapter 4, I will show you a Visual Basic custom class called **classUpdateCust**. I will then show you how to write code to expose the properties of that class and reuse it in another class.

If there were a fourth "pillar" of object-orientation, it would be *multiple inheritance*. Multiple inheritance is the process of inheriting from two or more objects to create a new object comprised of the base objects (it's kind of like inheriting from "tractor" and "trailer" to create a tractor-trailer). It is a confusing concept not implemented in languages that are otherwise fully object-oriented. Ironically, although Visual Basic does a poor job of "simulating" inheritance, its process of combining classes and achieving reuse via delegation is actually a pretty good stab at multiple inheritance.

The only true way to reuse code in Visual Basic 5 is by encapsulating the functionality that you need to reuse in a user class or standard module, save that class or module separately, and add it to other projects as needed. Now let's look at encapsulation.

Encapsulation

Encapsulation is another of the pillars of object-oriented development. Encapsulation refers to the process of hiding attributes from prying eyes. Imagine you have a routine that accepts an encrypted string and decrypts it to verify that a password is correct. You don't want the unencrypted data visible to unauthorized use. So you create an object—perhaps a user class—in which you have a routine with the sole purpose of decrypting a password and comparing it to what is stored in the database. To the extent that you do not make the class' variables public, the object "owns" the data and it is "hidden" from others.

 When I teach college students or lecture in the corporate environment, I often liken a properly constructed object to a selfish child—it does not allow others to play with its "toys" without first asking permission. An object owns data and other objects have to go through the first object to access that data.

Encapsulation is extended to ownership of properties and methods. Assume you have a form with a command button named Sort. You also have a menu choice named Sort. The purpose of both is to sort the data in an array. You might be tempted to write a routine for the command button's **Click** event and to cut and paste the routine into the equivalent menu's **Click** event. That's reuse, right? Well, maybe.

Let's back up and examine the nature of the data and the principles of object orientation. To whom does the array belong? Almost certainly the form. To the extent that the array is a form-level object, the only entity that has any business operating on it is the form itself. So, you create a form module routine to sort the array and call it from both the command button and the menu. Now, the data and the routine that operates on the data is encapsulated to the form itself. Further, and not coincidentally, if the routine needs to be modified, it only has to be changed in one place.

Recall from Chapter 2 our discussion of visibility or scope. I discussed, what are called in object-oriented development terms, *access modifiers* such as **Public** and **Private**. These allow you to properly protect attributes from unauthorized and (more importantly) unintended use.

Recall also that the access modifiers were not restricted to only variables. You could also indicate the scope of subs and functions. By making a form's procedures visible, another object can invoke those procedures to modify the data, while ensuring that the form has complete control over the process.

You really tame the encapsulation tiger when you encapsulate your data, methods, and so on, into a class module. Much of Chapter 4 is devoted to this subject.

Polymorphism

The third pillar of object orientation is the difficult-to-grasp term polymorphism. It refers to a process whereby an object invokes a method of another object in a common manner, without understanding or caring how it is accomplished. For instance, assume that you have a form with two OLE objects: a Microsoft Word document and a Microsoft Excel spreadsheet. You wish to send the objects to the printer. To do so, you merely "tell" each object (the document and the spreadsheet) to "print" themselves. The objects are "expressing" polymorphic behavior in that they both handle the chores of sending output to the printer and they are doing so in a common manner (by using the same method: **Print**). So, the application does not have to concern itself with how output is sent to the printer; it relies on the OLE objects to handle that. The application uses the same "command" (**Print**) to accomplish the task regardless of what object is actually being sent to the printer.

You even see polymorphism implemented in standard Visual Basic controls. For instance, you can invoke the **SetFocus** method of a CommandButton or a TextBox not caring how the control invokes the method, only that it is done.

Visual Basic Procedures

In Visual Basic, a *procedure* is a logical component of an application that can be called by name to perform one or more specific operations. For instance, you could write a procedure to compute the total of two numbers. You might give it the name: **Add2**.

All procedures can accept arguments (I discuss the rules for doing so in the section "Functions And Sub Procedures"). The procedure uses these arguments in its internal computations. Using the addition example from above, **Add2** would have two arguments: **Add2 (8, 16)** would mean that the procedure **Add2** is going to sum the numbers 8 and 16.

A procedure that returns a result is known as a function while a procedure that does not return a result is known as a sub procedure (often just called a sub). If **Add2** were defined to return a result, it would be called with syntax similar to:

```
myResult = Add2 (8, 16)
```

Visual Basic makes another distinction when referring to procedures. An *event procedure* is any code that is attached to an event. When you write code to handle the clicking of a command button, the code is an event procedure. If the command button's name is **Command1**, the name of the procedure is

Command1_Click (). Like functions and subs, event procedures may accept arguments. A *general procedure* is any procedure that you write that is not specifically related to a control or object.

> In Windows development, the terminology is sometimes seemingly contradictory. In the Windows API, everything is called a function whether it returns a value or not. If you search through the Help file for the term "method," you will find a definition: "An invocable function that is defined to be a member of an interface." This is really a referencing to the underlying nature of the object or control because each is derived from the Windows API. VB methods do not truly return values, so they are not functions in the VB sense. For purposes of the certification exam, you should use the definitions that I have just supplied (functions return values, procedures do not). Throughout this book, I attempt to use the VB terminology and point out where I am departing from that terminology.

Functions And Sub Procedures

In Chapter 2, I showed you the syntax to declare a sub or function within your VB program concentrating on the issue of scope. Now, let's examine the syntax of the arguments supplied and the return value:

```
[Private | Public | Friend] [Static] Sub subname [(arglist)]
[Private | Public | Friend] [Static] Function subname _
    [(arglist)] [As type]
```

In Chapter 2, I discussed the use of the declarative statements **Private, Public, Friend,** and **Static.** A function must return one value whose data type is specified by the **As** clause. Each may take arguments defined with the following syntax:

```
[Optional] [ByVal | ByRef] [ParamArray] varname[( )] _
    [As type] [= defaultvalue]
```

ByVal and **ByRef** are mutually exclusive; **ByRef** is the default. **ByVal** means that you are passing a copy of the variable, and **ByRef** means that you are passing an address to the variable. The implication is that by using **ByRef,** the procedure can alter the value of the variable. **As** defines the data type of the variable being passed.

You can define a default value for the variable being passed as an argument if the **Optional** clause is used. If the variable being passed is any type of object (including a VB control), the only acceptable default value is **Nothing.**

Optional indicates that the arguments following it are not required. If you use **Optional** and do not supply a default value, the arguments are assigned as a type **Variant** with the value **Empty**. You can use the **IsMissing** function to test for arguments not provided. **Optional** can appear anywhere in the argument list unless **ParamArray** is used.

ParamArray allows you to define a procedure with a variable number of arguments. You cannot use **ByVal** or **ByRef** with **ParamArray**.

The following snippet of code illustrates use of **ParamArray**.

```
' a function to add some numbers using ParamArray
Function AddEmUp (ParamArray iVars ()) As Integer
   Dim vNumber As Variant
   Dim iRslt As Integer
   For Each vNumber In iVars
       iRslt = iRslt + vNumber
   Next
   AddEmUp = iRslt
End Function
```

Note that you use the **For...Each** construct to iterate through the arguments. **For...Each** is discussed in Chapter 4 in the discussion of collections.

You may use *named arguments* when calling procedures. This is also illustrated and discussed in the Chapter 4 discussion of collections.

GoSub Procedures

The object of a **GoSub** statement, is not a procedure in the strict sense of the word because it does not accept arguments and cannot be called outside of the procedure in which it resides. Further evidence is that it is not named. That is, the argument to **GoSub** is a line label or a line number.

Of Modules And Forms

So, now we get to the nitty-gritty. What is a module anyway? In the following sections, I will discuss the various types of Visual Basic "code modules" and the implications of using each. The certification exam will expect you to have mastered the use of the three main types of code modules. It will also expect that you thoroughly understand what happens when a VB application is invoked and begins to run.

Visual Basic Startup

When running a VB application, the most common sequence of events is that a standard module is loaded, which then opens the first form.

When you create a Visual Basic project, by default VB creates a standard module with a single procedure **Sub Main()**. VB also generates a single default form. The **Sub Main()** procedure opens the default form.

You can display the properties of a VB project by selecting Project|*projectname* Properties from the main menu. A property page similar to that shown in Figure 3.6 is displayed. Here you can name your project something meaningful, rather than the annoying "Project1" that VB uses as a default. Also, you can specify where your program starts. The default is **Sub Main()**. This can exist anywhere in your project, but you can have only one. If you have more than one, the compiler generates an "ambiguous name" error. Alternatively, you can specify any form in your project to be the startup file.

A typical **Sub Main()** procedure looks like the following:

```
' this is in the declarations section
Option Explicit
Public fMainForm As frmMain

Sub Main()
    Set fMainForm = New frmMain
    fMainForm.Show
End Sub
```

But this does not necessarily have to be the case. A Visual Basic application does not need to contain a form. The typical "Hello World" program, without a form, would look similar to:

```
Sub Main ()
    MsgBox "Hello World!")
End Sub
```

The odds are very high that your exam will have one or more questions that deal with the confusing topic of how a form is instantiated, so be sure to familiarize yourself with the "rules." When *form*.**Show** is issued, Visual Basic does an implicit **Load** first, which creates an instance of the form in memory but *does not display it*. Next, the **Initialize** event of the form is executed, followed by the **Load** event. If there is any code attached to these events, then it (the code) is run prior to the form being displayed. After that, the form is finally made visible. You can load a form (**Load *formname***) without displaying it. This causes all variables and controls in the form to be initialized. If an attribute of a form is referenced (**form.*variablename* = *value***), the form is loaded but not displayed.

Form Modules

A *form* is a Visual Basic object that is analogous to a window in other programming environments (although note that the operating system considers *all* controls to be windows). The form contains other Visual Basic controls and it exposes various methods, properties, and events.

 A Visual Basic form is an object. This means that a form, as with any other object, may be passed to a sub or function as an argument.

Each form in your project is a module. The form module contains code to react to various events (event procedures), and also *general procedures*, which are subs

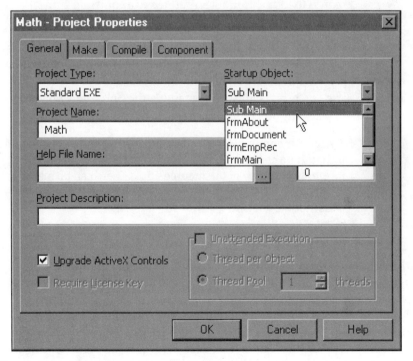

Figure 3.6   The Project Properties dialog.

and functions not related to any individual control. In object-oriented development terms, general procedures are methods of the form itself. Forms typically contain form-level declarations of constants, variables (including user-defined types), and external procedures (discussed in Chapter 5).

Standard Modules

Standard modules were referred to as *code modules* prior to version 4 of Visual Basic. Because standard modules, form modules, and class modules may also contain code, they are collectively known as code modules in VB versions 4 and 5. A standard module is a collection of Visual Basic procedures, declarations, and so on. It can have subs and functions, but unlike a form module, data in a standard module defaults to program scope. Further, procedures in a standard module default to **Public** visibility, whereas form-level subs and functions default to **Private** visibility. Of course, use of the **Private** keyword in standard module declarations allows you to make items module level in scope.

If a general procedure is not unique to the form—that is, it could be used elsewhere—it should be put into a standard code module. Remember our discussion of encapsulation. Only that which belongs to a control should be added to a control.

Except perhaps in your startup module, you should avoid making any references to forms. This allows you to reuse the code in other projects, fulfilling some of the promises of object orientation. In those modules that do need to reference a form (such as the module containing the **Sub Main()** procedure), you should not place any other procedures that could be used in other projects.

A key difference between a standard module and a class module is that there can only be one instance of the former and, therefore, only one copy of the module's data. There can be many instances of a class module and, therefore, many copies of the class module's data.

Class Modules

Recall the definition of a *class*: a class is an object, including its methods, properties, and attributes.

A form is also an object. And so is a list box. But there is nothing in the definition of an object that dictates that it have a visible component. A *class module* is essentially a user-defined control that does not require a visible component or manifestation. At its simplest, a class module's data are the variables declared within it, and its methods are the subs and functions declared within it. In that sense, it has more in common with a form module than it does with a standard module. Like a form, it does not expose its data nor its methods unless explicitly declared that way.

There can only be one instance of the data encompassed in a standard module because there can be one and only one instance of the module itself. However, you can have multiple instances of a form and, thus, multiple instances of the form's data. The same duplication is true of a class.

In Chapter 4, I will review the construction and instantiation of a class. I will also discuss how to add properties and methods, as well as how to combine it with other classes. In addition, I will discuss some of the specialized classes provided by Visual Basic.

Other Coding Topics

As noted at the beginning of this chapter, there are books a thousand pages thick that teach basic and advanced VB development. This chapter seeks to highlight those development issues you are most likely to see on the certification exam, not to teach you how to program.

The remainder of this chapter is devoted to key development concepts and terms you are likely to encounter on the exam.

Binding

Visual Basic documentation often mentions mysterious terms such as *early binding* and *late binding*, yet a search of VB's Help file will only yield information about binding data to controls. That's not exactly the same thing.

In compiler jargon, *binding* refers to the timing of when an item is resolved. For instance, if you declare a constant in your program, its value is *resolved* at compilation and the compiler actually stores the value in the program code. The advantage is that code runs faster, while the trade-off is loss of flexibility: the value of the variable cannot be changed at runtime.

When we get to Visual Basic, the concepts of *early binding* versus *late binding* refer to when an object's identity is resolved. If you declare a variable to be type **Object** (and then later use the **Set** statement to associate the variable with a specific object), the compiler cannot resolve the identity of the object, and so, adds overhead to resolve this at runtime. Assigning a variable to a specific object is called early binding and allows the VB compiler to determine at compilation what properties and methods need to be associated with that variable. Declaring a variable generically to be of type **Object** causes late binding because the compiler cannot know ahead of time what specific object will be created.

The Nature Of Null

Null is the absence of any data at all. Empty strings are said to be *null strings*; however, they do not equate to the **Null** keyword in the eyes of Visual Basic and are not literally null strings. In communicating with external modules, you pass a "null" string as the Visual Basic constant **vbNullString** or **vbNullChar**.

 Do not use **IfNull** to determine if a string is null. Instead, use **vbNullString: If myString = vbNullString**.

Do not confuse null with **Nothing** or **Empty**. **Nothing** indicates that an object variable does not reference anything and **Empty** denotes a **Variant** to which no data has been assigned (see Chapter 2).

 The constant **vbEmpty** is *not* an empty string; it is used to assign the value **Empty** to a **Variant**.

The Visual Basic keyword **Null** refers to the value of a **Variant**, which contains no *valid* data. The **IsNull** function evaluates a **Variant** to determine if its value is:

```
Null: If IsNull (myVar) Then ...
```

IsNull is the only way that you can test for **Null**. Because the statement

```
If myVar = Null
```

is **Null** itself, it always returns **False** regardless of the actual value of **myVar**.

MDI And SDI

A Multiple Document Interface (MDI) always has one and only one MDI *frame*, known as an *MDI form* in Visual Basic. The only purpose of the MDI form is to serve as a container for child forms. To designate a form as an MDI child, set the **MDIChild** property to **True**.

An MDI child cannot exist outside of the MDI form. If the form is closed, all of the child forms are closed also. A child form cannot be moved beyond the boundaries of the MDI form. If you minimize a child form, its icon appears on the form itself.

Toolbars and menus are housed on the frame; they relate to whichever child form is active at the moment. If the child has a menu, its menu replaces the form's menu when the child becomes the active form. Menus are added via Tools|Menu Editor on the menu. The Toolbar control is part of the Microsoft Common Controls OCX and must be added to the project by selecting Project|Components from the VB menu and checking the appropriate box. The controls available in the OCX are then added to the toolbox.

 To add buttons to your toolbar, use the toolbar **Add** method. To program the toolbar, add code to the **ButtonClick** event, which evaluates which button in the array was clicked. Most typically, the buttons will correspond to menu choices, and so should fire the code behind the appropriate menu item.

MDI forms can only have Menu, Toolbar, and PictureBox controls on them. You can add a custom control as long as it has an **Align** property. You normally do not place any controls (except Menu and Toolbar) on an MDI form, but if you need to do so, you can place a PictureBox on the MDI form and then place other controls inside of the PictureBox.

A Single Document Interface (SDI) application can have multiple forms, but they exist outside of the context of other forms. If you close one form, others stay open. The more modern approach to Windows programming is to make all but single-form applications MDI. A form is SDI by definition if its **MDIChild** property is **False**.

The **Screen** Object

The **Screen** object allows the Visual Basic developer to control visible manifestation of the entire Windows environment, even non-Visual Basic programs. Put another way, the "**Screen** object is the entire Windows desktop" (quoted from the VB5 Help file).

It has a number of properties that are useful:

➤ **ActiveControl** Returns the currently active control (which may or may not be a VB control). This is a convenient way to access a control's properties and methods because it also represents a reference to the active control.

➤ **ActiveForm** Provides a reference to whichever form currently has focus (if the form is an MDI form, then the active **MDIChild** is returned).

➤ **FontCount** Returns the number of fonts currently available for the display, while **Fonts** enumerates them.

➤ **Height** Returns the height of the **Screen** object in units of *twips*. A twip is 1/1440 of an inch or 1/567 of a centimeter.

➤ **Width** Returns the width of the **Screen** object in units of twips.

➤ **TwipsPerPixelX** Used with the **Width** property to determine the **Screen** object's current resolution height. This is done by performing the following formula: **Screen.Width / Screen.TwipsPerPixelX**.

➤ **TwipsPerPixelY** Used with the **Height** property to determine the resolution height of the **Screen** object. This is done by performing the following formula: **Screen.Height / Screen.TwipsPerPixelY**.

➤ **MousePointer** Allows you to change the current pointer.

➤ **MouseIcon** Allows you to load an icon or cursor file and use it as a new cursor, as seen in this example:

```
MouseIcon = LoadPicture ("c:\windows\cursors\mygarish.cur")
```

 The **ActiveControl**, **ActiveForm**, **MousePointer**, and **MouseIcon** properties also apply to forms.

Visual Basic Operators

As the last topic in this chapter, the Visual Basic operators are summarized in Table 3.2. Visual Basic *promotions* ("behind the scenes" conversion of one data type to another) are summarized in Table 3.3. It is crucial to the successful developer that he or she fully grasp the subtleties of these (you have already seen how the plus operator can work differently in different contexts). It can't hurt come exam time either.

Table 3.2   Visual Basic operators.

Operator	Use
-	Indicate a number is negative: -1. Subtract one number from another: **a = b - c**.
+	Add two numbers together: **a = b + c**. Concatenate two strings but is unreliable (use "&" instead): **string3 = string1 + string2**.
*	Multiply two numbers together: **a = b * c**.
/	Divide one number by another: **a = b / c** where c is the divisor and b is the numerator.
\	Divide one number by another: **a = b \ c** (b and c are rounded down to integers first).
^	Raise a number by the exponent: **a = b^c** where c is the exponent.
MOD	Divide two numbers and return the remainder (**3 MOD 2** returns .5): **a = b MOD c**.
<	Less than comparison operator: **If a < b Then** (for numbers or strings).
>	Greater than comparison operator: **If a > b Then** (for numbers or strings).
<=	Less than or equal to comparison operator: **If a <= b Then** (for numbers or strings).
>=	Greater than or equal to comparison operator: **If a >= b Then** (for numbers or strings).
=	Equals comparison operator: **If a = b Then** (for numbers or strings). Assignment operator: **a = b** (for numbers or strings).
<>	Does not equal comparison operator: **If a <> b Then** (for numbers or strings).
AND	Perform logical conjunction of two variables: **a = b And c** or **If b AND c Then**.
NOT	Perform logical negation: **a = Not b** or **If Not b**.
OR	Perform logical disjunction of two variables: **a = b Or c** or **If a OR b Then**.
XOR	Perform exclusive Or on two variables (result has to be numeric): **a = b XOr c** or **If b XOr c Then**.
EQV	Perform logical equivalency on two variables: **a = b Eqv C** or **If b Eqv c**.
IMP	Performs logical implication on two variables: **a = b Imp c** or **If b Imp c Then**.
&	Concatenation of two strings: **a = b & c**.

Table 3.3	Variable conversions and promotions resulting from operations.
Operation	**Result**
Compare	All numbers promoted to the more complex data type. Example: If compare **Single** to **Double**, **Single** is converted to a **Double**.
Variant Compare	If the underlying data types are the same, comparisons work as in Table 3.1.
	If one is a number and the other is a string, the number is less than.
	If one **Variant** is **Empty** and the other is a number, compares as though the **Empty Variant** = 0.
	If one **Variant** is **Empty** and the other is a string, compare as though the **Empty Variant** = "".
Concatenate	If either variable being concatenated is a **Variant**, result is **Variant**.
+ and -	If first **Variant** is numeric, result is numeric.
	If first **Variant** is **String**, result is concatenated **String**.
	If either **Variant** is **Empty**, result Is equal to other variable.
	If either variable is **Null**, result is **Null**. **Single** and **Long** = **Double**.
	If result overflows, convert to **Double**.
+, -, * or /	If result is **Byte** but overflows, convert to **Integer**.
	If result is **Integer** but overflows, convert to **Long**. **Date** plus any other data type results in a **Date**.
* and /	If either variable is **Single** or **Long**, result is **Double**.
	If result is **Variant Single**, **Double**, or **Date**, result is **Variant Double**.
/ or MOD	If any variable is **Null**, result is **Null**. Otherwise, it's the smallest of **Byte**, **Integer**, or **Long** that will contain result.
^	If any variable is **Null**, result is **Null**. Otherwise, **Double** or Variant **Double**.

Exam Prep Questions

Question 1

> Assuming that **frmCstMaint** is part of the current project, what will be displayed?
>
> ```
> Dim vVar As Variant
> Set vVar = frmCustMaint
> MsgBox vVar.Name
> ```
>
> ○ a. Nothing will be displayed
>
> ○ b. **frmCustMaint**
>
> ○ c. If **frmCustMaint** is already loaded, then **frmCustMain**, otherwise nothing
>
> ○ d. Error: Object's Property Not Set

The correct answer is b. *vVar* now references *frmCustMaint* and the *Name* property of *frmCustMaint* is *frmCustMaint*. Answer a is wrong because even if an object itself is **Nothing** in value, it has a **Name** property. Answer c is incorrect because it is irrelevant if the form has been previously loaded. Answer d is wrong because there is no such error message.

Question 2

> A function is: [Check all correct answers]
>
> ❑ a. Another type of module
>
> ❑ b. A procedure
>
> ❑ c. Different from a sub in that it must return a value
>
> ❑ d. Different from a sub in that it allows arguments or parameters

The correct answers are b and c. Answer b is correct because both subs and functions are procedures. Answer c is correct because functions require return values while subs do not allow them. Answer a is incorrect because a function is not a module; it is a part of a module. Answer d is incorrect because functions also allow arguments.

Question 3

> For the procedure prototype given, what code snippets are valid
> and will display the message box if the value of **DoSomeStuff** is
> **Null**?
>
> ```
> Function DoSomeStuff (a As String, b As
>     String, c As String, d As String)
>     As Variant
> ```
>
> ○ a.
> ```
> If IsNull (DoSomeStuff("cat","dog","rat", _
>     "turtle")) Then
>    MsgBox "It's Done1!"
> End If
> ```
>
> ○ b.
> ```
> If DoSomeStuff (b:="dog", c:="rat", _
>     d:="turtle", a:="cat") = vbEmpty Then
>    MsgBox "It's Done1!"
> End If
> ```
>
> ○ c.
> ```
> If DoSomeStuff (b:="dog", c:="rat", _
>     "cat", "turtle") = vbEmpty Then
>    MsgBox "It's Done1!"
> End If
> ```
>
> ○ d.
> ```
> If DoSomeStuff (a:="cat", b:="dog", _
>     c:="rat", d:="turtle") = Null Then
>    MsgBox "It's Done1!"
> End If
> ```

Answer a is correct because the *IsNull* **function is used correctly to evaluate the
result of the function, which you have been told is** *Null*. **Answer b is incorrect
because Null is not the same as Empty (as denoted by the vbEmpty constant).
Answer c is incorrect for the same reason as b, plus it will not run because of the
mixed named arguments and non-named arguments. Answer d is incorrect because of the comparison to Null, which is always False.**

Question 4

Assuming that **form1** is a valid form, which of the following code snippets in the **form1** module will run correctly? [Check all correct answers]

❏ a.
```
Form1.PictureBox = LoadPicture _
    ("c:\icons\myicon.ico")
Form1.Enabled = True
Form1.Show = True
```

❏ b.
```
Show
Hide
Enabled = True
```

❏ c.
```
With Form1
    PictureBox = LoadPicture _
        ("c:\icons\myicon.ico")
    Enabled = True
    Show = True
End With
```

❏ d.
```
With Form1
    Show
    Hide
    Enabled = True
End With
```

Answers b and d are correct. Answer b is correct even though it looks unusual. Without object qualifiers, properties and methods interact with the *Me* object, which is the form itself. Answer d is also correct: It uses the *With* object construct to accomplish the same thing as answer b. Answer a is incorrect because there is no **PictureBox** property and because **Show** is a method and not a property. Answer d is incorrect because **Show** is a method. You cannot invoke a method using the **With** construct.

Question 5

Assume you have an application with an MDI form named **frmMDI**. Your application loads a form, **frmNoChild**, with the **MDIChild** property of **False**. Code in that form opens another form, **frmAlsoNoChild**, with a **MDIChild** property that is also **False**. Finally, that form loads **frmChild** with a **MDIChild** property that is **True**. You close **frmMDI**. Which forms remain open?

○ a. No forms remain open.

○ b. **frmAlsoNoChild**.

○ c. **frmNoChild** and **frmAlsoNoChild**.

○ d. **frmNoChild**, **frmAlsoNoChild**, and **frmMDIChild**.

○ e. They all remain open because child forms were opened.

Answer c is correct because the actions of an MDI form have no effect on non-*MDIChild* forms (*frmChild* is closed because its *MDIChild* property is *True*). Answer a is incorrect because some forms are open. Answer b is incorrect because frmNoChild is also open. Answer d is incorrect because closing frmMDI also closes any forms that have **MDIChild** set to **True**. Answer e is incorrect because the existence of other forms does not preclude you from closing any forms. (For those who have programmed in other languages, Visual Basic does not have the equivalent of a true, non-MDI child window.)

Question 6

What is the result of the following computation?

```
Dim a, b, c, d
a = "7"
b = 7
c = "seven"
d = a + b + c
```

○ a. A **Variant String**: "77seven"

○ b. A **Variant Integer**: 7

○ c. A **Variant Double**: 7

○ d. A **Variant Integer**: 14

○ e. You will get a Type Mismatch error

Answer e is correct. The variables are all *Variant*s. Because the first variable (a) contains a number inside of the string, VB attempts to perform arithmetic instead of concatenation. Because the third variable (c) is a string, an error results. Answer a is wrong because VB will not concatenate a numeric data type (variable b). Answers b and c are wrong because neither takes into account that VB is trying to do an arithmetic operation.

Question 7

What is the result of the following computation?

```
' in the declarations section
DEFInt A - Z
' the following code is in a procedure
DIM a, b, c, d
a = 10
b = 2.5
c = 2
d = (a / b) * c
MsgBox d & TypeName (d)
```

- O a. **8Single**
- O b. **8Integer**
- O c. **8Variant**
- O d. **10Integer**
- O e. You will get a Type Mismatch error

Answer d is the correct answer. Because all of the variables are defined as *Integer*, each gets rounded down, so the computation of variable d is (10 / 2) * 2 = 10. Answer a is wrong because there is no promotion to **Single**. Answer b is wrong because it does not take into account that the second variable (b) gets rounded down. Answer c is wrong because of the **Variant** assignment and the miscomputation. Answer e is wrong because there is no error.

Question 8

Which line of code will execute?

```
Dim a as boolean, b as boolean
If a XOr b Then
    ' line1
    GoTo OuttaHere
else
     ' line 2
    GoTo OuttaHere
End If
' line 3
OuttaHere:
```

- ○ a. line 1
- ○ b. line 2
- ○ c. line 3
- ○ d. None of the above

Answer b is the correct answer because booleans are initialized to *False*. **When you** *XOR* **two** *False* **values, the result is** *False*, **causing the** *If* **test to fail.** Answer a is wrong because the **If** test fails (is not **True**). Answer c is wrong because program flow is directed to the line "OuttaHere" regardless of whether the **If** test is **True** or **False**. Answer d is wrong because the correct choice is provided. This is an example of a question where you should have been able to at least guess with a 50 percent chance, because only answers a and b are conceivable. Even if you did not understand **XOR**, program flow would branch to "OuttaHere" regardless of how the **If** statement evaluated, and so answer c is impossible. Likewise, either a or b has to be correct because the test is a simple **If...Else.**

Question 9

> You create a new project and then create an MDI form. How do
> you add a toolbar?
>
> ○ a. Use the Components dialog under the Project menu to
>   find Microsoft Common Controls.
>
> ○ b. Use the References option in either the Object Browser or
>   under the Project menu and check Microsoft Common
>   Controls.
>
> ○ c. It's already in the toolbox. Just draw it like any other
>   control.
>
> ○ d. You can only add a toolbar to an MDI child.

Answer a is correct. You add a toolbar through the Components dialog under the Project menu. Answer b is incorrect because although it exposes controls in the Common Controls library, that does not necessarily make the toolbar available. Answer c is incorrect because the control needs to be added, it is not part of the Standard toolbox. Answer d is incorrect because you can attach a toolbar to an MDI form.

Question 10

> Which of the following code snippets are valid [Check all correct
> answers]
>
> ❏ a.
> ```
> If TypeOf myObject = CommandButton Then
> End If
> ```
>
> ❏ b.
> ```
> If TypeOf (myObject) = CommandButton Then
>     myString = "ABC"
> End If
> ```
>
> ❏ c.
> ```
> Select Case TypeOf myObject
>     Case = CommandButton
>         myString = "ABC"
> End Select
> ```
>
> ❏ d. None of the above

Answer d is the correct answer because none of the choices provided is valid.
Answer a is wrong because you need to use the keyword **Is** instead of using the
equals sign. Answer b is wrong for the same reason as a, and because you do
not enclose the object in parentheses. Answer c is wrong for the same reason as
a, and also because you can only use **TypeOf** in an **If...Then...End If** construct.

Need To Know More?

 Aitken, Peter: *Visual Basic 5 Programming EXplorer*. Coriolis Group Books, Scottsdale, AZ, 1997. ISBN 1-57610-065-0. Chapter 1 provides a good overview of the VB environment and Chapter 2 delves into the subject of properties, methods, and procedures.

 Harrington, John, Mark Spenik, Heidi Brumbaugh, and Cliff Diamond: *Visual Basic 5 Interactive Course*. Waite Group Press, Corte Madera, CA, 1997. ISBN 1-57169-077-8. Chapters 4, 6, and 14 provide a good overview of Visual Basic modules, functions, and so on. It is also a good source for many of the basics of VB development.

 McKinney, Bruce: *Hardcore Visual Basic*. Microsoft Press, Redmond, WA, 1997. ISBN 1-57231-422-2. In particular, Bruce discusses the ins-and-outs of object-oriented development with Visual Basic in Chapter 3.

Collections, Classes, And Objects

Terms you'll need to understand:

- √ Collection class
- √ Forms collection
- √ Controls collection
- √ Property procedures
- √ Class events
- √ Enumeration
- √ Named arguments
- √ Implements keyword
- √ Containment and delegation
- √ Let, Set, and Get

Techniques you'll need to master:

- √ Creating a standard module that can be reused
- √ Creating a class module with appropriate encapsulation
- √ Instantiating and referencing multiple instances of forms and other objects
- √ Creating and traversing a collection
- √ Using the Forms collection and Controls collection
- √ Using the Class Builder utility
- √ Demonstrating containment and delegation
- √ Creating a user control
- √ Adding properties, methods, and events to a user control

Visual Basic provides you with some heavy artillery and, yes, you can do a lot of damage if you are not quite sure of what you are doing. In this chapter, I'll concentrate on building and using classes and mastering techniques to make more robust form modules and standard modules.

The Collection Class

The VB definition of a collection is "an ordered set of items that can be referred to as a unit." I did not discuss collections in Chapter 2 when I talked about arrays because it is neither an array nor a data type. However, the *members* of a collection are, themselves, **Variant**s.

 A further distinction between arrays and collections is that the latter do not need to be re-dimensioned. It grows and shrinks as necessary.

Because a collection is a class, when instantiated, it becomes an *object* and must have attributes. Actually, the implementation of collection is rather simple. It has one property and three methods, as seen in Table 4.1.

Let's start with the **Count** property. At all times, this returns the number of items in the collection. By default, **Count** is zero-based, meaning that the first item is number 0, the second item is number 1, and so on. This provides you with a convenient means to iterate through all of the items in the collection. There are two methods for doing this, both of which are discussed in the next section.

Iterating Through A Collection

Using the standard VB **For...Next** loop, you can reference the **Count** property to easily iterate through any collection

```
For iCtr = 0 To collection.Count - 1
```

Table 4.1	The Collection class attributes.	
Attribute	**Type**	**Description**
Count	Property	Returns the number of items in the collection
Item	Method	References an item by index or key
Add	Method	Adds an item to the collection
Remove	Method	Removes an item from the collection

where *collection* is a valid Visual Basic collection. However, there is an even better way, as seen in the following code snippet:

```
' declare a variable of type variant
Dim vVar As Variant
' colObjects is a collection of objects previously declared
For Each vVar In colObjects
    MsgBox vVar.Name
Next
```

This time, we have used the **For Each...Next** construct, which is actually much more efficient to display the name of each object in a message box.

Of course, we can loop through an array using a **For...Next** loop. What makes a collection different? When you loop through any set of data via some sort of an index (such as the subscript of an array), the process is known as *enumeration*. You are enumerating each member of the set. However, every collection contains an *enumerator* that guarantees that the next item retrieved is, in fact, the next item in the collection. Suppose you have a collection containing the strings: **Red Sox, Yankees,** and **Mets.** You enumerate it, and while doing so, you delete the despised (at least here in Boston) **Yankees.** The collection guarantees that you will not skip over **Mets.** Further, it is essentially an indexed pointer into the collection, which means that, just as indexing a column on a SQL table yields quicker **Select** statements, so, too, does the enumerator in a collection. I will examine this further when I discuss the **Item** and **Add** methods.

To reference an item during the enumeration process, you need to designate a variable to temporarily store the item in the collection. In this case, we have created a variable, **vVar,** of type **Variant.** We then reference that "holder" variable in the body of the loop.

 We could have created an enumerator variable of type **Object** and achieved the same result in the previous code snippet because the collection contained objects. However, recall that all items in a collection are of type **Variant** (in this case, with an underlying data type of **Object**). It is more customary to use a **Variant**—it is also safer because there is less likelihood of introducing a bug because you are using a consistent method to enumerate.

Every item in a collection is 16 bits long because each is a **Variant** that references some other object. The object may be any Visual Basic object, such as a control or a form, or it may be any valid data type, such as a **String** or a **Date,**

with one limitation: it must be supported by the **Variant** data type. Thus, user controls cannot be part of a collection. (But Visual Basic *does* have a built-in **Controls** collection on each form. See the section titled "The Controls Collection" later in this chapter.)

Four bytes of the **Variant** are used as a pointer to the address of the underlying item if the data is stored somewhere else. This is true for **Object, String, Date** data types, and arrays. Numeric data is stored directly in the **Variant**.

Collection Methods

The three methods of the collection allow you to manipulate individual items. The **Item** method allows you to locate a specific item either via its index or its key. The *index* is simply the equivalent of a subscript in an array. Thus, the fifth element in a collection (remembering the collection is zero-based) is item number 4.

When adding items to a collection, you can specify both the index and the key, which we will see in just a moment. The key provides a very efficient way to look up an item in the collection. Assume we have a collection of customers. We can find any item in the collection using the **Item** method, supplying either a numeric argument—**colCustomers.Item (33)** retrieves the thirty-fourth item—or a string that we have previously assigned as a key:

```
colCustomers.Item ("Jones, Sally")
```

In this example, Sally Jones is element number 33 and has a key of "Jones, Sally".

 You can also find an element omitting the keyword **Item**, because this is the default method of the class:

```
colCustomer (33) or colCustomer ("Jones, Sally")
```

If you use a numeric variable as a key, then you must first convert it to a string when retrieving:

```
colCustomer.Item (CStr (myNumber))
```

Placing a numeric literal inside of quotes is not the same as converting a numeric literal to a string using the **CStr** function.

To assign an item from a collection to another variable, you use the **Set** keyword because you are referencing a class, as seen in the following code snippet:

```
Dim vMyVar As Variant
Set vMyVar = colCustomer (33)
```

You use the **Add** method to insert an item into a collection. Because a collection is not an array, it grows and shrinks dynamically. (If you are a C programmer, you can think of a collection as similar to a linked list.)

You have a lot of control over where an item can be inserted in the collection. However, bear in mind that if you specify a numerical placement, it may only be valid until the next time an item is added. For instance, if you specify that an item is the eighth in the list, and then you insert another item before it, the first item you added will then be ninth.

The syntax of **Add** is as follows:

```
collection_name.Add item [,key_value] _
   [,before_value | after_value]
```

where *collection_name* is any valid Visual Basic collection. *Item* is a value of any valid VB data type. The other arguments (*key_value*, *before_value*, and *after_value*) are optional. *Key_value* must be a string; it serves as a way to find an item in the collection (see the **Item** method in Table 4.1). It must be unique (no other *key_value* in the collection can have the same value). The *before_value* and *after_value* clauses may be either numeric or **String** types. If numeric, they must be in the range of 0 to *collection*.**Count** − 1. If they are **Strings**, they must be valid keys previously entered. These allow you to specify in which position in the collection an item is to be inserted. You can specify the *before_value* or *after_value*, but not both.

The code in Listing 4.1 shows how to set up a collection. The output of the code is shown in Figure 4.1.

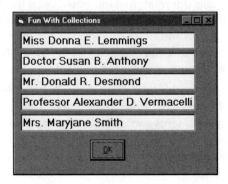

Figure 4.1   Members of a collection.

Listing 4.1   Populating a Collection.

```
' create an array of strings
Dim sCusts(5) As String
' populate the array
sCusts(1) = "Mrs. Maryjane Smith"
sCusts(2) = "Miss Donna E. Lemmings"
sCusts(3) = "Professor Alexander D. Vermacelli"
sCusts(4) = "Doctor Susan B. Anthony"
sCusts(5) = "Mr. Donald R. Desmond"

' create a collection - the New keyword is mandatory
Dim colCustomers As New Collection

' add the items to the array with keys and positionally
colCustomers.Add Item:=sCusts(1), Key:="Mary"
colCustomers.Add sCusts(2), Key:="Donna", Before:="Mary"
colCustomers.Add sCusts(3), Key:="Alex", After:="Donna"
colCustomers.Add sCusts(4), Key:="Sue", Before:="Donna"
colCustomers.Add sCusts(5), Key:="Don", After:="Sue"

' create a variable to loop through the collection
Dim vVar As Variant
Dim iCtr As Integer
' loop through the collection
For Each vVar In colCustomers
' assumes an array of txtResult text boxes!
    txtResult(iCtr) = vVar
    iCtr = iCtr + 1
Next
```

I have, in a number of examples, used a peculiar looking syntax for function arguments called *named arguments*. With named arguments, you specify the argument name followed by a colon and equals sign, and then the actual value (i.e., **before:=** **"Smith"**). You can use this syntax where the values being passed to a function, sub, or method may be ambiguous in their position (meaning that Visual Basic cannot determine the intended arguments from the values supplied).

In the case of the **Add** method of collections, Visual Basic has no way of knowing that the strings being passed correspond to certain arguments and it assumes, in the absence of further guidance, that you are passing them from left to right. Put another way: the **Add** method allows for four arguments: *item*, *key*, *before*, and *after*. If you pass two arguments without specifying what those arguments are for, VB assumes you are using the first two and omitting the last two. In the following example, I show two functionally equivalent statements to add a Form to a collection specifying only two of the four valid arguments to the **Add** method. The first uses named arguments while the second does not. In the second statement, Visual Basic assumes that the first two of the four valid arguments are being used. Thus

```
colMDIChild.Add Item:=frmCustChild, _
    key:=sLName & ", " & sFName
```

is the same as:

```
colMDIChild.Add frmCustChild, _
    sLName & ", " & sFName
```

The **Remove** method, as its name implies, removes items from a collection. There is a little more here than meets the eye though. Let's say you have a collection of forms and then unload one of them (by using the **UnLoad** method). The form is actually not destroyed until you also remove (using the **Remove** method) it from the collection! It stays in memory as though you had executed a **Load** without showing it (using **Show**). Likewise, if you declare an array of **String**s, for instance, and then iterate through them adding them to a collection, they are not removed from memory if you then **Erase** the array! They still exist in the collection.

The **Remove** method has a syntax similar to the **Item** method: *object*.**Remove** *key*, where *object* refers to a valid Visual Basic collection and *key* refers to a valid key or index in that collection, as seen here

```
colCustomers.Remove "Donna"
```

or:

```
colCustomers.Remove 3
```

The **Forms** Collection

The **Forms** collection includes every form loaded into your application, whether they are shown or not. These include MDI, MDI child, and non-MDI forms. The collection name is **Forms** and it has the same property and methods as any other collection. Thus, **Forms.Count** returns the number of form instances in your application or project. Note the use of the phrase *form instances*: you may have multiple instances of the same form (through use of the **New** keyword); Visual Basic returns the number of *all* instances. You can iterate through all of the forms as in any other collection, as seen here:

```
' create a variable to enumerate the collection
Dim vVar As Variant
' enumerate through all the loaded forms
For Each vVar In Forms
    ' show the form
    vVar.Show
Next
```

The **Controls** Collection

Each form has a **Controls** collection, which includes every control on the form. It has the same attributes as the **Forms** collection (and any other collection). You can iterate through it using the **For Each...In...Next** loop or a standard **For...Next** loop, referencing the **Count** property (you can also do this with the **Forms** collection), as shown in this code snippet:

```
' create a counter variable
Dim iCtr As Integer
' loop through all the controls on the current form
For iCtr = 0 to controls.Count - 1
    ' make the control visible
    controls(iCtr).Visible = True
Next
```

You can reference the **Controls** collection on another form by supplying a reference to the form:

```
If TypeOf frm.controls (3) Is CommandButton Then
```

You can also omit the word "controls" when referencing a form because **Controls** is the default attribute of a form:

```
frmMath (6).Caption = "OK"
```

 You can pass an item from a collection to a procedure as an argument that includes any object or variable.

Twin Forms!

In Chapter 3, I discussed the difficulties of obtaining a reference to a form (or any other object) when more than one form of the same name exists in memory. There are actually several ways that multiple forms of the same name could exist in memory at the same time. The most common is by using the **New** or **Set** keyword.

The New Keyword

I touch upon this useful variation of the Visual Basic declaration statement in Chapter 2. **New** causes an *implicit* creation of an object. (You will recall in Chapter 2 that an *explicitly* declared variable is one that is created at the same time it is declared. When **New** is used in the declaration, the object or variable is not created until it is first referenced. When it is referenced, it is said to be *implicitly* created.)

Assume that **frmMath** is a valid form in our project. We can declare a new reference to it with the **New** keyword:

```
Dim frmMathNew As New frmMath
```

frmNewMath does not actually exist until we reference it:

```
frmNewMath.Show
```

New can only be used with objects. It cannot be used to create intrinsic data types, such as **Integer** and **String**.

The Set Keyword

Set is an often misunderstood Visual Basic statement. In fact, the Visual Basic Help file is incorrect. If the object being referenced already exists, it creates a second *reference* to an object but not a second object. If the object does not exist, it is created. When used with the optional argument **New**, a new instance of the object is *always* created. Confusing.

Read through Listing 4.2 to see the **New** keyword at work. The comments preceding each line reveal what is going to happen. The line numbers are for reference only.

Listing 4.2   Fun with **Set** and **New**.

```
1  ' show a form
2  frmMath.Show
```

```
3  ' create a variable of type form
4  Dim frmNewForm As Form
5  ' this creates a new reference but not a new form
6  Set frmNewForm = frmMath
7  ' prove it--only one form is open so hide it
8  frmNewForm.Visible = False
9  ' unload the form
10 UnLoad frmNewForm
11 ' disassociate the variable
12 Set frmNewForm = Nothing
13 ' this creates the form!
14 Set frmNewForm = frmMath
15 ' Show it
16 frmNewForm.Show
17 ' create a second form variable
18 Dim frmNewForm2 As Form
19 ' Thus creates a second instance of the form
20 Set frmNewForm2 = New frmMath
21 ' show it
22 frmNewForm2.Show
```

That's not too tough to fathom. But, let's examine what happens when we use the other optional argument to **Set**, which is the **Nothing** keyword seen in line 12 of Listing 4.2. This frees up any reference between the variable and the argument. In this case, we had just unloaded the form being referenced (in line 10). What would happen, though, if we add **Set frmNewForm = Nothing**?

This will destroy our valid reference to the form. Let's say we then code:

```
frmMath.Caption = "Where Am I?"
```

What happens? We actually have loaded two instances of form **frmMath** into memory. Visual Basic finds the first form and changes its **Caption** property. The second instance of the form that loaded, the one to which **frmNewForm2** had been pointing, is now seemingly out of reach! How can we change its **Caption** or unload it?

Recall our conversation about the **Forms** collection. Through this convenience, Visual Basic always provides a means to find a reference to any form that is loaded. We will explore this subject next.

Telling Your Forms Apart

Assume you have an MDI application. One of the forms is **frmCustMaint**, which displays and maintains any customer in the database. Your user wants to be able to load multiple occurrences of **frmCustMaint** in order to maintain one customer and work on others as phone calls come in. This situation is seen in Figure 4.2, where we show five instances of the same form open. The **New** keyword can be used to obtain a reference to each one.

In this case, we start off by defining a collection to hold all our MDI child forms:

```
Dim colMDIChild As New Collection
```

Then, when a form is opened, it is added to the collection **colMDIChild**:

```
colMDIChild.Add Item:=frmCustChild, key:=sLName _
    & ", " & sFName
```

Note that **Key** is set to the customer's last name, followed by a comma and the first name.

Now, when we need to access a particular form, we have an easy reference to it (recall that *reference* merely means a way to address it in our code). Assume that we want to manipulate the third form shown in Figure 4.2. First, declare a variable:

```
Dim frmGrab As Form
```

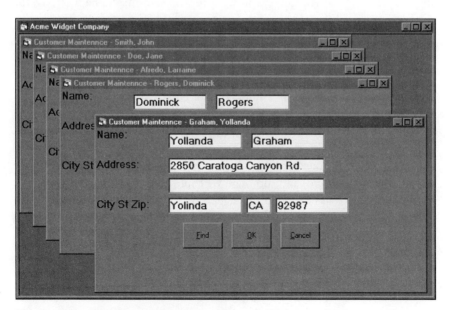

Figure 4.2   The Acme Widget Company's Customer Maintenance forms.

Next, associate it with the form in question:

```
Set frmGrab = colCustMain.Item (sName (3))
```

At this point, you can reference the variable as though it were the form itself. To change the **Caption** property, code:

```
frmGrab.Caption = "New Caption"
```

Remember that because the form is now referenced in a collection, unloading the form does not remove it from memory. You must also remove reference to it from the collection:

```
colCustMain.Remove (sName(3))
```

 Obtaining references to instances of objects, as shown, is a very powerful programming technique. Even more, it is almost certain to appear in some of your exam questions!

Custom Classes

We have already seen that we cannot name an object at runtime (see "Examining The Identity Of An Object" in Chapter 3). A form's **Name** property, for instance, can be changed only at design time.

Or, can it? We will explore this weighty issue in the next section, "Class Modules Revisited."

In Chapter 2, I discussed user-defined data types. Although they are useful, they do not always give us all of the programming power and flexibility that we might need. Imagine a user-defined data type that equates to a customer record. It is instantiated as **strCust**. One of the fields is **strCust.age**. We do not wish this value to be less than zero. The **Type** cannot enforce this rule (that the age cannot be less than zero) and, although we could place code in every procedure that updates **strCust** to validate the age, this is hardly convenient or productive. A user-defined object in the form of a custom class provides us with the tools we need to encapsulate the data and thus provide a ready means to enforce the integrity of the data (i.e., by not allowing age to be less than zero). I will also expand upon this in the next section.

Class Modules Revisited

In Chapter 3, I introduced you to class modules (see "Of Modules And Forms" and "Class Modules"). In this section, I will guide you through the use of class modules in the creation of what is known as a *custom class*. Recall that a class is essentially the definition of an object. Visual Basic provides us with many pre-built classes, such as forms and command buttons. VB also allows us to create a class from scratch, providing us with the capabilities to define properties and methods, and to fully encapsulate logic to protect internal data structures.

Think of the properties of the command button. **Default** is a property that defines whether the Enter key will invoke the command button's **Click** event. It has two possible values: **True** and **False**. The logic to enforce this is *encapsulated* within the command button—there is no way to alter the value of **Default** without accessing the command button itself. If we build a custom class, we can similarly protect data values by encapsulating them within the class. It is in this way that we, as I will show you, protect the "age" field mentioned at the end of the last section from inappropriate changes.

 When I teach these concepts in the classroom, I tell my students to think of a custom class as they might think of a child with his or her toys: The child states that the toys are his (or hers) and that no one can play with them without his or her permission. The analogy is that the class is the child and the data is the toy.

You use the Project|Add Class Module menu choice to insert a new class module into your project. This is the basis for your new class. You will be presented with a dialog, from which you should choose Class Module. The class module looks like a standard module because neither has a visual component.

In Figure 4.3, I have created a class module called **classUpdateClass**. Notice that it has only one property, **Name**, in the object drop-down list, as well as in the properties dialog. A class module is completely user-defined except for this one property. As can be seen, I named the class **classUpdateCust**.

I also created a form, which can be seen in Figure 4.4.

Data needs to be declared before you can encapsulate it into a custom class. The rules for doing so are the same as for any other type of module (see "Variable Declaration" in Chapter 2). For the following example, I placed a Visual

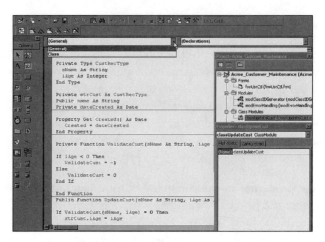

Figure 4.3   Constructing a class module.

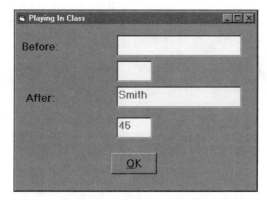

Figure 4.4   The working Customer Validate application.

Basic user-defined **Type CustRecType** in the declarations section of the class module and instantiated it as **strCust**. I also created two other variables, **Name** and **dateCreated**, as seen in Listing 4.3.

Listing 4.3   Declarations for the custom class.

```
Private Type CustRecType
  sName As String
  iAge As Integer
End Type
```

```
Private strCust As CustRecType
Public name As String
Private dateCreated As Date
```

Because the **CustRecType** and **strCust** are defined as part of the class module, they are unavailable to the rest of the application. (Recall that you cannot have a **Public** user-defined type in a class module.) The customer data belongs to the class module and cannot be acted upon without invoking methods of the class module. This is encapsulation! (See the sections titled "Object-Oriented Development" and "Encapsulation" in Chapter 3 for a discussion of encapsulation.)

Because **strCust** is invisible to the rest of the project, I added a publicly available function **UpdateCust** to expose it, as seen in Listing 4.4.

Listing 4.4   The **UpdateCust** function in the custom class.

```
Public Function UpdateCust(sName As String, iAge As Integer) _
    As Integer
 If ValidateCust(sName, iAge) = 0 Then
   strCust.iAge = iAge
   strCust.sName = sName
  ' update the database
   UpdateCust = 0
 Else
  UpdateCust = -1
 End If

End Function
```

The function exposes **strCust** via the arguments **sName** and **iAge**. It returns an **Integer** to the caller that designates success (the update worked) or failure (the update did not work). The function, in turn, calls another function, which is declared as **Private**. It is available only within the class module and is seen in Listing 4.5.

Listing 4.5   The **ValidateCust** function in the custom class.

```
Private Function ValidateCust(sName As String, iAge As Integer)_
    As Integer

 If iAge < 0 Then
   ValidateCust = -1
 Else
```

```
    ValidateCust = 0
  End If

End Function
```

The function verifies that the customer's age is not less than zero.

The form that I developed (seen earlier in Figure 4.4) allows the modification of customer information, but it cannot directly update this information because **strCust** is encapsulated in this custom class. In order to use the class, the form must first declare a reference to it. This is done in the declarations section of the form:

```
Private objUpdCust As classUpdateCust
```

Next, the **Set** keyword is used to create an instance of the class in the **Load** event of the form:

```
Set objUpdCust = New classUpdateCust
```

The **Private** variable **objUpdCust** is a reference to the newly created object of type **classUpdateCust**.

To update the customer information, code in the form module must call the custom class' **UpdateCust** function

```
If objUpdCust.UpdateCust (txtCustData(0), _
   Val(txtCustData (1))) = 0 Then
```

where **objUpdCust** is the reference to the class, and the two arguments **txtCustData(0)** and **Val(txtCustData(1)** are values from text boxes on the form.

Adding Properties To A Custom Class

The three variables defined in Listing 4.3: **strCust**, **Name**, and **dateCreated**, are properties of the newly created object. Notice that **Name** is defined to be **Public**. It can be altered by any object in the current project. This **Public** variable is *not* the same as the **Name** property of the class **classUpdateCust**. It is a property of the instantiated object **objUpdCust**, which is of *type* **classUpdateCust**. However, it does provide us with a method to have a unique "name" for each instance of objects of type **classUpdateCust**. You can, of course, assign the name in your code, but you can also allow the user of the application to create the name him- or herself:

```
objUpdateCust.Name = InputBox ("Enter the name:")
```

The **dateCreated** variable was defined as **Private** in Listing 4.3. It is also a property of the class (and the newly created object) and can be set in the **Initialize** event of the object:

```
dateCreated = Now
```

You use the **Property** keyword to define a *property procedure*. This, then, becomes a method of the object to manipulate in some way an object's properties. There are three methods of declaring a **Property**, depending on what it is that is being accomplished, as shown in Table 4.2.

These variations on declaring a property procedure look suspiciously like the variations on assigning a value to a variable. (The keyword **Let** is an optional method of assigning values [**Let** A = B] that is seldom used.)

In the case of property procedures, things work almost identically, except we are allowed to embed any number of statements into a **Property...End Property** construct, which takes the generalized form

```
[scope] Property Get | Let  propertyname ([arglist,] _
   [As datatype])
```

or

```
[scope] Property Set propertyname ([arglist,] reference)
```

followed by:

```
    [statements]
    [EXIT PROPERTY]
END PROPERTY
```

Table 4.2   Property statements.

Variation	Syntax	Comments
Get	[scope] Property Get propertyname [(arglist)] [As datatype]	Use to retrieve a value
Let	[scope] Property Let propertyname [(arglist)] [As datatype]	Use to assign a value
Set	[scope] Property Set propertyname ([arglist,]reference)	Use to set a reference to a value

In all other respects, the syntax is the same as for declaring a variable. *Scope* is any valid visibility, such as **Public** or **Private**. Note that you can only use **Friend** in a class module. The **Get** form is used in a procedure to retrieve the value of a property. The **Let** form is used to set the value of a property. The **Set** form is used to set a reference to an object. The declaration must be followed by the **End Property** statement. There may be any number of statements in between **Property** and **End Property** including any number of **Exit Property** statements. In other words, this is also just like any other procedure.

It is important to remember that module-level procedures cannot be declared with the **Static** keyword. This has implications: Because there can be multiple instances of a class in memory at any one time, you may wish that certain properties or variables maintain a common value across each class. You may also desire that a variable retains its value between calls to a class module. The latter is a little simpler than the former because a variable's data is not destroyed until the class is destroyed. However, Visual Basic provides no method to store a common set of data between all instances of a class. The only way to get around this is to declare a publicly accessible variable (or object) in a standard module, and then to provide corresponding **Property** statements in the class module to retrieve and update the value. This, however, violates proper object-oriented techniques in that the data is no longer encapsulated: It is accessible outside of the classes because it is in a standard module.

In my Acme Widget company example from Figure 4.3, I added a property procedure to allow other modules to "see" the **dateCreated** property of the class. It is shown in this code snippet:

```
Property Get Created () As Date
   Created = dateCreated
End Property
```

Because it is declared **Public**, any other module in the project can access it with the syntax:

```
objUpdCust.Created
```

In turn, **Created** then is a method of the class.

Adding Events To A Custom Class

When created, a Visual Basic class has only two events: **Initialize** and **Terminate**. However, adding an event to a class is relatively simple. You do so by adding the **Event** statement in the declarations section. That statement has the following syntax:

```
Event eventname [(arglist)]
```

Events are always **Public**. Events cannot have named arguments, **ParamArray** arguments, or other types of optional arguments, and they cannot return values.

Declared events are called by using the **RaiseEvent** keyword. This has the syntax:

```
RaiseEvent eventname [(arglist)]
```

where *arglist* is a list of arguments that must be exactly the same as the list specified in the **Event** declaration. If you wish to fire an event of a class, you need to expose it via a **Public** procedure in the form of a sub or function, as seen in this snippet:

```
' this is in the declarations section of the class
Event Ouch (count As Integer)
' this is a sub in the class
Public Sub ItHurtsSoBad (a As Integer)
    If a < 0 Then
        Exit Sub
    End If
    RaiseEvent Ouch (a)
End Sub
```

An *event source* is an object that raises events. You can create an object to handle the events using the **With Events** clause: **Private With Events** *objectname* **As** *classname*. *Classname* must be a valid (already existing) class. The variable *objectname* must be a module level variable (such as a form or standard module). When added, the class' events are available from the procedure drop-down list in the code window when *objectname* is selected from the object drop-down list.

You can declare user-defined events in a form. However, you need to declare references to the form itself, rendering this a tedious task.

Who Said You Can't Inherit?

In Chapter 3, I discussed a method of reuse known as *delegation*. Class modules should be seen as building blocks that you can use to assemble applications. In this chapter, I have created a class that validates and updates the database with

customer information. Assume that I want to create another class—
classCustomer—that implements the logic in **classUpdateCustomer**. This isn't
quite as good as inheritance, but it's close! To do so, I add a second class module to the project and name it **ClassCustomer**. I then add the following two
lines of code to the declarations section of **ClassCustomer**:

```
Implements classUpdateCustomer
Private classUpdCustomer As classUpdateCustomer
```

Now, when I scroll down the object drop-down list in the editor,
classUpdateCustomer is part of the new class. The procedure drop-down list
has all the procedures of **classUpdateCustomer**, including those declared **Private**. In other words, **classUpdateCustomer** *is* part of the new class. The classes
that are implemented are known as *inner objects* and the container class is known
as the *outer object*. Each object can, in turn, contain other objects nested as
deeply as needed.

The *Implements* Keyword

The **Implements** keyword allows a Visual Basic application to access the exposed *interfaces* of various types of classes, such as those created in VB or those
in type libraries. When a method, property, or event is declared, the declaration becomes a *prototype* (it defines how the attribute is to be accessed). An
interface, then, is a collection of prototypes that are encapsulated by the class
referenced. Visual Basic requires that you implement all **Public** procedures of
an implemented class. You can, however, raise an error (**Const E_NOTIMPL
= &H80004001**) when a procedure that you do not want to be exposed is
called, so that the calling procedure knows that the procedure it called is not
implemented.

There are some restrictions concerning classes implemented by other classes.
The main restriction is that the exposed procedures cannot have an underscore
in their **Name** properties. You can create classes stored in type libraries through
the use of the Microsoft Interface Definition Language compiler or the VB
MkTypLib utility. For more information, use the "Find" tab in the Help Search
dialog and search for "Description Of Interfaces That Can Be Used With
Implements (Read-Me)." The subject is both outside the scope of the certification exam and this book.

The Class Builder Utility

In the preceding pages, I created a class called **classUpdateCustomer** that encapsulated the name and address of the Acme Widget Company's customers. I

created a second class called **classCustomer**, which incorporated the first class. The outer object can access the properties and methods of the inner object. The reverse is also true. I will be talking about what is known as an *object model*, which is most easily created and rearranged using the Visual Basic Class Builder utility. The end result can be likened to a tree that can be traversed in either direction. The outer container always knows what the inner containers are, but the reverse is not necessarily true. The inner objects do not need to know to whom they belong (recall our principles of object-oriented development), but instead, reference them through the **Parent** property. This returns a reference to the container object in the form *myObj*.**Parent**. To find the name of the container object then, you would use *myObj*.**Parent.Name**.

As you become more adept at object-oriented development, you will start to identify those procedures that can be *generalized* (applied to more than one situation) and move those particular procedures into class objects. Soon, you will have a nifty but unwieldy set of classes to use. Now, it is time to take the next step and assemble them into cohesive models. The Class Builder utility helps you do just that.

Imagine that your company verifies the ZIP code whenever a customer's address is maintained. You also do that whenever an employee's or vendor's address is changed. So, you have an excellent situation where a **classAddressVerify** object would come in handy and can be used in all three cases. Let's further assume that you have the need to update a SQL database, check the return code, and perform the appropriate actions if an error has occurred. It is obvious that this can be generalized and used in multiple instances. You can quickly assemble these and other objects into a class hierarchy that looks something like Figure 4.5.

This structure is easy to reproduce with the Class Builder utility. You invoke it by selecting Project|Add Class Module from the menu and selecting the Class Builder from the dialog box that follows. If you have any classes already in your project, they are included on the screen that follows (see Figure 4.6) but are not organized in any structure. You can move them around using drag and drop until you have achieved the structure that you want. Use the toolbar to add other classes or collections. You can see the events, properties, and methods in the right-hand pane and can edit any member by double-clicking on it.

User Controls

From the Project|Add User Control menu, you can add *user controls*. Generally, a user control is similar to a form: You can add other controls—and even

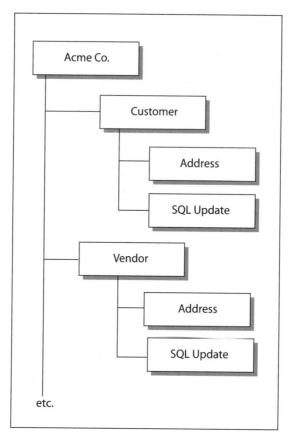

Figure 4.5 A typical object hierarchy.

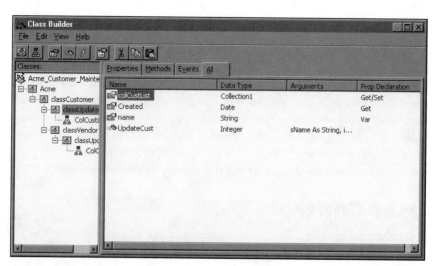

Figure 4.6 The Visual Basic Class Builder utility.

other user controls—to create a custom control that can be added to a form anywhere in your project. Additionally, the control is saved separately with the extension .CTL, giving you the ability to reuse a control from one project to the next.

A user control is most typically a cluster of controls that work in concert. Figure 4.7 shows a File Open dialog created as a user control and added to a form in the project. You can add the control to the toolbox dialog either by referencing the control in the design environment, or by selecting Project|Add File and choosing the control file. The simplest method, of course, is to simply use the Add User Control choice and select the Existing tab from the resulting dialog.

You can add user controls with no visible manifestation (that is, there is no visible component) as pure event handlers, making them similar to class modules in that respect. If you have the Professional or Enterprise editions of Visual Basic, an events user control is included. User controls also serve as the basis for custom ActiveX controls, which will be discussed in Chapter 9.

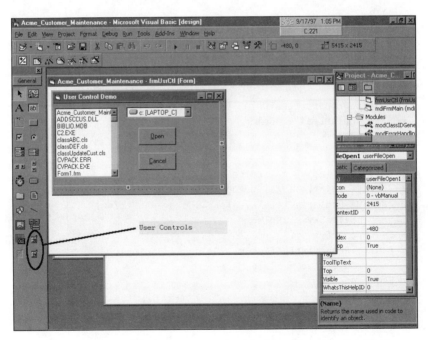

Figure 4.7   The userFileOpen control added to a form in the design environment. Notice that the toolbox shows available user controls at the bottom.

Exam Prep Questions

Question 1

You need to add two properties to a class. The **SkyColor** property is for use inside the class only, while the **LeafColor** property needs to be available to other objects. All data must be encapsulated to the class. Which accomplishes this?

○ a.
```
Private ColorSky As String
Public colorless As String
Private Property Let SkyColor (sColor As String)
     ColorSky = sColor
End Property
Public Property LeafColor (sColor As String)
     ColorLeaf = sColor
End Property
```

○ b.
```
Public ColorSky As String
Public ColorLeaf As String
Private Property Let SkyColor (sColor As String)
     ColorSky = sColor
End Property
Public Property LeafColor (sColor As String)
     ColorLeaf = sColor
End Property
```

○ c.
```
Private ColorSky As String
Private ColorLeaf As String
Private Property Let SkyColor (sColor As String)
     ColorSky = sColor
End Property
Public Property LeafColor (sColor As String)
     ColorLeaf = sColor
End Property
```

○ d.
```
Private ColorSky As String
Private ColorLeaf As String
Public Property Let SkyColor (sColor As String)
     ColorSky = sColor
End Property
Private Property LeafColor (sColor As String)
     ColorLeaf = sColor
End Property
```

Answer c is correct because both variables are defined as *Private*, thus accomplishing encapsulation. Further, only *LeafColor* is exposed (it is declared as *Public*) although *SkyColor* is *Private*. Answer a is incorrect because one of the variables is defined as **Public,** allowing other modules to change it directly. Answer b is incorrect because both variables are defined as **Public**. Answer d is incorrect because **SkyColor** is **Public** but **LeafColor** is **Private**.

Question2

Which routine is fired when another module attempts to set the value of **myVariant**, which is a property of type **Variant**?

○ a.
```
Public Property Let myVariant ( )
```

○ b.
```
Public Property Let myVariant _
    (vVal As Variant)
```

○ c.
```
Public Property Set myVariant ( )
```

○ d.
```
Public Property Set myVariant _
    (vVal As Variant)
```

Answer b is correct because *Let* is used for variables and a proper assignment argument has been provided. Answer a is wrong because no value is provided to set **myVariant**. Answer c is wrong for the same reason and also because the **Set** keyword is used instead of **Let**. Answer d is wrong because **Set** is used for objects (not variables) and has a different syntax.

Question 3

In the following code, you create two instances of **frmDoc**. Which instance(s) has (have) its (their) caption(s) updated?

```
Dim colTest As New Collection
Dim frmNew(1) As Form
Set frmNew(0) = New frmDoc
Set frmNew(1) = New frmDoc
colTest.Add frmNew(0), "first"
colTest.Item("first").Show
colTest.Add frmNew(1), "second"
colTest.Item("second").Show
colTest.Remove "first"
frmDoc.Caption = "New Caption"
```

○ a. The first instance

○ b. The second instance

○ c. Both the first and the second instances

○ d. Neither the first nor the second instance

Answer d is correct. For this question, you need to understand thoroughly how Visual Basic creates objects, specifically, in this case, forms. All of the code is "fluff" except the last line. Answers a, b, and c are all incorrect because the last line instantiates a *third* instance of **frmDoc**, even though it is only loaded and not displayed. The code is meant to trick you because removing one of the forms from the collection does not unload it from memory, thus distracting you from what is really going on.

Question 4

Assuming that every property in a class module has been declared **Public**, any module can than update all variables in that class module. True or False?

O a. True

O b. False

Answer b is correct. You need to have a *Property Let* statement to modify a variable in a class. The trick is that you need to watch out for superlatives—in this case, the "all variables" statement. The question is also written to intimidate you because of the second superlative "every property," which in this case, is meaningless. Answer a is incorrect because the mere fact that you have made all of your properties **Public** does not mean that you have a property for every variable. Any variable for which no **Property Let** statement has been defined is still protected (assuming it is declared as **Private**).

Question 5

Looking at the code provided, what will be in the list box **list1** (assuming its sorted property is set to **False**)?

```
Dim sNames (1 To 3) As String, vVar As String
Dim colNames As New Collection
sNames (1) = "Carrie"
sNames (2) = "Alice"
sNames (3) = "Bob"
colNames.Add Item:=sNames(1), _
   key:="Cancun"
colNames.Add Item:=sNames(2), _
   key:="Bermuda", Before:="Cancun"
colNames.Add Item:=sNames(3), _
   key:="Aruba", After:="Cancun"
For each vVar in colNames
   list1.AddItem vVar
Next
```

○ a. Cancun

   Bermuda

   Aruba

○ b. Bermuda

   Cancun

   Aruba

○ c. Carrie

   Alice

   Bob

○ d. Alice

   Carrie

   Bob

○ e. None of the above

Answer d is correct. Carrie is added first; Alice is added next but placed before Carrie; and Bob is added last and placed after Carrie. Thus, the order is: Alice, Carrie, and Bob. Answers a and b are both incorrect because it is the string's value that is added, not the key of the collection item. Answer c is wrong because it is in the incorrect order. Answer e is incorrect because the correct answer was given.

Question 6

> If an object of type **classA** implements an object of type **classB**, are **classB**'s methods and properties available to **classA**?
>
> ○ a. Yes
>
> ○ b. No
>
> ○ c. Yes, but only those declared **Public**
>
> ○ d. Yes, all methods are available, but the only properties that are available are those declared **Public**

Answer c is correct because the properties and methods of an inner object are only available to the outer object if they are declared *Public.* Answer a is wrong because not all properties and methods are necessarily available. Answer b is wrong because they're not necessarily all hidden. Answer d is wrong because there is nothing special about methods—they still need to be made publicly available to be accessed.

Question 7

> Which of the following code snippets from a class module is valid?
>
> ○ a.
> ```
> Public Event SetColor (color As String)
> Private Sub class_initialize ()
>     SetColor ("red")
> End Sub
> ```
> ○ b.
> ```
> Private Event SetColor (color As String)
> Private Sub class_initialize ()
>     SetColor ("red")
> End Sub
> ```
> ○ c.
> ```
> Public Event SetColor (color As String)
> Private Sub class_initialize ()
>     RaiseEvent SetColor ("red")
> End Sub
> ```
> ○ d.
> ```
> Private Event SetColor (color As String)
> Private Sub class_initialize ()
>     RaiseEvent SetColor ("red")
> End Sub
> ```

Answer c is correct because the event is properly defined and called using the *Raise Event* statement. Answer a is incorrect because a declared procedure must be called with **Raise Event**. Answer b is incorrect because a declared procedure must be called with **Raise Event** and because the event is declared as **Private,** which is illegal. Answer d is incorrect because the event is declared as **Private.**

Question 8

> The Class Builder utility can be used to assemble related:
>
> ○ a. Classes
> ○ b. Collections
> ○ c. Classes and collections
> ○ d. Classes and collections declared within those classes

Answer c is correct. The Class Builder utility is used to assemble related classes and collections into new classes. Answers a and b are both wrong because they specify classes and collections only, respectively. Answer d is wrong because the collections do not have to be specified in the classes in order to be added.

Question 9

> Assume you have a form **frm1**, a command button **cb1**, a collection **col1**, a **String s1**, and a **Variant v1**. Which of the following can be assigned to a variable of type **Object**? [Check all correct answers]
>
> ❑ a. **frm1**
> ❑ b. **cb1**
> ❑ c. **col1**
> ❑ d. **s1**
> ❑ e. **v1**

Answers a, b, and c are correct because they are valid objects. Answers d and e are wrong because they are both intrinsic data types, which cannot be assigned to an object.

Need To Know More?

 Jamsa, Kris and Lars Klander, *1001 Visual Basic Programmer's Tips.* Jamsa Press, Las Vegas, NV, 1997, ISBN 1-884133-56-8. This well-done book is not broken into chapters but rather into "tips." Tips 577 through 599 are an effective introduction to the creation and exploitation of classes. Tips 488 through 523 discuss the creation of collections and the use of many of the built-in VB collections.

 Mandelbrot Set, The: *Advanced Microsoft Visual Basic.* Microsoft Press, Redmond, WA, 1997. ISBN 1-57231-414-1. This book is broken into sections done by various authors (they are not listed on the cover). In Chapter 15, Chris Debollot and Steve Overall discuss the reuse aspect of classes, and in Chapter 16, Mark Sewell and Alan Inglis discuss many of the other topics covered in this chapter, particularly reuse, objects, and collections.

 McKinney, Bruce: *Hardcore Visual Basic, Second Edition* (which covers version 5). Microsoft Press, Redmond, WA, 1997. ISBN 1-57231-422-2. In Chapter 3, Bruce covers classes and objects at great depth, and in Chapter 4 he delves into collections.

 Swartzfager, Gene: *Visual Basic 5 Object-Oriented Programming.* Coriolis Group Books, Scottsdale, AZ, 1997, ISBN 1-57610-106-1. Gene has crafted a very nicely done volume on squeezing the most out of VB's limited object-oriented features. Chapters 1, 3, and 11 are particularly useful in reinforcing the concepts covered in this chapter.

 Search the online books on the VB CD for "Programming With Objects," which discusses the use of objects, collections, and classes at a fairly easy to digest level of detail.

 Microsoft places the most current Knowledge Base online at www.microsoft.com/support/. Enter search terms such as "class," "object," and "collection" to view articles detailing tips (and sometimes fixes) revolving around the issues discussed in this chapter.

There are a number of Web sites devoted to the subject of Visual Basic. Use a search engine such as Yahoo! (www.yahoo.com) or Hotbot (www.hotbot.com) with a search term such as "Visual Basic 5" (be sure to place the search term in quotes so that only pages containing the entire term as one string are returned). A well-done site with tips and sample code that I liked was the "VB Palace" at home.computer.net/~mheller/. Another site that was under "reconstruction" when I visited was a site hosted by Temple University at thunder.ocis.temple.edu/~shariq/vb/index.html.

Using External Modules

Terms you'll need to understand:

- √ API
- √ ActiveX control
- √ OLE Automation
- √ ImageList, TreeView, ListView, Slider, and UpDown controls
- √ ListImages, ListItems, and Nodes collections
- √ Child and Parent
- √ LoadPicture
- √ Buddy control
- √ Type library
- √ Early and late binding
- √ Declare
- √ Alias
- √ Any
- √ ParamArray
- √ ByVal and ByRef
- √ Overloaded function
- √ CreateObject and GetObject

Techniques you'll need to master:

- √ Using the TreeView control with the ListView control
- √ Using the Slider control
- √ Using the ImageList control to manage graphics
- √ Using the UpDown control
- √ Declaring an API function or procedure
- √ Using Any to call external procedures
- √ Using ParamArray as an argument
- √ Calling an API function or procedure
- √ Passing a null string to an external procedure
- √ Handling an error when calling an external procedure
- √ Creating an OLE Automation object

There are really three ways to add functionality to your project from outside of the Visual Basic environment. You are at least partly familiar with the first technique: the use of add-in ActiveX controls. The second is to access the API (Application Program Interface) of another process such as ODBC (Open Database Connectivity) or Windows itself. The third is via inter-application communications; OLE Automation is the most notable example of this. The Windows API is discussed in Chapter 7. This chapter will discuss all other aspects of using external modules.

ActiveX Controls

Visual Basic introduced the concept of "plug-in" controls with VBX files. These were replaced by OLE controls, with a file type of OCX, in Windows 95. These then became known as ActiveX controls, as methods to enable them in Web pages became available. The concept of plugging controls onto a form, and the use of pre-built objects in general, has become known as component-based development and is embraced in *COM* (Component Object Model) development. ActiveX is a piece of COM. The "old" term *OLE server* has been replaced by the more politically correct (according to Microsoft) term *ActiveX component*, which encompasses ActiveX documents and ActiveX DLLs.

 There are currently two competing standards for "distributed object" development. The Open Standards Group backs a standard called CORBA, while Microsoft, Hewlett Packard, and several others back a standard called DCOM (Distributed COM). Distributed object technology seeks to allow objects, such as ActiveX controls, to communicate with one another whether they are local (on the same machine) or remote (on another machine accessed over a network). You will likely see a question or two querying your knowledge of the goal of DCOM, but not its actual implementation, which is still evolving.

An ActiveX control is the most obvious example of using an external module, because it is not part of Visual Basic (it is an add-in). Chapter 9 covers Visual Basic 5's new ability to create ActiveX controls and ActiveX DLLs.

When you installed Visual Basic, it searched through your system for all registered OCX files. You can use any of them in your development environment by selecting Project|Components from the Visual Basic menu, and then selecting those that you wish to use. A collection of useful controls is also included with Visual Basic itself (and accessible from the VB menu). When selected, the tools are added to your toolbox, where you can use them in the same way as any standard control. Most typically, these controls have their own property sheets (in addition to those supplied by VB), because the controls can also be used in other development environments such as Visual C++.

Key ActiveX Controls

You may see a few questions on the certification exam about ActiveX controls. The specific ActiveX controls that you are most likely to see queried are: the CommonDialog control, which I discuss in Chapter 8 in "The CommonDialog Control"; the DBGrid control, which I discuss in Chapter 10 in "Data Bound Controls"; and the Winsock control, which I discuss in Chapter 12 in "The Winsock Control." In the following sections, I discuss other ActiveX controls that you may see on the exam.

The ImageList Control

As its main property, the ImageList control contains the **ListImages** collection, which contains **ListImage** objects. The ImageList control is basically a reference to images used by other controls. The images it references are Windows bitmaps, but you can use the **Extract** method of the **ListImage** object to convert the bitmap into an icon for those controls that expect an icon. For instance, assume you have a bitmap that you would like to use as your form's icon. You can do this with the following syntax:

```
Form1.Icon = ImageList1.ListImages(5).ExtractIcon
```

This example turns the bitmap referenced by the fifth **ListImage** object into an icon for use by the **Form** object.

To assign an image to a **ListImage** object, use the object's **Picture** property and the **LoadPicture** statement:

```
ImageList1.ListImages(3).Picture = LoadPicture _
   "C:\Graphics\Bitmaps\MyBitMap.BMP"
```

For more information, search for "ImageList Control" in the Visual Basic Help file.

The ListView Control

The ListView control is used to display information in a graphical format. It is often used in conjunction with the TreeView control, which I discuss next. Figure 5.1 shows the TreeView control in use in the left window and the ListView control in the right window.

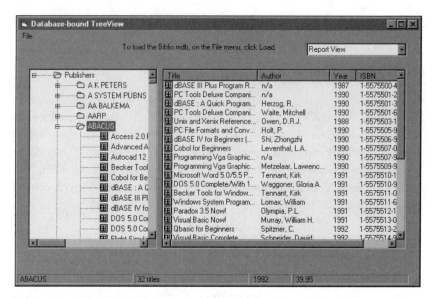

Figure 5.1   The TreeView control (left window) and the ListView control (right window) used in the DataView sample application supplied with Visual Basic.

The ListView control is contained in the COMCTL32.OCX file and can be added to your project by selecting Project|Components from VB's menu and choosing Microsoft Windows Common Controls 5.0. Several controls, including the ProgressBar, Slider, ImageList, and TreeView controls, are also added when you select this component.

The ListView control provides you with four presentation options: large icons, small icons, list, and report. This is governed by the **View** property using the VB constants **ivwIcon, ivwSmallIcon, ivwList,** and **ivwReport**, respectively. In report view, you can specify that column headings are displayed by setting the **HideColumnHeadings** property to **False**. (Figure 5.1 shows the report view with column headings displayed.)

To supply icons, you first associate the **Icons** and **SmallIcons** property with a valid ImageList control:

```
ListView1.Icons = ImageList1
```

Each ListView control has a **ListItems** property, which is a collection of type **ListItem**. This property corresponds to the actual contents of the ListView control. Each line in the right window of Figure 5.1 is a **ListItem**. Two of the properties of **ListItem** are **Icon** and **SmallIcon**. The preceding line of code associated a ListView control with an Image control via its **Icons** and **SmallIcons** properties, you can now assign a specific icon to any individual **ListItem**:

```
ListView1.ListItems(1).Icon = 1
```

This sets the **ListItem(1)**'s icon to the first icon in **ImageView1**.

The ListView control has a **ColumnHeaders** collection property comprised of **ColumnHeader** objects. **ColumnHeader** objects are quite powerful. For instance, a user can click on one to sort the report by that column.

For more information on the ListView control, search for "ListView Control," "ListItems collection," and "ColumnHeaders collection" in VB's online Help file.

The TreeView Control

A TreeView control is a hierarchical representation of data. Both the TreeView and ListView controls can be seen in Windows Explorer. The left window of Explorer (the Folders view), shows a TreeView control as it expands and collapses to show the drives and directories of a PC. The right window is a ListView control that shows the contents of the currently selected folder. Each item in the TreeView is called a *node*.

The TreeView control's main property is the **Nodes** collection. Each **Node** object within the collection contains an image and some text. To associate graphics, you associate the **Images** property of the ListView control with an ImageList control, similar to the way you associate the **Icons** and **SmallIcons** properties of the ListView control with an ImageList control. Then, you associate the **ImageView** property of each individual **Node** object with a specific image from the ImageList control, like this:

```
TreeView1.Nodes(1).ImageView = 4
```

This sets the **ImageView** property of the first **Node** object to the fourth icon of the associated ImageList control. To add text, use the **Text** property.

Each **Node** can contain other **Nodes**. The hierarchy of nodes is maintained by the **Child** and **Parent** properties of each **Node** object. To add a new node as a child of another node, you would use syntax similar to the following:

```
Dim newNode As Node
Set newNode = TreeView1.Nodes _
    (TreeView1.SelectedItem.Index).Child
```

This example uses the **Child** property of the currently selected **Node** object (determined by using the **SelectedItem** property of the TreeView control) to dynamically add the new **Node** object.

You use the **Sorted** property to sort the TreeView:

```
TreeView1.Sorted = True
```

For more information about the TreeView control, search for "TreeView control" and "Nodes collection" in the VB Help file.

The Slider Control

The Slider control is somewhat similar to an HScrollBar or VScrollBar control. It is a graphical representation of a "thumb" slider, which can be used to select either discrete values (such as 1, 2, 3, and so on) or a continuous range of values. Optional tick marks denote values. The **Max** and **Min** properties denote the maximum and minimum values. The **TickFrequency** property determines how many tick marks there will be. For instance, if the **Max** property is set to 10 and the **Min** property is set to 0, a **TickFrequency** of 2 will cause six ticks to be on the control (denoting the values 0, 2, 4, 6, 8, and 10). The **Value** property sets or returns the current value of the Slider control. An example of a Slider control is shown in Figure 5.2. You can use the **Orientation** property to set the control to a horizontal (**sldHorizontal**) or vertical (**sldVertical**) presentation.

The Slider control can be used to measure or alter a value. For instance, you can detect the alteration of the Slider control's **Value** property and use that value to alter something else, such as the size of a bitmap or the current position in a multimedia file. You use the **Change** event to detect a change in the **Value** property. A similar event, **Scroll**, may also be useful. The difference between the two events is that **Scroll** detects any movement of the Slider control, even if that movement does not result in a change in the control's **Value** property.

For more information, search for "Slider control" in the VB Help file.

The UpDown Control

The UpDown control presents a pair of arrow buttons that the user can click on to alter the contents of another control. The second control is known as a *buddy control*. A typical "pairing" of controls is a Textbox control with the

Figure 5.2   The Slider control.

UpDown control. You use the UpDown control's **BuddyControl** property to associate the TextBox control:

```
UpDown1.BuddyControl = Text1
```

Alternatively, you can use the **AutoBuddy** property to set the associated control. By setting this property to **True**, Visual Basic associates the control next lowest in the tab order as the buddy control. If there is no control lower in the tab order, VB uses the next control higher in the tab order. The **BuddyProperty** property determines which property of the buddy control is altered when the UpDown control is used. If the **BuddyProperty** property is not supplied, the buddy control's default property is used. If the **SyncProperty** property is set to **True**, VB will ensure that the values of both controls are synchronized. Thus, you can use an UpDown control to change the number presented in a TextBox control.

The **Min** and **Max** properties control the minimum and maximum values. **Increment** maintains the amount that the value changes every time an arrow is clicked. The **Value** control sets or returns the actual current value of the control.

The UpDown control is added with the Microsoft Windows Common Controls-2 5.0, available from the Project|Components menu.

Type Libraries

A *type library* (file extension .TLB) contains "Automation standard descriptions" of exposed properties and functions of other modules, such as the exported functions of DLL libraries (discussed in "Using The External Procedures Of An API" later in this chapter).

When you create an ActiveX control, a type library is also created, which allows other VB developers to browse its properties and methods in the environment. Further, the control can be directly accessed in code. (If no type library is provided, you will need to reference it via a generic variable of type **Object**.) This has binding implications: When a type library is supplied, VB can examine it and perform early binding, which means that the compiler can examine the control and include its properties and methods at compile time. Otherwise, VB does not "know" what properties and methods the control supports until you actually invoke a property or method at runtime. Because VB cannot include the properties and methods as part of the compiled program, it is forced to do late binding (essentially resolving references to the control at runtime), which is slower than access to early bound controls.

Using The External Procedures Of An API

Many applications expose their services via an *API* (Application Program Interface). These are sometimes referred to as external procedures or external functions. The process of exposing services is done via *exported* DLL (Dynamic Link Library) functions and procedures. An exported function or procedure is one whose *prototype* is visible to other programs (such as your VB applications). A prototype is a function or procedure definition similar to what you provide when you create a function or sub in your VB application; it defines the name of the function or procedure, the expected arguments and data types, and the type of value to be returned (if any). Chapter 10 reviews database access using Visual Basic code and controls. However, ODBC also exposes its functions and procedures via an API. You could list all available ODBC data sources using a function in ODBC32.DLL called **SQLDataSources**. Because the function is not part of Visual Basic, you need to create a function prototype that tells VB what arguments to send to ODBC32.DLL and what to expect in return.

The **Declare** Statement

To create the prototype, you use the **Declare** statement with the syntax as shown:

```
Public | Private Declare Function func_name Lib "lib_name" _
   [Alias "alias_name"] ([arg_list]) As return_type
Public | Private Declare Sub sub_name Lib "lib_name" _
   [Alias "alias_name"] ([arg_list])
```

Use the **Sub** form when the API call will not return a value. Use the **Function** form when a value will be returned.

The keywords **Public** and **Private** are, of course, mutually exclusive and refer to the visibility of **Declare**. If declared **Public**, all modules may access the declaration. If **Private**, only the module in which the declaration is defined can access the declaration. *Func_name* or *sub_name* is the name by which you will call the function or procedure. Unless you specify an alias (discussed shortly), it must be the same name as the function or procedure defined in the DLL being called. Note that the name is case-sensitive. Use **Lib** followed by *lib_name* to tell Visual Basic in which DLL to look for the API function.

Generally, it is not a good idea to supply a path as part of the *lib_name* because the file may be in different directories on different users' machines. Therefore, you should ensure that the DLL you want to reference is installed either in the application's directory or in the SYSTEM (SYSTEM32 on Windows NT) directory underneath the directory where Windows is installed. When you invoke the function, the operating system will look for the DLL file in the application's directory, the SYSTEM directory, and then the directories stored in the PATH environmental variable. The operating system will use whichever file it finds first. (If there are three copies of ODBC32.DLL on your PC, the operating system will use whichever it finds first.)

Alias supplies an alternate name for your program to use when invoking the DLL's function. If you create an alias, the "real" name of the function or procedure (as defined within the DLL) is supplied in quotes following the **Alias** keyword. The *func_name* or *sub_name* is the name you will use to call the function or procedure. Note that the name provided in **Alias** is case-sensitive. There are a few reasons you might need to supply the alias. If the DLL's function name contains characters that are illegal in Visual Basic (such as the dollar sign), then you will need to create an alias. Also, the function name may be the same as a Visual Basic reserved word or may be the same name as an existing variable or procedure. Again, you would then need to create an alias. Finally, some functions that return a string have two different versions: one for the ANSI character set and the other for the Unicode character set. (This topic is discussed in Chapter 7, in "Characters In The Windows API," but the same principles apply for DLLs that are not part of the Windows API.) In general, you should choose the form of a function that returns ANSI characters whether you are working in Windows 95 (which uses ANSI characters) or Windows NT (which uses Unicode characters).

Instead of a function or procedure name, you can provide a function or procedure *number*. In a DLL, all exported functions and procedures also have an *ordinal number*. The **SQLDataSources** function in ODBC32.DLL is also ordinal number 57. If using ordinal numbers in **Alias**, the first character must be the pound sign (#): "#57".

You must supply any necessary arguments enclosed within parentheses. If no arguments are expected, the parentheses should be left empty. If the function does expect arguments, you place them in the parentheses supplying both a variable name and data type using the **As** keyword to define the data type. This takes the form shown here:

```
[Optional] [ByVal | ByRef] [ParamArray] var_name [()] _
    As data_type
```

The keyword **Optional** tells Visual Basic the argument is optional and VB will not enforce its presence. **ByVal** and **ByRef** are mutually exclusive. **ByRef** causes a pointer to the actual variable to be passed to the function or procedure. This means that the DLL can change the value of the variable. When you see "LPSTR" (or similar) in the DLL's function or procedure prototype, you *must* specify **ByRef**. LPSTR is a "long pointer" to a string. I discuss these variable types in Chapter 7 in "Data Type Considerations." **ByVal** passes a copy of the variable—not the variable itself. Therefore, the DLL cannot alter the value of your VB variable. If omitted, **ByRef** is the default.

If used, **ParamArray** must be the last argument. It cannot be used with **ByVal** or **ByRef**. It specifies that the supplied variable is an **Optional** array of variants and allows the passing of a variable number of arguments. *Var_name* is the name of the variable being passed and *data_type* is the Visual Basic data type of the variable.

The function declaration for the **SQLDataSources** function mentioned earlier is:

```
Declare Function SQLDataSources Lib "ODBC32.DLL" _
(ByVal EnvironmentHandle As Long, ByVal Direction As Long, _
    ByVal ServerName As String, ByVal BufferLength1 As Integer, _
    ByVal NameLengthPointer1 As Integer, ByVal Description _
    As String, ByVal BufferLenhgth2 As Integer, ByVal _
    NameLengthPointer2 As Integer) As Integer
```

In this example, **SQLDataSources** is the name of the function. The library name is ODBC32.DLL. All of the arguments are passed **ByVal**, and the function returns a variable of type **Integer**.

You can see if a given DLL exports functions by right-clicking on it in Windows Explorer and selecting Quick View. The functions will be listed in a section called "Nonresident-Name Table (Exported Functions)." This does not, unfortunately, provide the function prototype. For that, you will need documentation from the author of the DLL or a third-party book that covers this.

The *Any* Keyword

Some object-oriented languages, such as C++ (with which most DLLs are developed), allow for a concept known as *function overloading*. With function overloading, a function or procedure behaves differently based on the number of arguments supplied and/or the data types of the arguments supplied. VB developers are sometimes confronted by this in API declarations, where the data type of an argument may vary depending on the context in which the function is used. This is common in the Windows API, where many functions require a string or an integer depending on the specific operation being performed.

When faced with the need for a variable number of arguments, the **ParamArray** keyword, outlined earlier, is used. Variable numbers of arguments are not common. Varying data types for a given argument are common. To support this requirement, Visual Basic provides the **Any** keyword as a "substitute" or "generic" data type. In the **Declare** statement, you would specify an argument similar to **myVar As Any**, which tells Visual Basic that the variable **myVar** can be of any data type. Because Visual Basic cannot perform validity checking on the data type, the VB developer needs to exercise extra caution when calling an API function using the **Any** keyword. If you pass a data type that the API function is not expecting, you may get anything from unexpected results to an operating system crash. Worse, if a crash does result, it may not happen until later in your program, making the connection between the system crash and your API call difficult to find.

Calling The API Function Or Procedure

After you have declared an external function, you invoke it much as you would any VB sub or function. The following snippet of code demonstrates a VB **Declare** followed by a function call:

```
Dim iRslt As Integer
' declare a reference to the function
Declare Function myAPICall Lib "some.dll" Alias "_a_function" _
    (myVar As Long) As Integer
' call the function
iRslt = myAPICall (99000)
```

In this example, the name of the function within the DLL is "**_a_function**". Because it begins with an underscore character (which is illegal in VB), I have used the **Alias** keyword. The function accepts an argument of type **Long** and returns a value of type **Integer.** To call it, I assigned the result to the variable

iRslt, which had been declared as an **Integer.** I passed the value 99000 as an argument.

Note that you can optionally use the **Call** keyword when invoking any function or procedure: **Call myProcedure (myVar)** is the same as **myProcedure (myVar).**

String Handling With External Modules

If you call a function that expects a string argument and you need to pass a null string, you can sometimes get away with declaring the variable as being of type **Any** in the **Declare** statement and then passing a value of zero when you call the function. This usually works because the function is generally expecting to receive the address of the string and, if that address is zero, the function "knows" that the string is null. This can occasionally lead to subtle behavioral differences. It is a better practice to use the Visual Basic constant **vbNullString** instead. A null string is not the same as an empty string ("").

 Knowing how to pass a null string to an external procedure is very likely to appear on the exam. You may be asked a question about passing a string to an external module where the string has a null value or where it has a value of zero. Null strings and zero-value strings are synonymous terms. Either way, call the function using the VB constant **vbNullString.**

The *LastDLLError* Property

Many external functions return a code to indicate success or failure. If the function failed, there is no Visual Basic error raised. However, the **LastDLLError** property of the **Err** object is filled in. Immediately after calling a function, the VB application should check this property and act accordingly. Use the DLL's documentation to determine the meaning of different return codes. I discuss the **Err** object in the next chapter, "Error Handling."

OLE Automation

Microsoft's COM model depends on OLE Automation. The Microsoft definition of Automation is "a technology that enables applications to provide objects in a consistent way to other objects, development tools, and macro languages." OLE stands for Object Linking and Embedding. Therefore, Automation is the means by which OLE objects communicate and are communicated with. Every object that supports Automation exposes (provides) at least one object. Microsoft Word provides the **Document** object. Excel provides the **Sheet** and **Chart** objects. Note that although these objects tend to be made up of other objects, the underlying objects are not Automation objects. As an example, **Range** is a **Sheet** object in Excel but it cannot be directly accessed via Visual Basic. It must be referenced via **Sheet**.

The **CreateObject** Function

CreateObject creates an Automation object within the VB application. You are required to supply the name of a class made up of an application and an object. To create an Excel **Sheet** object, you use the syntax:

```
Dim mySheet As Object
Set mySheet = CreateObject ("Excel.Sheet")
```

If the referenced application is not already running, it is invoked. The referenced object is then created. From that point, underlying objects, properties, and methods can be manipulated using dot notation

```
mySheet.SaveAs "C:\mysheet.xls"
```

to save the worksheet. To change the value of a cell in the worksheet, use the syntax:

```
mySheet.Cells (4,2) = "=sum(a1:a10)"
```

The **GetObject** Function

Use the **GetObject** function to obtain a reference to an existing Automation object. The following snippet of code obtains a reference to an already-running instance of Microsoft Excel and loads an existing worksheet:

```
Dim myObj As Object
myObj = GetObject ("\my documents\excel\mysheet.xls")
```

The OLE Control

Visual Basic provides an OLE control (sometimes called the OLE Container control) to house Automation objects directly on your form. The object reference within the OLE control is slightly different than that used with the **CreateObject** function. The control has a **Class** function that takes three parts (instead of the **CreateObject** function's two parts): *application.obect.version*, where *application* is the application that creates *object* and *version* is the version of the application. For instance, to create a document using Microsoft Word version 8 (Office 97), you would use the following syntax:

```
OLE1.Class = "Word.Document.8"
```

When you use the OLE control, you can either *link* an object or *embed* it. A linked object is actually stored by the target application (such as Microsoft Word). The application shows an image of the object's data, not the actual data itself. With an embedded object, the actual data is stored within the control. You use the **CreateEmbed** method to create an embedded object and the **CreateLink** method to create a linked object. You can determine whether an object is linked or embedded with the **OLEType** property. **vbOLELinked** indicates that the object is linked, while **vbOLEEmbedded** indicates the objects is embedded.

The **SourceDoc** property is used to set or return the document contained in the object:

```
OLE1.SourceDoc = "C:\mydoc.doc"
```

SourceItem is used to determine the data to be displayed in a linked (but not embedded) object. The actual value will vary from application to application. To display data from an Excel spreadsheet, use the syntax:

```
OLE1.SourceItem = "R1C1:R4C8"
```

At runtime, you can concatenate the **SourceDoc** and **SourceItem** properties into the **SourceDoc** property using an exclamation point (!) as a separator:

```
OLE1.SourceDoc = "C:\mySheet.XLS!R1C1:R4C8"
```

Every object has associated *verbs*, which are actions that the OLE object can perform. You can set the **AutoVerbMenu** to **True**, which causes a pop-up menu to be displayed at runtime when the user right-clicks on the control. This pop-up will generally be a context menu. If you embed a Microsoft Word document and run the application, the pop-up menu will offer two choices: Open and Edit. If the user chooses Edit, Word's menu replaces your application's menu when the control has focus. The **DoVerb** property performs actions that are valid in the context of the object (for instance, spellcheck is a valid action for a Word document but not for Microsoft Paint). Some verb actions are standard to most or all valid OLE objects and can be invoked using VB constants: **OLE1.DoVerb (vbOLEShow)** activates the object. Other constants are listed in the VB Help file (search for "DoVerb"). The **FetchVerbs** method queries the object for all valid verbs and stores them in an array in the **ObjectVerbs** property.

The **AppIsRunning** property returns **True** if the application that created the embedded object is running. You can set this value to **True** to cause the application to load, and to **False** to unload the application. The **Format** property sets or returns the data format used when receiving data from, or sending data to, the application that created the object in the OLE control. The valid values will vary by application and the valid data types can be queries using other properties. The **OLEAcceptFormatsCount** property returns the number of different formats supported by the embedded object. This, in turn, tells you how many items are in the array contained in the **OLEAcceptFormats** property. This property is a zero-based array containing Visual Basic constants of all valid data formats that the application accepts. Likewise, the **OLEGetFormatsCount** and **OLEGetFormats** properties return a count of the number of formats that the object can provide to the OLE control, and an array of what those formats are, respectively.

You can use the **MiscFlags** property to alter the OLE control object's functionality. To force all data into memory (instead of relying on disk swap files), set the property equal to **vbOLEMiscFlagMemStorage**. To override *in-place* Automation (which means that the object activates within the control), use **VbOLEMiscFlagDisableInPlace**, which causes activation to take place in a separate window.

For more information on the OLE control, search for "OLE" in the VB help file.

Exam Prep Questions

Question 1

> An ActiveX control is:
>
> ○ a. An Internet control that has been adapted to also work in the Visual Basic development environment.
>
> ○ b. An example of static linking of functionality (as opposed to the dynamic linking done with DLLs).
>
> ○ c. An OLE control.
>
> ○ d. A standard DLL with non-resident exported functions.

Answer c is correct. An ActiveX control is actually an OCX (or OLE control) file. Answer a is incorrect because although ActiveX controls can work on the Internet, they were adapted for that purpose and originally designed for Visual Basic (and other development environments). Answer b is incorrect because ActiveX is not an example of "static linking." Answer d is incorrect because an ActiveX control is not a "wrapper" (as this answer implies) around the non-resident exported functions of a DLL.

Question 2

> What control would you use to reference multiple graphic images to be used by other controls?
>
> ○ a. The ImageList control
>
> ○ b. An array of PictureBox controls
>
> ○ c. Any ActiveX control that has an **Images** collection property
>
> ○ d. The **Layers** property of the Image control to store an array of type **Graphic**

Answer a is correct because the ImageList control contains a *Pictures* collection, which contains a reference to various graphic objects. Answer b is incorrect because the question asked for one control and also because it is a very inefficient solution. The PictureBox is a control in its own right and actually displays graphics. Although a solution could be worked out using this control, this is not the purpose of the control. Answer c is incorrect because there is no such thing as an **Images** collection nor, if there were, would you use such a collection from one object to supply graphics to another. Answer d is incorrect because there is no **Layers** property for the Image control (or for any other control). The trick is not to look beyond the obvious and question what you already know. As phrased, an array of PictureBox controls may seem like a tempting choice, especially if you are not familiar with the ImageList control. Likewise, answer d is tempting also, because everyone knows that an Image control is more efficient than a PictureBox control (never mind the non-existent property).

Question 3

What actions can't you do with the **Node** object of the ListView control's **Nodes** collection?

○ a. Assign a reference to a VB intrinsic control

○ b. Assign some text

○ c. Assign an icon

○ d. All of the above

Answer d is correct. You cannot do any of the actions because a ListView does not have nodes. Answers a, b, and c are all incorrect because the ListView control does not have a **Nodes** collection nor a **Node** object. This is another trick question; it tries to throw you off course by supplying answer a as a reasonable answer. You cannot reference an intrinsic control with a **Node** object. The problem is only the TreeView control has nodes. Read each question very carefully and don't let the clock rush you into choosing the wrong answer for the right reason.

Question 4

> Which of the following is a valid **Declare** statement (assume the DLL is valid)?
>
> ❏ a.
> ```
> Static Declare Function myFunc Lib _
>     "ABC.DLL" (myVar As String) _
>     As Integer
> ```
>
> ❏ b.
> ```
> Public Declare Function myFunc Lib _
>     "ABC.DLL (ParamArray myVar () _
>     As Variant, myVar2 As String) _
>     As Integer
> ```
>
> ❏ c.
> ```
> Private Declare Function myFunc Lib _
>     "ABC.DLL" Alias (_otherfunc) () _
>     As Integer
> ```
>
> ❏ d.
> ```
> Public Declare Function myFunc Lib _
>     "ABC.DLL" Alias (As Any) _
>     (myVar As String) As Integer
> ```

Answer c is correct because there are syntax errors. The funny-looking function name in the *Alias* clause is valid because the function has been renamed. Answer a is incorrect because it uses **Static,** which is illegal for this type of function. Answer b is incorrect because the **ParamArray** must be last in the argument list. Answer d is incorrect because **As Any** is listed in the **Alias** clause—it should be listed as an argument, if used.

Question 5

> If an ActiveX control has no associated type library, what will happen at compile time?
>
> ○ a. You will get an "unresolved reference" error.
>
> ○ b. The control will be early bound.
>
> ○ c. The control will be late bound.
>
> ○ d. Because Visual Basic always creates a type library when creating an ActiveX control, this will never happen.

Answer c is correct because the absence of a type library forces the compiler to do late binding. Answer a is incorrect because no such error is generated. Answer b is incorrect because VB needs the type library to do early binding. Answer d is incorrect because, although VB will always create a type library, other tools that create ActiveX controls may not.

Need To Know More?

In addition to the resources mentioned here, you should review Chapter 7, "Accessing The Windows API," which is closely related because the Windows API is, itself, a series of external modules.

 Harrington, John, Mark Spenik, Heidi Brumbaugh, and Cliff Diamond: *Visual Basic 5 Interactive Course.* Waite Group Press, Corte Madera, CA, 1997. ISBN 1-57169-077-8. Chapter 15 discusses interfacing with other programs and Chapter 14 begins with a discussion of compatibility of VB data types and C data types.

 McKinney, Bruce: *Hardcore Visual Basic, Second Edition* (which covers version 5). Microsoft Press, Redmond, WA, 1997. ISBN 1-57231-422-2. This excellent volume does not devote any specific sections to the use of external modules. However, to illustrate many concepts in advanced VB development, Bruce makes use of external modules. Chapters 1 and 2 both discuss the **Declare** statement and **Alias** clause. Chapter 5 discusses the C language in comparison to VB, including special topics such as "Hammering Bits" (pages 271 through 281) and the implementation of external sorts (pages 282 through 296).

 Mandelbrot Set, The: *Advanced Microsoft Visual Basic.* Microsoft Press, Redmond, WA, 1997. ISBN 1-57231-414-1. This book is broken into sections done by various authors (they are not listed on the cover). Brant Vaughan's Chapter 13 discusses accessing data, including the bypassing of VB objects to get directly to the external libraries of ODBC functions.

 Search the online books on the VB CD-ROM for the terms "Declare" and "external module."

 Microsoft places the most current Knowledge Base on line at www.microsoft.com/support/. Enter search terms such as "external module," "DLL," "Declare," and so on, to view articles detailing tips (and sometimes fixes) revolving around the use of external modules.

Error Handling In Visual Basic

Terms you'll need to understand:

√ Err

√ Number

√ Description

√ Source

√ LastDLLError

√ HelpFile

√ HelpContext

√ Clear and Raise

√ On Error

√ Resume

Techniques you'll need to master:

√ Creating an error handler

√ Enabling and disabling error handling

√ Handling an error while the error handler is active

√ Using the built-in editor to minimize syntax errors

√ Raising an error

√ Manipulating and customizing the Err object

The handling of errors in Visual Basic is the subject of this important chapter. The fact that you will see it on your certification exam only adds to the weightiness of this topic. Visual Basic makes error handling rather easy, and the services it provides are robust. In this chapter, we'll look at how to keep your programs running as smoothly as possible when those dreaded errors crop up.

What Is An Error?

In a sense, nothing is an error if it is properly handled. In programming, as in life, the best-laid plans of mice and men do go astray. Except more so, for it is your pride that hangs in the balance when your program grinds to a halt.

Many things can go wrong in a program. Some of these things derive from logic flaws; you may not be able to do much about these except fix them as they are discovered. Others stem from the unexpected. Assume you are connecting to a database but the server isn't up. It's kind of silly to ignore that little fact and continue reading to and writing from the SQL tables. Errors that can be handled in your programs generally fall into four areas:

➤ Problems arising from external sources beyond your control, such as a printer jam.

➤ Problems arising from flaws in your code, such as a division by zero.

➤ Problems arising from circumstances that you did not envision (though these arguably often fall under the previous item). An example would be if a user runs an ill-constructed report that brings the network to its knees.

➤ Errors you deliberately create to avoid a worse situation. These are better classified under the category of error *handling* (rather than actual errors) because they usually arise out of a situation that you *did* anticipate.

What Is Error Handling?

Again, I like to think there are four areas of effective error handling, but they all have one thing in common: the graceful degrading of an application so that the integrity of data is maintained and so that users are not faced with a message such as the one seen in Figure 6.1. (The term "graceful degrading" is used to refer to a process whereby a program that encounters an error that cannot be resolved performs an orderly "shutdown" instead of an ugly "crash.")

The four areas of error handling are:

➤ Coding for the unexpected, such as the use of **Case Else**

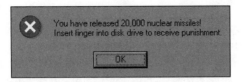

Figure 6.1   An error that was not handled well.

➤ Anticipating specific errors and providing specific remedies in the code (such as checking return codes before issuing a **Commit**, following a SQL update)

➤ Specific **On Error** routines to handle events that cannot be handled in code (such as routines written to handle the possibility of a paper jam in the printer)

➤ Generalized error handling routines so that the application exits gracefully and informs the user of what has happened

The bulk of this chapter will concentrate on these four areas (with most of the emphasis on the last two), with the caveat that ActiveX errors will be touched upon in Chapter 9 and database errors will be looked at more closely in Chapter 10.

The Err Object

The **Err** object is a structure provided by Visual Basic. It is populated with data that your application needs to know to properly react to an error. (Alternatively, the application can populate the **Err** object, for instance, when it deliberately invokes an error in the debugging process.) The **Err** object has six properties, which we'll look at in the next section.

In previous releases of Visual Basic, **Err** had only one property: **Error Number (If Err = 1 Then ...)**. **Number** is the default property of the **Err** object in VB5, however, so code written for previous releases will still execute correctly. Note also that **Err** had no methods in prior versions. To generate an error, the **Error** *error_number* statement was used. This still works, but using the **Raise** method is more flexible (and is discussed later in the chapter in the section titled "Raising Errors").

The properties of **Err** are cleared after an error has been handled, such as when a **Resume** statement is encountered. They are also cleared when the procedure in which the error has occurred ends. You can also use the **Clear** method (**Err.Clear**) to clear the properties manually.

Whenever an error is encountered, you will want to examine **Err** to determine what has happened, in order to intelligently continue processing. Finding documentation of Visual Basic's error codes is no easy feat (they are listed, rather non-intuitively, under "Trappable Errors" in the VB Help file). Visual Basic provides 117 trappable errors such as "Subscript out of range" (**Err.Number** = 9). Numbers 1 to 1,000 and all numbers over 31,000 are reserved by Visual Basic, although not all are used. Those numbers not used all equate to "application-defined" errors. Some of the more common VB errors are displayed in Table 6.1.

Properties Of The **Err** Object

The **Err** object's six properties provide the application developer with a rich set of information about what went wrong. The **Number** property is helpful, but only if the developer anticipates the particular error, and therefore provides the number in advance to the error-handling routine. Some errors simply can't reasonably be anticipated (such as **Err.Number** = 47, "Too many DLL clients"). So, the addition of new properties to **Err** (and, indeed, making it a full-fledged object) is very welcome.

Number is a **Long** in the range of 0 to 65,635. For each **Number**, there is an associated **Description**. If the VB error **Number** is not used, **Description** defaults to the string "Application-defined or object-defined error." The Visual Basic constant **vbObjectError** is used for creating user-defined errors, as we will see in the "Raising Errors" section later in this chapter.

Source is a string that contains the location where the error occurred. Unfortunately, this information is at a high level and does not tell you specifically at what line number and in what procedure the problem occurred. The actual contents of **Source** are dependent on where the error occurred. If it was in a standard module, the name of the project (as defined in project properties) is returned. If it occurred in a class module, however, the class' name is also returned in the form *project.class*. If the error happened outside of Visual Basic in an OLE operation, the application where that error occurred fills in its own **Number** and **Source**, such as Excel.Application for Microsoft Excel.

HelpFile is a string containing the fully *qualified* path (i.e., drive, folder, and file name) to a Help file. If a Visual Basic error occurs, the Help file will contain the path to the VBENLR3.HLP file.

The **HelpContext** is a string containing the Help Context ID associated with the error that occurred. If this field is blank, Visual Basic looks at the **Number** and uses the Help Context ID associated with that error. If the error is not a VB-trappable error, the VB Help Contents screen is displayed. The developer

Table 6.1   Common Visual Basic errors.

Error	Description
6	Overflow
7	Out of memory
9	Subscript out of range
10	This array is fixed or temporarily locked
11	Division by zero
13	Type mismatch
20	Resume without error
28	Out of stack space
35	Sub, Function, or Property not defined
52	Bad file name or number
53	File not found
55	File already open
57	Device I/O error
61	Disk full
68	Device unavailable
70	Permission denied
71	Disk not ready
75	Path/File access error
76	Path not found
91	Object variable or With block variable not set
92	For loop not initialized
337	ActiveX component not found
380	Invalid property value
422	Property not found
423	Property or method not found
438	Object doesn't support this property or method
450	Wrong number of arguments or invalid property assignment
482	Printer error
483	Printer driver does not support specified property

can populate the **HelpFile** and **HelpContext** properties in order to display appropriate application help.

Though **HelpFile** and **HelpContext** are read/write properties, they are of limited value in VB. When Visual Basic displays an error message box, you can press F1 for help. However, by the time a VB built-in dialog is presented, you no longer have access to the **Err** object. Your only alternative, then, is to present a message box with the **MsgBox** function, at which point it is easier to provide literals for the Help file and help context arguments than it is to pass the **Err** properties. The following code does this:

```
Dim sError As String
sError = "Error: " & Str(Err.Number) & ": " & _
    Err.Description
' Method 1:
Err.HelpFile = "c:\my path\my help file.hlp"
Err.HelpContext = 108024
MsgBox = sError, vbMsgBoxHelpButton, "Gawk!", _
    Err.HelpFile, Err.HelpContext
' Method 2:
MsgBox = sError, vbMsgBoxHelpButton, "Gawk!", _
    "C:\my path\my help file.hlp", 108024
```

When seeking to display help for an error, don't use the example provided by Visual Basic; it's incorrect! Use this one.

The last property of **Err**—**LastDLLError**—is useful, as we saw in the last chapter. This is a **Long** and contains the result code of the last external call you made (to the Windows API or another DLL).

An error in calling a DLL or in the execution of the procedure called does not raise a Visual Basic error event. Therefore, you should always examine the contents of **Err.LastDLLError** immediately after making an external call to ensure that you received the expected result or return code.

Methods Of The **Err** Object

Err has two methods associated with it. **Clear** was mentioned earlier in the chapter and behaves pretty much as you would expect: it clears (initializes) all of the properties of the **Err** object. **Raise** is used to deliberately invoke a runtime error and is discussed in more length in "Raising Errors" later in this chapter.

Preventing Errors

When errors do occur, you don't want your users looking at an incomprehensible message box and then turning off their computers in frustration. It is only slightly more embarrassing to generate "An Unexpected Application Error (UAE) in Module Unknown" error message. There are a number of strategies that you can use; the most effective is to prevent those errors that you can. The next best is "error anticipation" and the last is effective planning for errors. There are a number of error prevention strategies, which I will discuss in the following paragraphs.

The first is plain-old common sense. Imagine the rather unlikely application in Figure 6.2. Its whole purpose in life is to divide the number in the first text box by the number in the second, and to display the result in the third (and I paid *how* much for VB?):

```
' divide value in text1 by value in text2 and display result
Text3 = Str(Val(Text1) / Val(Text2))
```

The simplest approach would have been better coding:

```
' no division by zero errors!
If Val(text2) <> 0 then
  Text3 = Str(Val(Text1) / Val(Text2))
End If
```

Mainframe programmers like to brag that they had bugs long before PCs had mice. Unfortunately, PC applications have bugs, too. Drop-through code

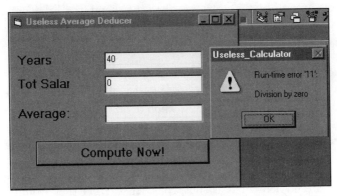

Figure 6.2 An unhandled error generates a message that is pretty meaningless to your user. Worse, this error could have been avoided.

resulted in hard-to-find bugs long before Microsoft sold its first product (a version of Basic for the Altec). The term "drop-through" code refers to poorly designed decision structures where the program does not anticipate the possibility of an unexpected condition. For example, a program might use an **If...Then** construct when handling customers to perform special processing on the postal code if the customer is Canadian, otherwise assuming the customer is American. What happens if an individual from Mexico places an order? The **If** statement tests to see if the customer is Canadian and, if he or she is not, "falls through" the code to perform the default logic as though the customer were American. The result at best is a fouled-up address. At worse is a program crash when a routine encounters an unexpected character in the postal code. It is a solid practice to always test for unexpected value with the **Else** statement in an **If** construct, **Case Else** in a **Select Case** construct, and so on.

> On the certification exam, read all code examples carefully looking for drop-through code possibilities. Microsoft will almost certainly try to trip you up on one or two questions in this manner.

The theme of these two simple error-handling approaches is to prevent errors in the first place. The single most commonly overlooked preventative measure (an ounce of prevention is worth...) is simply checking the return code of the operation being performed. There are three types of this: Visual Basic functions, custom functions (those that you write yourself), and database updates.

All Visual Basic functions return a result. Unfortunately, Visual Basic is also replete with statements that could be implemented better as functions. Consider the **MsgBox** function. It can optionally be used to return a result (which button was pressed by the user). On the other hand, the **FileCopy** function returns no result to indicate success or failure, relying instead on the generation of a runtime error.

What about procedures that we write ourselves? We need to check for any possible unexpected results and return a code to the calling routine as a status code. In Chapter 4, I discussed the encapsulation of an update procedure inside of a class module. The procedure performed some edits and returned to the caller (the procedure that "requested" the update) a code signifying success or failure.

The moral here is that we should look carefully at all of our procedures and, for those that are implemented as subs, consider whether they would be better implemented as functions. For some of them, of course, this would be overkill. The VB statement **GoTo** has no need to be implemented as a function because the program won't compile if there is a possible problem (i.e., the line label that is the object of **GoTo** is missing). Even so, we are trying to prevent major errors from happening by handling the minor errors. Returning to the class module example from Chapter 4, if the module had allowed an invalid "age" to be entered into the database, it would be possible to reach a point where either the program crashed or serious logic errors later occur (perhaps generating a pension check to someone 30 years before he or she actually retires).

The final area of error prevention is in the realm of database updates. I will cover this topic in much more detail in Chapter 10—however, it is imperative that every modification of the database be checked for success lest the data become corrupt. This is done by evaluating the SQL return code after each update and performing a **Commit** if there were no errors, otherwise performing a **Rollback** if any single update failed.

Other Error Prevention Strategies

In Chapter 3, I reviewed the Editor tab on the Options dialog, accessed via Tools|Options. It offers the following tools to help you while you are coding (though, as indicated in the earlier discussion, not all of them are perfect):

➤ **Auto Syntax Check** Informs you of errors like incomplete statements (such as a missing **Then** following an **If** statement), but it cannot report all syntactical errors, nor can it clue you in on any logic errors (such as division by zero).

➤ **Require Variable Declaration** Causes an **Option Explicit** statement to be generated in all modules. This forces you to declare all variables, thus preventing many errors arising out of the mistyping of variable names.

➤ **Auto List Members** Provides a useful drop-down list box of possible values in declaration statements. For example, if you type **Dim myVar As**, a drop-down list box is displayed, showing all the things (VB intrinsic data types, as well as project-specific variables) that **myVar** could be defined as (i.e., **Integer, frmMath**, and so on).

➤ **Auto Quick Info** Helps you complete VB statements by prompting you for required and optional arguments as you type. A small pop-up box lists the proper syntax to help guide you.

➤ **Auto Data Tips** Displays a variable's current value when "stepping" through code during debugging.

Handling Errors

As we have seen in the preceding pages, we're not always able to prevent the inevitable: something going wrong in our applications. That is where Visual Basic's rich error-handling routines come in handy.

On Error

The **On Error** statement tells Visual Basic what to do when an error has occurred. It takes the syntax:

On Error GoTo 0 | *linelabel* **| On Error Resume Next**

Either **GoTo** or **Resume Next** must follow **On Error**. If the former is used, either a valid line label within the current procedure, or 0, must be supplied. **On Error GoTo 0** has the effect of shutting off all error checking. **Resume Next** simply says that, if an error occurs, the program should execute the line immediately following the line in which the error occurred.

If you do not have error checking turned on, *all* runtime errors, regardless of their severity, are fatal!

All error-handling routines must end in a **Resume** statement. If the **On Error** statement does not have **Resume Next**, then **Resume** must be coded elsewhere. Its syntax is

Resume Next | *linelabel*

where *linelabel* is a valid label within the current procedure. **Next** causes execution to branch to the line immediately following the one where the error occurred.

Error handlers have three possible states. When not turned on (such as following an **On Error GoTo 0**), the error handler is *disabled*. Following the execution of an **On Error GoTo** *linelabel* or **On Error Resume Next** statement, the error handler is *enabled*. After an error has occurred, but before it has been handled (or before the current procedure had terminated), the error handler is *active*.

A properly constructed error handler will save the values of **Err**'s properties to program variables in case another error occurs.

> **TIP**
>
> Programmers generally put error-handling code at the end of the sub or function. Remembering the lesson we learned about drop-through code, we do not wish to execute any error handling code when, in fact, no error has occurred. Therefore, it is a wise idea to place an **Exit Sub** or **Exit Function** statement immediately above the error handler.

If a second error occurs while the error handler is active, the current error handler cannot process the second error. An error handler cannot handle an error while it is already handling another error! If this unfortunate circumstance should happen, control is passed to the procedure that called the current procedure. As an example, if **command1_click** called a function **Compute** (), control would pass back to **command1_click** if an error occurred in **Compute** () while the function's error handler was already active. If there is no enabled error handler in **command1_click**, a runtime error occurs. If there is an *active* error handler in **command1_click**, control is passed to whatever procedure called it (presumably a form module). Control keeps going up the line until either an error handler is found that is enabled but not active, or a runtime error occurs. Once the error is handled, execution resumes in the current procedure at the point designated by the **Resume** statement.

Planning A Specific Error Handler

The actual error handler is easy enough to write, though a bit tedious. What is more difficult is *planning* the error handler. There are a number of considerations in terms of how to handle errors and where to place the error handler.

It is not realistically practical to code a routine for every possible error in every sub or function. (If Visual Basic were truly object-oriented, this might be more realistic.) Therefore, it is more sensible to write a generalized routine to handle the unexpected, and specific routines to handle the anticipated problems.

Suppose you are generating a report to go to a printer. It is reasonable to assume that an "Out of Paper" error may occur. So, you will want to implement a routine that tests for those values of the **Number** property of **Err** having to do with conceivable printer problems. If this routine were at line label "PrintError:", you would turn on error checking with **On Error GoTo PrintError**. You will then evaluate the **Number** property with a **Select Case Err.Number** construct testing with statements such as **Case 483** ("Printer does not support this feature"). Of course, you also need to code a **Case Else** statement to handle problems for which you did not code.

Once the error has been intercepted, you can take appropriate action, such as asking the user to check the printer and click OK when ready to proceed (or click Cancel to abort).

There should always be a generic error handler turned on, and I will discuss that next.

Planning The Generalized Error Handler

A more generalized error handler is somewhat more difficult to write and plan. The situation I just discussed (with the printer error handling) was fairly simple, because we can say with some degree of certainty that if an error occurs while we are printing a form, the error is related to printing. That does not guarantee that another error hasn't occurred. Any veteran Windows programmer knows that all manner of demons haunt the real world with such tragedies as insufficient memory, filled hard disks, and other errors happening at inopportune times. So, our only reasonable option is to make sure that we have a generic error-handling routine enabled at all times, and graciously close the program, while alerting the user to what has happened.

There is a little more you can do to help yourself. You could create a routine to write the circumstances of the error to a file, for later analysis. Alternatively, you could write a more generic handler.

It's easy to gather information to write an error storage file. For instance, you might open a file in **Append** mode (see "Visual Basic And Flat Files" in Chapter 10) and use the **Write** statement to record: the time of the incident with the **Now** function; the problem description with **Err.Number** and **Err.Description**; the place the error occurred with **Err.Source** and form's **Caption**; and perhaps additional environmental information such as disk space free and so on.

VB does not allow us to create a generalized procedure in, say, a class module and it is not practical to code a routine to write errors to a file in every sub or function. The next base choice is to take advantage of Visual Basic's "promotion" of errors to calling procedures as discussed earlier.

Raising Errors

We can generalize error handling by employing the **Raise** method of the **Err** object. The syntax is:

Err.Raise Number [,Source, Description, HelpFile, HelpContext]

Raising an error in this manner is more flexible than using the **Error** statement, as we did earlier in the chapter. We are allowed to fill in the source, description, and so forth, as needed. This alone might give us reason to create our own error—we then have the option of providing even more rich information than that provided by VB. You might terminate an error condition by branching to a label where the only line is a **Raise** statement. Recall that if you do not **Clear** any properties of the **Err** object, they are intact. When we **Raise** an error, we are required to supply an error number, but all other information remains intact.

At this point, you could add the file-writing routine discussed in the last section ("Planning The Generalized Error Handler"), manipulate the values of the **Err** object that you have saved, and so on. In short, you have a lot of flexibility.

Still, it is a lot of trouble to code this into every single procedure. We can instead take advantage of the fact that control passes "up the food-chain" when an error occurs while the currently enabled error handler is active. Assume you have a standard module where your startup procedure (**Sub Main ()**)is located. You can place your generic handler here because, by definition, it is the "highest" on the "food-chain" (recall from Chapter 3 that **Sub Main ()** is the first procedure to run in your program and loads the first form). Then, in every module, you merely have to code a generic error handler that immediately invokes an **Err.Raise** statement to create a second error. Because, in each case, the error handler is active, control is automatically passed to the calling procedure, which eventually leads back to the startup module (such as **Sub Main ()**)! Here, you can record all of the information about the error in a file, and then do some meaningful error handling. This little tidbit is worth the price of this book alone (if I do say so myself), let alone to prep you for the certification exam!

Exam Prep Questions

Question 1

Assuming that you have Auto Syntax Check turned on, syntax errors are detected: [Check all correct answers]

- ❏ a. At design time.
- ❏ b. At runtime if an error handler is enabled.
- ❏ c. At runtime if no error handler is enabled.
- ❏ d. Only when Auto Syntax Check is turned on.

Answers a, b, and c are correct. Answer a is correct because Auto Syntax Check detects some, but unfortunately not all, syntactical errors at design time. Answers b and c are both correct but irrelevant because the existence of an error handler does not impact Visual Basic actually detecting an error (the existence of an error handler only impacts VB's handling of the error). Syntax errors *will* be detected by the fact that an error occurs regardless of whether you have error checking on or not. Answer d is, therefore, incorrect. This is a bit tricky in two regards. One is simply that Auto Syntax Check does not catch all errors. The second has to do with the nature of syntax errors. "Syntax" is best defined as the rules about how programming statements work. The **MsgBox** function requires certain arguments, and if they are not provided correctly, an error results. Although Auto Syntax Check catches most syntax problems, it does not catch all. The compilation process in turn catches most remaining syntax problems. Some slip through to running programs such as with late bound controls (discussed in the section titled "Binding" in Chapter 3) where the compiler can do no syntax checking for you. Thus, runtime errors result.

Question 2

Which error handler is valid (assume that **Generic_Error** and **Exit_The_Sub** are valid line labels)?

- ○ a. **On Error Resume Exit_The_Sub**
- ○ b. **Resume Generic_Error**
- ○ c. **On Error Resume Next**
- ○ d. None of the above

Answer c is the correct choice. A *Resume* statement that is part of the *On Error* statement can only be qualified with the *Next* keyword. Answers a and b are both incorrect because they specify a line label. Answer d is incorrect because a valid choice is provided.

Question 3

Examine the following code. Assume that **command1_click** is being executed. During the execution of which line(s) is the error handler enabled (turned on)?

```
' line numbers provided for reference only
1    Private Sub Command1_Click ()
2         Dim myVar1, myVar2, myVar3
3         myVar1 = 13
4         myVar2 = 0
5         ' calculate a result
6         myVar3 = Compute (myVar1, myVar2)
7    End Sub
8
9    Private Function Compute (a As Integer, _
         b As Integer)
10        Compute = a / b
11        Exit Function
12        On Error GoTo Division_Error
13        Division_Error:
14        MsgBox "Division by zero!", vbOK
15        Resume Next
```

○ a. During the execution of lines 12, 13, 14, and 15

○ b. During the execution of line 12 only

○ c. During the execution of line 14 only

○ d. None of the above

Answer d is correct. The error handler is never enabled (turned on) because it is never executed in this snippet. The error occurs before the error handler. Answers a, b, and c are all incorrect because the error handler is never enabled. Walking through the code, the **Function Compute** is called at line 6. At line 10, a division by zero error occurs. However, the error handler defined at line 12 never executes, and so, it is never turned on.

Question 4

> Which is not a property of the **Err** object?
>
> ○ a. **Clear**
>
> ○ b. **Description**
>
> ○ c. **Number**
>
> ○ d. **Source**
>
> ○ e. None of the above

The correct answer is a because *Clear* is a method, not a property, of *Err*. Choices b, c, and d are all incorrect because **Description, Number,** and **Source** are all valid properties of **Err.** Answer e is incorrect because a correct choice was provided.

Question 5

> Which message(s) is/are displayed?
>
> ```
> On Error GoTo Error_Handler
> MsgBox "Blue", vbOK, Str (8/0)
> On Error GoTo 0
> MsgBox "Green"
> Exit Sub
> Error_Handler:
> MsgBox "Red"
> Resume Next
> ```
>
> ○ a. Blue and Green
>
> ○ b. Green
>
> ○ c. Blue and Red
>
> ○ d. Red and Green

Answer d is correct because the division by zero error causes execution to branch immediately to *Error_Handler* (without displaying "Blue"), followed by *the On Error GoTo 0,* and then the "Green" *MsgBox.* Answer a is wrong because the "Blue" **MsgBox** never gets a chance to execute. Answer b is wrong because "Red" is also displayed (after the division by zero error). Answer c is wrong because the "Blue" **MsgBox** is never displayed.

Need To Know More?

 Aitken, Peter: *Visual Basic5 Programming EXplorer*. Coriolis Group Books, Scottsdale, AZ, 1997. ISBN 1-57610-065-0. Chapter 7 has a very nice discussion of error handling, the **Err** object, raising errors, and so on. It also has a good discussion of objects in general, including class modules, adding properties, and so on.

 Harrington, John, Mark Spenik, Heidi Brumbaugh, and Cliff Diamond: *Visual Basic 5 Interactive Course*. Waite Group Press, Corte Madera, CA, 1997. ISBN 1-57169-077-8. Chapter 10 provides a well-done, if brief, look at error handling.

 Jamsa, Kris and Lars Klander: *1001 Visual Basic Programmer's Tips*. Jamsa Press, Las Vegas, NV, 1997. ISBN 1-884133-56-8. This well-done book is not broken into chapters, but rather into "tips." Tips 55 and 255 deal with problems of logic errors. Tip 102 delves into overflow errors in specific. Tips 56 and 57 discuss error trapping while Tip 291 discusses the **Err** object and generic error handling.

 McKinney, Bruce: *Hardcore Visual Basic, Second Edition* (which covers version 5). Microsoft Press, Redmond, WA, 1997, ISBN 1-57231-422-2. Chapter 5 of Bruce's excellent (and entertaining) book has some discussion of raising errors.

 Mandelbrot Set, The: *Advanced Microsoft Visual Basic*. Microsoft Press, Redmond, WA, 1997. ISBN 1-57231-414-1. This book is broken into sections done by various authors (they are not listed on the cover). Error handling is a crucial issue in development and it is only fitting that this book begins with a detailed examination of the whole issue in Peter J. Morris's Chapter 1, "On Error GoTo Hell." The most meaningful pages in terms of the discussion in this chapter are on pages 2 through 24. In Chapter 5, Jon Burn discusses a "new approach" to Visual Basic programming, including a lot of discussion about class usage. In Chapter 8, Peter has a section ("Stuff About Types") that gets into object-oriented concepts and collections.

 Search the online books on the VB CD for "Handling Errors," which discusses error handling in general and the design of an error handler.

Microsoft places the most current Knowledge Base online at www.microsoft.com/support/. Enter search terms such as "Err," "error handling," and so on, to view articles detailing tips (and sometimes fixes) revolving around the issues discussed in this chapter.

 There are a number of Web sites devoted to the subject of Visual Basic on the Internet. Use a search engine such as Yahoo! (www.yahoo.com) or Hotbot (www.hotbot.com) with a search term such as "Visual Basic 5" (be sure to place the search term in quotes so that only pages containing the entire term as one string are returned). A well-done site with tips and sample code that I liked was the VB Palace at home.computer.net/~mheller/. Another site that was under "reconstruction" when I visited was a site hosted by Temple University at thunder.ocis.temple.edu/~shariq/vb/index.html.

Accessing The Windows API

Terms you'll need to understand:

- √ API
- √ ANSI and Unicode (wide) character sets
- √ Kernel, GDI, and User libraries
- √ Conditional compilation
- √ Declare
- √ Alias
- √ ByVal

- √ Space$
- √ hWnd
- √ hDC
- √ hInstance
- √ AddressOf
- √ GetSetting and GetAllSettings
- √ SaveSetting
- √ DeleteSetting

Techniques you'll need to master:

- √ Converting data types from C to Visual Basic
- √ Creating a Visual Basic Declare from a C function prototype
- √ Properly initializing a string variable for use by the Windows API
- √ Passing a null string to the Windows API
- √ Obtaining a handle to a Form object or control

- √ Obtaining a device context to a Form object
- √ Obtaining a reference to a running VB application
- √ Creating a user-defined type to handle a C structure
- √ Determining whether to use ANSI or wide character API functions.
- √ Manipulating INI files
- √ Manipulating the Windows Registry

Windows provides a wide variety of services to the developer. When we create a form in Visual Basic, the form is actually created by the operating system. VB merely "asks" Windows to create it. Windows exposes much of its functionality via its *API* (Application Programming Interface). The API is a series of functions and procedures that provide such diverse services as printing a document and playing a MIDI music file. (Throughout this chapter, I will refer to "procedures and functions" as "functions" because that is the convention in the world of API programmers.) The Visual Basic 5 certification exam will query your ability to use the Windows API, but not your knowledge of the individual function names or calling syntax. In this chapter, I introduce you to the basics of the Windows API and how to take advantage of it from Visual Basic. With that knowledge, you will be well prepared to handle the exam questions about the Windows API.

Overview Of The Windows API

Windows 3.0 consisted of about 300 API functions. Windows 3.1 and 3.11 added some 400 new functions. Windows 95 has more than 1,000 and Windows NT adds perhaps another 100. Both Windows 95 and Windows NT use what is called the *Win32* API; however, Windows 95 does not implement some of the Windows NT functions (mostly in the area of system security). The four broad areas of functionality provided by the Win32 API are:

➤ **System services** These are the fundamental services such as accessing files and allocating memory provided by the operating system. In general, Visual Basic provides all of these services already.

➤ **Graphic services** These services send drawing and painting functions to devices such as the monitor and printer attached to your computer.

➤ **Windows services** These services provide objects such as windows, text boxes, and command buttons to interact with the user. Security services also fall into this category.

➤ **Multimedia services** These services provide the functionality to "play" movies, sound files, and interact with a joystick, as well as interacting with the timer.

Because Visual Basic 5 only compiles to 32-bit applications, it only supports the Win32 API. Therefore, when I refer to the Windows API throughout the remainder of this chapter, I am referring to the Win32 API.

Through the years, there have actually been several versions of the Windows API. The Win16 API was introduced with Windows 3.0. The Win32s API is a subset of the Win32 API and was introduced to allow Windows 3.11 applications to perform some 32-bit operations (although Windows 3.x is a 16-bit operating system).

The Windows API is implemented in a series of DLLs (Dynamic Link Libraries). The Windows "core" is considered to be the KERNEL32.DLL, GDI32.DLL, and USER32.DLL. These provide most of the system, graphics, and windows services respectively. Multimedia services are implemented in a file called MMSYSTEM.DLL. These, and several other files that provide additional functionality, are located in the System directory (typically \Windows\System). The entire suite of API functions is sometimes referred to as the *API Library*.

Characters In The Windows API

Since the inception of MS-DOS in the early 1980s, Microsoft operating systems have used a single byte to represent a character. For instance, a byte with a decimal value of 65 is used to represent the letter "A". This can be seen with the function: **Chr(65)**, which returns the letter "A". Microsoft operating systems have conformed to a standard known as *ASCII* (American Standard Code for Information Interchange) that defines a seven-bit code. Using 7 bits yields $128(2^7)$ possible characters. With the English language, 128 is large enough to represent the 52 alphabet characters (26 uppercase and 26 lowercase letters) plus the various numbers, punctuation characters, and so on. Windows 3.1 and Windows 95 actually use what is known as the *ANSI* (American National Standards Institute) character set, which uses the 128 ASCII characters and then adds 128 more special characters such as the "trademark" and "copyright" symbols.

Languages such as Mandarin have thousands of characters, which ANSI is not able to support (because there are only 256 possible characters). To handle this, Windows NT (and Windows 98, which had not been released at the time of this writing) use what is known as *Unicode* characters. Under Unicode, all characters are represented with two bytes using all eight bits of each byte. Because a character is now 16 bits long, $65,535(2^{16})$ characters can be represented. Unicode characters are often referred to as *wide* characters.

You may, in your reading, come across the term *DBCS*. This stands for *Double Byte Character Set*, which actually represents characters in one or two bytes. If the first byte is within a certain range, a second byte is used. These DBCS characters are then mapped internally, by the operating system, to Unicode characters. Windows NT uses DBCS, and Windows 98 is slated to be a DBCS operating system.

Visual Basic versions 4 and 5 both convert strings internally to Unicode format, whether the application is running on Windows 95 or Windows NT. However, VB then converts the strings back to ANSI when calling a Win32 API function.

Most API functions (that return a string) have two versions: ANSI and Unicode. They can be distinguished by a character added to the end of the function name: "A" for ANSI and "W" for Unicode (the "W" denotes wide characters). Because Visual Basic converts its internal Unicode strings to ANSI, you should call the ANSI version of these functions.

As an example, consider **GetWindowsDirectory**, which is one of the more commonly used functions. As its name implies, it returns the directory in which Windows is installed and where important files such as WIN.INI, SYSTEM.INI, and the Registry files are located. The function is contained in KERNEL32.DLL and has two versions: **GetWindowsDirectoryA** for ANSI character sets and **GetWindowsDirectoryW** for Unicode character sets. The **Declare** statement for this function is shown in the following snippet of code:

```
Declare Function GetWindowsDirectory Lib "kernel32" _
    Alias "GetWindowsDirectoryA" _
    (ByVal lpBuffer As String, ByVal nSize As Long) As Long
```

In this example, the name of the API function is **GetWindowsDirectoryA**, which means that the function has been written for the ANSI character set; there is an equivalent function—**GetWindowsDirectoryW**—written for the Unicode character set. In the **Declare** statement, we have aliased the function to use the more generic name **GetWindowsDirectory**. The **Lib** is "kernel32"— the .DLL extension is assumed.

Visual Basic Migration Issues

As noted earlier, Visual Basic 5 supports 32-bit Windows (Windows 95, 98, and NT) only. Visual Basic 4 supported both 32-bit and 16-bit Windows (Windows 3.1x). Unless specifically written for one target or another, VB had to use *conditional compilation* in order to ensure that the correct API library was called. If you are attempting to write applications for both 16-bit and 32-bit environments, you'll need to continue using conditional compilation and to use Visual Basic 4 for your Windows 3.1x environments and Visual Basic 5 for all others. An example is shown in the following snippet:

```
' see if 16-bit
#If Win16 Then
    Declare Function GetWindowsDirectory Lib "Kernel" _
      (ByVal sBuffer As String, ByVal nSize As Integer) _
      As Integer
' otherwise 32-bit
#Else
    Declare Function GetWindowsDirectory Lib "Kernel" _
      Alias "GetWindowsDirectoryA" _
      (ByVal sBuffer As String, ByVal nSize As Long) _
      As Long
#End If
```

 Visual Basic 4 can read VB5 module files (form modules, standard modules, and class modules), but not project files.

Visual Basic 5 is easier to use, in this case, than VB4 because the 16-bit option has been taken away. VB5 does not support the Win16 API. However, if migrating a 16-bit application to Visual Basic 5, the developer needs to be aware of some crucial changes in the API.

The first concern is that the Win16 and Win32 API DLL names are different. "KERNEL" becomes "KERNEL32," "GDI" becomes "GDI32," and "USER" becomes "USER32." Many integers, most notably *handles* (a handle is a number by which the operating system refers to open windows; it is similar to the file numbers by which VB developers refer to open files), become **Long** data types. (Data types are discussed in the next section.) Finally, some API functions have been replaced, deleted, or added. For more information, see the "Need To Know More?" section at the end of this chapter. You will need to keep these issues in mind and modify your API declarations, as well as the calls to the API functions, as necessary.

Data Type Considerations

The Windows API uses C language data types. Additionally, it uses some "derived" data types. These are roughly analogous to VB user-defined types. For instance, Windows API documents refer to **hWnd** (a handle to a window), which is a C **Long** data type "renamed" for the convenience of the programmer. The names of the data types differ from C to Visual Basic. Table 7.1 shows various data types used in the Windows API and their Visual Basic equivalents.

Table 7.1 Windows API data types and their VB equivalents.		
API Data Type	**VB Data Type**	**Comment**
* (any pointer)	Long	**Integer** in Win16
Bool	Boolean	
Byte	Byte	
Char	Byte	
Char *	String	Or an array of type **Byte**
Double	Double	
DWord	Long	"Double Word"
FarProc	Long	Pointer to a procedure or function
Float	Single	
Handle	Long	**Integer** in Win16
HInst	Integer	
HWnd	Long	**Integer** in Win16
Int	Long	**Integer** in Win16
Long	Long	
LPByte	ByVal Long	Pointer to a **Byte**
LPDWord	ByVal Long	Pointer to a **DWord**
LPInt	ByVal Long	Pointer to an **Int**
LPLong	ByVal Long	Pointer to a **Long**
LPStr [1]	ByVal String	Pointer to a **String**
LPVoid	ByVal Long	Pointer to a **Void** function
LPWord	ByVal Long	Pointer to a **Word**
Short	Integer	
TChar	Byte	
Unsigned Int	Integer	Also **UInt**
Unsigned Long	Long	
Unsigned Short	Integer	
Variant [2]	Variant	OLE only
Word	Integer	

[1] There are many variations of pointers to strings, such as **LPTSTR** and **LPCTSTR**. For all, pass a string to the API using **ByVal**.

[2] The Windows API does not support the **Variant** data type but any API written specifically for OLE does.

Table 7.2	Visual Basic data types and their C equivalents.	
VB Data Type	**C Data Type**	**Comment**
Byte	Char	
Boolean	Bool	
Currency	N/A	There is no C equivalent
Date	N/A	There is no C equivalent
Decimal	N/A	There is no C equivalent
Double	Double	
Integer	Int and Unsigned Int	
Long	Long	
Object	Long	As a pointer to the object
Single	Real	
User defined	Struct	
Variant	N/A	There is no C equivalent (but OLE, not really a part of the Windows API, does have a **Variant** data type)

Table 7.2 lists the Visual Basic data types and their C equivalents. Note that not every VB data type has a C equivalent.

Also note that although **Void** looks like a data type, it is actually used to denote a function that does not return a value (a sub in VB).

Though the naming conventions may look strange, most C data types map easily to VB data types. Strings, however, need special consideration.

Strings And The Windows API

Visual Basic is different from most other programming languages because it maintains an internal table of strings, including a memory address of where the string begins, as well as the string's length. C, on the other hand, uses "null-terminated" strings that rely on null characters (ASCII value 0) to mark the end of a string. Therefore, a Visual Basic program needs to ensure that a string used to call the Windows API allows room for a null character at the end. In other words, VB programs need to allow for an extra character. So, if a variable needs to contain the string "Visual Basic", it should be able to accommodate 13 characters (12 characters for "Visual Basic" and an extra character for the null terminator). This is usually a consideration only with fixed-length strings.

You must properly initialize any string that is to be passed to the Windows API. In the context of Visual Basic and the Windows API, the string must either be a fixed length at least one character longer than the anticipated string length (to accommodate the null character), or a variable-length string padded with spaces using the **Space$** function, as seen in this snippet of code:

```
Dim myString As String
' allocate 255 characters
myString = Space$(255)
```

 Visual Basic has introduced many "string" functions that have two forms: one for the **String** data type and one for the **Variant** data type with an underlying type of **String**. Functions that end in a dollar sign ($) are for data type **String**, while those that don't are for data type **Variant**. Examples are **Space** and **Space$**; **Mid** and **Mid$**, and so on. Most functions that end in a dollar sign have an equivalent function for variants that does not end in a dollar sign.

Windows Objects

Every item in Windows is an object; command buttons are objects, so are menus and list boxes. (In the parlance of the Windows API, all objects are windows, but that starts to get confusing and so I will use the more generalized term *objects*.) Every object also has a handle, which is a pointer to the object. A *pointer* is an address and a *handle* is a type of address. When you use the **ByVal** keyword to pass a variable to a function or procedure, you are actually passing a pointer to the variable. In the case of an object, we refer to the address of the object as its handle. Much as we create a variable in Visual Basic to reference a form or command button, the handle of an object is the API's reference to the object.

All Visual Basic controls and objects have an **hWnd** property, which returns a handle to the control or object. Because handles to controls and objects can change, you should not store the value of a handle in a variable. Instead, use the property directly. The following code snippet uses the **hWnd** property of a form to find the text stored in the **Caption** property:

```
Declare Function GetWindowText Lib "user32" _
    Alias "GetWindowTextA" (ByVal hWnd As Long, _
    ByVal lpString As String, ByVal cch As Long) _
    As Long

Dim lRslt As Long
Dim sVar As String * 101
```

```
lRslt = GetWindowText(hWnd, sVar, 100)
MsgBox (sVar)
```

In this code, **cch** is a variable used to define the length of **lpString**. Because the API expects a null-terminated string, the variable **sVar** has been defined as one byte longer than **cch**. Note also that **hWnd** has been passed, but no reference to the form was made. When a property or method is used without referencing an object, VB assumes you are referencing the form.

Visual Basic controls and objects are not really part of the Windows API per se. Though VB is ultimately using the API to "create" the controls and objects, Microsoft has chosen to hide this fact from the developer. Therefore, it is not possible to obtain a handle to a Form object or Command Button control.

If you use the Windows API to create an object, however, the API function will generally return a handle to the new object.

Windows Tasks

Windows defines a task a little differently than you might expect. Any running application is a task, which seems natural enough. However, any loaded DLL, font, and so on, is also a task. Each task has an associated task ID. In API parlance, the task ID is known as an instance. Each instance is similar to a handle because it defines a memory address (and thus needs to be stored as a **Long**). To obtain the instance of the currently running VB application, access the **hInstance** property of the **App** object:

```
' Display the current app's handle
MsgBox App.hInstance
```

Callback Considerations

Some Windows API functions are callback procedures—they call themselves recursively, interacting with the calling program. Visual Basic does not directly support this. However, you may pass the address of a Visual Basic procedure to the API in a standard module using the **AddressOf** function. The syntax is:

```
AddressOf procedurename
```

This is potentially dangerous unless you thoroughly understand the workings of the API function. When you pass the address of a VB procedure to an API function, the API function will call your procedure. If there is any kind of bug in your program, it is possible to crash or make the operating system unstable. Because the Windows API function is invoking your procedure, the debugging support within VB is minimal. Callback procedures are outside of the scope of this book. For purposes of the exam, it is enough to know how to use the **AddressOf** function.

When discussing callback procedures, the most often cited example in the Windows API is **EnumFont**.

Device Context

Windows performs its graphical chores using *device contexts*. Various drivers enable Windows to draw or print to different types of devices such as screens and printers. The link between Windows and the specific device is called a device context. If you are going to use the Windows API to output graphics, you need to reference the appropriate context ID. (A thorough discussion of Windows graphics is beyond the scope of this book and not required for the VB exam.) Every Form object in VB has a device context associated with it defined by the **hDC** property (literally, a handle to the device context). The following snippet of code draws an ellipse on the current form by obtaining its device context. **X1, X2, Y1,** and **Y2** form a rectangle within which the ellipse will be drawn.

```
Public Declare Function Ellipse Lib "gdi32" _
    (ByVal hDC As Long, ByVal X1 As Long, _
    ByVal Y1 As Long, ByVal X2 As Long, _
    ByVal Y2 As Long) As Long

Dim lRslt As Long
' Set the form to use pixels
ScaleMode = vbPixels
' Set the form's foreground color
ForeColor = vbRed
lRslt = Ellipse(hDC, 1, 1, 200, 200)
```

Messages

When we make a form invisible (**Form1.Visible = False**), VB is actually sending a message to the form via the Windows API. When we tell a control to set focus to itself, VB is also using the Windows API to send a message to that control. A message may alter a property of an object or it may invoke a method of the object. The following code snippet uses the **SendMessage** API function to set focus on the Command Button control **command2**. The message being sent is **WM_SETFOCUS** (note that messages are expressed as VB constants and that the Windows convention is to use all uppercase characters):

```
Public Const WM_SETFOCUS = &H7
```

```
Declare Function SendMessage Lib "user32" Alias "SendMessageA" _
    (ByVal hWnd As Long, ByVal wMsg As Long, _
    ByVal wParam As Long, lParam As Any) As Long

lRslt = SendMessage(Command2.hwnd, WM_SETFOCUS, 0, 0)
```

The API has several thousand separate messages organized into related groups; messages beginning with **WM_** are window messages while those beginning with **BM_** are button messages.

Windows API Structures

Often, a Windows API function needs to reference a structure. The equivalent in Visual Basic is a user-defined data type. A common structure is **PointAPI**, which is used to describe any point on a graphic output (such as a screen or a printed page) in terms of its X and Y coordinates. The VB equivalent is shown in the following code snippet:

```
Type POINTAPI
        X As Long
        Y As Long
End Type
```

To pass the VB **Type** to an API function, use a VB user-defined data type, in this case **PointAPI**. The following code snippet shows the VB **Declare** for the **PolyLine,** which requires the **PointAPI** structure:

```
Declare Function PolyLine Lib "gdi32" _
    Alias "PolyLine" (ByVal hDC As Long,
    lpPoint As POINTAPI, ByVal nCount As Long)
    As Long
```

Using The Windows API

Most Visual Basic programs will seldom need to directly access the Windows API. However, VB developers should have a basic familiarity with the API and how to use it for those instances when functionality not implemented by VB is required. For instance, although the message box is implemented with the **MsgBox** function in VB, there are additional message box capabilities in the API that VB does not directly support.

Calling a Windows API function is identical to calling the exported functions of any other DLL. This is reviewed in Chapter 5 in "Using The External Procedures Of An API."

Generally, when you use a product that has an exposed API, it is accompanied by documentation that specifies how to make calls to the functions and procedures. Not so with the Windows API. Microsoft gives little to no guidance about using the Windows API and you need to turn to a third-party source that documents the calling syntax. (I list several good books at the end of this chapter.) Further, most guides are oriented to the C programming language, forcing you to "translate" the C syntax into VB syntax. (Tables 7.1 and 7.2 do most of this for you by listing equivalent data types.) Once you have a handle on getting from the C data types to the VB data types, translating the calling syntax is straightforward.

Consider the following API call:

```
DWord GetPrivateProfileString (LPCTSTR
   lpszSectionName, LPCTSTR lpszKeyName,
   LPCTSTR lpszDefaultValue, LPTSTR lpszReturnBuffer,
   DWord dwcBuffer, LPCTSTR lpszIniFileName)
```

Notice that it begins with **DWord**. This is the function's return data type. If the function had begun with **Void**, it would indicate that the function had no return value (in other words, that the function was actually a sub in Visual Basic terms). Using Table 7.1, we see that **DWord** is implemented in Visual Basic as a **Long**. There are several **Long** pointers to strings, such as **LPCTSTR**, in the function. Again referring to Table 7.1, we see that we need to use **ByVal String** to create the VB **Declare** statement that calls this Windows API function. The function happens to be in the KERNEL32.DLL library. The translated function in VB is:

```
Declare Function GetPrivateProfileString Lib _
   "kernel32" Alias "GetPrivateProfileStringA" _
   (ByVal lpApplicationName As String, ByVal _
   lpKeyName As Any, ByVal lpDefault As String, _
   ByVal lpReturnedString As String, ByVal nSize _
   As Long, ByVal lpFileName As String) As Long
```

In the example, because the API function has a return value, we declare a function (instead of a sub). The function's return type is **As Long**. The long pointers to strings are implemented as **ByVal** *variable* **As String** (*variable* is one of the variables listed in the function declaration). The **DWord dwcBuffer** becomes **ByVal nSize As Long**. The reason the latter was declared as **ByVal** is that the API will update this value.

The function is aliased because the Windows API provides both an ANSI and a Unicode version. The ANSI version is **GetPrivateProfileStringA**. If in doubt, refer to one of the books mentioned at the end of this chapter (see "Need To Know More?"), use the API Viewer application (see "Using The API Viewer" in the next section), or use Quick View to directly examine the DLL file.

To do the latter, right-click on KERNEL32.DLL in Windows Explorer and select Quick View. Scroll down until you find the Export Table section. Here you will find all the available functions listed by name, ordinal offset number, and entry points (the address within the file). As seen in Figure 7.1, **GetPrivateProfileStringA** and **GetPrivateProfileStringW** are both listed. Because VB uses the ANSI version of Windows API function calls, you need to use **GetPrivateProfileStringA**. Similarly, you can examine GDI32.DLL and USER32.DLL for their exported functions. Unfortunately, Quick View only shows the name of the functions—not how to use them.

The presence of a long pointer with the characters "CT" in it (**LPCTSTR**) is generally a giveaway that the function is implemented as both ANSI and Unicode. "CT" stands for character translation.

```
KERNEL32.DLL - Quick View                                                  _ □ ×
File  View  Help

   016e     0002f801     GetPrivateProfileSectionNamesA
   016f     000242a1     GetPrivateProfileSectionNamesW
   0170     00034fb9     GetPrivateProfileSectionW
   0171     00021d16     GetPrivateProfileStringA
   0172     0001bac6     GetPrivateProfileStringW
   0173     00023f3c     GetPrivateProfileStructA
   0174     00021396     GetPrivateProfileStructW
   0175     00021d51     GetProcAddress
   0176     0002e9bb     GetProcessAffinityMask
   0177     0001bb4d     GetProcessFlags
   0178     0002dc56     GetProcessHeap
   0179     00034fef     GetProcessHeaps
   017a     00034fd4     GetProcessShutdownParameters
   017b     00034fd4     GetProcessTimes
   017c     00034fd4     GetProcessVersion
   017d     00007ca3     GetProcessWorkingSetSize
   017e     00034d96     GetProductName
   017f     0002d383     GetProfileIntA
   0180     0002d3c5     GetProfileIntW
   0181     0002d3a2     GetProfileSectionA
   0182     0002d3e4     GetProfileSectionW

To edit, click Open File for Editing on the File menu.
```

Figure 7.1   Quick View of the KERNEL32.DLL file with the cursor pointing to the **GetPrivateProfileStringA** function.

Using The API Viewer

Visual Basic bundles a convenient application, API Viewer, in the VB\WINAPI directory as APILOAD.EXE. This utility, shown in Figure 7.2, provides the VB syntax for most API functions, messages, and structures. To use it, start the application and select File|Load Text File from the menu. When you do so, you can convert the loaded text file (stored in the same directory as WIN32API.TXT) into an Access database file by selecting File|Convert To Database from the menu. The database file will be stored in the same directory as WIN32API.MDB. In the future, you will then be able to load either the text file or the database file. The latter is marginally faster.

On the View menu, you can choose Line Item, which displays only the name of the functions, or Full Text, which displays the entire **Declare** syntax.

Use the API Type drop-down list to choose Constants, Declares, or Types. You can scroll through the top window, Available Items, and select those that you want to use in your VB application. Click the Add button to select an item. It will be added to the Selected Items window. When you have selected all of the items that you require, click the Copy button to copy the syntax to the clipboard. Paste them into a standard module or into your procedure. Alternatively, you can view the text file directly using any text editor, such as WordPad.

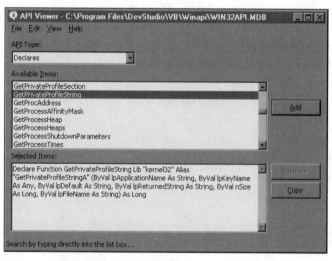

Figure 7.2 The API Viewer program.

Do not use the Add File function in VB to load the entire API file into a module. It is almost 700 KB long and will make your application slow to load and cause sluggish performance. Additionally, it will bloat the file size and memory requirements of your program.

INI Files

Under Windows 3.1x, programs maintained various settings in INI files. Windows itself maintained most of its settings in WIN.INI and SYSTEM.INI. Although the Windows Registry has replaced many of these INI files, many applications (including most 16-bit apps) continue to use these files. In fact, Windows 95 and Windows NT have not entirely divorced themselves from INI files. As an example, WIN.INI is still used, though not as extensively as it was under Windows 3.1x.

INI files are broken into "sections" and "settings," as seen in the following example from part of my WIN.INI file:

```
[Windows Telephony]
TelephonINIChanged=1997-09-19 12:32:06

[DrawDib]
pnpdrvr.drv 800x600x8(0)=55,0,0,0
pnpdrvr.drv 800x600x24(BGR 0)=37,5,5,5
pnpdrvr.drv 640x480x16(565 0)=37,5,5,5
```

Unfortunately, VB5 does not provide support for INI files. Although the documentation refers to the fact that **GetSetting** (and several other VB functions) work with INI files for 16-bit applications, VB does not generate 16-bit applications. You need to use Windows API functions to work with, set, or retrieve settings in an INI file. Consider the section of my WIN.INI file. To retrieve the setting **TelephonINIChanged** from the Windows Telephony section, use the **GetProfileString** function. For non-Windows INI files, use the **GetPrivateProfileString** function. Check the books listed at the end of this chapter for more information.

The Windows Registry

Visual Basic applications should store program settings in the Windows Registry. When doing so, the settings will be within the key HKEY_CURRENT_USER\SOFTWARE\VB AND VBA Program Settings.

Assume you want to store some colors for your program. To do so, use the **SaveSetting** statement:

```
SaveSetting "MyApp", "Colors", "Favorite", "Red"
SaveSetting "MyApp", "Colors", "Other", "Green"
```

The first argument is the application's name ("MyApp"). This is the key in the Windows Registry (underneath "VB AND VBA Program Settings"). If it does not already exist, it will be created. "Colors" is the section and appears underneath "MyApp" in the Registry. "Favorite" and "Other" are both values. "Red" and "Green" are settings. The results in the Registry are shown in Figure 7.3.

To retrieve a value, use the **GetSetting** function, which returns a string:

```
Dim myString As String
myString = GetSetting("MyApp", "Colors", "Favorite", "Not Found")
MsgBox myString
```

"MyApp", "Colors", and "Favorite" are the application's name, key, and setting, respectively. "Not Found" is a value to be returned if the setting is not found.

To retrieve all settings, use the **GetAllSettings** function, which returns a two-dimensional array of type **Variant**. Do not define the variable as an array—VB

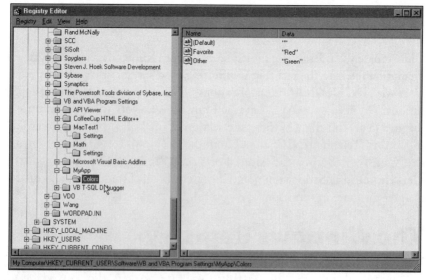

Figure 7.3 Saved settings in the Windows Registry.

converts it when the function is called. An example is shown in the following snippet of code:

```
Dim myVar
myVar = GetAllSettings("MyApp", "Colors")
MsgBox myVar(1, 0) & " " & myVar(1, 1)
```

To delete a setting or section, use the **DeleteSetting** statement. To delete all of the Colors section, use the syntax:

```
DeleteSetting "MyApp", "Colors"
```

To delete just an individual setting, also supply the setting name:

```
DeleteSetting "MyApp", "Colors", "Other"
```

Exam Prep Questions

Question 1

> Which is not a functional area of the Windows API?
>
> ○ a. Data services (DAO32.DLL)
>
> ○ b. Graphical services (GDI32.DLL)
>
> ○ c. System services (KERNEL32.DLL)
>
> ○ d. Windows services (USER32.DLL)
>
> ○ e. None of the above

Answer a is correct. Data services is not part of the API and DAO is a Visual Basic term—not a Windows API term. Answers b, c, and d are incorrect because graphical services, system services, and windows services are all provided by the Windows API by GDI32.DLL, KERNEL32.DLL, and USER32.DLL respectively.

Question 2

> The Windows API provides two different functions to return the directory where Windows files are located. Which two functions are they? [Check all correct answers]
>
> ○ a. **GetWindowsDirectory**
>
> ○ b. **GetWindowsDirectoryA**
>
> ○ c. **GetWindowsDirectoryU**
>
> ○ d. **GetWindowsDirectoryW**
>
> ○ e. **GetINIDirectory**

Answers b and d are correct because Windows provides an ANSI and a "wide character" version of the function denoted by the "A" and the "W" characters at the end of the function names. Answer a is incorrect because you need to use the ANSI or wide character naming convention. Answer c is incorrect because the suffix for Unicode functions is "W" (wide character) and not "U". Answer e is incorrect because there is no such function. The trick to this question is to reason out the correct answer, even if you do not know the names of all the API functions (though this is perhaps the most commonly used one). You are told that there are two correct answers. The fact that there are so many variations of **GetWindowsDirectory** clues you in to the fact that you need to choose from these. Further, any function that returns a string will always have an ANSI and a wide character version. If Windows provides an ANSI version, it always provides a wide character version. Answer e was added to throw you off a little bit. An INI Directory (if there were such a thing) would not necessarily have to be the Windows directory. Although the certification exam will not expect you to memorize the names of the API functions, you may encounter a question asking you to reason out which one(s) you might use from a supplied list of names.

Question 3

The following is the Windows API definition of the **MessageBoxEx** function.

```
Int MessageBoxEx (hWnd hwndOwner, LPCTSTR _
    lpszText, LPCTSTR lpszCaption, uInt _
    uStyle, Word wLanguageID)
```

Which is the correct VB declaration?

○ a.
```
Declare Function MsgBox Lib "user32" _
    Alias "MessageBoxExA" (ByVal hwnd As _
    Long, ByVal lpText As String, ByVal _
    lpCaption As String, ByVal uType As _
    Long, ByVal wLanguageId As Long) _
    As Long
```

○ b.
```
Declare Function MessageBoxExA Lib _
    "user32" Alias "MessageBoxEx" _
    (ByVal hwnd As Long, ByVal lpText As _
    String, ByVal  lpCaption As String, _
    ByVal uType As Long, ByVal wLanguageId _
    As Long)  As Long
```

○ c.
```
Declare Function MessageBoxEx Lib _
    "user32" Alias "MessageBoxExA" _
    (ByVal hwnd As Long, ByVal lpText As _
    String, ByVal lpCaption As String, _
    ByVal uType As Long, ByVal wLanguageId _
    As Long) As Long
```

○ d.
```
Declare Function MessageBoxExA Lib _
    "user32" Alias "MessageBoxExA" _
    (hwnd As Long, lpText As String, _
    lpCaption As String, uType As Long, _
    wLanguageId As Long) As Long
```

Answer c is correct because it accurately aliases the name of the function. Answer a is incorrect because it aliases the function as **MsgBox**, which is a VB reserved word. Answer b is incorrect because the function name and alias are backwards. When aliasing a function, include the "real" name (the name as defined in the Windows API) following **Alias**. Answer d is incorrect mainly because none of the variables being passed has the **ByVal** keyword. In particular, all strings need to be passed **ByVal**. Interestingly, if you attempt to type the declaration in this way, VB will delete the alias after you press Enter because the alias and the function name are the same.

Question 4

Assume you want to send a message to a command button on your VB form. Which of the following will you need to pass to the Windows API function?

○ a. **Form1.hWnd.Command1.hWnd**

○ b. **Command1.hWnd**

○ c. **Form1.hInstance.Command1.hInstance**

○ d. **Command1.hInstance**

○ e. **AddressOf Command1**

Answer b is correct. Every VB control (except the OLE control), as well as the Form object and MDIForm object, has an *hWnd* property, which is a handle to the control. To send a message to the control, you need to tell the Windows API what the control's handle is. Answer a is incorrect because you do not need to pass a handle to the form and also because it shows the command button as a "property" of the form's **hWnd** property. Answer c is incorrect both because you do not need to reference the form containing the command button, and because the answer uses **hInstance**, which is not a valid property of a Form object or of a Command Button control. It returns a handle or instance of the application itself and is a property of the **App** object. Answer d is incorrect because it also uses the **hInstance** property, which is invalid. Answer e is incorrect because **AddressOf** is used to return the address of a VB procedure (not a control).

Question 5

> Assume you want to use the Windows API to draw on a form. Which property of the Form object might you use?
>
> ○ a. **hDC**
>
> ○ b. **DeviceContext**
>
> ○ c. **X1** or **Y1**.
>
> ○ d. **Shape (type As Long)**

Answer a is correct because *hDC* **returns the form's device context.** Answer b is incorrect because **DeviceContext** is not a valid property. Answer c is incorrect because neither **X1** nor **Y1** is a valid property. Answer d is incorrect because **Shape** is not a property of a Form object (it is a control) and because properties are never expressed as functions (with parameters enclosed by parentheses).

Need To Know More?

 Appleman, Daniel: *Dan Appleman's Visual Basic 5.0 Programmer's Guide to the Win32 API.* Ziff-Davis Press, Emeryville, CA, 1997. ISBN 1-56276-446-2. Dan, president of Desaware Software, has been involved with Basic and Visual Basic for many years. This excellent volume is devoted exclusively to the subjects covered in this chapter. Of particular interest in prepping for the certification exam are Chapters 1, 2, and 3, where Dan lays down the groundwork for communicating and exploiting the Windows API. If you happen to own the VB4-specific edition of this book, there is not a whole lot different in the VB5 edition. This book should be part of any VB developer's basic reference library.

 Harrington, John, Mark Spenik, Heidi Brumbaugh, and Cliff Diamond: *Visual Basic 5 Interactive Course.* Waite Group Press, Corte Madera, CA, 1997. ISBN 1-57169-077-8. Chapter 14 begins with a discussion of the use of the Windows API at an introductory level, as well as a discussion of the differences of passing variables by value or by reference.

 Jamsa, Kris and Lars Klander: *1001 Visual Basic Programmer's Tips.* Jamsa Press, Las Vegas, NV, 1997. ISBN 1-884133-56-8. This well-done book is not broken into chapters but rather into "tips." Tips 364 through 377 provide an introduction to the use of the Windows API.

 Jerke, Noel and Eric Brierly: *Visual Basic 4 API How-To: The Definitive Guide to Using the WIN32 API with Visual Basic 4.* Waite Group Press, Corte Madera, CA, 1997. ISBN 1-57169-072-7. Though this book has not been updated for Visual Basic 5 (as of this writing), the text is nevertheless relevant. It takes a "problem/solution" format using the Windows API to solve various programming problems with source code and discussion. Chapter 1 also introduces the methodology of accessing the Windows API from Visual Basic.

 MacDonald, Michael: *Powerbuilder & Java Developer's Journal, Signature Software,* St. Paul, MN. *PB&J* is an electronic magazine available for free (you do need to register) at www.pbmag.com. The December, 1997, issue has an article that I wrote, "PowerBuilder and the Windows API." Although the article is geared to PowerBuilder (another programming language), it explains much of the theory of the use of the API and the declarations are almost identical to Visual Basic.

 Mandelbrot Set, The: *Advanced Microsoft Visual Basic*. Microsoft Press, Redmond, WA, 1997. ISBN 1-57231-414-1. This book is broken into sections done by various authors (they are not listed on the cover). Brant Vaughan's Chapter 13 discusses accessing data including the bypassing of VB objects to get directly to the external libraries of ODBC functions.

 Simon, Richard: *Windows 95 Common Controls & Messages API Bible*. Waite Group Press, Corte Madera, CA, 1997. ISBN 1-57169-010-7. This book, the second of a three-volume set, discusses all of the Windows messages and the common controls available to VB from the Project|Components menu. This book is an essential resource because it explains the meaning of those thousands of constants listed in the VB API Viewer utility, and it also illustrates the process of creating through API calls all of the controls in the Microsoft Common Controls libraries. Volume 1 of this series is listed next. Volume 3 discusses multimedia and ODBC.

 Simon, Richard, Michael Gouker, and Brian Barnes: *Windows 95 Win32 Programming API Bible*. Waite Group Press, Corte Madera, CA, 1997. ISBN 1-57169-009-3. The definitive resource for Win32 development. This book, despite its title, is a valuable resource for NT developers that covers all WIN32 APIs common to Windows 95 and Windows NT, as well as a discussion of how they differ. The book is geared to the C developer, but it still belongs on the reference shelf of most VB developers. The function prototypes given are easy enough to translate into VB **Declare** statements. This is the first of a three-volume library.

 Search the online books on the VB CD-ROM for the terms "DLL" and "API." There are several chapters dealing with how and when to use the Windows API. Also, search for "ByVal" and "ByRef."

 Microsoft places the most current Knowledge Base online at www.microsoft.com/support/. Enter search terms such as

"Win32," "Windows API," and "DLL" to view articles detailing tips (and sometimes fixes) revolving around the use of the Windows API.

Components And Controls

Terms you'll need to understand:

- √ Object
- √ Component
- √ Control
- √ ZOrder
- √ TabIndex
- √ SetFocus
- √ GotFocus
- √ LostFocus
- √ KeyUp

- √ KeyDown
- √ KeyPress
- √ KeyPreview
- √ Image control
- √ PictureBox control
- √ ActiveX control
- √ CommonDialog Control
- √ DDE and OLE
- √ OLE Container control

Techniques you'll need to master:

- √ Establishing the ZOrder of layered controls
- √ Establishing tab order at design time and runtime
- √ Setting focus on a control and getting and losing focus
- √ Intercepting and handling keystrokes

- √ Dynamically creating Visual Basic controls
- √ Dynamically altering the Class property of ActiveX controls
- √ Creating and using the CommonDialog control

Microsoft pioneered the current *IDE* (Integrated Development Environment)—seen in most modern Windows development tools—with the introduction of Visual Basic 1.0. An essential component of the IDE was the toolbox consisting of various controls that could be placed on a Form. The toolbox could be customized with additional VBXs (Visual Basic controls), which spawned an entire third-party industry to meet the demand for enhanced controls. Visual Basic soon took advantage of other ways to add power to applications with DDE (Dynamic Data Exchange) and then OLE (Object Linking and Embedding), creating the capability to embed Microsoft Word and Excel documents directly onto a Form. Visual Basic 4 and Windows 95 saw the switch from VBXs to OCXs (OLE Custom Controls are now known as ActiveX controls). In this chapter, we'll survey some of the tools available, the methodology to customize the toolbox, and show how to establish OLE automation in your application.

Mastery of Visual Basic components and controls is not a huge portion of the certification exam, but is a huge portion of mastering Visual Basic (which, in turn, is the key to successfully passing the exam). What I have attempted to do with this chapter is select those topics that you are most likely to encounter (such as **ZOrder** and **TabIndex**), while outlining the key issues of VB controls and components.

The Intrinsic Controls

When you perform Visual Basic 5's standard installation, VB includes a set of more than 20 controls (referred to as *intrinsic controls*) that are innate to Visual Basic itself. All except the Menu, Form, and MDIForm are available from the toolbox. It is outside of the scope of this book to discuss the properties, methods, and events of each control. This material is available in the Help file or in any number of fine books (see "Need To Know More?" at the end of this chapter). I will, however, take a brief look at some of the selected topics and the OLE Container control. To prepare for the exam, you should create a test application and paste each of the controls onto a Form. Then, quickly familiarize yourself with the methods, events, and properties of each so that you don't get tripped up by questions listing nonexistent attributes. Pay particular attention to the "important attributes" listed in Table 8.1. In the following section, I will discuss a few of the attributes that you are most likely to run into on the certification exam.

Table 8.1   Visual Basic intrinsic controls and the Form and MDIForm objects.

Control	Purpose	Important Attributes	Type
Check Box	Set an option	**Caption**	Property
		Style	Property
		Value	Property
Combo Box	Combine a ListBox and a TextBox	See ListBox	
Command Button	Initiate a process	**Caption**	Property
		Default, **Cancel**	Properties
		Click	Event
Data	Manipulate database records	**Connect**	Property
		Database, **DatabaseName**	Properties
		Exclusive	Property
		RecordSet, **RecordSource**	Properties
		RecordType	Property
		UpdateRecord	Property
		Validate	Event
DirListBox	Display hierarchical list of directories	**List**, **ListCount**, **ListIndex**	Properties
		Path	Property
		Refresh	Method
		Click	Event
DriveListBox	Display a list of disk drives	See DirListBox	
FileListBox	Display a list of files	Same as DirListBox, plus:	
		Pattern	Property
		PathChange	Event
		PatternChange	Event
Form	Act as the interface for the application	**ActiveControl**	Property
		AutoRedraw	Property
		Caption	Property
		Controls	Property
		CurrentX, **CurrentY**	Properties
		Enabled	Property
		Height, **Width**	Properties
		hWnd	Property
		Icon	Property
		MDIChild	Property
		Visible	Property
		Add	Method
		Hide	Method
		Move	Method

(continued)

Table 8.1 Visual Basic intrinsic controls and the Form and MDIForm objects (continued).

Control	Purpose	Important Attributes	Type
		PopUpMenu	Method
		PrintForm	Method
		Refresh	Method
		Show	Method
		Activate, Deactivate	Events
		Initialize	Event
		Load, UnLoad	Events
		QueryUnLoad	Event
		ReSize	Event
		Terminate	Event
Frame	Group related controls, particularly Option Buttons	Caption	Property
HScrollBar	Scroll horizontally or represent relative position	LargeChange	Property
		SmallChange	Property
		Max, Min	Properties
		Change	Event
		Scroll	Event
Image	Display a graphic	Picture	Property
		Click, DblClick	Events
Label	Display text	Alignment	Property
		Caption	Property
Line	Display a line on the Form	DrawMode	Property
		X1, Y1, X2, Y2	Properties
ListBox	Display data in scrolling box	ItemData	Property
		List, ListCount, ListIndex	Properties
		MultiSelect	Property
		NewIndex	Property
		Selected, SelCount	Properties
		Sorted	Property
		Text	Property
		AddItem, RemoveItem	Methods
		Clear	Method
		RemoveItem	Method
		Click, DblClick	Events
		ItemCheck	Event
		KeyDown, KeyPress	Events
		Scroll	Event

(continued)

Table 8.1   Visual Basic intrinsic controls and the Form and MDIForm objects *(continued)*.

Control	Purpose	Important Attributes	Type
MDIForm	Act as an MDI frame for the application	**ActiveControl**	Property
		ActiveForm	Property
		AutoShowChildren	Property
		Caption	Property
		Controls	Property
		CurrentX, CurrentY	Properties
		Enabled	Property
		Height, Width	Properties
		hWnd	Property
		Icon	Property
		Picture	Property
		Visible	Property
		Arrange	Method
		Hide	Method
		Move	Method
		PopUpMenu	Method
		Show	Method
		Activate, Deactivate	Events
		Initialize	Event
		Load, UnLoad	Events
		QueryUnLoad	Event
		ReSize	Event
		Terminate	Event
Menu	Display a custom menu	**Caption**	Property
		Checked	Property
		Enabled	Property
		NegotiatePosition	Property
		Shortcut	Property
		WindowList	Property
		Click	Event
OLE Container	Add insertable objects to Forms	**Action**	Property
		ApplsRunning	Property
		AutoActivate	Property
		Class, Container	Properties
		MiscFlags	Property
		FileNumber	Property
		SourceDoc, SourceItem	Properties
		Close	Method
		Copy	Method
		DoVerb, FetchVerbs	Methods

(continued)

Table 8.1	Visual Basic intrinsic controls and the Form and MDIForm objects *(continued)*.		
Control	**Purpose**	**Important Attributes**	**Type**
		InsertObj	Method
		SaveToOLE1File	Method
		Click, DblClick	Events
		Updated	Event
Option Button	Select mutually exclusive options	See Check Box	
PictureBox	Display graphic; more functional than Image	**CurrentX, CurrentY**	Properties
		Image	Property
		Palette	Property
		Circle, CLS, Point, PSet	Methods
		PaintPicture	Method
		Click	Event
		Paint	Event
Shape	Place a geometric shape on a Form or control	**BackColor, ForeColor**	Properties
		DrawMode	Property
		FillColor, FillStyle	Properties
		Shape	Property
		Refresh	Method
TextBox	Display or capture data	**DataChanged**	Property
		DataRecord, DataSource	Properties
		Enabled, Locked	Properties
		Multiline	Property
		PassWordChar	Property
		SelLength, SelStart	Properties
		SelText	Property
		Text	Property
		Change	Event
Timer	Execute code at regular intervals	**Interval**	Property
		Timer	Event

Selected Attributes Likely To Be On The Test

In the following sections, I will discuss some of the methods, properties, and events that you are likely to run into on the certification exam.

ZOrder Method

ZOrder refers to the order in which items are layered on the Form from front to back. For instance, you typically place option buttons on top of a frame. Therefore, the frame is behind the option buttons. To place a control at the top (front) of the ZOrder, use the syntax *object*.ZOrder 0. To place it in the back, use *object*.ZOrder 1. Zero is the default. The method applies to every Visual Basic control.

TabIndex Property

TabIndex refers to the order in which controls are entered as the user presses the Tab key to move around the Form. It applies to all controls except Menu, Data, Line, Shape, Image, and MDIForm. You set the TabIndex at design time or runtime. If you change the TabIndex of a control, all other controls on the Form are automatically reindexed. If you delete a control and then select Edit|Undo, all properties except TabIndex are restored. If TabIndex is zero, the user cannot tab to that control. A value less than zero causes an error. To change the order programmatically, use the syntax *control*.TabOrder = *n* where *n* is any positive number or zero. This is a likely exam question.

SetFocus Method

Any control that can be navigated to with the Tab key (plus the Form and MDIForm objects) can also receive *focus*. This means the object (that is, the control, or the Form or MDIForm object) is the current object, and is usually visually denoted by a dashed box on the control. (Figure 6.1 in Chapter 6 shows an example of a message box with the Command Button having focus.) You can make an object receive focus programmatically by employing its SetFocus method using the following syntax: *object*.SetFocus. The object or control must be visible to receive focus.

GotFocus And LostFocus Events

When a control no longer has focus, the LostFocus event occurs. Every control that can receive focus (plus the Form object, but not the MDIForm object) has a LostFocus event. Further, if you create a dialog in a DLL with Visual Basic and display it, it also has a LostFocus event. When a control gets focus, the GotFocus event occurs. Every control that has a LostFocus event also has a GotFocus event. LostFocus is typically used to provide a place to perform an action, such as programmatically validating the contents of a TextBox that has just lost focus. GotFocus may be used to signal the program to initialize a field.

KeyDown, KeyUp, And KeyPress Events

When a control has focus and a key is pressed, three events are triggered. **KeyDown** occurs when the user presses a key but has not yet released it. **KeyUp** occurs when the user has released the key. **KeyPress** occurs after the user has pressed *and* released the key. All controls that can receive focus can receive these events. However, there are special rules for Form controls: In order to receive the **KeyDown** and **KeyUp** events, there must be no visible and enabled controls on the Form. In order to receive the **KeyPress** event, either there must be no visible and enabled controls on the Form or its **KeyPreview** property must be set to **True.**

The **KeyPress** event is defined as a sub procedure

```
Sub object_KeyPress (keyAscii As Integer)
```

where *keyAscii* is the ASCII value of the key pressed. To determine the character itself, use the syntax: **Chr (*keyAscii*)**. **KeyPress** detects all printable characters, the Ctrl key combined with any alphabetic character, and the Enter and Backspace keys (in other words, ANSI characters). You can use the **KeyPress** event to test for characters keyed in, and change them (by altering *keyAscii*) before they are echoed to the control.

KeyDown is defined as a sub procedure:

```
Sub object.KeyPress (keycode As Integer, shift As Integer)
```

KeyUp is also defined as a sub procedure:

```
Sub object.KeyUp (keycode As Integer, shift As Integer)
```

Both indicate which key was pressed. **KeyPress** is more flexible for standard ANSI characters. *Keycode* is returned as a Visual Basic constant, such as **vbKeyF1** for the F1 key. This means that alphabetic characters are not distinguished as upper- or lowercase. Shift evaluates to 1 if the Shift key was pressed; 2 if the Ctrl key was pressed; and 4 if the Alt key was pressed. To determine if a combination of these keys were pressed, add the results together. Thus, if *shift* returns 7, the Shift, Control, and Alt keys were all pressed. (Note: You can also use the Visual Basic constants **vbShiftMask, vbAltMask,** and **vbCtlMask** to evaluate *shift*.) **KeyDown** and **KeyUp** aren't invoked if Enter is pressed for a Command Button control that has its **Default** property set to **True,** or if the Escape key is pressed for a Command Button control that has its **Cancel** property set to **True.** The events are also not triggered when the Tab key is pressed.

KeyPreview Property

The **KeyPreview** property applies to Form and user objects. It alters the behavior of **KeyDown, KeyUp,** and **KeyPress.** If **KeyPreview** is set to **True** for the Form or user object that contains the control that would normally receive the keystrokes, the events are invoked on the Form instead. This is useful to intercept keycodes before they are echoed to the control. You can change *keyAscii* for **KeyPress,** and *keycode* for **KeyDown** and **KeyUp,** to alter the character echoed. You can also set them to zero to prevent the character from being echoed. In addition, **KeyPreview** is useful to set up a generic key handling event at the form level, rather than giving each control identical code to process keystrokes. For instance, you may wish to intercept the F1 key to trigger Help. Note that **KeyPreview** does not intercept arrow keys in a ListBox, nor does it intercept the Enter or Esc keys for Command Buttons whose **Default** or **Cancel** properties are set to **True.**

Index Property

As discussed in Chapter 2, you can create an array of controls that all share the same **Name** property. You may change this at design time and read or write at runtime. To address a control that is part of an array of controls, use the syntax: *control (index),* where *control* evaluates to the control's **Name** property and *index* is a positive **Integer** (0 to 32,767). Specifying an invalid *index* causes a runtime error. As mentioned, unlike regular arrays, the indexes for arrays of controls do not have to be sequential. Note that every control also has a **Tag** property of type **String** that Visual Basic does not use for any purpose. You may use the **Tag** property to identify a control (or for any other suitable purpose).

 You can use the **Index** property to create a new instance of a control using the **Load** statement. Assuming you have an array of a TextBox control named **txtResult,** you can add a new one dynamically using the syntax: **Load txtResult (*newIndex*),** where *newIndex* is an unused index number.

Selected Controls

As noted at the beginning of the chapter, it is impossible to predict with certainty what might be encountered on the certification exam. In general, if you are familiar with the basic arsenal of intrinsic controls and their key attributes (see Table 8.1), you will be in good shape. However, I have highlighted some specific controls that, in my experience, VB developers are not always up to speed on and that are likely to appear on the exam.

Image Vs. PictureBox Controls

Visual Basic developers often confuse these two controls because their functionality overlaps. The Image control is used to display a graphic (such as a bitmap, icon, and so on). It has less features than the PictureBox control. However, an Image control uses fewer resources than the PictureBox control and refreshes more rapidly. It can react to **Click, DblClick,** and the usual drag-and-drop events. PictureBox will do all of this and more. For instance, it will clip a graphic if it is not the same size as the control. PictureBox can be used to house graphic methods, such as **Circle, PSet,** and so on, that are used to draw images programmatically. It can also act as the target for another control's **Print** method. You can place a PictureBox control on a MDIForm to act as a container for other objects, and it can be part of a DDE communication. PictureBox has an **AutoSize** property, which, when set to **True,** causes the control to adjust its size to match the graphic's size.

ActiveX Controls

You can add ActiveX controls to your project and make them available via the toolbox for use in your development. To do so, use Project|Components and select those controls that you wish to use. Figure 8.1 shows this process. Figure 8.2 shows an application running with an unlikely mix of ActiveX controls. The chessboard is the QuantamX ActiveX Game Control, from Brilliance Labs, Inc., available at www.brlabs.com. The calendar is the Microsoft Access Calendar Control, Microsoft Corporation. The slider is the ctSlide OCX Control from Gamesman, Inc., available at www.kwanza.com. The data grid is the DBGrid developed for Microsoft by Apex Software Corporation. The movie control is the Microsoft ActiveMovie Control. The graph is the Microsoft Chart Control from Visual Components, Inc. Depending on which version of Visual Basic you have installed, you may have all of the Microsoft controls.

 Those controls that you are likely to run into on the certification exam are referenced where appropriate in the book. The "data aware" ActiveX controls (such as DBGrid) are covered in Chapter 10. Others are discussed in Chapters 5 and 9.

The CommonDialog Control

Visual Basic's CommonDialog control is a Windows dialog customized by the parameters and messages sent to it. Visual Basic shields the developer from most of the complexities involved in setting up the dialog by providing a number of methods to perform the desired service(s), which I will discuss in a moment. In

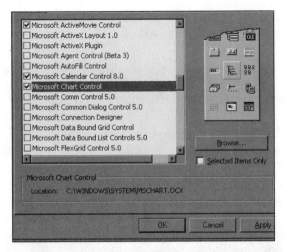

Figure 8.1   Adding ActiveX controls to a Visual Basic project.

general, the dialogs that you present to your users are identical to those presented by other Windows applications, lending your application a professional and common "look and feel."

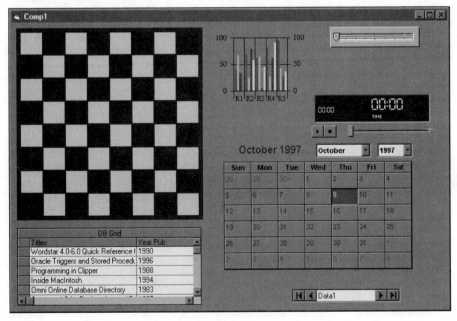

Figure 8.2   Some ActiveX controls in use.

To add the CommonDialog control to your project, select Project|Components and then choose Microsoft CommonDialog Control 5.0. The control is then included in the toolbox. To use it, you should place it on the Form in which it is going to be used. An icon—not visible at runtime—appears on the Form.

The actual dialog that is presented is dictated by which of the CommonDialog's methods you invoke. The CommonDialog has a number of properties summarized in Table 8.2, but it has no events associated with it. (Properties related to Help are listed in Chapter 11 in the section titled "Using The CommonDialog To Display Help.") None of the control's methods return a value. To determine what the user has selected from the dialog presented, the application has to query the control's properties, as I outline in the following sections.

Table 8.2 Key CommonDialog properties.

Property	Value	Meaning
Action	0	No Action.
	1	Displays Open dialog box.
	2	Displays Save As dialog box.
	3	Displays Color dialog box.
	4	Displays Font dialog box.
	5	Displays Printer dialog box.
	6	Runs WINHLP32.EXE.
CancelError	True	Generate error if user clicks Cancel.
	False	Do not generate error if user clicks Cancel.
DefaultExt	String	Default file extension to display.
FileName	String	Name of the file(s) that the user selected delimited by a space.
Filter	String	Define a filter to control what file(s) to be displayed, such as:"*.DOC".
Flags	cdlOFNAllowMultiselect	Allow multiple selections.
	cdlOFNCreatePrompt	Prompt the user to create a file.
	cdlOFNExplorer	Present an Explorer-like dialog box.

(continued)

Table 8.2   Key CommonDialog properties (continued).

Property	Value	Meaning
	cdlOFNExtensionDifferent	Indicates extension entered by user different than default extension.
	cdlOFNFileMustExist	Permits the user to select an existing file only.
	cdlOFNHelpButton	Display a help button.
	cdlOFNHideReadOnly	Hide the Read Only checkbox.
	cdlOFNLongNames	Allow long file names.
	cdlOFNNoChangeDir	Restore current directory to what it was when dialog opened.
	cdlOFNNoLongNames	Disallow long file names.
	cdlOFNNoReadOnlyReturn	Turn off Read Only attribute of selected file.
	cdlOFNNoValidate	Allow invalid file name characters.
	cdlOFNOverwritePrompt	Generate message if file already exists.
	cdlOFNPathMustExist	Disallow entry of invalid file paths.
	cdlOFNReadOnly	Set Read Only checkbox to checked.
	cdlOFNShareAware	Ignore sharing violations.
InitDir	String	Specify the initial directory.

Open, Save, and Save As

Perhaps the most common use of the CommonDialog control is to present an Open File, Save File, or Save File As dialog box. These are invoked by using the **ShowOpen** or **ShowSave** methods of the control as shown:

```
' Prompt the user to save a file
CommonDialog1.ShowSave
```

Alternatively, you can use the control's **Action** property to dictate what dialog will be displayed. The use of **Action** is included for backwards compatibility with prior versions of Visual Basic and does not provide all of the functionality of CommonDialog's various methods. (The valid **Action** values are listed in Table 8.2.)

An example of using the **Action** property to display a Save As dialog box is shown in this snippet:

```
CommonDialog1.Action = 2
```

To determine the name of the file to open or the file to save, you need to query the **FileName** property of the CommonDialog control. If the user selected or typed in a valid file name, this property will contain a fully qualified path and file name. It is the application's responsibility to actually open or create the file.

About Box

The CommonDialog Control displays an "About Box" by invoking the **AboutBox** method:

```
CommonDialog1.AboutBox
```

The **AboutBox** is not well documented in the VB Help file (if you search on "AboutBox," the resulting help page does not list the CommonDialog as being a control that supports this method) and is of limited value in that the resulting display yields an About Box for the CommonDialog control itself (most ActiveX controls have this method).

Show Fonts

The **ShowFont** method (**CommonDialog1.ShowFont**) displays all of the fonts installed on the user's PC or printer. However, you must supply a constant to the **Flags** property of the CommonDialog control. These constants are not valid with other methods of the control. The valid constants are:

➤ **CdlCFScreenFonts** Display the PC's screen fonts.

➤ **CdlCFPrinterFonts** Display the installed printer fonts.

➤ **CdlCFBoth** Display both screen and printer fonts.

Other CommonDialog Methods

Besides the CommonDialog methods previously reviewed, the following methods are used to show available printers and available colors:

➤ **ShowPrinter** Displays a list of available printers.

➤ **ShowColor** Allows the user to select a color from the system color palette. To determine the color selected, query the **Color** property (**myColor = CommonDialog1.Color**).

The CommonDialog control also has a **ShowHelp** method, which I discuss in Chapter 11 in the section titled "Using The CommonDialog To Display Help."

Interapplication Communications

In 1990, Bill Gates made a speech at Comdex in which he espoused his "document-centric" philosophy for the future of computing (and, not by coincidence, Microsoft Windows). Under this doctrine, the user need only be concerned with the document being worked on and not with the application(s) used to create that document. Thus, if a presentation at a board meeting requires the use of a word-processing document, spreadsheet, and a graph, the user should be able to perform all of these functions from one interface, not knowing or caring what applications are actually doing the work. The original implementation of this was through DDE (Dynamic Data Exchange). DDE has been succeeded by OLE (Object Linking and Embedding), though DDE is still widely used.

Dynamic Data Exchange

Under DDE, the two applications that are communicating both need to be running when the conversation is initiated. The source application is known as the *DDE client* and the destination application is known as the *DDE server*. Visual Basic can act as both a client and a server in a DDE conversation.

There are three types of DDE communication: cold link, warm link, and hot link. In a cold link, communications are opened, data is exchanged, and the channel is closed. In a warm link, the channel remains open and the client is notified of any changes. In a hot link, the channel remains open and the client is automatically updated when there are any changes. These are implemented with the Visual Basic **LinkMode** keyword using the syntax

```
object.LinkMode = n
```

where *object* is a Form object, MDIForm object, Label control, TextBox control, or PictureBox control. The valid values for *n* are:

➤ **0** Close communications

➤ **1** Automatic update (hot link)

➤ **2** Manual, updated only when **LinkRequest** is issued (cold link)

➤ **3** Notify, update only when **LinkRequest** is issued (warm link)

The syntax for the **LinkRequest** method is: *object*.**LinkRequest**, where *object* is a Label, TextBox, or PictureBox control (the Form and MDIForm objects do not have the **LinkRequest** method). The method causes the control to ask the source application (the DDE client) to update its (the control's) contents. To use this method, the control must be involved in the DDE conversation as a client (DDE server). In the case of the Label control, the **Caption** property is updated. For the TextBox control, the **Text** property is updated. The **Picture** property is updated for the PictureBox control.

LinkTopic is used to describe the destination and **LinkItem** describes the data being requested. Thus, the following snippet of code will keep a text box updated automatically whenever the contents of an Excel spreadsheet cell changes:

```
' describe the destination
Text1.LinkTopic = "Excel|Sheet1"
' establish the link
Text1.LinkItem = "R1C1"
' open the channel
Text1.LinkMode = 1
```

Object Linking And Embedding

OLE technology is fully supported in Visual Basic, allowing a VB project to act either as a server or client. When VB is the server, another application acts as the client and requests and receives data from the VB application. When VB is the client, it establishes communications with another application and receives data from that application. Further, the OLE server exposes its functionality to the client. Thus, you can embed a Microsoft Word document into your VB application and, when that document is active, Word's menus replace your own. For all practical purposes, when the document is active, the user is working inside of Microsoft Word. Visual Basic implements OLE client technology through the use of the OLE Container Control.

OLE Container Control

There are two methods of creating an OLE object in your application. The first is to select Project|Component and then select the Insertable Objects tab. This brings up a list of OLE objects that can be inserted into your project, as seen in Figure 8.3. Select those items that you will be using and they will be added to the toolbox. Figure 8.4 shows the VB environment with several OLE objects added to the toolbox, and several controls painted onto the screen (a Microsoft Word document, a Microsoft Photo graphic, and a Microsoft Excel worksheet and chart).

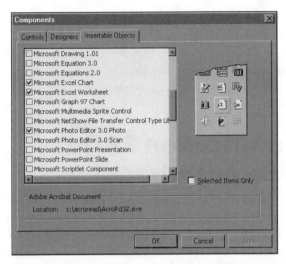

Figure 8.3   Use the Project menu to add OLE controls to the toolbox.

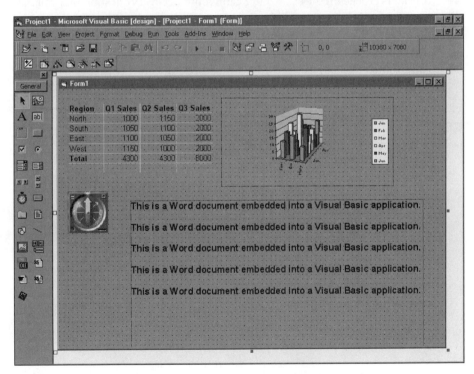

Figure 8.4   Some OLE objects embedded into a form.

Alternatively, you can use the OLE Container icon directly from the toolbox to draw a container onto the Form. When you do so, Visual Basic prompts you for the object, as seen in Figure 8.5. You may create a new object or create an object from an existing file. You may also choose not to specify the object at this time, instead assigning it at runtime through the object's **Class** property (see Figure 8.6).

The Certification Exam And VB Controls

Visual Basic supports a wide array of control-driven functionality, along with exposing the whole world of OLE via the OLE Container control. Ironically, the certification exam concentrates on areas other than controls, making it difficult to anticipate those few questions that you are likely to see. I have attempted to recount what appears to me to be those areas that Microsoft considers crucial on the exam, but I cannot predict every question that you may encounter. My recommendation is to know the basics of using OLE automation, as described in this chapter, and to familiarize yourself with the controls that are available, along with the most frequently used properties, methods, and events. The key is not to be tripped up by controls that don't exist or confusing the properties of one control with those of another.

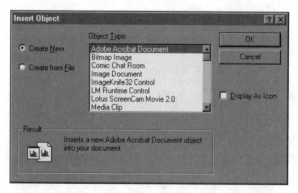

Figure 8.5   Create an insertable object by using the OLE Container control from the toolbox.

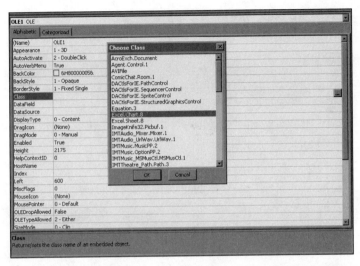

Figure 8.6 You may dynamically create an insertable OLE object at runtime or at design time through the OLE Container control's **Class** property.

Exam Prep Questions

Question 1

Which controls can receive focus on a Form?

- ○ a. All controls except the Form itself
- ○ b. All controls except Shape
- ○ c. All controls that have a **TabIndex** property
- ○ d. All controls that have their **CanReceiveFocus** property set to **True**

Answer c is correct. If a control can be tabbed into, it can receive focus. Answer a is incorrect because some controls cannot receive focus. Answer b is incorrect because Shape is not the only control that cannot receive focus. For instance, the Line control also cannot receive focus. Answer d is incorrect because there is no **CanReceiveFocus** property.

Question 2

You have a Form with four text boxes on it and need to intercept keystrokes for all four text boxes. What is the best method of doing this?

- ○ a. Use the **KeyPreview** method of the Form.
- ○ b. Use the **TestKey** event of the OLE keyboard object inserted into the Form.
- ○ c. Use the **KeyDown** or **KeyPress** events of each of the text boxes.
- ○ d. Use the **KeyDown** or **KeyUp** properties of the Form.
- ○ e. None of these.

Answer c is correct because it is the only one that will work. The best way to do this is to use the **KeyPreview** property of the Form, but this option was not provided. The trick to this question is being familiar with properties, methods, and events, and then choosing among only the feasible solutions. Answer a is incorrect because, though it looks tempting, **KeyPreview** is a property, not a method. Don't let yourself make a mistake by quickly jumping to the "obvious" answer without carefully reading the choices. Answer b is also wrong because there is, in fact, no OLE keyboard object. Answer d is incorrect because **KeyDown** and **KeyPress** are events, not properties. Answer e is incorrect because there is a valid choice provided.

Question 3

> Your Form has two TextBox controls occupying the exact same space (one is on top of the other). Assuming the following snippet of code, with which one can the user interact?
>
> ```
> Private Sub Form_Load()
>     Text2.ZOrder 1
>     Text1.ZOrder 0
> End Sub
> ```
>
> ○ a. Both
>
> ○ b. Text2
>
> ○ c. Text1
>
> ○ d. The one with the lowest **ZOrder** property, assuming the **TabOrder** for both is non-zero

Answer a is correct. As odd as it may sound, each control can still receive focus and even have data entered into it. The user just cannot see what is being typed. The trick here is that answer a seems implausible while answers c and d seem very plausible. This is another case where the choices have to be read very carefully. The only reason that d is incorrect is because **ZOrder** is a method and not a property. Answers b and c are both incorrect because both controls can, in fact, be edited. However, although answer b even looks wrong (because we have set its **ZOrder** to 1), answer c is a logical but incorrect guess. It is logical because its **ZOrder** is 0, and it is incorrect because both TextBox controls can receive focus and be edited.

Question 4

> What steps must you take to change the tab order of controls at runtime?
>
> - ○ a. It can't be done at runtime.
> - ○ b. Invoke the **ReTab** method for each control utilizing the Form's **Controls** collection.
> - ○ c. Alter the **TabIndex** property of the control or controls that need to be resequenced and all others will resequence themselves accordingly.
> - ○ d. Invoke the **TabOrder** method of the Form (using the **Controls** collection if desired) except that arrays of controls have to be sequenced at design time.

Answer c is correct. You alter the *TabIndex* of any control and other controls move to reflect the change. Answer a is incorrect because the **TabIndex** is not a read-only property. Answer b is incorrect because there is no **ReTab** method. Answer d is incorrect because the Form has no **TabOrder** method and arrays of controls can be resequenced as any other controls.

Question 5

> How do you change the target of an OLE Container?
>
> - ○ a. Alter the control's **Class** property.
> - ○ b. At design time, remove the control and reinsert or, at runtime, invoke a new **OLETopic**.
> - ○ c. Invoke the control's **OLESetNew** method.
> - ○ d. It can't be done.
> - ○ e. None of the above.

Answer a is correct. You can dynamically alter the class of an OLE Container control's *Class* property to assign the OLE object. Answer b is incorrect because there is no **OLETopic**. Answer c is incorrect because there is no **OLESetNew** method. Answer d is incorrect because it can be done, and answer e is wrong because the correct choice is provided.

Question 6

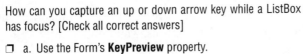

How can you capture an up or down arrow key while a ListBox
has focus? [Check all correct answers]

❒ a. Use the Form's **KeyPreview** property.

❒ b. Use the ListBox's **Scroll** event.

❒ c. Use the ListBox's **KeyPress** event.

❒ d. Use the ListBox's **KeyDown** or **KeyUp** events.

Answers b and d are correct. The ListBox's *Scroll* event is triggered when an
arrow key is pressed, thus allowing you to react to it. Likewise, the *KeyDown*
and *KeyUp* events can be used to intercept an arrow key. Answer a is incorrect
because the Form cannot intercept an arrow key in a ListBox. Answer c is
incorrect because the **KeyPress** event is not invoked with the arrow keys.

Need To Know More?

Because the nature of this chapter is so far-reaching, it is difficult to point the reader to any specific sources to learn "all there is." Instead, the following sources provide some good overviews of VB controls. More important, I highly recommend that you develop an inventory of those intrinsic controls you are not familiar with. Then, write a small application manipulating those controls to ensure that you have a basic understanding. Add to the intrinsic controls the CommonDialog control and create some OLE objects with the OLE Container control.

 Aitken, Peter: *Visual Basic5 Programming EXplorer*. Coriolis Group Books, Scottsdale, AZ, 1997, ISBN 1-57610-065-0. Chapter 3 provides an introduction to the more often used intrinsic controls.

 Harrington, John, Mark Spenik, Heidi Brumbaugh, and Cliff Diamond: *Visual Basic 5 Interactive Course*. Waite Group Press, Corte Madera, CA, 1997. ISBN 1-57169-077-8. Chapter 5 outlines the usage of the more often used intrinsic controls, while Chapter 8 discusses the CommonDialog and other Windows 95 controls. (The latter are from the Microsoft Common Components version 5 which I discussed in Chapter 5.)

 Jamsa, Kris and Lars Klander: *1001 Visual Basic Programmer's Tips*. Jamsa Press, Las Vegas, NV, 1997. ISBN 1-884133-56-8. This well-done book is not broken into chapters but rather into "tips." Tips 428 through 526 are a continuing discussion centering around the Form object and its various methods and properties and then discussing the CommonDialog control. Tips 621 through 629 deal with graphic controls and scroll bars.

 McKinney, Bruce: *Hardcore Visual Basic, Second Edition* (which covers version 5). Microsoft Press, Redmond, WA, 1997. ISBN 1-57231-422-2. Chapter 7 provides more than you ever wanted to know about drawing and painting in Visual Basic, and thus discusses those controls that Bruce refers to as "canvas objects" (controls that have graphic methods). These include the Form object, and PictureBox, Image, Shape, and Line controls.

Search the online books on the VB CD for "controls." The four main topics of interest are "Controls For Displaying And Entering Text," "Controls That Present Choices To The User," "Controls That Display Pictures And Graphics," and "Additional Controls." Separate subjects include "Understanding Focus" and "Setting The Tab Order."

 Microsoft places the most current Knowledge Base online at www.microsoft.com/support. Enter search terms such as "control" to view articles detailing tips (and sometimes fixes) revolving around the issues discussed in this chapter.

 There are a number of Web sites devoted to the subject of Visual Basic on the Internet. Use a search engine such as Yahoo! (www.yahoo.com) or Hotbot (www.hotbot.com) with a search term such as "Visual Basic 5" (be sure to place the search term in quotes so that only pages containing the entire term as one string are returned). A well-done site with tips and sample code that I liked was the VB Palace at home.computer.net/~mheller/. Another site that was under "reconstruction" when I visited was a site hosted by Temple University at thunder.ocis.temple.edu/ ~shariq/vb.

Visual Basic And ActiveX

Terms you'll need to understand:

- √ ActiveX component
- √ In-process and out-of-process servers
- √ Asynchronous and synchronous communications
- √ Component Object Model (COM)
- √ Distributed Component Object Model (DCOM)
- √ OLE server
- √ ActiveX control
- √ Extender
- √ Container
- √ PropertyBag
- √ PropertyPage
- √ ActiveX EXE
- √ ActiveX Document EXE
- √ Instancing property
- √ Modal and modeless
- √ Enumeration and Enum keyword
- √ UserDocument
- √ Hyperlink
- √ ActiveX DLL

Techniques you'll need to master:

- √ Creating ActiveX controls
- √ Adding properties, methods, and events to ActiveX controls
- √ Adding property pages to ActiveX controls
- √ Debugging an ActiveX control
- √ Creating an ActiveX server (ActiveX EXE and ActiveX DLL)
- √ Creating an ActiveX Document (ActiveX Document EXE and ActiveX Document DLL)
- √ Testing ActiveX servers

In this chapter, I discuss a technology that is critical both in terms of Visual Basic development and in successfully completing the Microsoft Visual Basic certification process. Because ActiveX is so central to Microsoft's vision of future technology, the term and the technologies are by necessity discussed in most chapters in this book. Here, I discuss the basis of the technology, its use, and how to develop ActiveX components with Visual Basic.

ActiveX Components

ActiveX components are essentially a by-product of object-oriented development. Whereas object-oriented development seeks to create reusable objects, *component-based development* seeks to exploit those objects by reusing them in multiple applications. In Visual Basic, this means that development includes assembling prebuilt components and customizing their behavior to match the needs of the application being developed. This is accomplished with Microsoft's ActiveX technology.

The advantage of ActiveX is that any development tool that supports the technology can use the same objects. Most modern development tools (including Visual Basic) support ActiveX-based component development.

In-Process And Out-Of-Process Servers

ActiveX components run as either in-process or out-of-process servers. The distinction lies in where the objects of the ActiveX component are created. In the case of an ActiveX DLL, objects are created in the same address space as the application that is using them and are thus called *in-process* servers. An ActiveX EXE runs in its own memory space. It is called an *out-of-process* server because it does not run in the same memory space as the application that is accessing its objects.

An application can invoke the services of an object within an out-of-process server *asynchronously*—this means that the application can continue processing while the server performs the requested task. For example, an application can invoke the print services of a Microsoft document object and continue processing without waiting for the document to print. With an in-process server, the application communicates *synchronously*, which means that the application must wait until the server completes its task before continuing.

ActiveX Vs. OLE

OLE (Object Linking and Embedding) allows for interapplication communication. The first model for OLE was DDE (Dynamic Data Exchange). I discuss the mechanics of both in the "Dynamic Data Exchange" and "Object Linking And Embedding" sections of Chapter 8.

Since OLE version 2 was introduced, Microsoft has embraced its COM (Component Object Model) technology proposal to establish standards for interobject communication. Under COM, all applications, documents, and so on, can be thought of as objects. DCOM (Distributed Component Object Model) is an extension of COM; this standard specifies that objects can communicate with each other regardless of their locations. The components can be on the same PC or reside in different places on a network (including the Internet).

The "X" in ActiveX is derived from the name of the file extensions given to controls that can be reused in the development environment. VBX files are Visual Basic controls and OCX files are OLE controls; these extensions were so named by Microsoft. The "Active" in ActiveX reflects Microsoft's attempt to make the Internet a more interactive (as opposed to static) experience with active servers and active clients (I discuss these in more detail in Chapter 12, "Visual Basic And The Internet").

ActiveX technology builds upon, rather than replaces, OLE technology, but OLE controls have been renamed ActiveX controls.

An OLE server is a piece of code that reacts to the requests of other applications. Visual Basic can act as an OLE server or an OLE client (again, discussed in the "Object Linking And Embedding" section of Chapter 8). However, in keeping with Microsoft's technology shift, OLE servers have been redubbed ActiveX components. An ActiveX control is a type of ActiveX component, as are ActiveX documents and Active X DLLs.

ActiveX Controls

ActiveX controls can be built with several different development tools, including Visual Basic. They can be deployed in a wide variety of development environments in addition to Visual Basic. Although most controls that are added to a VB project have a visible component, it is not necessary. (The Internet Transfer control is an example of an ActiveX control that does not have a visible component.) The control can be merely a block of code meant for reuse in other applications. For example, an ActiveX control can be developed to perform statistical calculations. The control's methods would be those calculations, such as computing a standard deviation, that it supports.

VB developers can, with the release of VB5, develop ActiveX controls to use in other VB projects or in other development environments such as Microsoft

Visual C++. The process is straightforward and not much different than developing a form in VB. Select File|New from the VB menu and, at the New Application prompt, select ActiveX Control. The resulting screen is the same as the screen for creating a user control (which I reviewed in the "User Controls" section of Chapter 4). If the control is to have a visible component, draw other controls such as TextBoxes and Command Buttons on it. You can also add other ActiveX controls to it. You can manually add properties and methods in the same manner as you would to a class object. I discussed adding properties in Chapter 4, also, in the "Adding Properties To A Custom Class" section. The control's methods will be those subs and functions you define in your code.

Alternatively, you can use the ActiveX Control Interface Wizard to add properties, methods, and events. Select Add-Ins|ActiveX Control Interface Wizard from the VB menu.

Figure 9.1 shows the initial dialog of the ActiveX Control Interface Wizard opened in the Visual Basic development environment. The control shown is a small MIDI file player (MIDI is a music file format). The control itself has the Microsoft Multimedia Player 5.0 ActiveX control embedded in it, along with the DriveListBox, DirListBox, FileListBox, and Command Button VB controls. The Control Interface Wizard presents two scrollable list boxes, which you use to build a list of attributes (properties, methods, and events) for the

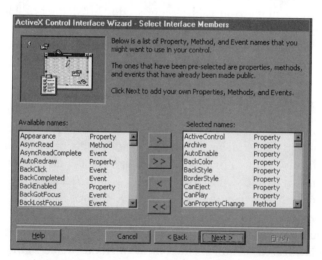

Figure 9.1 From the ActiveX Control Interface Wizard, choose the interface members for the new control.

new ActiveX control. These attributes are referred to as the *interface members*. In the Selected Names list box, Visual Basic initially provides a bare minimum of attributes such as **KeyDown** and **KeyUp**. In the Available Names list box, Visual Basic provides a list of all the attributes of the individual controls embedded in the new ActiveX control. Using the arrow buttons between the two list boxes, you can add and remove attributes as needed.

After choosing those "built-in" attributes (that is, those attributes that are native to the individual VB controls) that you need, you can use subsequent dialogs to add custom properties, methods, and events.

Figure 9.2 shows a subsequent dialog needed to tell Visual Basic how to "map" each attribute. The attribute names are listed in the Public Name list box. The names are called public because they are the names that the control will expose—as opposed to the names of the attributes of the embedded controls (although the names will often be identical). In the figure, I have mapped the **PlayEnabled** property of the new ActiveX control to the **PlayEnabled** property of the embedded multimedia control. Thus, when the control is used in an application and the **PlayEnabled** property is modified, the modification will affect the underlying multimedia control. Not all attributes should be mapped to underlying controls—often, the attributes apply to the entire control. For instance, a property **Visible** would not map to an underlying control—it refers to the entire new ActiveX control.

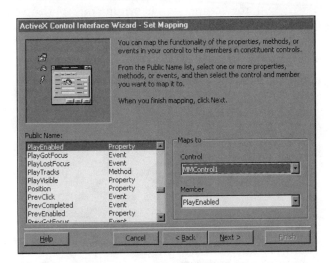

Figure 9.2   Mapping the public names of the new ActiveX controls to attributes of the individual embedded controls.

In a new ActiveX control project, there will often be embedded controls with duplicate attribute names (for instance, both the DirListBox and FileListBox controls have **Refresh** methods). Because you can map the public names to only one embedded control, you may need to create new members (attributes) to map to other embedded controls. For instance, if I needed to expose the **Refresh** methods of both the DirListBox and FileListBox controls, I would have to create attributes that map to each.

In Figure 9.3, I am specifying the attributes of the public name that I had earlier added as a method of the new ActiveX control. I defined **PlayTracks** to return a **Boolean** and accept an argument named **Tracks()** as a **ParamArray**. This allows the ActiveX control to play a variable number of tracks when used in a VB application.

After defining all the attributes of the code, you write all necessary scripts and compile it. You need to specify that the project type is an ActiveX control using the Project Properties dialog, as seen in Figure 9.4. The Upgrade ActiveX Controls checkbox specifies that when a program is launched using the new ActiveX control, the program will check to see if a newer version has been installed on the computer and, if so, automatically upgrade to the newer version. The Require License Key option specifies that the user of the control must have a license to use it. Visual Basic creates a VBL file that is packaged with the control during the setup process. The VBL file contains an entry to the user's registry with the license key. The Setup program that you create to distribute the control will update the user's registry with this information. The

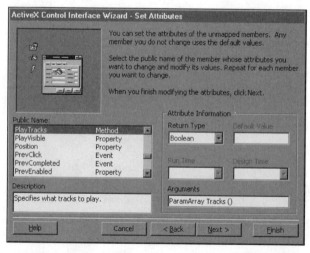

Figure 9.3   Specifying the attributes of the custom **PlayTracks** method.

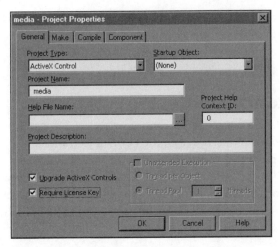

Figure 9.4   The Project Properties dialog for an ActiveX control.

compilation process is discussed in detail in Chapter 14. Use of the Setup program is discussed in more detail in Chapter 15.

As noted earlier, an ActiveX control does not need a visible component; it simply can be a VB script. This is a convenient way to "package" logic that can be reused from application to application. Figure 9.5 shows an application using a simple ActiveX control with no visible component. The name of the control is Permutations. I defined it to have one method, **Compute**, which accepts two arguments of type **Long**. Using a lottery as an example, it determines how many possible variations of six digits can be computed from forty numbers.

ActiveX controls that you create can be used and added to the toolbox like any other ActiveX controls. Select the control from Project|Components (from the VB menu) and it's added to the toolbox. Click the control on the toolbox

Figure 9.5   The Permutations ActiveX control in use.

and add it to the form. In Figure 9.5, I had named the control **PermCtl1**. To use it, I simply referenced the **Compute** method:

```
text3 = Str (PermCtl.Compute(Val(Text1), Val(Text2)))
```

The Extender Object

When you place a Visual Basic control or ActiveX control onto a form, it derives some of its properties from the Form object, which is a container. The **Top** and **Left** properties of any control describe, as X and Y coordinates, where the control is located on the container. Clearly, these properties of the control are not functions of the control itself but of its container. The container maintains an **Extender** object, which exposes these extender properties, methods, and events to the control.

 In addition to the Form object, Visual Basic provides two other types of containers: the Frame control and the PictureBox control. Each can contain other controls, so they are called container objects.

Not all containers have the same extender properties. For instance, your ActiveX control could be used in a Microsoft Visual C++, Borland Delphi, or Powersoft PowerBuilder application—these will not necessarily provide the same properties as does Visual Basic. Because Visual Basic has no way of knowing on what container a control will be placed, the **Extender** object is not available during the **Initialize** event of the control. It is available during the **InitProperties** and **ReadProperties** events.

All containers provide several standard properties of the **Extender** object:

➤ **Cancel**

➤ **Default**

➤ **Name**

➤ **Visible**

Visual Basic provides the following additional properties, methods, and events for the **Extender** object:

➤ **Container** (property)

➤ **DragIcon** (property)

➤ **DragMode** (property)

➤ **Enabled** (property)

➤ **Height** (property)

➤ **HelpContextID** (property)

➤ **Index** (property)

➤ **Left** (property)

➤ **TabIndex** (property)

➤ **TabStop** (property)

➤ **Tag** (property)

➤ **ToolTipText** (property)

➤ **Top** (property)

➤ **WhatsThisHelpID** (property)

➤ **Width** (property)

➤ **Drag** (method)

➤ **Move** (method)

➤ **SetFocus** (method)

➤ **ShowWhatsThis** (method)

➤ **ZOrder** (method)

➤ **DragDrop** (method)

➤ **DragOver** (method)

➤ **GotFocus** (method)

➤ **LostFocus** (event)

The ActiveX control developer must be aware of the possibility that certain properties, methods, and events may not always be present, depending on which container object holds the control.

The *Extender* Property

All ActiveX controls have the **Extender** object as a property; this returns a reference to the object providing the container properties. To determine the **Extender** object for a given control, use the following code:

```
Dim myObject As Object
myObject = myActXCtl.Extender
```

The **Container** Property

Every Visual Basic control (except for the Form and MDIForm objects) has a **Container** property. Additionally, all ActiveX controls used in a Visual Basic project have access to a **Container** property via the **Extender** object. The **Container** property can be read to determine which object contains the control. Only the Form itself and the Frame and PictureBox controls can be containers. The **Container** property can also be used to move a control from one container to another within the Form object. For instance, if **command1** is a control on **form1**, it can be "moved" to **frame1** with the following code:

```
Set command1.Container = frame1
```

The **PropertyBag** Object

The **PropertyBag** object is another service provided by a container. It can be thought of as similar to a "shopping cart" in online shopping services. If you go to a commercial Web site, such as www.amazon.com, you can browse items for sale and when you decide you want to purchase one, you can add it to the "shopping cart." When you are finished shopping, you can purchase all of the items in the shopping cart at once. With an ActiveX control, the container provides the **PropertyBag** as a place for the control to read and write information about its state (that is, the values of its properties). This is done via the **PropertyBag's ReadProperty** and **WriteProperty** methods. Let's assume a control has a property called **TextColor**. The control can save the current value of this property using the following syntax:

```
Private Sub UserControl_WriteProperties(PropBag As PropertyBag)
    PropBag.WriteProperty "TextColor", TextColor, Black
End Sub
```

The **WriteProperties** event is called by the developer when properties of the object need to be saved. The **PropertyBag** object is passed to the event as the variable **PropBag**.

The first argument is a "data name," a key by which to retrieve the data later, similar to the **Key** property of the **Collection** object. The second argument is the value (**TextColor**) being stored (in other words, the actual property). The third argument is optional; it provides a default value. This is supplied so that if the value being saved is the same as the default value for the property, it will not be written to a file. Then, when the control is re-created at some time in the future, the property bag is smaller and the control initializes faster because it does not have to process redundant information. In the previous example, if

. . . .

the value saved for **TextColor** is **Black** (the same as the default value), then the information is not written to the **PropertyBag** object. Thus, the ultimate purpose of the **PropertyBag** object is to save the state (values of the properties) of the control between invocations.

The **ReadProperty** method is used to read from the property bag. To retrieve the fictitious **TextColor** property, we would use the syntax:

```
Private Sub UserControl_ReadProperties(PropBag As PropertyBag)
    PropertyBag.ReadValue "TextColor", Black
End Sub
```

The first argument is the data name, as in the **WriteProperty** method. The second argument is again a default, except this time it is the value to be returned if the data name is not found in the property bag.

The **ReadProperties** event is automatically invoked following the **Initialize** event and the **PropertyBag** property is passed to the event as the variable **PropBag**.

Adding Property Pages

Before you distribute your control, you need to provide the user with a means to set its properties at design time. When you use a VB control, Visual Basic provides the property window for this purpose. However, when you use an ActiveX control, the control generally provides its own dialog, in the form of a tabbed dialog, to customize its properties. To build a property page for your control, choose Project|Add Property Page from the VB menu. When you do so, you will be given the option of invoking the Property Page Wizard. If you choose the Wizard, VB will examine your control for all properties that you have defined as public and available at design time. VB will then walk you through the process of creating one or more property pages to manage these properties.

Each property page represents a single **PropertyPage** object.

It is a straightforward process to manually create a property page. Add the new property page and then create appropriate dialogs for the properties to be listed on that page. For instance, if the property has a **True** or **False** value, use a checkbox to indicate the range of possible values. Use the **SelectionChanged** and **ApplyChanges** events of the **PropertyPage** to set the values of the properties for the page. The **SelectionChanged** event is where you set the values of the controls on the property page, as shown in the following snippet:

```
chkNextVisible.Value = _
    (SelectedControls(0).NextVisible And vbChecked)
chkPauseVisible.Value = _
    (SelectedControls(0).PauseVisible And vbChecked)
```

In this example, there are two checkboxes to represent the values of the
NextVisible and **PauseVisible** properties of the media control that I built in
Figures 9.1 through 9.4. Here, if the value of the property is **True**, the checkbox
is checked.

The **ApplyChanges** event is where you add code to set the value of properties
based on the values of the controls on the page as in this short example:

```
SelectedControls(0).NextVisible = (chkNextVisible.Value = _
    vbChecked)
SelectedControls(0).PauseVisible = (chkPauseVisible.Value = _
    vbChecked)
```

The property pages become available after you compile the control into an
OCX file. An example of the media control's property dialog in the development environment is shown in Figure 9.6.

Debugging An ActiveX Control

Debugging an ActiveX control presents special problems since you cannot simply run the control in the development environment (the control must be added
to a Form object before it can be run). To get around this, we need to debug the
control while another Form-based project is running in the development envi-

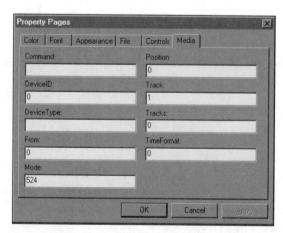

Figure 9.6 The property dialog for the media ActiveX control.

ronment. To do so, select File|Add Project from VB's menu while the ActiveX control project is open. You will be presented with a dialog where you can create a new project or open an existing one. You will then have two projects open at once.

 The new project will become the startup project since an ActiveX control project cannot be a startup project. In the Project Explorer dialog, the startup project is boldfaced.

You should save your "workspace" as a project group by selecting File|Save Project Group from the VB menu.

If you bring the design window for the control to the foreground, its icon on the toolbox becomes disabled. The control is now said to be in design mode. If you go back to the Form object, the ActiveX control's icon becomes enabled again, showing that the control is now in run mode. Place the control on the form as normal. While the control is in design mode, run the project as you normally would and you can step through the control's code, use the watch and intermediate windows, and so on. (Debugging techniques are discussed in Chapter 13, "Debugging And Testing.") When you are satisfied that the control's code has been debugged, you can then remove the Form-based project by selecting File|Remove Project from the VB menu. You can then compile or recompile the control.

ActiveX EXEs And ActiveX Document EXEs

If you select File|New from the VB menu, you are presented with a choice of project types, including ActiveX EXE and ActiveX Document EXE. An ActiveX Document is an application that runs inside of a Web browser as either an ActiveX EXE or ActiveX DLL. An ActiveX Document EXE is a **UserDocument**-based (as opposed to Form-based) ActiveX EXE.

ActiveX EXEs encapsulate data, but make it available to other programs. It can be thought of as an extension to what was formerly called an OLE server. Microsoft Word is an example of an ActiveX EXE, because it exposes its data via VBA (Visual Basic for Applications). An ActiveX Document is a **UserDocument** object that can be added to any ActiveX EXE project. ActiveX EXEs and ActiveX DLLs are programs (I use the word "program" loosely to also include dynamic link libraries) that have been modified to work within a Web browser. (A discussion of ActiveX Document creation follows, but addi-

tional detail can be found in Chapter 12.) An ActiveX Document EXE is
essentially an ActiveX EXE with one or more **UserDocument** objects.

ActiveX EXE

An ActiveX EXE can do most anything that a standard EXE can do except
that it cannot contain an MDIForm object. It can, however, do some things
that a standard EXE cannot do: It can contain **UserDocument** objects and it
can have public classes. Unlike a standard EXE, it has no default startup object
and the start mode is always an ActiveX component. If the EXE is to be used
on the Web, it cannot have Form objects and if it is to be run outside of a
browser, it cannot have user documents.

When you create an ActiveX EXE project, VB automatically adds a class with
a single property: **Instancing**.

The *Instancing* Property

The **Instancing** property determines whether a publicly available class can be
created outside the scope of the current project and, if so, how it can be uti-
lized. The settings are listed here:

➤ 1 **Private:** The class is for internal use only and other applications
cannot create instances of it.

➤ 2 **PublicNotCreatable:** Other applications can access the class but only
if it is first created by the application. Other applications cannot create
instances of the class.

➤ 3 **SingleUse:** Other applications can create the class but, in doing so,
they create a new instance of the ActiveX component. (Not allowed in
ActiveX DLL projects.)

➤ 4 **GlobalSingleUse:** Same as **SingleUse** except that properties and
methods of the class are invoked as though they are public functions.
(Not allowed in ActiveX DLL projects.)

➤ 5 **MultiUse:** Other applications can create the class but only one
instance of the ActiveX component is created.

➤ 6 **GlobalMultiUse:** Same as **MultiUse** except that properties and
methods of the class are invoked as though they are public functions.
The class does not need to be explicitly created—this happens automatically when a function is invoked.

Forms In An Active EXE project

An out-of-process server (recall that Active EXE components are always out-of-process servers) can show both *modal* and *modeless* forms. A modal form prevents any other process within the application from continuing until the form is closed. A typical example is a message box, which requires the user to close it before doing anything else in the application. (In Windows, there is also a *system modal* window, which prevents any application from being used until the window is closed. However, Visual Basic does not support this. The VB modal is often called *application modal* outside of Visual Basic.) A modeless form is one that has no mode—processing can continue while the form is open.

Visual Basic supports modality with optional arguments to the **Show** method of the Form and MDIForm objects:

```
object.Show style, owner
```

In this example, *object* is the Form or MDIForm being opened. *Style* is either 0 (modeless) or 1 (modal). Alternatively, you can use the VB constants **vbModeless** or **vbModal**. *Owner* refers to the "owner" of the Form that is being opened. This would be most useful with child forms which Visual Basic does not support. (Most Windows development tools support the concept of a "child window" which is "owned" by a main window. With this type of relationship, if the main window closes, all child windows close also.) In VB, each Form object owns itself, so you should leave the argument blank or use the **Me** keyword.

 Me is a move in the right direction towards true object-orientation for Visual Basic. You can use **Me** as a convenient way to call a procedure in another module that expects a form as an argument. Assume that a standard module contains a procedure to set the font for controls on a form. You might call the procedure with the syntax: **SetFont Me**.

Enumeration

You can use a process, called *enumeration*, to create publicly available constants. In the case of the VB constants **vbModal** and **vbModeless**, you may wish to expose your own set of constants to other processes that use your ActiveX server. (This is a good idea because the application may be used from within a development environment other than Visual Basic, which would not "know" what **vbModal** and **vbModeless** mean.) You enumerate your own constants with the **Enum** keyword. By adding the following code to the class in your ActiveX server that VB automatically generates, the new constants **enuModal** and **enuModeless** become part of the "global name space" of the ActiveX EXE (entries made to the global name space of a server are available to all applications). The following code should be added to the Declarations section of the class:

```
Public Enum enuModality
  enuModal = vbModal
  enuModeless = vbModeless
End Enum
```

Each **Enum** must have a name. In this case, the name is **enuModality** (the "enu" prefix is my naming convention that specifies the variables as enumerated constants). The Visual Basic online books show a very similar example (see "Showing Forms From The CoffeeMonitor Class") but recommend against the use of a prefix to indicate enumeration. It is a matter of personal preference and will not affect the application's behavior.

The project has no startup module since it is an out-of-process server. Applications that invoke services of the ActiveX EXE actually invoke one of its classes. If a form is to be loaded, it must be done from a class within the server.

Testing An ActiveX EXE

Because an ActiveX EXE runs out-of-process, it cannot be tested from within the same Visual Basic environment in which it is being developed. (Put another way, the ActiveX EXE cannot run within the same memory space as the Visual Basic development environment.) To test the EXE, you need to create another instance of Visual Basic. Further, because it is an out-of-process server, the second instance of Visual Basic needs to have a reference to the ActiveX component in the same way that you need to reference other ActiveX EXE servers, such as Microsoft Word and Microsoft Excel. This further implies that before you can test the ActiveX EXE, it needs to be compiled. I will walk through this critical process with a simple example application.

Figure 9.7 shows a very simple application that displays a form with a RichTextBox ActiveX control (supplied with Visual Basic) and a menu to supply basic word processing services. The name of the form is **frmRTF**. The project also has one class, **clsRTF**. The name of the project is "ActXRTF." On the project options dialog, I specified a Project Type of ActiveX EXE. For Start Mode I have specified ActiveX Component. This indicates that when the application is started, it becomes an ActiveX server. Stand Alone (the other option for Start Mode) indicates that the program is independent of any other process. The project options dialog also allows the specification of Remote

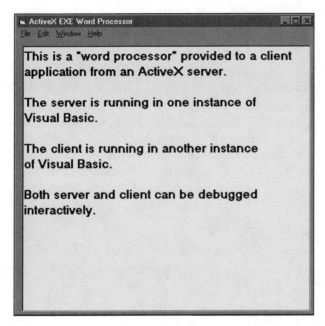

Figure 9.7   A client invoking a service from an ActiveX server.

Server Files (Enterprise edition only), which creates the necessary files to allow the ActiveX EXE to be an ActiveX server on a remote computer.

The following code opens **frmRTF** from **clsRTF**. It is a sub within **clsRTF**.

```
Public Sub ShowRTF
    Dim frmNew As New frmRTF
    frmNew.Show
End Sub
```

When another application needs a "word processor," it can invoke the **ShowRTF** method, as I will discuss in a moment.

The form needs to reference the class. This is done first by creating a public variable within the Declarations section of the form:

```
Private ActXRTF As clsRTF
```

The variable **ActXRTF** becomes a reference for the class **clsRTF**. When the form is loaded, a new instance of the class is created with the following code placed in the **Form_Load** event:

```
Set ActXRTF = New clsRTF
```

To use the ActiveX server, another application must be created to call it. If you are going to use Microsoft Word as an ActiveX server, you will need to reference it using Tools|References from the VB menu and then check Microsoft Word. I had to do the same thing in the test application that I created in Figure 9.7. As seen in Figure 9.8, I added a reference to **ActXRTF**. Before a component is available as a reference, it needs to be compiled. Visual Basic then adds the ActiveX server to the list of available references.

After I compiled the project, I ran a second instance of Visual Basic and created a new project using the Standard EXE project type (a standard Visual Basic application). I added a form with one command button. In the form's declaration section, I added a reference to the class within the ActiveX server:

```
Dim actXTest As clsRTF
```

In the form's **Load** event, I added a reference to the ActiveX Server references in Figure 9.8:

```
Set ActXTest = New clsRTF
```

On the command button's **Click** event, I added the following code to invoke the services of the ActiveX server using the variable I just created:

```
ActXTest.ShowRTF
```

ShowRTF is the name of the procedure on the server that loads the "word processor" form. The result can be seen in Figure 9.7.

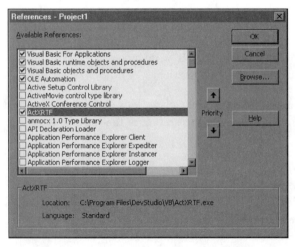

Figure 9.8 Adding a reference to the ActiveX component.

At this point, both client and server can be debugged as needed. Once the ActiveX EXE has been fully tested, it is no longer necessary to run a second instance of Visual Basic.

 Knowing how to run multiple instances of Visual Basic, creating an ActiveX server, and testing the ActiveX server is a critical pathway to passing the Certification Exam.

ActiveX Document EXE

To create an ActiveX Document EXE, select File|New from the VB menu and choose ActiveX Document EXE. You will be presented with a screen that looks like any standard EXE except that the "form" is now called a **UserDocument**. ActiveX documents have most of the events of a Form object, but not all. Unlike a Form object, the ActiveX document—called a **UserDocument**—does not have the following events:

➤ Activate

➤ Deactivate

➤ LinkClose

➤ LinkError

➤ LinkExecute

➤ LinkOpen

➤ Load

➤ QueryUnload

➤ Unload

However, it does have these events, which a Form object does not have:

➤ AsyncReadComplete

➤ EnterFocus

➤ ExitFocus

➤ Hide

➤ InitProperties

➤ ReadProperties

➤ Scroll

➤ Show

➤ WriteProperties

Unlike the Form object, **UserDocument** does not have the **Show** method.

You can place any control on a **UserDocument** object except embedded objects (such as Microsoft Word document) or an OLE Container control.

The finished application runs inside of a Web browser. To test it, run the application from the VB development environment. When you do, your user document(s) are saved with the extension .VBD. (There is no visible component of the application within the VB development environment.) Next, you need to launch Internet Explorer 3.0 or a later version (Internet Explorer is included on the CD-ROM with Visual Basic). Figure 9.9 shows a small database application that I wrote to run within Internet Explorer 4.0. Its menu has been merged with Internet Explorer's menu. When the ActiveX document is running, the client machine is termed the container—it contains the document.

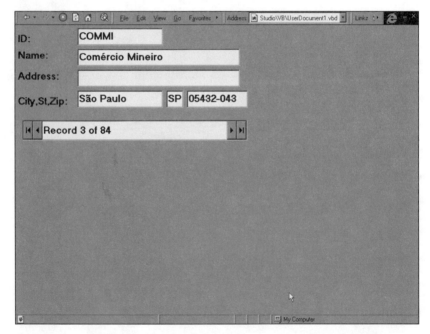

Figure 9.9 An ActiveX document running within a Web browser.

Navigating ActiveX Documents

In a standard EXE project, it is easy to open multiple forms by using the **Show** method of forms. You cannot do this in an ActiveX Document EXE project. The browser determines which documents to open. Instead, you must link from one document to another via a hyperlink, as you would move between Web pages. However, the project is an actual application. The **UserDocument** needs to be able to control the navigation to another document. Visual Basic supplies the **Hyperlink** object for this purpose.

Before proceeding, you need to understand how Visual Basic handles directories in an ActiveX Document EXE project. When running an application in the development environment, VB creates a VBD file for each document in the VB directory. However, when you compile the project, you have more latitude about where the VBD files are located. VB's default is to place them in the application's executable directory. If you accept this default behavior, you can reference the application's **App.Path** property and the file name with the **Hyperlink** object's **NavigateTo** method. If you install the VBD files into a different directory, you will need to hardcode the path to the VBD files.

Here is an example of navigating to another document:

```
UserDocument.Hyperlink.NavigateTo App.Path & "UserDocument2.vbd"
```

The **Hyperlink** object has two other methods: **GoBack** and **GoForward**. Each operates as you would expect, going backward or forward through the Web document history in the same manner as Internet Explorer operates. You should be sure to perform error checking in case there is no history item, as shown in the following example:

```
On Error GoTo NoPage
UserDocument.HyperLink.GoBack
Exit Sub
NoPage:
Resume Next
```

Adding Properties To An ActiveX Document

As with an ActiveX control, you can customize an ActiveX Document by adding and exposing properties. To do so, you need to add a declaration for a variable to the Declarations section of the document:

```
Public myProperty As String
```

Once you have added the variable, you can create the **Property Get** and **Property Let** procedures. Alternatively, you can select Tools|Add Procedure from the VB menu, supply the name of the variable, and Visual Basic will create the procedures for you. You can also use the same dialog to add methods and events to the document.

You can read properties from and save properties to the property bag in the same manner as you do with an ActiveX control. See "The PropertyBag Object" earlier in this chapter.

Debugging The ActiveX Document EXE
Debugging an ActiveX Document is almost the same as debugging a standard EXE project. You can set breakpoints, use the Intermediate window, and so on. However, you need to keep in mind that using the VB development environment to terminate an ActiveX document EXE application that is running within a browser will cause an error in the browser and possibly make the operating system unstable. Therefore, you should refrain from any debugging activities that could cause the project to be reset (which causes the application to end and restart). The most common example of this is when altering declaration statements, particularly for variables.

Converting Form-Based Projects To User Document-Based Components
You may have already written an application that you wish to convert for use on the Internet or perhaps to run locally within a Web browser. Visual Basic makes this easy through the use of the ActiveX Document Migration Wizard, available from the Add-Ins menu in VB. The wizard essentially does all the work for you, converting your forms to user documents (the forms are not destroyed). If there is any incompatible code, VB will comment it out and will optionally generate a text file outlining what steps need to be completed before the application can run as an ActiveX Document EXE.

ActiveX DLL
The final type of ActiveX component is the ActiveX DLL. Unlike an ActiveX EXE, an ActiveX DLL is an in-process server, which means that it runs in the same memory space as the application invoking its services. (This is true of all DLLs, whether they are ActiveX components or not.)

To create an ActiveX DLL project, select File|New from the VB menu. You then have the option of creating an ActiveX DLL or an ActiveX Document

DLL. The differences between the two are essentially the same as with an ActiveX EXE and an ActiveX Document EXE. The ActiveX DLL can contain forms but not user documents. The ActiveX Document DLL can contain user documents but not forms. See my previous discussions of ActiveX EXEs and ActiveX Document EXEs for more information.

ActiveX DLLs normally do not have a startup module. However, if you need to perform some initializations, you can do so in a **Sub Main ()** procedure. This is an option in the Project Options dialog.

Because the ActiveX DLL runs in the same memory space as the application invoking its methods, you can test both in the same instance of Visual Basic. To do so, add a second project (normally the project type would be Standard EXE) to the ActiveX DLL project. Make the new project the startup project. If the ActiveX DLL is not an ActiveX document, you can test it in the same manner as you would an ActiveX EXE, discussed earlier in this chapter. Otherwise, test it in the same manner as an ActiveX Document EXE.

ActiveX DLLs are persistent, which means they stay in memory until all applications have released references to them. When this occurs, the DLL will unload and all memory will be released.

Because ActiveX technology is such a key piece of Visual Basic, the topic is widely discussed throughout the book. Chapter 4 expands on the discussion of classes. Chapter 8 discusses the use of key ActiveX controls in your project. Chapter 12 delves deeper into the subject of ActiveX and the Internet. Chapter 14 expands on the subject of compilation and Chapter 15 covers distribution.

Exam Prep Questions

Question 1

> An ActiveX server is: [Check the best answer]
>
> ○ a. An in-process server.
>
> ○ b. An out-of-process server.
>
> ○ c. Either an in-process server or an out-of-process server.
>
> ○ d. An in-process server unless the ActiveX component is defined as a standard EXE.

Answer c is correct. If the ActiveX server is a DLL, it is an in-process server. If it is an EXE, it is an out-of-process server. Answer a is incorrect because an ActiveX server is not necessarily an in-process server. Answer b is incorrect because an ActiveX server is not necessarily an out-of-process server. Answer d is incorrect because an ActiveX server can never be defined as a standard EXE.

Question 2

> When invoking a service of an in-process server, how does communication proceed?
>
> ○ a. In a manner consistent with the **Connect** object's **Async** property
>
> ○ b. Asynchronously regardless of any other settings
>
> ○ c. Syncopathically
>
> ○ d. Synchronously unless the **Async** property is set to **True**

Answer b is correct—any communications with an in-process server occur asynchronously. Do not let the rest of the statement "regardless of any other settings" throw you—it is totally irrelevant. Answer a is incorrect because there is no **Async** property. Answer c is incorrect because there is no such communication mode as "syncopathically." Answer d is incorrect because there is no **Async** property and because communications are never synchronous with an in-process server.

Question 3

> What VB controls have a **Container** property and can thus act as a
> container for other VB controls? [Check all correct answers]
>
> ❏   a. ActiveX controls
>
> ❏   b. PictureBox controls
>
> ❏   c. Image controls
>
> ❏   d. Frame controls
>
> ❏   e. Form objects

Answers b and d are correct. The PictureBox control and Form object can act as containers for other controls. Answer a is incorrect because an ActiveX control (which is a **UserControl** object plus any other controls added to it) does not have a **Container** property and thus cannot act as a container for other controls. Likewise, answer c is incorrect because the Image control cannot act as a container for other controls. Answer e is also incorrect. Though you place controls on a form, it also does not have a **Container** property and is not a container for controls.

Question 4

Assume that the ActiveX control **myControl** has three text boxes named **text1**, **text2**, and **text3** and that the control is placed on a form named **form1**. Which code snippet will initialize or restore the **Text** properties of the three text boxes?

○ a.
```
Private Sub UserControl_ReadProperties _
   (Stuff As PropertyBag)
      text1 = Stuff.ReadProperty _
         ("text_one", "ABC")
      text2 = Stuff.ReadProperty _
         ("text_two", "DEF")
      text3 = Stuff.ReadProperty _
         ("text_three", "GHI")
End Sub
```

○ b.
```
Private Sub UserControl_Initialize _
   (PropBag As PropertyBag)
      text1 = PropBag.ReadProperties _
         ("text_one", "ABC")
      text2 = PropBag.ReadProperties _
         ("text_two", "DEF")
      text3 = PropBag.ReadProperties _
         ("text_three", "GHI")
End Sub
```

○ c.
```
Private Sub UserControl_Initialize
   Open "values.txt" For Input As #1
   Input #1, text1
   Input #1, text2
   Input #1, text3
   Close 1
End Sub
```

○ d.
```
Private Sub UserControl_GetProperties _
   (Properties As StoredProps)
      text1 = Properties (0)
      text2 = Properties (1)
      text3 = Properties (2)
End Sub
```

Answer a is correct even though the syntax looks odd. After an ActiveX control initializes, its *ReadProperties* event occurs. The *PropertyBag* object becomes available at that point and is automatically passed to the event as an argument. VB defaults to casting the object as variable *PropBag* but the code snippet shown has changed the variable name to *Stuff*. The renamed variable is then used in the code statements that look for stored keys "text_one", "text_two", and "text_three". If not found, the defaults "ABC", "DEF", and "GHI" are used. This is all perfectly valid. Answer b is incorrect because it uses the control's **Initialize** event to populate the text boxes. The **PropertyBag** object is not available at that time. Answer c is incorrect although it could conceivably work if the file "values.txt" existed. However, that cannot be guaranteed and reading values from a file is not the most efficient way to set the properties, in any case. Answer d is incorrect because there is no **GetProperties** event and there is no **Properties** object. The trick to this question is the confusing manner in which the correct choice, a, was written and the fact that the **PropertyBag** is being used for an unusual purpose (to set the text attributes of embedded controls). However, if you are well versed on how to use the **PropertyBag** object to save and retrieve properties of the control between uses, you should be able to quickly eliminate other choices and come up with the correct answer.

Question 5

> You have created an ActiveX control to be used in non-Visual Basic development environments. How do you provide the user of the control (the developer) a means to customize the properties of the control at development time?
>
> ○ a. Because the control will be used in non-VB projects, the developer will be forced to set the properties of the control at runtime in code. The properties cannot be made available at development time.
>
> ○ b. Use the ActiveX Control Migration Wizard to add Visual Basic's Property dialog as a hidden control on the ActiveX control. The developer will then be able to right-click on the Property control to set the properties.
>
> ○ c. Add one or more **PropertyPage** objects to the control. On each **PropertyPage**, add type-appropriate controls (such as a checkbox for true/false values) and code to read and set the ActiveX control's properties.
>
> ○ d. ActiveX controls created in Visual Basic 5 cannot be used in projects outside of Visual Basic.

Answer c is correct. To expose properties of the ActiveX control in non-VB projects, create property pages in which you code the logic to set the properties of the ActiveX control. Answer a is incorrect because the properties of the control *are* available at design time in non-VB projects. Answer b is incorrect because there is no ActiveX Control Migration Wizard and there is no hidden Property control that can be added to an ActiveX control. Answer d is incorrect because ActiveX controls created in Visual Basic can be used in any development environment that supports ActiveX controls. This includes Microsoft Visual C++, Powersoft PowerBuilder, Borland Delphi, and many others.

Question 6

Assume you have created an ActiveX DLL. What is the best way to test it?

○ a. Compile the ActiveX DLL. Then, create the appropriate **Declare** statement to invoke any of the ActiveX DLL's exposed procedures. (You cannot invoke any procedures declared as **Private**.)

○ b. Add to the ActiveX DLL project a standard EXE project. In the new project, declare a reference to a class object within the ActiveX DLL and invoke (from the standard EXE) procedures of the class.

○ c. Run the ActiveX DLL from within the Visual Basic environment. Then, open Microsoft Explorer and open the VBD file created when the ActiveX DLL is run.

○ d. Run the ActiveX DLL from within the Visual Basic environment. Then, open a second instance of Visual Basic and create a standard EXE project that references the ActiveX DLL.

Answer b is correct. Because an ActveX DLL is an in-process server, it can be tested in the same instance of the Visual Basic development environment as the application that is using it. The standard EXE merely declares a reference to the class object in the ActiveX DLL. Then, it uses the reference obtained to invoke procedures of the class. Answer a is incorrect because you cannot use **Declare** to make references to an ActiveX DLL as you would to non-ActiveX DLLs. Answer c is incorrect because you cannot "run" an ActiveX DLL in the development environment and VB does not generate a VBD file as it does for ActiveX Document EXEs. Answer d is incorrect because you do not need to create a second instance of the VB development environment as you would with out-of-process servers.

Need To Know More?

 Aitken, Peter: *Visual Basic 5 Programming EXplorer*. Coriolis Group Books, Scottsdale, AZ, 1997. ISBN 1-57610-065-0. Chapter 6 introduces OLE, COM, and ActiveX, and discusses Visual Basic's project types. It then walks through the process of creating ActiveX components.

 Harrington, John, Mark Spenik, Heidi Brumbaugh, and Cliff Diamond: *Visual Basic 5 Interactive Course*. Waite Group Press, Corte Madera, CA, 1997. ISBN 1-57169-077-8. Chapter 16 provides an overview of the process of creating ActiveX controls. Appendix B provides an overview of Internet Explorer.

 Jamsa, Kris and Lars Klander: *1001 Visual Basic Programmer's Tips*. Jamsa Press, Las Vegas, NV, 1997. ISBN 1-884133-56-8. This well-done book is not broken into chapters but rather into "tips." Tips 600 through 603 introduce the concepts of ActiveX technology. Tips 801 through 871 provide a fairly thorough overview of creating ActiveX controls, ActiveX EXEs, and ActiveX DLLs, as well as how to use all three.

 Mandelbrot Set, The: *Advanced Microsoft Visual Basic*. Microsoft Press, Redmond, WA, 1997. ISBN 1-57231-414-1. This book is broken into sections written by various authors (they are not listed on the cover). In Chapter 15, Chris Debelliot and Steve Overall discuss advanced subjects in ActiveX control design, property bag usage, and more. In Chapter 3, Clive Hubbard discusses ActiveX EXEs and ActiveX DLLs. Several other chapters discuss ActiveX technology relating to other subjects, such as in Chapter 5 where Kevin Houston explores ActiveX controls while discussing migration (from Visual Basic 4) issues.

 McKinney, Bruce: *Hardcore Visual Basic, Second Edition* (which covers version 5). Microsoft Press, Redmond, WA, 1997. ISBN 1-57231-422-2. Chapter 10 of this excellent book covers COM in depth. Bruce also covers the exploitation of ActiveX technology throughout the book, particularly in Chapter 3 (pages 128 through 132).

Swartzfager, Gene: *Visual Basic 5 Object-Oriented Programming*. The Coriolis Group, Scottsdale, AZ 1997. ISBN 1-57610-106-1. This very well-written book discusses ActiveX technology throughout most chapters: Chapter 3 discusses the creation of ActiveX EXEs and ActiveX DLLs; Chapter 4 discusses using a form in an ActiveX component; Chapter 5 discusses the public interface of ActiveX components, and so on.

 Search the online books on the VB CD for the term "ActiveX." There are numerous chapters dealing with the subject including step-by-step "how-to's" detailing the creation and use of various ActiveX components.

 Microsoft places the most current KnowledgeBase online at www.microsoft.com/support/. Enter search terms such as "ActiveX" to view articles detailing tips (and sometimes fixes) concerning compilation and distribution. Also, explore the site for new ActiveX controls that can be used in your projects.

 Use any popular search engine such as www.yahoo.com, www.hotbot.com, and so on, to locate many articles on ActiveX technology, as well as sources of ActiveX controls. Use the terms "+Visual +Basic +ActiveX" to return a large listing. (The search criteria will vary at different sites. The plus sign is usually used to denote that the word must appear in the search result. Placing quotes around "Visual Basic" will generally force the requirement that the two words appear together. Use the search engine's Help page for hints on narrowing your searches.)

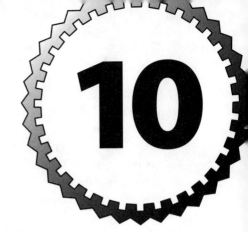

Data Handling

Terms you'll need to understand:

√ Open and Close

√ Output, Input, Append, Random, and Binary

√ Structured Query Language (SQL)

√ Commit and Rollback

√ ODBC, ODBCDirect, and Microsoft Jet

√ RecordSet

√ Workspace

√ DAO and RDO

√ QueryDef

√ DBEngine

√ Transaction

√ Asynchronous

√ Data control

√ Data bound controls

√ RecordCount

√ RecordSetType

√ Dynaset-, snapshot-, table-type recordsets

Techniques you'll need to master:

√ Opening and closing flat files

√ Understanding the use of SQL

√ Committing and rolling back changes to the database

√ Managing a transaction

√ Creating and manipulating DAO objects

√ Creating and manipulating RDO objects

√ Using the Data control

√ Using data bound controls

√ Moving around in and manipulating recordsets

√ Choosing an appropriate workspace

The ultimate purpose of any program is to handle data, whether that data is an employee record or a file to be compressed. It should be no surprise then that this chapter will provide you with a big bang for your exam buck, because a relatively important portion of the exam is on this crucial topic. In general, data handling refers to your ability to access a file and process it. Of more importance is your ability to open a database via the *ODBC* (Open Database Connectivity) standard, manipulate a dynaset, use the Data control, and so on.

The Nature Of Data

Not so many years ago, all data was stored in sequential files, often on magnetic tape. These files consisted of fixed length records and, within the records, fixed length fields. That was followed by the navigational model, where you found a record by navigating through a file. The classic example of this is the binary search model often called "B-Tree." This was succeeded by today's relational database model. Visual Basic provides tools to access all three of these data models and, through the use of ODBC, can almost transparently connect to any compliant database. Visual Basic 5 Enterprise edition also includes native drivers to access Microsoft SQL Server and Oracle databases.

Database Basics

Along with the advent of the relational model comes the usual plethora of terms. *RDBMS* refers to any relational database management system. In an RDBMS, data is organized into *tables*, which is analogous to files. We might have a Customer table and an Orders table. A table consists of *columns* and *rows*, which correspond to records and fields. A table has a *primary key*, which is a unique identifier for any row in a table (i.e., a Customer number on the Customer table). *Referential integrity* (RI) refers to a database-enforced mechanism to constrain relationships between tables. For instance, the database can enforce the requirement that all records on the Order table have a valid corresponding customer on the Customer table. A *foreign key* is the mechanism to enforce referential integrity. A foreign key is defined on the Cust_No column in the Orders table "referencing" the primary key of the Customer table, which is, of course, also Cust_No. This is a departure from prior data models, which placed the burden of enforcing such "business rules" on the program instead of the database.

SQL (Structured Query Language) is the language that is used to access the database. There are three types of SQL:

➤ **DDL (Data Definition Language)** Consists of statements that create, alter, and delete the database structures.

➤ **DCL (Data Control Language)** Consists of statements that administer access (that is, security) to the database.

➤ **DML (Data Manipulation Language)** Includes statements to manipulate the data, such as retrieving rows or inserting new rows.

Programs will generally use DML; the *DBA* (Database Administrator) handles the DDL and DCL.

A *query* is a request of the database to supply some data. In other words, we ask the database to *retrieve* certain rows of data from one or more tables in the database, in the form of a SQL **Select**. The database engine then processes the SQL statement and sends the answer set to the requesting program. The SQL **Select** statement is the one your application will perform most often. SQL syntax is outside of the scope of this book. Depending on the **Workspace** (the **Workspace** object is discussed in "Data Access Objects," later in this chapter) you choose, you can opt to have Visual Basic shield you from the need to write SQL statements yourself. For instance, if you connect a Data control to a database, the SQL syntax to move from record to record or to update a record can be generated behind the scenes.

If you do write your own SQL statements, the four that you are most likely to use (**Select, Insert, Delete**, and **Update**) are listed in the sections that follow.

An *index* is an object that can be created on the database to speed access to a table. For instance, we can create an index on the Cust_Last_Name column of the Customers table to speed **Select**s based on a customer's last name or to sort a report by last name. Indexes may be defined as *unique*, meaning that no duplicate values are allowed, or *non-unique*, meaning that duplicate values are allowed.

A *client/server* environment is one in which a client program (for instance, the Visual Basic application) is running as a separate process from the database. Generally, the database *engine* is a separate program running on a remote server connected to the client by some sort of network. For instance, a database such as Microsoft SQL Server runs as a separate program, "listening" for requests from client programs.

Two of the most powerful aspects of programming with SQL are the ability to manage *transactions* and to discard or make permanent changes to the database.

Transaction management is beyond the scope of the book but, in brief, it refers to two concepts. The first is the length of time that an "active" connection to the database is maintained. Because resources on a database are limited, you generally want to keep the duration of a transaction as brief as possible. Transaction management also refers to the issue of *concurrency*. Concurrency problems arise when two or more users are trying to update the same record at the same time.

SQL supports the **Rollback** and **Commit** keywords to discard all changes made to the database during the current transaction or to make them permanent. A transaction ends when either a **Rollback** or **Commit** is issued. Generally, if you are updating SQL tables, you will want to make sure that the updates worked (that is, there were no errors) and, if they did not, you will want to issue a **Rollback**.

The *Select* Statement

Select is the most commonly used SQL statement. The syntax is as follows:

```
Select column1, column2, ... | *
From table1, table2, ...
[Where condition1, condition2, ...]
[Group By column1, column2, ...]
[Having condition1, condition2, ...]
[Order By column1, column2, ...]
```

The only two clauses required are the **Select** and **From** clauses. After **Select**, you must provide a comma-separated list of columns that you wish to be returned by the database. If you want all columns to be returned, you may use the asterisk (*) as an abbreviation (**Select * From…**). The **From** clause is used to supply a comma-separated list of tables from which to obtain the columns. If more than one table is listed, you need to provide a *join* to tell the database how the two tables are related. For instance, if you list the Customer and Orders tables, you need to join them by the column that they have in common (the Cust_No column). You do this in the **Where** clause (**…Where Customer.Cust_No = Orders.CustNo…**). You also use the **Where** clause to supply other selection criteria to specify the row(s) that you want returned from the database. For instance, if you wanted only female customers, you might specify:

```
Where Customer.Gender = 'F'
```

The **Group By** clause is optional and specifies how you want to summarize rows in the report if you are performing functions on the data. SQL allows you, in your **Select** clause, to apply functions to individual columns such as Sum (**Select Sum (Orders_Amount) From…**). The **Having** clause allows you to further restrict rows by specifying that only those results of functions meeting certain conditions be returned. For instance, if you wanted only those orders totaling more than $100, you might specify:

```
... Having Sum(Orders.Amount) > 100
```

The **Order By** clause allows you to sort your result set by providing a comma-separated list of columns to sort by. If you wanted to sort by last name and then by first name, you might specify:

```
... Order by Customer.Last_Name, Customer.First_Name
```

The *Insert* Statement

To add rows to the database, you use the SQL **Insert** statement with the following syntax:

```
Insert Into table [column1, column2 ...]
Values (value1, value2 ...)
```

Table must be a valid table on the database. You supply a comma-separated list of the column names in which to insert the data. If you want to insert data into all of the columns on a table, you may omit the column list. In parentheses, you supply a comma-separated list of the actual values, surrounding non-numeric data with single quotes.

The *Delete* Statement

The SQL **Delete** statement is used to delete rows (records) from the database. It takes the syntax:

```
Delete From table
[Where condition1, condition2 ...]
```

You specify one table from which to delete row(s). The **Where** clause specifies what row(s) to delete such as:

```
Delete From Customer Where Customer.Cust_No = 1018
```

If you omit the **Where** clause, all rows are deleted.

The *Update* Statement

The SQL **Update** statement allows you to update one or more columns on one or more rows of a table. It takes the syntax:

```
Update table
SET column1 = value1, column2  = value2…
[Where conition1, condition2 ...]
```

You must provide a valid table name, along with one or more columns to alter. The **Where** clause specifies what row(s) to update and, if omitted, causes all rows to be altered. The **Set** clause tells SQL what columns to update. To change the gender of a customer in the table, you might specify:

```
Update Customer Set Gender = 'M' Where Customer.Cust_No = 1018
```

Visual Basic And Flat Files

For purposes of this discussion, a *flat file* is any file that is accessed directly (i.e., without using a Visual Basic control, such as the Data control, or through a database engine). For instance, if we open a text file and read it using the **Input** keyword, the text file is a flat file.

Visual Basic allows you to process flat files either *sequentially* or *randomly*. When a file is read sequentially, the program reads or writes one record at a time and cannot directly access any record in the file without first reading all prior records in the file. Random access allows the program to directly access any individual record or byte in the file.

In order to access a file, it must first be opened using the **Open** keyword. The syntax is as follows:

```
Open filename For mode [Access access] [lock] _
    As [#] filenumber [Len = record length]
```

You must supply a fully qualified file name, including the path to the file if appropriate. *Mode* refers to how the file is to be processed. The options are listed in Table 10.1. In **Random** mode, you must also supply a *record length*, because file access is done by supplying the record number within the file. Therefore, all records must be of the same length. **Binary** mode allows you to move to any byte within the file by supplying a byte *offset* relative to the beginning of the file. Supplying a *record length* has no effect. *Record length* cannot be supplied in any of the sequential modes (**Append**, **Input**, and **Output**). If the file does not exist, **Append**, **Binary**, **Output**, and **Random** cause the file to be created.

Access is optional. If not supplied, the file is opened as **Read Write**, meaning that the file may be read from or written to. If **Read** is specified, the file may be read but not updated. If **Write** is specified, the file may be updated but not read.

Table 10.1	Visual Basic file open modes.
Mode	**Usage**
Append	File is opened for sequential output. Any output is added to the end of the file.
Binary	File is opened for random input/output. A byte offset into the file must be supplied.
Input	File is opened for sequential input.
Output	File is opened for sequential output. Any output overwrites the file.
Random	Default setting. File is opened for random input/output. A record offset and record length must be supplied.

Lock is also optional and specifies what access to the file other processes may use. Valid values are:

➤ **Shared**

➤ **Lock Read**

➤ **Lock Write**

➤ **Lock Read Write**

The file number, called a *file handle*, must be a value between 1 and 511. Further activity against the file is done by referencing the file number. You may use the **FreeFile** function to obtain a file number. **FreeFile** returns a number between 1 and 255. You may provide an optional argument, "1," (**FreeFile (1)**) to return a number from 256 to 511. Unlike earlier versions of Visual Basic, the pound sign (#) preceding the file number is optional.

Each file opened must be closed using the **Close** statement. You can provide the file number as an argument to specify which file to close (**Close #1**). Omitting the argument causes all currently opened files to be closed.

To read a file opened sequentially, use the **Input** statement

```
Input #1, myVar
```

where *myVar* is a valid Visual Basic variable into which the record is stored. Visual Basic will read data from the current position in the file, up to the first comma or carriage return/line feed characters. If a comma is embedded in quotes, everything within the quotes is read. A variation on **Input** is **Line**

Input, which causes Visual Basic to read everything until a carriage return/line feed sequence. To write to a file opened sequentially, use the **Write** statement:

```
Write #1, myVar
```

If the file was opened for **Output,** the file is overwritten (all data is destroyed). If the file was opened for **Append,** the record is written to the end of the file. To read from a file opened for **Random** or **Binary,** use the **Get** statement

```
Get #1, position, myVar
```

where *position* is a record number (in **Random** mode) or byte number (in **Binary** mode) in the file. If *position* is omitted, Visual Basic reads the next record or byte. In the case of **Random,** *myVar* must be a variable with a length at least two bytes longer than the **Len** specified in the **Open** statement. Visual Basic reads one record and puts it into *myVar.* In the case of **Binary,** Visual Basic uses the length of *myVar* to determine how much data to read. If *myVar* is a fixed length string of 256 characters, Visual Basic places 256 characters beginning at *position* into *myVar.* To write to a file opened as **Random** or **Binary,** use

```
Put, position, myVar
```

where *position* is the record or byte offset into the file. If omitted, data is written from the current position in the file. If the length of the variable is less than **Len** in **Random** mode, the record is padded with spaces. If the length is greater than **Len,** a runtime error occurs.

Visual Basic And Database Access

Visual Basic provides many methodologies and controls to access data. Microsoft Jet is the most commonly used method to access the database, but you may use *ODBC Direct* instead. The Visual Basic SQL Libraries (VBSQL) provide a *direct connection* to Microsoft SQL Server. (When using Microsoft Jet or ODBCDirect, Visual Basic communicates with the database through a series of drivers. With VBSQL, Visual Basic communicates directly with the database without the use of intermediary drivers. Sometimes, this is called a *native connection.* Generally, direct connections are somewhat more efficient.)

Visual Basic provides the ability to place a Data control that lets your program quickly and easily manipulate the database. Although this provides a very rapid method to develop a database application, it is also somewhat less functional than what can be done in program code. In the following sections, I will discuss the various methods of accessing and manipulating databases.

The Visual Basic certification exam puts a lot of emphasis on these topics. Although no areas are less important than others, my experience indicates that the areas most likely to be questioned are those involving the **RecordSet** object and, more generally, the Data Access Objects (DAO).

Data Access Objects

Data Access Objects (DAO) are a collection of different object types used to connect to and manipulate the database.

There are 17 different DAO objects, each of which has collections, methods, and properties. The objects represent a hierarchy with the **DBEngine** object being the "highest" or "top" object. **DBEngine** has three collections, one of which is **Workspaces**. Each **Workspace** object, in turn, has four collections, each of which also has "lower" collections. It is roughly analogous to the **Forms** collection discussed in Chapter 4. Each member of **Forms** has a **Controls** collection. Because they are valid Visual Basic collections, they can be iterated as outlined in Chapter 4 (see the section titled "The Collection Class"). The objects hierarchy is shown in Figure 10.1.

I will discuss the key DAO objects in the following sections.

Key DAO Objects

Figure 10.1 illustrates how the DAO objects relate to one another. Although you can write effective applications without fully appreciating all aspects of this hierarchy, the more you understand, the better equipped you are to write programs that access the database efficiently and with flexibility.

As we review the key DAO objects, we will keep an eye towards those items you are likely to see on the certification exam.

The *DBEngine* Object

Unlike other DAO objects, there can be only one **DBEngine** object. All other DAO objects are derived from **DBEngine**. It has three collections: **Properties**, **Errors**, and **Workspaces**.

One of **DBEngine**'s properties is **DefaultType**, which provides a default every time a new **Workspace** is created. Valid values are **dbUseJet** and **dbUseODBC** (see "The Workspaces Collection" later in this chapter). The **DefaultUser** and

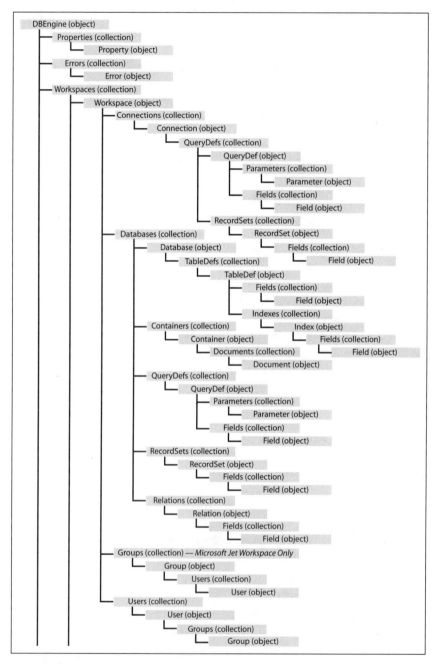

Figure 10.1 The DAO hierarchy.

DefaultPassWord properties provide a default user and default password to use when connecting to the default **Workspace**.

The **CreateWorkspace** method creates a new **Workspace** object (which becomes part of the **Workspaces** collection). You may override the **DefaultType**, **DefaultUser**, and **DefaultPassword** properties by specifying the optional arguments. The syntax is:

```
Set workspacename = CreateWorkSpace (workspacename [,user] _
    [,password] [,type])
```

You supply *workspacename* to name the **Workspace** object.

The **OpenDatabase** method opens a database using the following syntax:

```
Set database = [workspace.]OpenDatabase (dbname [,options] _
    [,read-only] [,connect])
```

Database is the name of a valid **Database** object within *Workspace*. The string *dbName* is the database to open. *Options* is either **True** or **False** for a Microsoft Jet workspace; **True** indicates that the database should be opened in *exclusive* (single-user) mode. For ODBCDirect workspaces, there are various constants that can be supplied, such as **dbDriverPrompt**, which tells Visual Basic to prompt the user for connection information. See the Visual Basic Help file under "OpenDatabase Method" for more information. To open the database in read-only mode, *read-only* is set to **True**. The *connect* string supplies various connection parameters. These vary by database.

The *Properties* Collection

Every DAO object except **Connection** and **Error** has a **Properties** collection. The collection is comprised of objects of type **Property**. The **Properties** collection object is essentially the properties of the underlying object. For instance, the **Properties** collection of the **DBEngine** object includes **Property** objects that correspond to the **DefaultType** and **DefaultPassword** properties of **DBEngine**.

The **Properties** collection, like most DAO collections, is not *persistent*. A persistent object is "updated" as required. For instance, if you add a new form to your project, the form is added to the **Forms** collection automatically. The **Properties** collection is not persistent—it is created in memory only when needed. Therefore, you need to invoke the collection's **Refresh** method (**Properties.Refresh**) before accessing it to be sure that you have the most current collection of objects.

The only DAO objects that *are* persistent are:

➤ **Connections**

➤ **Databases**

➤ **RecordSets**

➤ **Workspaces**

➤ **Connections** (collection of **QueryDefs** only)

Additionally, each **Property** object itself has four properties. The **Name** property is the name of the underlying property (such as **DefaultType**). The **Type** property returns a Visual Basic constant that indicates the data type of the underlying property. The **Value** property returns a **Variant** with the value of the underlying property. The **Inherited** property returns a boolean indicating whether the property is inherited from another object.

The *Errors* Collection

The **Errors** collection is comprised of **Error** objects. Each DAO operation can result in an error and, when this occurs, a new **Error** object is inserted into the **Errors** collection. It is possible that a single operation can result in multiple errors. For instance, if you attempt to insert a row into a database before connecting to the database, several errors will occur indicating that the insert failed, that the database is not connected, and so on. Visual Basic refers to these as lower-level and higher-level errors. **Error** objects are inserted in the order in which they are received. Thus, when connecting to an Oracle database via Microsoft Jet, you may get errors from several of the drivers involved. You need to iterate through the **Error** objects to determine their cause and take corrective action.

The **Error** object has several properties. **Description** returns a string describing the error. **Source** contains the name of the object that generated the error. **Number** is a DAO error number similar to the **Err** object's **Number** property. For instance, error number 3006 indicates that the database being accessed is exclusively locked. For a complete list of these error numbers, see "Trappable Microsoft Jet And DAO Errors" in the Visual Basic Help file.

The *Workspaces* Collection

Workspaces is the default property of **DBEngine**. A **Workspace** object represents an active session with a database. There are two types of **Workspace** objects supported by DAO:

➤ Microsoft Jet **Workspace** is used to connect to:

 ➤ Microsoft Jet databases (those created by Microsoft Jet). These databases have an extension of .MDB (Microsoft Access format).

 ➤ Microsoft Jet-connected ODBC (Open Database Connectivity) databases. These are ODBC data sources (defined with the Control Panel's 32-bit ODBC Administrator applet). Virtually all RDBMSs are accessible via ODBC.

 ➤ Installable ISAM (Indexed Sequential Access Method) databases. These are non-relational databases accessed via a driver supplied by Microsoft Jet that allows access using SQL. Examples include Paradox and Btrieve.

➤ ODBCDirect **Workspace** is used to connect to an ODBC database, directly bypassing Microsoft Jet.

A **Workspace** must be opened before being used and must be closed when done. The workspace is opened when created and closed with the **Close** method, as seen in the following code snippet. You have to add each **Workspace** object to the **Workspaces** collection using the **Append** method. The following snippet of code illustrates each of these operations:

```
' declare the Workspace objects
Dim wrkJetExample As Workspace
Dim wrkODBCExample As Workspace
' Create the Jet workspace
Set wrkJetExample = CreateWorkSpace ("MyJetWorkSpace", _
  "dba","sql",dbUseJet)
' Create the ODBCDirect workspace
Set wrkODBCExample = CreateWorkSpace ("MyODBCWorkSpace", _
  "dba","sql",dbUseODBC)
' append the Workspaces to the collection
Workspaces.Append wrkMyJetExample
Workspaces.Append wrkMyODBCExample
' Close them
wrkMyJetExample.Close
wrkMyODBCExample.Close
```

In addition to the **OpenDatabase** method (see "The DBEngine Object" earlier in this chapter), you need to invoke the **OpenConnection** method if you are using ODBCDirect. This allows you (for ODBCDirect only) to have multiple connections to the database using the same workspace. The syntax is as follows:

```
Set connection = [workspace].OpenConnection (name [,options] _
   [,read-only] [,connect])
```

Connection is the name of a previously declared **Connection** object (see the example code snippet that follows). *Workspace* is the name of a valid, already created **Workspace** object. If omitted, the default workspace is used. *Name* is any valid *Data Source Name* (DSN) as defined in the 32-bit ODBC Administrator available in the Control Panel. *Options* contains one or more Visual Basic constants (see "OpenConnect Method" in the Visual Basic Help file) such as **dbDriverPrompt**, which causes the database driver to prompt the user for any missing connection information. If set to **True**, *read-only* causes the database to be opened in read-only mode. *Connect* is a string of selection parameters that varies from database to database. An example of using this method is shown in this code snippet:

```
Dim conMyCon1 As Connection
Dim conMyCon2 As Connection
' this assumes that the workspace is already created
' open the first connection
Set conMyCon1 = wrkMyODBCExample.OpenConnection _
  ("First", dbDriverPrompt, _
  "ODBC;Database=myDBTest;UID=dba;PWD=sql;DSN=myODBCDataSource")
' open a second connection read only
Set conMyCon1 = wrkMyODBCExample.OpenConnection _
  ("First", dbDriverPrompt, True, _
  "ODBC;Database=myDBTest;UID=dba;PWD=sql;DSN=myODBCDataSource")
```

The **Workspace** object has a **BeginTrans** method that enables you to manage transactions. You can then commit or roll back changes made to the database going back to the beginning of the current transaction. A **Commit** or **Rollback** ends the current transaction. To commit changes, use the **CommitTrans** method. To roll back changes, use the **Rollback** method. You can nest transactions within one another and, if you commit changes in the inner transaction, you can roll back the outer transaction, which will "undo" the commit of the inner transaction.

To begin a transaction, specify *workspace*.**BeginTrans** where *workspace* is the name of the valid **Workspace** object. To commit a change, specify *workspace*.**CommitTrans**. To roll back changes, specify *workspace*.**Rollback**. Be careful with ODBCDirect workspaces: A transaction applies to all open **Connection** objects for that workspace. Thus, if you issue a **CommitTrans**, it will commit the changes in *all* **Connection** objects.

The *Connections* Collection

The **Connections** collection is valid for ODBCDirect workspaces only. When you open a connection, a **Database** object is created and appended to the **Databases** collection.

The **OpenRecordSet** method creates a **RecordSet** object. This method is also supported in the **Database, QueryDef, RecordSet**, and **TableDef** objects, but for **Connection** and **Database**, it takes the form:

```
Set recordset = object.OpenRecordSet (source [,type] _
    [,options] [,lockedits])
```

(See "The QueryDefs Collection" later in this chapter for the other syntax of **OpenRecordSet**.) *Recordset* is a valid **RecordSet** object, and *object* is a valid **Connection** or **Database** object. *Source* is a string containing a table name, query name, or an SQL **Select** statement. *Type* is the type of **RecordSet** (see "The RecordSets Collection" later in this chapter). *Options* describes how the **RecordSet** object is to behave and is also documented later in this chapter under "The RecordSets Collection." *Lockedits* takes one of the following Visual Basic constants:

➤ **dbReadOnly** Prevents updates to the RecordSet and is the default with ODBCDirect. This can be used in either options or lockedits, but not both.

➤ **dbPessimistic** Dictates that a database page is to be locked as soon as the RecordSet's Edit method is invoked. This is the default for Microsoft Jet workspaces.

Databases employ different schemes to lock rows when a record is being updated. Most lock an entire *page* at a time. A page is a block whose size is typically defined when the database is created. The page contains multiple rows. Some RDBMSs, most notably Oracle, do row-level locking, which means that only the one row is locked. Microsoft SQL Server 6.5 does *pseudo-row-*level locking, which means that the row immediately prior to and after the current row is also locked.

There are various schemes that determine how *optimistic* the database is about locking. In *pessimistic* locking, the page is locked as soon as it is selected for update. In *optimistic* locking, the page isn't locked until it is being updated. The safest method is to use pessimistic locking because it guarantees that no one can read and subsequently overwrite the changes made to a record. But it can impact performance, because any users

> attempting to access other rows on that page are locked out. Optimistic locking offers better performance but creates concurrency issues because it is possible for two users to "grab" the same record and overwrite each other's changes.

➤ **dbOptimistic** Dictates that the page will not be locked until the **Update** method is invoked.

➤ **dbOptimisticValue** Employs an optimistic locking scheme but then verifies that the rows have not changed between reads and updates. (Available only for ODBCDirect workspaces.)

➤ **dbOptimisticBatch** Employs an optimistic locking scheme using batch updating. (Available only for ODBCDirect workspaces.)

 New to VB5: With ODBCDirect workspaces, you can use a method of updating the database called *batch* updates, where updates are cached in memory for performance reasons. You need to specify **dbOptimisticBatch** and you also need to specify **dbUseClientBatchCursor** for the **DefaultCursorDriver** property of the **Workspace** object to get the benefits of batching.

The **DefaultCursorDriver** property is specified by the **OpenConnection** or **OpenDatabase** methods. An SQL *cursor* is a "pointer" used to move through result sets from SQL queries. In Visual Basic, a **RecordSet** is considered to be a cursor. Various databases and database connection drivers support differing levels of cursor functionality. For instance, some support moving (**Fetch** in SQL vernacular) forward a row, backward a row, to the first row, and to the last row. See "DefaultCursorDriver Property" in the Visual Basic Help file for the different values you can use.

The *QueryDefs* Collection

The **QueryDef** object is an SQL query that returns a record(s) from the database. The result of the query is called a *result set*. If you set the **Name** property of the **QueryDef** object, it is automatically appended to the **QueryDefs** collection and is saved to disk (and thus may be reused). A named **QueryDef** is said to be permanent; a non-named **QueryDef** is said to be temporary.

As with any other DAO object, it must be declared and then created before it can be used. It is declared as any other type of object variable and created with the **CreateQueryDef** method. An example is shown in this code snippet:

```
' declare the QueryDef object
Dim qdfMyQuery As QueryDef
```

```
' dbsBiblio is an existing database object
' create a new querydef and name it
Set qdfMyQuery = dbsBiblio.CreateQueryDef ("MyNewQuery", _
    "Select * from title")
```

If you do not supply the SQL statement when you create the **QueryDef** object, you can provide it after the fact using the **SQL** property:

```
qdfMyQuery.SQL = "Select * from title"
```

The **Execute** method causes the SQL statement to be executed:

```
qdfMyQuery.Execute options
```

Options is one or more Visual Basic constants that determine how the statement is to be executed. These are shown here (note that the **dbConsistent** and **dbInconsistent** constants are mutually exclusive):

➤ **dbDenyWrite** Microsoft Jet only. Do not allow others to update the result set.

➤ **dbConsistent** Microsoft Jet only. When the **QueryDef** involves two or more joined tables, only allow consistent values between joined columns. For instance, if two tables are joined on the Cust_No columns in each table, do not allow updates where Cust_No is different on the two tables.

➤ **dbInconsisten** Microsoft Jet only. Allow inconsistent result sets. See **dbConsistent**.

➤ **dbSQLPassThrough** Microsoft Jet only. When the **Workspace** object is connected to an ODBC data source, pass the SQL statement directly to the database instead of having Jet process it.

➤ **dbFailOnError** Microsoft Jet only. If the update fails, roll back all changes automatically.

➤ **dbSeeChanges** Microsoft Jet only. If another user is changing the data you are changing, create a runtime error.

➤ **dbRunAsync** ODBCDirect only. Execute *asynchronously* (which means that processing continues although the SQL result set has not yet been returned).

The **Cancel** method can be used to halt a currently executing asynchronous query. This method is supported only with ODBCDirect workspaces where **dbRunAsync** has been specified.

The **StillExecuting** property returns **True** if an asynchronous query is still executing. Other properties of the object cannot be accessed until **StillExecuting** returns **False**. You should examine the **RecordsAffected** property of **QueryDef** after invoking the **Execute** method to determine how many records were inserted, deleted, or updated following an *action* query. Action refers to the **QueryDef** object's **Type** property, which is set to one or more Visual Basic constants. **dbQAction** is used to denote an action query that is any query that changes or copies data. See the VB Help file under "Type Property" for a list of the possible values.

The **MaxRecords** property is used to limit the number of rows that will be returned in a query. When set to zero, there is no limit. Otherwise, it can be set to any valid **Long** and the database will stop returning rows when this limit has been reached.

The **Prepare** property is used with ODBCDirect workspaces only and determines whether a query is to be *prepared* on the database before being executed. Most RDBMSs will compile a query, referred to as "preparing," before running it. The ODBC API supports the **SQLPrepare** call to cause a query to be prepared before being run, and the **SQLExecDirect** call, which causes the query to be run without preparing it. You can override this by setting **Property** equal to **dbQUnPrepare** to cause the query to be run without preparation. **dbQPrepare** is the default and causes the query to be prepared prior to being executed.

You can use **QueryDef** to open a recordset using the **OpenRecordSet** method. The following syntax is used also with the **OpenRecordSet** method of the **RecordSet** and **TableDef** objects. An alternative syntax is supported for the **Connection** and **Database** objects, which was discussed earlier in this chapter (see "The Connections Collection"):

```
Set recordset = object.OpenRecordSet ([type] _
    [,options] [,lockedits])
```

Recordset is a previously declared **RecordSet** object. *Object* is any valid **QueryDef**, **RecordSet**, or **TableDef** object. The use of *type*, *options*, and *lockedits* was documented under "The Connections Collection" earlier in this chapter.

The *RecordSets* Collection

The **RecordSets** collection is comprised of one or more **RecordSet** objects. The **RecordSet** object is the DAO object most often asked about on the certification exam.

Any time you open a **RecordSet**, the **RecordSets** collection is automatically updated to reflect the new object. Any time you close a **RecordSet** object, it is automatically removed from the collection. You will use the **RecordSet** almost exclusively to actually manipulate records from the database. Different **RecordSet** objects can be used to access the same tables, queries, and so on, as other **RecordSet** objects without conflicting with each other.

The hierarchy of DAO objects seems unnecessarily complicated. However, it is with the **RecordSet** object that we can see how it all comes together. Recall from Figure 10.1 that the **RecordSets** collection is a property of the **Database** object. Each **Database** object is comprised of the **TableDefs**, **Containers**, **QueryDefs**, **Relations**, and **RecordSets** collections. Recall that a **Database** object is simply a representation of an open database. Each of the collections listed represent things that you can do with a database. The **QueryDefs** collection, for instance, is comprised of **QueryDef** objects representing different queries that can be used on the open database. Visual Basic's **RecordSet** object provides the developer with the interface needed to interact with the database.

The **Type** property determines the type of **RecordSet** that is opened. There are five possible values as outlined below:

➤ **dbOpenTable** Microsoft Jet only. Represents all of the columns in a single table. This is referred to as a table-type **RecordSet** object.

➤ **dbOpenDynamic** ODBCDirect only. Referred to as dynamic-type **RecordSet** object, this represents one or more columns from one or more tables derived from a database query. The updates, inserts, and deletes from other users also appear in the recordset.

➤ **dbOpenDynaset** The dynaset-type **RecordSet** object is a flexible recordset representing one or more columns from one or more tables. Movement within the recordset is unrestricted (that is, you can move from any record to any record).

➤ **dbOpenSnapshot** The snapshot-type **RecordSet** object contains one or more columns from one or more tables but the data is *static* (it cannot be updated). It is most useful for generating reports because it is more efficient than updateable types of recordsets. (Note: with some ODBCDirect drivers, limited updating of snapshots is available. Refer to the driver's documentation. You may also reference the **RecordSet's** **Updateable** property, which will be **True** if the recordset can be updated.)

➤ **dbOpenForwardOnly** The forward-only-type **RecordSet** object is
identical to a snapshot except that you can only scroll forward through the
records (no cursor is provided). This recordset type is useful for generating
reports where you need to make only one pass through the data.

Table 10.2 lists which **RecordSet** methods are supported by each of the recordset
types.

Table 10.3 provides a cross-reference of the **RecordSet** properties that are available
for each recordset type.

Table 10.2	RecordSet methods supported for each of the record set types. "Jet" means Microsoft Jet only. "ODBC" means ODBCDirect only.				
Method	**Table**	**Dynaset**	**Snapshot**	**Forward-Only**	**Dynamic**
AddNew	Jet	Yes	ODBC [1]	ODBC	ODBC
Cancel	No	ODBC	ODBC	ODBC	ODBC
CancelUpdate	Jet	Yes	ODBC [1]	ODBC	ODBC
Clone	Jet	Jet	Jet	No	No
Close	Jet	Yes	Yes	Yes	ODBC
CopyQueryDef	No	Jet	Jet	Jet	No
Delete	Jet	Yes	ODBC [1]	ODBC	ODBC
Edit	Jet	Yes	ODBC [1]	ODBC	ODBC
FillCache	No	Jet	No	No	No
FindFirst	No	Jet	Jet	No	No
FindLast	No	Jet	Jet	No	No
FindNext	No	Jet	Jet	No	No
FindPrevious	No	Jet	Jet	No	No
GetRows	Jet	Yes	Yes	Yes	ODBC
Move	Jet	Yes	Yes	Yes [2]	ODBC
MoveFirst	Jet	Yes	Yes	No	ODBC
MoveLast	Jet	Yes	Yes	No	ODBC
MoveNext	Jet	Yes	Yes	Yes	ODBC

(continued)

Table 10.2	**RecordSet** methods supported for each of the record set types. "Jet" means Microsoft Jet only. "ODBC" means ODBCDirect only *(continued)*.				
Method	**Table**	**Dynaset**	**Snapshot**	**Forward-Only**	**Dynamic**
MovePrevious	Jet	Yes	Yes	No	ODBC
NextRecordset	No	ODBC	ODBC	ODBC	ODBC
OpenRecordset	Jet	Jet	Jet	No	No
Requery	Jet	Yes	Yes	Yes	ODBC
Seek	Jet	No	No	No	No
Update	Jet	Yes	ODBC[1]	ODBC	ODBC

[1] Snapshots may be updateable with ODBCDirect workspaces depending on the ODBC driver.

[2] Only forward moves and only when no bookmark offset is used.

Table 10.3	**RecordSet** properties supported for each of the recordset types. "Jet" means Microsoft Jet only. "ODBC" means ODBCDirect only. "Read" means read-only. "Write" means read-write.				
Property	**Table**	**Dynaset**	**Snapshot**	**Forward-Only**	**Dynamic**
AbsolutePosition	No	Write	Write	No	Write ODBC
BatchCollisionCount	No	Read ODBC	Read ODBC	Read ODBC	Read ODBC
BatchCollisions	No	Read ODBC	Read ODBC	Read ODBC	Read ODBC
BatchSize	No	Read ODBC	Read ODBC	Read ODBC	Read ODBC
BOF	Read Jet	Read	Read	Read	Read ODBC
Bookmark	Write Jet	Read	Read	Read	Read ODBC
Bookmarkable	Read Jet	Read	Read	No	Read ODBC
CacheSize	No	Write Jet Read ODBC	Read ODBC	No	Read ODBC
CacheStart	No	Write Jet	No	No	No
Connection	No	Write ODBC	Write ODBC	Write ODBC	Write ODBC
DateCreated	Read Jet	No	No	No	No

(continued)

Table 10.3 RecordSet properties supported for each of the recordset types. "Jet" means Microsoft Jet only. "ODBC" means ODBCDirect only. "Read" means read-only. "Write" means read-write (continued).

Property	Table	Dynaset	Snapshot	Forward-Only	Dynamic
EditMode	Read Jet	Read	Read	Read	Read ODBC
EOF	Read Jet	Read	Read	Read	Read ODBC
Filter	No	Write Jet	Write Jet	Write Jet	No
Index	Write Jet	No	No	No	No
LastModified	Read Jet	Read	Read ODBC	No	Read ODBC
LastUpdated	Read Jet	No	No	No	No
LockEdits	Write Jet	Write Jet Read ODBC	Write Jet Read ODBC	No	Read ODBC
Name	Read Jet	Read	Read	Read	Read ODBC
NoMatch	Read Jet	Read Jet	Read Jet	No	No
PercentPosition	Write Jet	Write	Write	No	Write ODBC
RecordCount	Read Jet	Read	Read	Read	Read ODBC
RecordStatus	No	Read ODBC	Read ODBC	Read ODBC	Read ODBC
Restartable	Read Jet	Read	Read	Read	Read
Sort	No	Write Jet	Write Jet	No	No
StillExecuting	No	Write ODBC	Write ODBC	Write ODBC	Write ODBC
Transactions	Read Jet	Read Jet	Read Jet	Read Jet	No
Type	Read Jet	Read	Read	Read	Read ODBC
Updateable	Read Jet	Read	Read	Read	Read ODBC
UpdateOptions	No	Write ODBC	Write ODBC	Write ODBC	Write ODBC
ValidationRule	Read Jet	Read Jet	Read Jet	Read Jet	No
ValidationText	Read Jet	Read Jet	Read Jet	Read Jet	No

You will want to be familiar with the important methods and properties of the RecordSet object listed in Table 10.4. Critical usage notes on some of these methods and properties follow. For more information, refer to "RecordSet Object" in the VB Help file.

Table 10.4 Key RecordSet methods and properties.		
Method or Property	**Type**	**Use**
AbsolutePosition	Property	Relative record number of the recordset.
AddNew	Method	Insert a new record into the recordset.
BOF	Property	**True** means that the current position is before the first record.
Bookmark	Property	Used to set a **Variant** so that you can return to any given record.
Cancel	Method	Halt an asynchronous query.
CancelUpdate	Method	Cancel any pending updates for the recordset.
Clone	Method	Create an exact duplicate of a recordset.
Close	Method	Close a recordset.
Delete	Method	Delete the current record.
Edit	Method	Begin editing the current record.
EditMode	Property	**dbEditNone** indicates no edit is in process. **dbEditAdd** indicates the **AddNew** method has been invoked. **dbEditInProgress** indicates the **Edit** method has been invoked.
EOF	Property	**True** indicates that the current position is after the last record.
Filter	Property	A string value that restricts the records in a recordset.
FindFirst	Method	Find the first record that matches the criteria supplied.
FindNext	Method	Find the next record that matches the criteria supplied.
FindPrior	Method	Find the prior record that matches the criteria supplied.
FindLast	Method	Find the last record that matches the criteria provided.
GetRows	Method	Copy the recordset into an array in memory.
Move	Method	Move the number of rows indicated in the recordset.

(continued)

Table 10.4	Key **RecordSet** methods and properties (continued).	
Method or Property	**Type**	**Use**
MoveFirst	Method	Move to the first record of the recordset.
MoveNext	Method	Move to the next record in a recordset.
MovePrior	Method	Move to the prior record in a recordset.
MoveLast	Method	Move to the last record in a recordset.
NextRecordSet	Method	With multiple Selects, get the rows from the next **Select** statement.
NoMatch	Property	**True** indicates that the record searched for wasn't found.
PercentPosition	Property	The approximate position within the recordset, expressed as a percentage.
RecordCount	Property	The number of records in the recordset that have been accessed.
RecordStatus	Property	Indicates the status of the current record.
Requery	Method	Get a new set of records based on the querydef supplied.
Seek	Method	Find a record within the recordset based on the supplied criteria.
Sort	Property	A string specifying the sort order of a subsequently opened recordset.
StillExecuting	Property	**True** indicates that an asynchronous query is still executing.
Transactions	Property	**True** indicates that the underlying database supports transactions.
Update	Method	Save changes to the database.
UpdateOptions	Property	Indicates how the database will be updated.

The **FindFirst**, **FindNext**, **FindPrior**, and **FindLast** methods accept a string argument that is similar to the SQL **Where** clause. In a recordset, to find the next record in where the name of the country is "Canada" (assuming the column name is Ctry_Name), specify:

```
FindNext "Ctry_Name = 'Canada'"
```

If no record is found, the **NoMatch** property is set to **True**.

The **Move** method is similar except that it accepts an *offset* argument specifying how many records to move. The number supplied may be positive (move forward) or negative (move backward). You may also optionally supply the name of a bookmark variable, which will cause **Move** to begin relative to the bookmarked record instead of the current record. To move to the fifth record before the current record, specify: **Move -5**.

RecordCount does not contain an accurate count of all of the records in a recordset until all have been accessed. To quickly determine the number of records, use the **MoveLast** method to move to the last record in a recordset. The **RecordCount** property will then reflect the number of records in the recordset.

The **Update** method saves pending changes to the database. If you invoke the **Edit** or **AddNew** methods, and then move to another record, set a bookmark, or close the recordset, the changes will be lost unless you invoke the **Update** method. **Update** accepts two arguments, both of which are optional: *Type* is a Visual Basic constant and *Force* is a **Boolean** indicating whether to force changes to the database even if another user has already altered the records (use **True** to force the changes). The valid constants for *type* are:

➤ **dbUpdateRegular** The default. Specifies that changes are not cached—they are written to disk immediately.

➤ **dbUpdateBatch** Indicates that all changes pending in the cache are written to disk.

➤ **dbUpdateCurrentRecord** Indicates that only changes to the current record are to be written to disk (other cached changes remain cached).

You may use the other two constants only if batch updating is enabled.

The **Update** property tells the database how to construct the **Where** clause when applying updates. **dbCriteriaKey** specifies that only the key column(s) are to be used. For instance, if the "Customer" table has a primary key of Cust_ID, then the **Where** clause will state:

```
Where Cust_ID = ...
```

dbCriteriaModValues dictates that the **Where** clause will use the key column(s) and any columns that were updated. **dbCriteriaAllCols** specifies that all columns are to be used in the **Where** clause. **dbCriteriaTimeStamp** specifies that, if available, only the time stamp column will be used. **dbCriteriaDelteInsert**

specifies that the original row will be deleted and a new row inserted. Normally, this is used where the primary key is to be updated. **dbUpdate** is the default and specifies that the row be updated (instead of being deleted and a new row inserted in its place).

The Data Control

The Data control implements most of the functionality of DAO and is very easy to use.

To place a Data control onto a form, select it from the toolbox. It consists of a textbox in the middle with two "arrows" buttons on both sides of the textbox. The button on the left is the Move First button and is used to move to the first record in the recordset. The next button is the Move Prior button, which moves the record immediately before the current record. On the right side of the textbox are Move Next and Move Last buttons. Figure 10.2 shows the control being used in a simple application.

The action of the Data control's Move First button is defined by the **BOFAction** property. The default value, 0, specifies that the first record in the database is displayed. If repeatedly pressed, the first record remains the current record. With a value of 1, second and subsequent presses of this button cause the file pointer to move *prior* to the first record, triggering a **Validate** event on the first record followed by the **Reposition** event on the invalid record. The Move Prior button on the Data control is then disabled.

The action of the Move Last button is defined by the **EOFAction** property. The default value, zero, specifies that the last record in the database be displayed. If

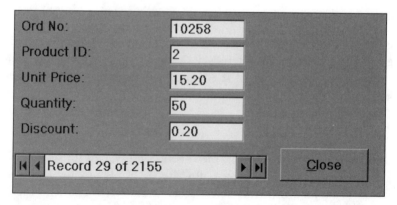

Figure 10.2 The Data control and several textboxes bound to the database.

repeatedly pressed, the last record remains the current record. With a value of 1, however, the second press of the button causes the file pointer to move beyond the end of the recordset. This triggers the **Validate** event on the last record and a **Reposition** event on the new invalid record (the new record is invalid because it is beyond the end of the recordset). The Move Next button is disabled. If the property is set to a value of 2, the **Validate** event occurs for the last record, followed by an automatic **AddNew**, creating a new record, followed by a **Reposition** event on the new record. This represents an easy way to automatically add new records to the database and have them automatically receive focus.

The Data control has a number of properties that need to be set in order to use it. The essential properties are discussed in the following sections. After that, we'll look at the important events of the Data control.

The **Connect** Property

The **Connect** property specifies what database format you will be using. See "The Workspaces Collection" earlier in this chapter for a discussion of the different types of connections that can be made. It can be set at design time, via the Properties dialog, or at runtime, via the syntax:

```
object.Connect = databasetype; parameters.
```

In the case of native format, omit *parameters* and simply specify "Access." Otherwise, specify a valid database type (such as "ODBC;" or "dBase 5.0;"). The semicolon is used to separate the database type from optional parameters:

```
database= pubs;uid=sa;pwd=;dsn=Publishers
```

These values will typically coincide with what you have set up in the Windows "32-bit ODBC Administrator" applet (see your database documentation or the help file in the ODBC administrator for specific guidance). Figure 10.3 shows a simple application connected to a Sybase SQL Anywhere database via ODBCDirect. One of the textboxes shows the connect string and another textbox shows the SQL Select.

The **DatabaseName** Property

In the **DatabaseName** property, you need to specify a fully qualified path to your database such as *object*.DatabaseName = "C:\Program Files\DevStudio\ VB\NWIND.MDB". The example given is the Northwind database supplied with Visual Basic 5.

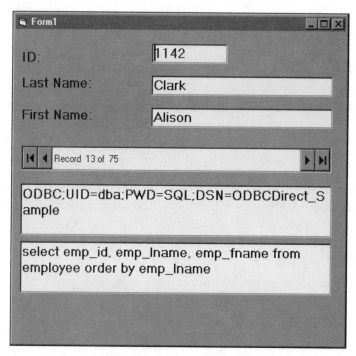

Figure 10.3   An application showing a record along with a **Connect** string and SQL **Select** statement.

The **RecordSetType** Property

In the **RecordSetType** property, you may specify one of three values in the form:

```
object.RecordSetType = value
```

Valid values are the Visual Basic constants:

➤ **vbRSTypeTable** A table-type **RecordSet**

➤ **vbRSTypeDynaset** The default **Dynaset**

➤ **vbRSTypeSnapShot** A snapshot-type **RecordSet**

These recordset types were discussed under "The RecordSets Collection" earlier in this chapter. You cannot create a forward-only or dynamic-type recordset with the Data control.

When using the Jet engine, a **RecordSet** object is created of the type specified by the control's **RecordSetType** property. Table-type **RecordSets** are most efficient when you need add, update, and delete capabilities but are selecting from no more than one table and do not need the added functionality provided by the **Dynaset**. Unlike the other two **RecordSetType**s, table-types are not stored in memory.

The snapshot **RecordSetType** is used when you need to access records that will not change such as when creating a report. The records can come from more than one table.

The **Dynaset** has the most features of the **RecordSetType**s and is also the most expensive to use in terms of application efficiency.

The **RecordSource** Property

In the **RecordSource** property, you specify the source of the data for the underlying recordset—in other words, to which table within the database is the Data control to be connected. You use the following syntax:

```
object.RecordSource = "Order Details"
```

The specification for **RecordSource** is dependent on the **RecordSetType**. With the table-type, only one table may be specified. With the Dynaset or snapshot types, you can specify an SQL query returning more than one table. If using Microsoft Jet, you may also specify only a table name. With ODBCDirect, you specify an SQL Query. The **RecordSource** for the application we saw in Figure 10.2 is Order Details (a table in Northwind sample database). The **RecordSource** for the application in Figure 10.3 is the SQL **Select** statement, shown in the bottom textbox in the figure.

Recordsets

With Microsoft Jet workspaces, the **RecordSet** created by the Data control is automatically populated. This means that the **RecordCount** property is accurate without having to access every record in the **RecordSet**. With ODBCDirect, you need to perform a **MoveLast** (**Data1.RecordSet.MoveLast**) in order to get an accurate **RecordCount**.

All properties and methods of the **RecordSet** object are available to the Data control using dot notation (*datacontrol.RecordSet.method_or_property*). See "The RecordSets Collection" earlier in this chapter for a discussion of the methods and properties.

The **Validate** Event

Whenever the Data control moves to a new record, the **Validate** event occurs. It occurs before the new record becomes the current record, and before the **Update**, **Delete**, **Unload**, and **Close** operations. The **Validate** event is where you will place program code to edit changes made to the record. If no action is performed by the application, the changes are automatically applied to the database.

The syntax for the **Validate** event is

```
object_Validate (action As Integer, save As Integer)
```

where *object* is the Data control, *action* is a Visual Basic constant informing the application of what event occurred to trigger the **Validate** event, and *save* is a **Boolean** indicating whether any data has changed or not. Valid *actions* are shown in Table 10.5. You can query the *action* to determine what occurred to trigger the **Validation** event, for instance, the user scrolling to a new record or perhaps attempting to close the form. This is your only opportunity to edit all of the data fields for validity and cancel the update if needed.

You can cancel the change by setting *action* to zero. You can also query all controls that are bound to the database to determine which ones have been modified. The **DataChanged** property of individual controls will be **True** if the data was changed. You may cancel those individual changes by setting the property to **False**.

Table 10.5   Actions triggering the Validate event.

VB Constant	Value	Event occurred
vbDataActionCancel	0	End of sub
vbDataActionMoveFirst	1	**MoveFirst** method
vbDataActionMovePrevious	2	**MovePrevious** method
vbDataActionMoveNext	3	**MoveNext** method
vbDataActionMoveLast	4	**MoveLast** method
vbDataActionAddNew	5	**AddNew** method
vbDataActionUpdate	6	Update invoked
vbDataActionDelete	7	**Delete** method
vbDataActionFind	8	**Find** method
vbDataActionBookmark	9	**Bookmark** property set
vbDataActionClose	10	**Close** method
vbDataActionUnload	11	Form in process of being unloaded

The **Error** Event

It is possible for an error to occur when your code is not running. For instance, the user may click on one of the Data control's move buttons and a database error may ensue. The **Error** event will then be triggered. It has the syntax:

```
datacontrol_Error (dbError As Integer, response As Integer)
```

dbError is an error number returned from the **Database** object (See "The Databases Collection" earlier in this chapter), and *response* is a number indicating how you wish to respond to the error. The Visual Basic constant **vbDataErrContinue** will cause the program to continue execution; **vbDataErrDisplay** will cause an error message to be displayed.

The **Reposition** Event

The **Reposition** event occurs whenever a new record replaces the current record. It offers you the opportunity to perform any needed calculations based upon the data currently being displayed.

Data Bound Controls

Most Visual Basic controls can display data from the database. This process is known as *data binding*; each bound control displays one column from the current record in the recordset. Controls that can be bound to the database are:

➤ Check Box

➤ Combo Box

➤ DBCombo

➤ DBGrid

➤ DBList

➤ Image

➤ Label

➤ ListBox

➤ Masked Edit

➤ PictureBox

➤ ProgressBar

➤ RichTextBox

Two properties need to be set in order to bind a control. The **DataSource** must be set to the desired Data control. As an example:

```
Text1.DataSource = Data1
```

You must then set the **DataField** property to one of the fields in the **RecordSet** property of the Data control. The first textbox in Figure 10.3 was set with the syntax:

```
Text1.DataField = "Emp_ID"
```

Different controls behave differently when displaying data. The DBList control differs from the ListBox control in that it is automatically populated by all the values in the **RecordSet** field to which it is bound. For instance, if the DBList control were bound to the Emp_ID field from Figure 10.3, the control would be populated with all of the employee IDs, whereas the ListBox must be manually populated (via program code).

Likewise, the DBCombo control is different from the ComboBox control because the latter must be populated using the **AddItem** method, whereas the DBCombo is automatically populated.

The DBGrid control is a flexible control that can display multiple columns at once. When drawing it on the form, you can right-click on it and select Retrieve Fields to automatically add all of the **RecordSet** fields to the control. An example of the DBGrid control is shown in Figure 10.4.

Remote Data Object (RDO)

A powerful feature of Visual Basic is its Remote Data Object (RDO). It is essentially a "wrapper" around the ODBC API that offers the simplicity of Microsoft Jet without the performance penalty. Although you can use RDO to access desktop databases such as Microsoft Access (as long as they provide an ODBC driver), it is really intended to take advantage of the power of remote databases such as Oracle or Microsoft SQL Server.

RDO is similar in most respects to DAO but some of the object names differ. Figure 10.5 lists the RDO hierarchy and the DAO equivalent. Like DAO, RDO is organized into collections and objects.

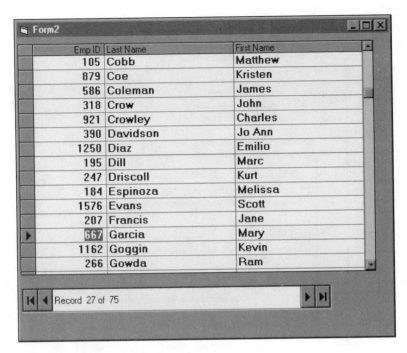

Figure 10.4 The DBGrid control.

Beyond the name differences of the collections and objects, the methods and properties of RDO and DAO objects are essentially equivalent. A notable exception is that the **rdoResult** object does not have the **RecordSet** object's **FindFirst, FindNext, FindPrior,** or **FindLast** methods.

The Remote Data Control

The Remote Data control, sometimes referred to as the RDC, is similar but not identical to the Data control. The essential difference is that you need to supply an SQL query to the control's **SQL** property (which is the Data control's **RecordSource** property). To use the Remote Data control, select Project|Components from VB's menu and choose Microsoft Remote Data Control 2.0. An example of the Remote Data control in action is seen in Figure 10.6.

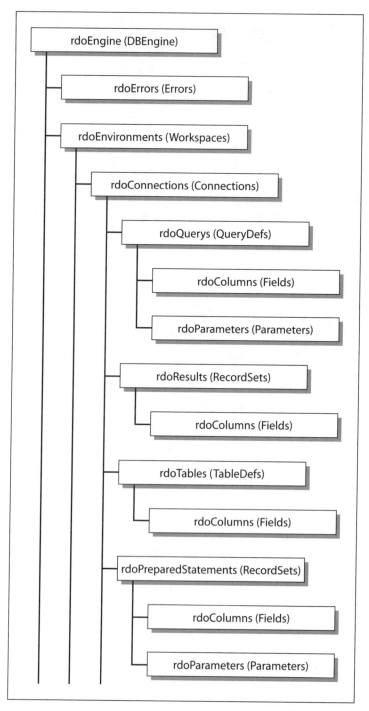

Figure 10.5 The RDO hierarchy (with DAO equivalents in parentheses).

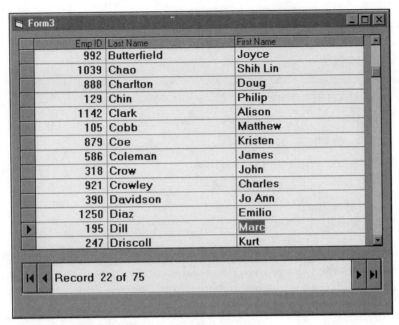

Figure 10.6   The Remote Data control, used in the same way as the Data control from Figure 10.4.

Exam Prep Questions

Question 1

> What is the Data control used for? [Check all correct answers]
>
> ☐ a. Any file opened for **Random** or **Binary**
>
> ☐ b. Any dynaset-type **RecordSet**
>
> ☐ c. Any forward-only-type **RecordSet**
>
> ☐ d. Any snapshot-type **RecordSet**
>
> ☐ e. Any valid DAO or RDO object

Answers b and d are correct. Answer b is correct because you can open a dynaset with the Data control. Answer d is correct because you can open a snapshot with the Data control. Answer a is incorrect because you cannot use a Data control for files opened in **Random** or **Binary** mode. Answer c is incorrect because the Data control does not support the forward-only type RecordSet. Answer e is incorrect because the Data control does not support all DAO objects (for instance, the **TableDef** object) and it does not support any RDO objects.

Question 2

> Which property of the Data control will return the number of records in the recordset?
>
> ○ a. The **RecordSet** property
>
> ○ b. The **RecordCount** property
>
> ○ c. The **RecordsAffected** property
>
> ○ d. None of the above

Answer d is correct because none of the supplied answers will provide the number of records in the recordset. Answer a is incorrect because the RecordSet property does not provide the count of records. Answer b is incorrect because RecordCount is not a property of the Data control, it is a property of RecordSet. Answer c is incorrect because RecordsAffected does not give a record count and is not a property of the Data control. To get the count of all records, you must specify: *datacontrol*.RecordSet.RecordCount.

Question 3

> Which of the following **RecordSet** object's methods will prevent
> an update?
>
> ○ a. **Cancel**
>
> ○ b. **CancelUpdate**
>
> ○ c. **EditUnDo**
>
> ○ d. **Rollback**

Answer b is the correct answer because the *CancelUpdate* **will stop the** *RecordSet* **from sending the update to the database.** Answer a is incorrect because **Cancel** stops a currently executing asynchronous query. Answer c is wrong because there is no such property. Answer d is incorrect because **Rollback** is not a property of the **RecordSet** object.

Question 4

Consider the following code snippet:

```
' line numbers are for reference only
1  Dim wrkMyWork As Workspace
2  Dim dbsMyDB As Database
3  Dim rstMyCust As Recordset
4  ' Create a default workspace.
5  Set wrkMyWork = DBEngine.Workspaces(0)
6  ' open the database
7  Set dbsMyDB = OpenDatabase("Orders.mdb")
8  ' open the recordset
9  Set rstMyCust = _
10    dbsMyDB.OpenRecordset("Customers")
11 wrkMyWork.BeginTrans
12 rstMyCust.Edit
13 rstMyCust.Update
14 wrkMyWork.Rollback
15 dbsMyDB.Close
```

Referring to the line numbers, at what line does the transaction end?

O a. Line 12

O b. Line 13

O c. Line 14

O d. Line 15

Answer c is correct because *Rollback* (or *CommitTrans*) ends the current transaction. Answers a and b are incorrect because **Edit** and **Update** are both part of the transaction. Answer d is incorrect because the transaction has already ended.

Question 5

In a Data control, what property or method determines the action to be taken if the user attempts to move to a record before the first record?

O a. The **BOFAction** property

O b. The **Error** property

O c. The **InsertNew** method

O d. None of the above; it is not possible to move something before the first record

Answer a is correct because the *BOFAction* property determines how the Data control responds to the Beginning Of File button. Answer b is incorrect because no error is generated nor is **Error** a property of the Data control. Answer c is incorrect because **InsertNew** is not a valid method (the correct method is the **AddNew** method of the **RecordSet** object). Answer d is incorrect because the correct answer is provided.

Question 6

```
Given the following code snippet, what will happen to the
AUTOEXEC.BAT file?

Open "C:\Autoexec.Bat" For Output As 1
Dim sVar As String
Write #1, sVar
Close
```

○ a. The first character of the file will be overwritten.

○ b. The last character of the file will be overwritten.

○ c. A space will be added to the end of the file.

○ d. The entire file will be overwritten.

Answer d is correct because when a file is opened for output, anything written to the file overwrites the previous contents. Answers a, b, and c are all incorrect because the entire file is destroyed (not just one character).

Question 7

```
Which of the following controls cannot be bound to the database?
```

○ a. Check Box

○ b. Data

○ c. PictureBox

○ d. TextBox

Answer b is correct because you do not bind a Data control to the database. Answers a, c, and d are all incorrect because the Check Box, PictureBox, and TextBox controls all can be bound to the database.

Need To Know More?

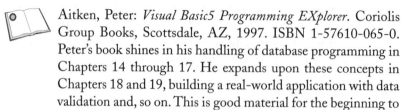

Aitken, Peter: *Visual Basic5 Programming EXplorer*. Coriolis Group Books, Scottsdale, AZ, 1997. ISBN 1-57610-065-0. Peter's book shines in his handling of database programming in Chapters 14 through 17. He expands upon these concepts in Chapters 18 and 19, building a real-world application with data validation and, so on. This is good material for the beginning to intermediate developer or those who need a brush-up.

Harrington, John, Mark Spenik, Heidi Brumbaugh, and Cliff Diamond: *Visual Basic 5 Interactive Course*. Waite Group Press, Corte Madera, CA, 1997. ISBN 1-57169-077-8. Chapter 12 discusses the ins-and-outs of file access and Chapter 13 builds upon this with a well-done discussion of database access techniques.

Jamsa, Kris and Lars Klander: *1001 Visual Basic Programmer's Tips*. Jamsa Press, Las Vegas, NV, 1997. ISBN 1-884133-56-8. This well-done book is not broken into chapters but rather into "tips." Tips 646 through 750 are a fairly thorough discussion of using databases from within Visual Basic from a good discussion of SQL to the Data control to remote data objects. Even experienced developers can glean some insights from this book.

Mandelbrot Set, The: *Advanced Microsoft Visual Basic 5*. Microsoft Press, Redmond, WA, 1997. ISBN 1-57231-414-1. This book is broken into sections done by various authors (they are not listed on the cover). In Chapter 9, Mark Mayes discusses Year 2000 issues in Visual Basic, which includes some database topics. Brant Vaughan's Chapter 13 is a very thorough overview of the various data access options, including a nice evaluation of the merits of DAO versus RDO and moving from there into some very advanced topics.

McKinney, Bruce: *Hardcore Visual Basic, Second Edition* (which covers version 5). Microsoft Press, Redmond, WA, 1997. ISBN 1-57231-422-2. Bruce has written an excellent book on squeezing the most out of Visual Basic. He uses Chapter 11 as his forum for all of the those subjects he did not cover in other chapters. This includes a nice sequence on files, particularly on pages 658 through 678.

Search the online books on the VB CD-ROM for the term "database." The VB Help file is a good resource also, with a well-ordered presentation on the subject. Search for "DAO" and then for "RDO."

 Microsoft places the most current Knowledge Base online at www.microsoft.com/support/. Enter search terms such as "DAO," "RDO," and "ODBC" to view articles detailing tips (and sometimes fixes) revolving around the use of external modules.

Implementing Help

Terms you'll need to understand:

√ Context-sensitive help

√ ToolTip

√ What's This Help

√ WhatsThisMode

√ StatusBar control

√ Panel object

√ Panels collection

√ CommonDialog control

Techniques you'll need to master:

√ Displaying context-sensitive ToolTips help

√ Invoking WhatsThisMode and displaying WhatsThisHelp

√ Displaying various status items using the StatusBar control

√ Using the CommonDialog control to display help contents, index, and topical search

Close to 10 percent of the VB certification exam will deal with implementing help for the users of your application. Fortunately, Visual Basic makes the implementation of user help easy. The subject of creating the Help file is outside the scope of the test and this book. In the following pages, we'll look at the application side of generating help.

Overview Of User Help

When designing your application, you want to think as though you are a first-time user of the program: How do I print that document? How do I save this file? What is the purpose of this button? Visual Basic provides five methods of providing this type of feedback to your users.

ToolTips

A ToolTip is sometimes known as "balloon help." When implemented, a small box appears when the user pauses with the mouse pointer over a Window's icon, toolbar button, and so on For example, when you move the pointer over the controls on the toolbox in the Visual Basic development environment, a ToolTip pops up saying "FileListBox" or "DriveListBox," and so on.

ToolTips are easy to implement via the **ToolTipText** property of any control that can receive focus plus the Form object (but not the MDIForm object). The property is a string value, which should consist of no more than five or six words. It can be updated at design time via the properties dialog, or at runtime via the syntax:

```
object.ToolTipText = "tool tip text"
```

If the control has a menu shortcut, it should be included. For example, if the user held the mouse pointer over the Exit button, the ToolTip would say "Exits the application (Ctrl + Q)". An example of a ToolTip is shown in Figure 11.1.

What's This Help

What's This Help displays a box of help text that is more detailed than ToolTips, but not as detailed as a Help file. An example is shown in Figure 11.2. With What's This Help, your user invokes the feature by clicking a toolbar icon or a menu selection. The mouse pointer turns to a question mark and arrow. The user then clicks on the control of interest to bring up the pop-up box.

To implement What's This Help, you need to enable it at the form level first. You do this by setting the **WhatsThisHelp** property to **True**. You can

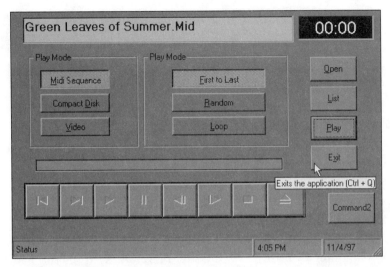

Figure 11.1   ToolTip help implemented via the **ToolTipText** property
of a Command Button control.

optionally set the **WhatsThisButton** property to **True**. Doing this causes a
What's This icon to appear on the caption. However, if you do this, you must
either set the **BorderStyle** property to 3 (**Fixed Dialog**), 2 (**Sizable**), or 1 (**Fixed
Single**). You must also set the **MinButton** and **MaxButton** properties to **True**
with the **ControlMenu** property also set to **True**. When the user clicks the
What's This button, the form invokes its **WhatsThisMode**, which changes
the cursor to the What's This pointer.

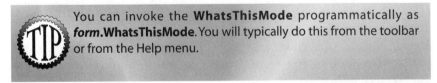

You can invoke the **WhatsThisMode** programmatically as
form.**WhatsThisMode**. You will typically do this from the toolbar
or from the Help menu.

Next, each control for which you want to invoke What's This Help must have
its **WhatsThisHelpID** set to a valid context ID for your Help file. (A context

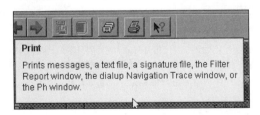

Figure 11.2   What's This Help text from Eudora Pro.

ID is created when you create your Help file. It can be thought of as a help subject number or a page number. Each topic in your Help file has a context ID.)

If you create a toolbar, you should assign one of the buttons for What's This Help. You should also add a selection for What's This Help under the Help menu.

Note that Windows 95 and Windows NT applications tend to invoke this feature inconsistently, if at all. For instance, Microsoft Word only has a menu choice. Ironically, it doesn't seem that Visual Basic itself implements What's This Help at all.

The StatusBar Control

You can add a StatusBar control to your application by adding Microsoft Windows Common Controls 5.0 (COMCTL32.OCX) from the Project| Component menu. The control will then appear on your toolbox. Select it and place it on the form.

 Be sure to draw the control at the bottom of the form because, in my experience, it is a little buggy when you attempt to move it.

Right-click on the control to bring up its properties dialog box, as shown in Figure 11.3. You can create up to 16 "panels." Each of these can have different uses. In this example, I have reserved two panels for displaying the time and date, by setting the **Style** properties to 5 (**SbrTime**) and 6 (**SbrDate**), respectively.

You should add some code into the **GotFocus** event so that when the user clicks on a control, the text in the status box is altered. You do this through the **Panel** object or **Panels** collection.

Panel Object And Panels Collection

Much like every form has a **Control** collection, each StatusBar control has a **Panels** collection. The **Panels** collection contains **Panel** objects (much as the **Controls** collection for any given Form contains all of the controls on that form). Like any other collection, it has a **Key** property and **Add**, **Remove**, and **Clear** methods (see the section titled "The Collection Class" in Chapter 4). To obtain a reference to it, you use the status bar's **Panels** property as shown:

```
Dim vPanel As Variant
' iterate through all of the Panel objects
```

```
For Each vPanel In StatusBar1.Panels
    vPanel.Text = "This is a control"
Next
```

You can explain its functionality in the **GotFocus** event of a given control. The following assumes that the first panel is used to display help:

```
' display status help
StatusBar1.Panels(1).Text = "Opens a file"
```

You can use the **Style** property to display different system information in each panel as shown:

```
' Use the With method to iterate through the collection
With StatusBar1.Panels
    ' today's date
    .Item(2).Style = sbrDate
    ' the current time
    .Item(3).Style = sbrTime
    ' state of the insert key
    .Item(4).Style = sbrIns
End With
```

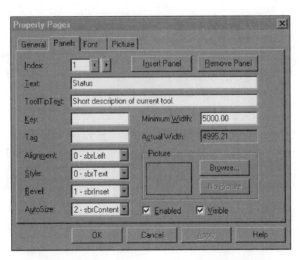

Figure 11.3   Use the StatusBar control from the Microsoft Common Controls OCX to add status help to your application.

Help Files

The most comprehensive help that you can display is contained in a Help file. As noted previously, when you open a Help file, you need to supply the help context ID so that the correct topic is displayed. Every control has a **HelpContextID** property, which can contain any string holding a valid help context ID. The Help file is specified as a property of the **App** object as:

```
app.HelpFile = "c:\myhelp.hlp"
```

When the HelpFile and HelpContextID properties are set, Visual Basic launches the Help file whenever the user presses F1.

 In the interests of being "user friendly," you should think in terms of context-sensitive help. Every object to which a user can tab should have its **HelpContextID** property set.

If a control's **HelpContextID** is set to zero, Visual Basic looks at the control's container (a command button's container is typically a form). If the container's **HelpContextID** is also set to zero, Visual Basic looks at the container's container (and so on). If a non-zero **HelpContextID** cannot be found, the F1 key is ignored and help is not presented to the user.

Visual Basic Professional and Enterprise editions include the Windows 32 Help Compiler. You should practice creating a small Help file before taking the exam, paying particular attention to assigning help context IDs.

Using The CommonDialog To Display Help

The CommonDialog control, available to your application by selecting Project|Components, provides a flexible means to present help data to your users. The control has four properties related to the display of help: **HelpContext;** **HelpCommand; HelpKey;** and **HelpFile.** There is a single method, **ShowHelp,** which interacts with all of these properties. To set the properties, right-click on the control and select the Help tab, as seen in Figure 11.4.

The **HelpCommand** property of the CommonDialog control dictates in what manner the Help file will be displayed when the **ShowHelp** method is invoked. The property is set to one of the constants listed in Table 11.1. (Note that these constants are not additive—they cannot be added together because they are largely mutually exclusive.)

HelpCommand works in concert with the **HelpContext, HelpKey,** and **HelpFile** properties under certain circumstances. When the **cdlHelpContext**

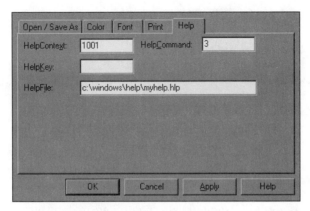

Figure 11.4   The Help properties page of the CommonDialog control.

constant is used (usually to display context-sensitive help), the context ID in **HelpContext** determines which topic will be displayed. Therefore, you should set this property first. When **cdlHelpKey** is used, the string supplied to the **HelpKey** property determines which topic is searched for. If **cdlHelpPartialKey** is used, a partial key search is done by displaying the "topics box" (the "Index" tab of the Help Search dialog). To display the contents of the Help file, you would code (assuming the CommonDialog control was named **comdlg1**):

Table 11.1   Constants for the HelpCommand property of the CommonDialog control.

Constant	Value	Purpose
cdlHelpCommand	258	Executes a help macro
cdlHelpContents	3	Displays help contents
cdlHelpContext	1	Displays context-sensitive help
cdlHelpContextPopup	8	Displays help in a pop-up window
cdlHelpForceFile	9	Ensures that Winhlp32 displays proper Help file
cdlHelpHelpOnHelp	4	Displays help for using help
cdlHelpIndex	3	Displays help index
cdlHelpKey	257	Displays help for a keyword
cdlHelpPartialKey	261	Displays topic keyword list
cdlHelpQuit	2	Quits help
cdlHelpSetContents	5	Determines which topic is displayed when the F1 key is pressed
cdlHelpSetIndex	5	Sets the current context ID as the index to use for the Help file

```
' set the properties
comdlg1.HelpFile = "c:\windows\help\myhelp.hlp"
cmddlg1.HelpCommnd = cldHelpContents
' display the Help file contents topic
cmndll.ShowHelp
```

The **ShowHelp** method of the Common Dialog control provides a lot of functionality in terms of displaying help. You invoke the **ShowHelp** method with the syntax:

object.ShowHelp

where *object* is a valid CommonDialog control created in your program. The use of the **ShowHelp** method invokes WINHLP32.EXE, which in turn displays the Help file indicated by the **HelpFile** property of the CommonDialog control.

Exam Prep Questions

Question 1

> Which control offers a high degree of flexibility in presenting user help?
>
> ○ a. TextBox via the **ShowHelp** method
>
> ○ b. Combo Help control via the **ShowHelp** method
>
> ○ c. Combo control via the **ShowHelp** method
>
> ○ d. CommonDialog control via the **ShowHelp** method

Answer d is correct because it is the only control listed that offers special help functionality. Answers a and c are incorrect because neither control implements any help functionality, and neither has a **ShowHelp** method. Answer b is incorrect because there is no Combo Help control.

Question 2

> Which controls can display ToolTip help? [Check all correct answers]
>
> ❏ a. TextBox
>
> ❏ b. Menu
>
> ❏ c. MDIForm
>
> ❏ d. Shape

Answer a is the only correct answer because TextBox is the only control listed that implements and supports ToolTip help. Answers b, c, and d are all incorrect because the controls do not have a **ToolTipText** property.

Question 3

> You need to display context-sensitive help in a pop-up window. How would you do this?
>
> ○ a. Using the CommonDialog control, invoke the **ShowHelp** method, setting the **HelpCommand** property to **cdlHelpContext + cdlHelpPopUp**.
>
> ○ b. Display a small form with an OK command button to act as a modal window. Then set the form's **Print** method to **object**.ShowHelp, where *object* is a valid CommonDialog, and its **HelpCommand** property has been properly set.
>
> ○ c. Set the control's **WhatsThisProperty** to the constant **vbMultiLine** and the **WhatsThisHelpID** to a valid help context ID.
>
> ○ d. None of the above.

The correct answer is d because none of the answers supplied solve the problem. Answer a is incorrect because constants are not additive (that is, they cannot be added together) for the CommonDialog control. In this case, **cdlHelpContext** has a value of 1 and **cdlHelpPopUp** doesn't exist. **cdlHelpContextPopUp** does exist though. If we were to use that—it has a value of 8—we would add the two together to get a value of 9, which would cause the Windows help system to verify that the correct Help file was being displayed (see Table 11.1); hardly what we wanted. Answer b is incorrect because, besides being awkward, the form's **Print** sends an image of the form to the printer. Answer c is incorrect because there is no **WhatsThisProperty**.

Question 4

> Which of the following can you do with a StatusBar control ? [Check all correct answers]
>
> ❏ a. Add a panel at design time.
>
> ❏ b. Display the status of the Insert, Scroll Lock, and Num Lock keys.
>
> ❏ c. Add new panels at runtime.
>
> ❏ d. Iterate through the panels with the **For Each** construct.

The correct answers are a, b, c, and d. Answer a is correct because you can add a panel at design time through the control's property page. Answer b is correct because you can display the status of various keys, such as the Insert, Num Lock, Scroll Lock, Caps Lock, and so on. Answer c is correct because new panels can be added at runtime. Answer d is also correct because the StatusBar control has a *Panels* collection through which you can iterate, as with any other control.

Need To Know More?

 Search the online books on the VB CD for "ShowHelp," which discusses usage of the CommonDialog control in implementing help systems and "Designing A User Assistance Model," which provides an overview of user help with links to other subjects.

 Microsoft places the most current Knowledge Base online at www.microsoft.com/support/. Enter search terms such as "help," "context sensitive," and so on, to view articles detailing tips (and sometimes fixes) revolving around the issues discussed in this chapter.

 There are a number of Web sites devoted to the subject of Visual Basic on the Internet. Use a search engine such as Yahoo! (www.yahoo.com) or Hotbot (www.hotbot.com) with a search term such as "Visual Basic 5" (be sure to place the search term in quotes so that only pages containing the entire term as one string are returned). A well-done site with tips and sample code that I liked was the VB Palace at home.computer.net/~mheller/. Another site that was under "reconstruction" when I visited was a site hosted by Temple University at thunder.ocis.temple.edu/~shariq/vb/index.html.

Visual Basic
And The
Internet

Terms you'll need to understand:

- √ File Transfer Protocol (FTP)
- √ Hypertext Transfer Protocol (HTTP)
- √ World Wide Web (WWW)
- √ Hypertext Markup Language (HTML)
- √ HTML tag
- √ Active server and active client
- √ VBScript
- √ <OBJECT> tag and <PARAM NAME=> tag
- √ MSComm control
- √ Winsock control

- √ TCP and UDP
- √ RemoteHost, RemotePort, and LocalPort properties
- √ Accept, Listen, Connect, GetData, and SendData methods
- √ Bind method
- √ Internet Transfer control
- √ OpenURL and Execute methods
- √ UserName and Password properties
- √ Uniform Resource Locator (URL)
- √ URL property
- √ StateChanged event

Techniques you'll need to master:

- √ Understanding the basics of embedding an ActiveX control in an HTML page
- √ Using the MSComm control

- √ Using the Winsock control to establish a client-host connection and peer-to-peer communication.
- √ Using the Internet Transfer control to retrieve files from Web and FTP servers.

297

Visual Basic has transformed itself into a Web and internet development tool and Microsoft has not ignored that fact on the certification exam. In this chapter, I discuss the use of VB5 and the Internet.

Where Does The Internet Fit In?

The term "client/server" has been a buzzword for most of the 1990s. In Chapter 10, I discussed data access using Visual Basic with an emphasis on client/server operations. Briefly, a client/server application is broken into at least two independent processes. The classic implementation is a client developed with a tool such as Visual Basic that communicates with a database engine such as Microsoft SQL Server, typically over a network.

The Internet itself is a large network connecting many millions of computers around the world and, as such, is a suitable platform for client/server development (though not without special considerations). With Visual Basic 5, we can not only develop applications *for* the Internet, we can make the Internet part *of* our applications.

Although the World Wide Web brought the Internet to the masses, it is one of the Internet's newest components. The following sections will give you a quick overview of the terms you'll need to master the certification exam questions relating to Visual Basic and the Internet.

File Transfer Protocol (FTP)

File Transfer Protocol, usually referred to as FTP, was the original application on the Internet when UCLA was brought online in 1969 (there were four nodes by the end of that year). FTP provides a means to transfer files from a host computer to a client computer. Host computers are known as FTP servers.

Email

The ability to send email (electronic mail) was a natural and early application of the Internet (actually known as ARPANET until the early 1980s). Email takes advantage of the "language" of the Internet—TCP/IP—to find its destination. The Department of Defense funded research for the Internet, seeking to find a network that could withstand interruptions such as a nuclear explosion. With TCP/IP, data packets are addressed in terms of a server and a user. The packets are transmitted from one station to the next, meandering their way through the network. They do not depend on any particular server (except the destination, of course).

Usenet

The Usenet (User Network) consists of Usenet servers hosting theme-oriented chat areas or bulletin boards where participants can post messages on subject areas as diverse as Visual Basic and Brad Pitt. The Usenet, an outgrowth of email, became perhaps the first killer application for the Internet when scientists, using the federally funded network, formed groups to discuss Star Trek plots. Today, there are over 20,000 Usenet groups. Listservs (List Servers) are private discussion groups included under the Usenet "umbrella."

Gopher

The concept of the Gopher server came into vogue in the 1980s as a way to master the deluge of FTP servers coming online. The term is not an acronym; rather, it refers to "go for this and go for that." Gopher servers sought to catalog the documents stored on other servers in one accessible and indexed location so that someone seeking a particular document did not need to search through all of the FTP servers and their directories.

World Wide Web

The World Wide Web was based on a 1980 program—Enquire—and was proposed in 1989 by Tim Berners-Lee of the European Particle Physics Laboratory. The first Web site went online in June of 1991. The Internet grew quickly in popularity in 1993 and 1994 with the introduction of commercial Web browsers such as Mosaic and Spry's Internet-In-A-Box. Today, Netscape Communication's Communicator and Microsoft Internet Explorer dominate the Web browser market.

HTML

Web servers send Web pages to client Web browsers. Web pages are written entirely in *Hypertext Markup Language* (HTML), a still-evolving standard for presenting documents with embedded graphics and controls. The primary purpose of HTML is to present a point-and-click environment to the user so that he or she can link to other pages on the same server, or a remote server, merely by clicking on a hypertext link. HTML pages include embedded "tags" to control formatting. To begin a section of boldfaced text, the <**B**> tag is used. The end of the boldfaced text is denoted with a </**B**> tag. It is the browser's job to interpret the tags and display the page appropriately, taking into account screen resolution, and so on.

Presently, there is a new standard emerging for Dynamic HTML (DHTML), which allows the HTML page to behave more like a program.

Java And The World Wide Web

Sun Microsystems introduced the Java programming language, which makes it possible to create Java *applets*—small programs that are downloaded to the client's PC each time a page is visited. These applets are run in the browser's Java Virtual Machine (JVM). The JVM essentially interprets the Java code much as Basic interpreters did with GW-Basic in the 1980s. Java applets allow HTML pages to be less static, giving them the ability, for instance, to animate objects. However, because Java applets are interpreted and downloaded every time a page is visited, they can often slow down the Web experience. On the other hand, the Java language contains restrictions that make downloaded applets relatively harmless to a user's PC.

ActiveX And The World Wide Web

Through the use of active technology, Visual Basic can make the Internet experience more rich than is possible with Java applets. Active technology is both the bedrock of Microsoft's DCOM (Distributed Component Object Model) and an extension of Visual Basic's ActiveX controls. With active technology, the client PC is referred to as an *active client* and the host is referred to as an *active server*.

ActiveX Technology And The Internet

Microsoft's vision of the Internet, naturally enough, is a universe in which all clients use Microsoft Internet Explorer and all servers run Microsoft Internet Information Server (IIS). Active server pages are different than static pages because the server itself is running processes in addition to those run by the client, much as a database server runs a database engine in a traditional client/server system.

ISAPI (Internet Server Application Program Interface) is an API exposed by IIS that enables active server pages. This frees up resources on the client and allows the client to run more robust applications than is feasible with downloaded Java applets.

Active Servers

Active server pages have an extension of .ASP (whereas static HTML pages have an extension of .HTM or .HTML). Visual Basic can create programs that run as active server pages by creating an ActiveX DLL that invokes the services of OLEISAPI2.DLL. This DLL acts as a "bridge" from your VB program to ISAPI. Documentation for this is included in the Tools directory on the VB CD-ROM (this should not be on the certification exam). By definition, an active server page is one that is running some code above and beyond that necessary to fulfill HTML page requests. This could be an ActiveX DLL, VBScript, JavaScript, or a Java application (as opposed to an applet). However, also inherent in the definition of an active page is that the object running on the server (for instance, an ActiveX DLL) can have its methods called from the client PC using information in an HTML page.

Active Client

An active client is dynamic, running script rather than merely reacting to received HTML pages. In its documentation, Microsoft implies that Java applets embedded in HTML are included in the definition of static HTML, and thus, do not constitute an active client. Visual Basic supports the creation of active clients in two ways:

➤ You can "embed" ActiveX controls into a Web page to offer additional functionality. Although the pages are still constructed from HTML, special object tags (<**OBJECT**> and </**OBJECT**>) denote the use of embedded ActiveX controls, such as those used in VB development. (The page does not physically contain the control—the <**OBJECT**> and </**OBJECT**> tags contain a reference to the control and the location from which it can be downloaded). When the page is downloaded to the user's PC, the browser checks to see whether the control has been downloaded before. If not, it is downloaded and installed into the user's Windows\System (or WindowsNT\System) directory. There are two advantages to this approach: Because the controls are compiled, they execute faster than equivalent Java applets; and, because the control is downloaded only once, the developer can build more functionality into the control. The disadvantage to this approach is that because the ActiveX control is essentially a fully functional program, the developer has to be extra wary about potentially causing harm to the user's PC. (Also, because the control is developed for the Windows environment, its portability to other operating systems is limited.)

➤ You can create an ActiveX document, which is essentially a VB application designed to run within a Web browser such as Microsoft Internet Explorer. Most functionality that can be built into a VB application can also be supported in an ActiveX document. I discussed the creation of ActiveX documents in Chapter 9.

Active Servers And Active Clients

When an active server is communicating with an active client, each can leverage the power of the other to create true client/server applications across the Internet. Further, the model supports a three-tiered architecture, providing a great deal of *scalability*. Scalability refers to the ability of an application to grow to support more users. In this context, three-tiered refers to the Web browser as the client tier, the Web server as the middle tier, and the database server as the third tier. As an example, you might develop a Visual Basic application that displays a user interface and some degree of data validation on the client side. This would be deployed as an ActiveX document running within a browser. It would then communicate with an ActiveX DLL running on the Web server, which would be responsible for formulating SQL requests and possibly other chores not handled by the client. It would communicate with a database engine such as MS SQL Server, which is responsible for processing SQL requests, running stored procedures, performing some of the data validation, and so on.

Exploiting The Internet With Visual Basic

In the remaining portion of this chapter, I will discuss how to use the Internet from Visual Basic and how to make the Internet part of your Visual Basic application.

VBScript

VBScript is a Web page scripting language that can be embedded in HTML documents to perform server side processing. It is essentially Microsoft's response to JavaScript. VBScript is a subset of VBA (Visual Basic for Applications), the most notable difference is VBScript's absence of file I/O statements (omitted as a security precaution to minimize the risk to client PCs). VBScript can be used to access the properties and methods of an ActiveX control embedded in an HTML page. Currently, only Internet Explorer supports VBScript (however, you may want to search the World Wide Web for plug-ins to Netscape products that support VBScript).

VBScript is placed between the HTML tags **<SCRIPT>** and **</SCRIPT>**. A tutorial on VBScript usage is outside of the scope of the book. However, I raise the subject because I will make occasional reference to it when discussing ActiveX controls and components.

ActiveX Controls

In Chapter 9, I detailed the creation of an ActiveX control and introduced its use. An ActiveX control can be embedded in an HTML page. When a user visits a Web page, the browser sees references to the control between the HTML page's <OBJECT> and </OBJECT> tags. The browser then checks to see if the control is already installed on the user's PC and, if not, downloads it. The <OBJECT> and </OBJECT> tags actually specify the control's **CLASSID**, which is how the control is installed into the Registry. The **CLASSID** can be seen in the sample HTML file generated during the setup process (discussed in the "Internet Download Setup" section of Chapter 15) or by examining your own Windows registry. When you embed the control in an HTML page, certain properties of the control become a function of the HTML page and are embedded in the <OBJECT> tag itself. Other properties specific to the control are inserted into a special <PARAM NAME> tag with a VALUE= clause. The HTML code that follows shows how to embed a control, with two values assigned via the <PARAM NAME> tag. Notice that numeric values (as well as character values) are surrounded by quotes. The HTML was generated using Microsoft Front Page Express:

```
<html><head><title>Rich Text Control Example</title></head>
<body bgcolor="#FFFFFF">
<p><object classid="clsid:3B7C8860-D78F-101B-B9B5-04021C009402"
border="0" width="523" height="316" multiline="1"
text="Sample Text">
<PARAM NAME NAME="FontSize" VALUE=" 18">
<PARAM NAME NAME="FontBold" VALUE= "1"></object></p>
</body></html>
```

There are a number of good tutorials on the Web to teach you HTML. Alternatively, you can use a tool such as Microsoft Front Page to generate Web pages for you.

ActiveX Components

An ActiveX component is an ActiveX EXE ActiveX DLL, or ActiveX control. Each was formerly known as an OLE automation server, but have been redubbed as ActiveX components. I discuss the mechanics of creating and using ActiveX components in detail in Chapter 9.

The MSComm Control

The MSComm control is the granddaddy of VB communication controls. It allows you to directly manipulate data coming into and going out of the COM (serial) port, and thus, allows you to create a communications program entirely within VB. You can use the control's one event, **OnComm**, to trap the arrival of characters or changes in communication status such as Carrier Detect or Request To Send (RTS). Use the **CommEvent** property to determine what communications event has just taken place. For more information about the property and its possible values, search the VB Help file for "CommEvent Property." The **CommPort** property sets the COM port to which the control is attached. You can only use one COM port per control. The **PortOpen** property sets and returns the state of the communications port and also allows the port to be opened and closed. Use the **Settings** property to set parity, baud rate, and other communication settings. Use the **Input** property to read characters received and use the **Output** property to send data out of the COM port.

By and large, it is no longer necessary to write your own communications I/O with Visual Basic. It is easier to use built-in Windows functions such as Dial-Up Networking.

The Winsock Control

The Winsock control provides accesses to TCP and UDP services. To use the Winsock control in a project, select Microsoft Winsock Control 5.0 from Project|Components on the VB menu.

TCP (Transfer Control Protocol) allows communications between two computers and is the "language" of the Internet (though you can use it to communicate on TCP networks). UDP (User Datagram Protocol) is a lower-level protocol. Using UDP, computers do not need to establish a connection. Before you use the Winsock control, you must specify the protocol using the **Protocol** property:

```
'specify TCP
Protocol = sckTCPProtocol
'specify UDP
Protocol = sckUDPProtocol
```

Generally, where a connection needs to be maintained (such as when moving large volumes of data or when communicating frequently), you will use TCP. Otherwise, you will use the less resource intensive UDP.

TCP Applications

A TCP application can be either a client or a server app. If writing a client application (such as a Web browser), you need to know the server's IP Address (explained in the next paragraph) or computer name (on a TCP network). You also need to know the port on which the server will be listening.

The **RemoteHost** property is where you specify the IP address or computer name of the server with which the client application will be communicating. An IP address has four numbers separated by periods with each number having a range of 0 to 255. The computer name will usually be in the form of protocol://address such as "HTTP://www.coriolis.com" or "FTP://ftp.coriolis.com", where HTTP (Hypertext Transfer Protocol) and FTP (File Transfer Protocol) specify the local protocol and the remainder of the string is the computer name. An example is shown in this snippet (assuming the name of the Winsock control is **winsock1**):

```
winsock1.RemoteHost = "http://www.coriolis.com"
```

Fortunately, local port assignments are pretty much standardized. If connecting to a World Wide Web page (HTTP server), use port number 80. For FTP servers, use port 21. An example is shown here:

```
winsock1.RemotePort = 80
```

Once you have specified the **RemoteHost** and **RemotePort** properties, you can connect to the remote host using the **Connect** method:

```
winsock1.Connect
```

To send data from the TCP client to the host, use the **SendData** method of the Winsock control:

```
Dim myVar As String
myVar = "Text to send"
winsock1.SendData myVar
```

You can measure the status of data that is being sent with the **SendProgress** and **SendComplete** events. **SendProgress** maintains a counter of bytes transmitted since the last time the event was invoked. It also maintains a counter of how many bytes remain to be sent. This makes the event an ideal place to monitor a file send status such as with this simple code:

```
Public Sub SendFile (success As Boolean)
   Dim sBuffer As String * 1000

   Open "SomeText.Txt" For Binary As 1
```

```
    ' assumes the file is 1000 bytes long!
    Get #1,, sBuffer
    Close 1
    ' Send the file
    winsock1.SendData sBuffer
    Call winsock1_SendProgress
End Sub

Public Sub winsock1_SendProgress (bytesSent As Long, _
    bytesRemaining As Long)

    Do Until bytesRemaining = 0
        frm_progress.Caption =
            frm_progress.Caption & _
            str (int(bytesRemaining / 1000)) & "%"
        frm_Progrss.progressBar1.Value = _
            bytesRemaining / 1000
    Loop
Exit Sub

Public Sub winsock1_SendComplete
    Unload frm_progres
    MsgBox "Transfer Complete"
End Sub
```

This code loads a file into a string variable (to keep the size of the code down, the file size is assumed to be exactly 1000 bytes) and then uses the **SendData** method to transmit the data to the host. The **SendProgress** event is invoked and that loops until the transfer is complete. A form, **frm_Progress**, is updated, complete with a ProgressBar control. The progress of a transfer can be seen in Figure 12.1.

To create a TCP server application, you need to set the **LocalPort** property and then invoke the **Listen** method. Typically, this will be done in the **Load** event of the form containing the Winsock control. A typical snippet might be:

```
winsock1.LocalPort = 21
winsock1.Listen
```

Figure 12.1   The progress of a file being downloaded using the Winsock control.

To detect data being received, use the **DataArrival** event. To retrieve the data use the **GetData** method:

```
Public Sub winsock1_DataArrival (ByVal bytesTotal As Long)
    Dim myString As String
    winsock1.GetData myString
End Sub
```

You can also use the **PeekData** method to look at the data received without removing it from the input buffer.

UDP Applications

When two computers are communicating using UDP they are establishing a "peer-to-peer" relationship. Neither one is a client or a server. The **RemotePort** of one computer is set to the value of the **LocalPort** of the other computer. The **RemoteHost** of each computer is set to the "name" of the other computer.

 To determine the name of a computer, open the Network applet in the Windows Control Panel. Click on the Identification tab and check the value in the Computer Name textbox.

Once the **RemotePort**, **LocalPort**, and **RemoteHost** properties of the Winsock control have been set on both computers, use the **Bind** method from one computer to communicate with the other computer. There is no active connection as there is with TCP. The following code snippet shows a computer connecting to another computer named "Remote," with a **LocalPort** of 1001. To use the **Bind** method, you bind the Winsock control to the **LocalPort** as seen:

```
winsock1.LocalPort = 1002
winsock1.RemotePort = 1001
winsock1.RemoteHost = "Remote"
' bind to the local port
winsock1.Bind 1002
```

Sending and receiving data are then done in the same manner as under TCP using the **SendData** and **GetData** methods and the **DataArrival** event.

With UDP, you can change the **RemoteHost** and **RemotePort** properties whenever you wish to communicate with another computer. With TCP, you must first close the communication link using the **Close** method.

The Internet Transfer Control

The Internet Transfer control is an ActiveX control and so must be added from Project|Components on the VB menu. Select Microsoft Internet Transfer Control 5.0.

The Internet Transfer control implements Hypertext Transfer Protocol and the File Transfer Protocol, thus allowing you to connect your application to World Wide Web and FTP servers. You then retrieve documents or files using either the **OpenURL** or **Execute** methods. With WWW servers, you may need to set your user ID and password (for some restricted servers). For FTP servers, you usually supply a user ID of "anonymous" and a password of whatever your mail ID is (for instance, username@isp.com). Some FTP servers have restricted access, in which case you will have to use the user ID and password given to you by the server administrator. To set the user ID, use the Internet Transfer control's **UserName** property. To set the password, use the **Password** property. The **URL** property specifies the server that you will be connecting to.

Always set the **URL** property *prior* to the **UserName** and **Password** properties. When you set the value of **URL**, the **UserName** and **Password** properties are cleared. The following code will retrieve the base directory from Coriolis' FTP server (assuming the name of the Internet Transfer control is **Inet1**):

```
inet1.URL = "FTP://ftp.coriolis.com"
inet1.Password = "username@isp.com"
inet1.UserName = "anonymous"
' load the directory into a textbox
text1.Text = inet1.OpenURL
```

Alternatively, you can supply the URL (Uniform Resource Locator) as an argument to the **OpenURL** method. A second optional argument specifies whether to retrieve the data as a string or as an array of type **Byte**. These options are **icString** and **icByte** respectively; **icString** is the default. If you are retrieving binary data, you need to use the **icByte** options. The following will retrieve the file MYPROGRAM.EXE from the fictitious FTP server ftp.myftp.com:

```
Dim bBuffer () As Byte
Dim sURL As String
sURL = "FTP://ftp.myftp.com"
bBuffer () = inet1.OpenURL (sURL, icByte)
Open "C:\myprogram.exe" For binary As 1
Put #1,, bBuffer ()
Close 1
```

The **OpenURL** method communicates synchronously; the **Execute** method communicates asynchronously. Therefore, other processes can occur while the **OpenURL** method is executing. With **Execute**, the application has to wait until the request is completed before it (the application) can continue processing.

Some methods of the Internet Transfer control work differently or not at all depending on which protocol you use. The **Execute** method, for instance, supports different commands for HTTP than it does for FTP. The supported commands are listed in Tables 12.1 and 12.2. Consult an HTTP and an FTP guide for more explanation about how to use these commands.

The **GetHeader** method works only with HTTP servers and returns a portion of or all of the URL page's header information. The following code snippet returns the name of the server:

```
Dim myVar As String
myVar = inet1.GetHeader(server)
```

If no argument is supplied, all header information is returned. For other arguments, refer to the VB Help file under "GetHeader Method."

The Internet Transfer control has an **AccessType** property to determine how a connection is made. Use the VB constant **icDirect** for a direct connection (such as when the network is connected to the Internet or with an existing dial-up connection); **icNamedProxy** when connecting through a proxy server (in which case it uses the server specified by the **Proxy** property); or **icDefault** to use the default settings from the registry.

Use the **Document** property to determine which document the **Execute** method will retrieve.

The **Protocol** property specifies (or retrieves) the protocol to be used. It has one of the following values:

➤ **icUnknown** Protocol is unknown

➤ **icDefault** Use the default protocol

➤ **icFTP** FTP protocol (FTP)

➤ **icHTTP** HTTP protocol (HTTP)

➤ **icHTTPS** Secure HTTP (HTTPS)

Use the **RequestTimeOut** property to set the time, in seconds, at which an error will occur if the current request has not been completed. A VB error will

Table 12.1 Supported HTTP commands.

Command	Purpose
GET	Retrieve all data from the specified URL.
HEAD	Send request headers.
POST	Post data to the server.
PUT	Replace the page specified in the data argument.

Table 12.2 Supported FTP commands.

Command	Purpose
CD *dir*	Change to the specified directory.
CDUP	Change to the parent directory.
CLOSE	Close the FTP connection.
DELETE *file*	Delete the specified file.*
DIR *dir*	Perform a directory operation using *dir* as an argument (passwords are allowable but work differently on different operating systems). Use the **GetChunk** method to retrieve the data.
GET *from to*	Download the file specified as *from* and save it as the file specified by *to*.
LS *dir*	Perform a list operation using *dir* as an argument (passwords are allowable but work differently on different operating systems). Use the **GetChunk** method to retrieve the data.
MKDIR *dir*	Make the specified directory.*
PUT *from to*	Upload the file specified as *from* and save it as the file specified by *to*.*
PWD	(Print Working Directory) Generates the name of the current directory. Use the **GetChunk** method to retrieve the data.
QUIT	Terminate the current user.
RECV *from to*	Same as GET.
RENAME *from to*	Rename the remote file specified as *from* to the name specified as *to*.*
RMDIR *dir*	Remove the specified directory*.
SEND *from to*	Same as PUT.
SIZE *dir*	Return the size of the specified directory.

* Success is determined by your privileges on the server.

be generated if the **OpenURL** method was used for the request. If **Execute** was used, the **StateChanged** event will occur with an error code, listed in Table 12.3.

The Internet Transfer control has the same **RemoteHost, RemotePort,** and **StillExecuting** properties as the Winsock control, though you generally do not need to configure the remote host or port.

The Internet Transfer control has one event: **StateChanged**, which happens when the state of the current connection occurs. A **state** variable is passed to the event signifying what has happened. These are listed in Table 12.3.

If the **state** becomes **icError**, you should check the control's **ResponseCode** property for a numeric error code from the server. The **ResponseInfo** property will provide a textual description of the error.

The **StateChanged** event is used to monitor requests made with the **Execute** method. Because this is done asynchronously, the program can perform other tasks while the request is being processed. (With **OpenURL,** the program cannot do anything else until the request has completed.) If you set up a loop inside of the event to monitor the progress of the request, be sure to provide the **DoEvents()** function to allow other processes to continue.

Table 12.3 **StateChanged state codes.**	
State	**Meaning**
icNone	No change
icHostResolvingHost	Looking up the IP address of the host computer
icHostResolved	Found the IP address of the host computer
icConnecting	Connecting to the host computer
icConnected	Connected to the host computer
icRequesting	Sending a request to the host computer
icRequestSent	Request sent
icReceivingResponse	Receiving a response from the host computer
icResponseReceived	Received a response from the host computer
icDisconnecting	Disconnecting from the host computer
icDisconnected	Disconnected from the host computer
icError	An error has occurred
icResponseCompleted	Request has been fulfilled

Exam Prep Questions

Question 1

A remote computer has connected to your VB application using TCP and wants to send a stream of data. Which of the following scenarios can you use to successfully receive the data?

○ a. Use the Winsock control. Set its **RemoteClient** property to the name or IP address of the client (remote) machine. Invoke the **Listen** method of the Winsock control.

○ b. Use the Winsock control. Use the control's **Listen** and **Accept** methods to listen for connection requests and to accept incoming data.

○ c. Use the Winsock control. Use the control's **Listen** and **Accept** methods to listen for connection requests and to accept the connection request. Use the **DataReceive** method to receive the data.

○ d. Use the Winsock control. Use the control's **Listen** and **Accept** methods to listen for connection requests and to accept the connection request. Use the **DataArrival** event to determine how much data is being received and use the **GetData** method to retrieve the data from the input buffer.

Answer d is correct. The *Listen* method continually listens for requests. The *Accept* method accepts connection requests. The *DataArrival* event indicates how much data has been received and the *GetData* method actually retrieves the data from the input buffer. Answer a is incorrect because there is no **RemoteClient** property and because the **Listen** method does not accomplish the data retrieval. Answer b is incorrect because **Accept** permits a connection; it does not accept data. Answer c is incorrect because **DataReceive** is not a valid method of the Winsock control.

Question 2

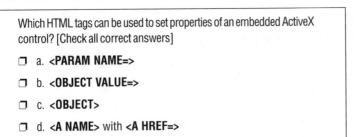

Which HTML tags can be used to set properties of an embedded ActiveX control? [Check all correct answers]

- ❐ a. <PARAM NAME=>
- ❐ b. <OBJECT VALUE=>
- ❐ c. <OBJECT>
- ❐ d. <A NAME> with <A HREF=>

Answers a and c are correct. The <*OBJECT*> tag allows the specification of many ActiveX control properties. Those specified with the <*PARAM NAME*=> tag can be read by VBScript to directly manipulate property values of the ActiveX control. Answer b is incorrect because there is no <**OBJECT VALUE**=> tag. Answer d is incorrect because the <**A**> tag provides references to HTML objects. (The **HREF**= option provides a link to other HTML documents.)

Question 3

What type of VB project can run as a service of Microsoft IIS (Internet Information Server)?

- ❐ a. VBScript applets
- ❐ b. ActiveX Controls
- ❐ c. ActiveX DLLs
- ❐ d. ActiveX EXEs

Answer c is correct. By invoking the services of OLEISAPI2.DLL, the ActiveX DLL can communicate directly with Microsoft IIS to create applications that run on the Web server, performing most tasks that a VB application running locally can do. Answer a is incorrect because VBScript is not a valid Visual Basic project and because applets run on a client machine—not on the server. Answer b is incorrect because ActiveX controls are run on local machines as part of a Web page. Answer d is incorrect because ActiveX EXEs are run within a Web browser—not on the server in conjunction with Microsoft IIS.

Question 4

> Which of the following code snippets will correctly fulfill a peer-to-peer communications request?
>
> ○ a.
> ```
> winsock1.LocalPort = 1002
> winsock1.RemotePort = 1001
> winsock1.RemoteHost = "Remote"
> ' bind to the local port
> winsock1.Bind 1002
> ```
>
> ○ b.
> ```
> winsock1.LocalPort = 1002
> winsock1.RemotePort = 1001
> winsock1.RemoteHost = "Remote"
> ' bind to the local port
> winsock1.Bind 1001
> ```
>
> ○ c.
> ```
> winsock1.LocalPort = 1002
> winsock1.RemotePort = 1001
> winsock1.Listen
> winsock1.Accept
> ```
>
> ○ d.
> ```
> winsock1.LocalPort = 1002
> winsock1.Listen
> winsock1.Accept
> ```

Answer a is the right choice because it correctly establishes a connection using UDP. The question specified a peer-to-peer connection, which requires UDP (TCP is used for a host-client type of connection). The local machine must specify the name of the remote machine, as well as on which port it will be listening. It must also specify the local port to use and then bind to that port using the *Bind* method. Answer b is incorrect because the control is binding to the **RemotePort** when it should be binding to the **LocalPort**. Answer c is incorrect because it is establishing a TCP connection. (The specification of the **RemotePort** is redundant.) Answer d is incorrect because it is also establishing a TCP connection.

Question 5

> What are the valid values of the Internet Transfer control's **Protocol**
> property? [Check all correct answers]
>
> ☐ a. **icFTP**
>
> ☐ b. **icHTTP**
>
> ☐ c. **icTCP**
>
> ☐ d. **icUDP**

Answers a and b are correct. *icFTP* and *icHTTP* are valid protocols of the
Internet Transfer control. (There are a few other valid values—see "The
Internet Transfer Control" section of this chapter.) Answers c and d are incorrect because **icTCP** and **icUDP** are not valid values of the **Protocol** property.
The property specifies HTTP or FTP and not TCP or UDP. When a secure
HTTP site is encountered, the value reflects HTTPS.

Need To Know More?

 Aitken, Peter: *Visual Basic5 Programming EXplorer.* Coriolis Group Books, Scottsdale, AZ, 1997. ISBN 1-57610-065-0. Peter discusses the use of the MSComm control in Chapter 12, and in Chapter 22 discusses the use of ActiveX controls on the Web.

 Harrington, John, Mark Spenik, Heidi Brumbaugh, and Cliff Diamond: *Visual Basic 5 Interactive Course.* Waite Group Press, Corte Madera, CA, 1997. ISBN 1-57169-077-8. Chapter 19 covers communications including use of the MSComm control, connecting to the World Wide Web and use of the Internet Transfer control.

 Jamsa, Kris and Lars Klander: *1001 Visual Basic Programmer's Tips.* Jamsa Press, Las Vegas, NV, 1997, ISBN 1-884133-56-8. This well-done book is not broken into chapters but rather into "tips." Tips 759 through 768 discuss the MSComm control. Tips 669 through 775 discuss the Winsock control, and Tips 776 through 786 cover the Internet Transfer control. Tips 851 through 871 cover VBScript, HTML (as it relates to ActiveX controls), and the use of ActiveX controls within a browser.

 Mandelbrot Set, The: *Advanced Microsoft Visual Basic.* Microsoft Press, Redmond, WA, 1997. ISBN 1-57231-414-1. This book is broken into sections done by various authors (they are not listed on the cover). Chapter 4, written by Adam Magee and Karen Field, is a superb discussion of the Internet as it relates to Visual Basic as well as use of the Internet Transfer control.

 Search the online books on the VB5 CD-ROM for the terms "Internet," "Winsock," "HTTP," and "TCP" and you will receive an extensive list of topics on using the Internet with Visual Basic.

 Microsoft places the most current Knowledge Base on line at www.microsoft.com/support/. Enter search terms such as "Internet," "Winsock," and "World Wide Web" to view articles detailing tips (and sometimes fixes) revolving around the use of the Internet with Visual Basic.

Debugging And Testing

Terms you'll need to understand:

- √ Debug
- √ Watch window
- √ Watch expression
- √ Locals window
- √ Immediate window
- √ Call Stack window
- √ Print and Assert

Techniques you'll need to master:

- √ Suspending program execution conditionally and absolutely
- √ Changing the values of variables while the program is executing
- √ Using the Immediate window to print and execute procedures
- √ Monitoring and interpreting the Call Stack window
- √ Using the Print and Assert methods of the Debug object
- √ Creating an Assert sub

Few activities are more important and less practiced than thorough testing. Visual Basic provides a number of tools to make sure your programs run smoothly. Debugging a program in Visual Basic is largely a process of halting execution at appropriate places to see what is going on as your application is running and taking corrective action. You will find several questions on the certification exam designed to judge your familiarity exploiting these tools. Debugging and testing is the topic of this chapter on your road to VB certification.

The Debug Toolbar

Visual Basic provides a good selection of debugging aids under the Debug menu and makes them conveniently available on the Debug toolbar. If the toolbar does not show in your IDE, right-click in the toolbar area and select Debug. It is shown in Figure 13.1.

The most useful debugging feature may well be the Breakpoint. By placing your cursor on a line of code and clicking the toolbar (or pressing F9), the breakpoint is toggled on or off. When on, the program automatically stops immediately *before* executing that line.

Step Into (F8) executes the next line of code and then pauses execution, even if that line of code is in another procedure. Step Over (Shift+F8) executes the next line of code but does not enter other procedures. This means that other procedures are executed in their entirety as though they were one line of code. Step Out (Ctl+Shift+F8) is an underused option that will cause all remaining lines in a procedure to be executed and pause execution on the next line of the calling procedure.

Not found on the Debug toolbar is Run To Cursor (Ctl+F8), which causes execution to continue until the line where the cursor is placed is encountered. Also not found on the toolbar are the Set Next Statement (Shift+F9) and Show Next Statement (available only under the Debug menu) options. The former allows you to change the order of statements, while the latter, as its name implies, shows you which statement will execute next.

The other buttons are covered in the next several sections.

The Debugging Process

You can set a breakpoint on any line, as we have already seen. You can also press Ctrl+Pause at any time to suspend execution. Visual Basic even allows you to alter many (but not all) statements while the programming is running. The most notable exceptions to this are declarative statements. Adding or modifying a declaration will almost always cause VB to restart the program from the beginning.

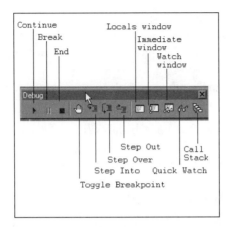

Figure 13.1 The Visual Basic Debug toolbar.

Many program bugs come from problematic variables. If you knew what the values of your variables were at all times, you would not need to debug. In Chapter 6, I gave you many pointers on preventing syntax errors and handling runtime errors. However, except for those of us who are perfect (such as myself), logic errors are a fact of life in programming.

Let's assume you are dividing values and get our "division by zero" friend as an error message. There are a number of tactics you can employ to determine where that nasty zero in the divisor is coming from.

The Watch Window

A topic you are sure to see on your exam is the Watch window, shown in Figure 13.2. You can add a watch on any variable or expression, which will cause a break (suspend program execution) when the expression is true or when the value changes. You can simply "watch" the variable. In all cases, VB continually displays the value of the variable (or expression). In Figure 13.2, an expression is set to break when the expression **dDivisor = 0** evaluates to **True**. While the program is executing, but suspended, you can click the current value to change it, or click the watch expression to edit it. Right-clicking in the Watch window allows you

Figure 13.2 The Visual Basic Watch window.

to add, edit, or delete a watch. Note that variable values are not available while "out of scope." Thus, if you are "watching" a variable defined in one procedure, it is not available while another procedure is being executed.

The Locals Window

The Locals window is a "built-in" version of the Watch window. While stepping through code, you may select View|Locals Window at any time. A Watch window titled "Locals" will be displayed containing all "in scope" variables (that is, all variables that are visible from the procedure currently being executed).

The Immediate Window

Another topic that you are very likely to encounter on the exam is the use of the Immediate window (you mainly need to know that it is available and how to use it). In this window, you can type any valid Visual Basic line of code, but you cannot declare a new variable or object. The code is always executed in the context of the current procedure. This means that any statement behaves as though it were part of the code of the current procedure. Thus, if you alter a variable, the most locally defined version of that variable is the one that is operated on.

To print to the Immediate window, you can use the **Print** method of any valid object or you can use **Debug.Print**. Output is sent to the Immediate window without breaking execution and without disturbing the application's display space. Figure 13.3 shows the results immediately after a **Debug.Print dDivisor** statement has been executed (the top line). Notice also that the values of **cmdGo.Caption** and **dNumerator** have been printed.

The Immediate window also allows you to call other procedures, but only if doing so would be valid within the current procedure.

 The Immediate window, available since Visual Basic 1.0 (and, back to its QuickBasic predecessors) has been primarily intended to be a debug time tool. However, VB5 now allows it to be used at design time to support ActiveX development.

```
Immediate
   2
print cmdGo.Caption
&Go
print dNumerator
   10
```

Figure 13.3 Outputting values to the Immediate window.

The Call Stack Window

While our mothers have advised us not to look back, it is often essential to know our roots in the debugging process. In this context, the Call Stack window is a useful, if imperfect, tool. It displays the name of all procedures executed, each preceded by the name of the object to which it belongs (i.e., frmMath.cmdGo_Click). This can be helpful when trying to follow complicated nested procedure calls. Unfortunately, if you have multiple occurrences of a given object, you cannot distinguish one from another. It would also be useful if you could examine the actual order in which specific lines of code are executed (Microsoft Professional Basic for MS-DOS allowed you to recall the last 10 lines executed). Still, when you are having trouble with the ultimate in nested procedures-recursive calls, this can be a handy tool.

The Debug Object

Debug is a unique Visual Basic object that exists only in the development environment (it is not available at runtime) to support development. Statements referencing the **Debug** object are automatically stripped out of code when an EXE file is created. It has two methods: **Print** and **Assert**.

We have already seen the **Print** method in action; its output always goes to the Immediate window.

Visual Basic already allowed for an **Assert** procedure. VB5 essentially makes it part of the development environment by providing it as a method of **Debug**. **Assert** allows the developer to conditionally halt execution when the **Assert** line is encountered. The syntax takes the form: Debug.Assert *expression*, where expression must evaluate to a **Boolean** (i.e., **True** or **False**).

 The **Assert** method must have been a late add-on to VB5 because the documentation within VB is weak, and a survey of some other reference guides shows inaccurate examples or no mention at all. A VB5 book from a publisher whom I generally trust makes the statement: "The **Debug** option has no properties and only one method, **Print**."

If you have not used assertions before, the syntax may be counter-intuitive. Execution halts (and the **Debug.Assert** line is highlighted) when the expression is **False**. What you are doing is *asserting* that a statement is true and then having the program tell you if you are wrong:

```
Debug.Assert dDivisor <> 0
```

In this example, we are asserting that **dDivisor** is any value but zero *when the line of code is executed*.

Further Asserting Yourself

As stated earlier, VB already allowed you to code an **Assert** sub. The **Debug**. **Assert** method is convenient because it is automatically stripped out of your executable. This may not be what you want, however. Therefore, you may wish to "roll your own":

```
Sub Assert (bExpr As Boolean, sMsg As String)
    If Not bExpr Then
        MsgBox (sMsg, vbOK, "Assert")
    End If
End Sub
```

To use the **Assert** sub:

```
Assert (dDivisor <> 0, "dDivisor = 0!")
```

You can eliminate this code with conditional compilation also:

```
#If fDebug Then
  Assert (dDivisor <> 0, "dDivisor = 0!")
#End If
```

The best way to become intimately familiar with what is available is to use the tools. Create a small program and step through the code. Use the Immediate window to make assignments. Use the Locals window to view and change values. Step through code and set break points. The "Debugging Your Code" topic in the online books provides an excellent overview of what is available. Also, review Chapter 6 if necessary, and then move on to Chapter 14, where compiler switches are discussed, including how they relate to debugging.

Exam Prep Questions

Question 1

> Under what conditions will the message box be displayed (that is, program execution is not halted)? [Check all correct answers]
>
> ```
> DeBug.Assert sVar <> "cat"
> MsgBox "Blue"
> ```
>
> ☐ a. In a compiled program
>
> ☐ b. In the development environment when **sVar** is equal to "cat"
>
> ☐ c. In the development environment when **sVar** is not equal to "cat"
>
> ☐ d. Always

Answers a and c are correct. Answer a is correct because the *Debug.Assert* statement is stripped out of the executable. Answer c is correct because in the development environment, *Assert* does not halt execution if the statement is false. Answer b is incorrect because execution would halt if sVar were equal to "cat." (that is, if the statement evaluates to **True**, program execution halts; if the statement evaluates to **False**, execution proceeds). Answer d is wrong because b and c are mutually exclusive choices; the message box will not display in the development environment under all conditions.

Question 2

> Assuming that your form has at least one enabled text box, where does the output of a **Debug.Print** statement go?
>
> ○ a. The first text box in tab order
>
> ○ b. The last text box in tab order
>
> ○ c. The Watch window
>
> ○ d. The Immediate window

Answer d is correct because *Debug.Print* is always displayed in the Immediate window. Answers a and b are both wrong because output is never sent to the form. Answer c is wrong because output never goes to the Watch window.

Question 3

> Assume the following line is in the **command1_click** event of your form:
>
> ```
> print label1.caption
> ```
>
> Where is the output displayed?
>
> ○ a. In the Immediate window
>
> ○ b. The *first* text box in tab order
>
> ○ c. The *last* text box in tab order
>
> ○ d. Directly on the form
>
> ○ e. Nowhere. Label controls do not have a **Print** method.

Answer d is correct. Output goes directly to the form. Answer a is wrong because output from the **Print** method in this case is *not* to the Immediate window. Similarly, b and c are wrong because output is not to any control except the form to which the control belongs. Answer e is incorrect because the fact that the Label control has no **Print** method is irrelevant. The trick to this question is, once again, to read the code snipped carefully and not jump to the obvious answer too quickly. Whenever you see a method (in this case, the **Print** method) being employed without being qualified, it is a method of the "containing" object. The code is at the form level (it is not at the Label control level) and so, **Print** is a method of the form. The output of the form's **Print** method goes to the form.

Question 4

> When is an entry added to the Call Stack window? [Check all correct answers]
>
> ❐ a. When the program starts.
>
> ❐ b. When a module level function is executed.
>
> ❐ c. When a procedure is executed, but only if it is called with the **Call** keyword.
>
> ❐ d. When every line of code (except nested statements) is executed.
>
> ❐ e. When any sub or event procedure is executed.

Answers **b** and **e** are correct. Answer **b** is correct because the **Call Stack** window records all executions of any procedure, including a function. Answer **e** is correct because an event procedure is no different than any other procedure and so is also recorded in the **Call Stack window.** Answer a is incorrect because the Call Stack window only records calls to procedures—the start of a program is not a call to a procedure. Answer c is incorrect because it specifies that the **Call** keyword must be used when it is optional. Answer d is incorrect because actual lines of code are (unfortunately) not recorded. The "except nested statements" comment was meant to confuse you.

Need To Know More?

 Aitken, Peter: *Visual Basic 5 Programming EXplorer*. Coriolis Group Books, Scottsdale, AZ, 1997. ISBN 1-57610-065-0. In Chapter 8, Peter devotes the first several pages introducing the mechanics of debugging.

 Harrington, John, Mark Spenik, Heidi Brumbaugh, and Cliff Diamond: *Visual Basic 5 Interactive Course*. Waite Group Press, Corte Madera, CA, 1997. ISBN 1-57169-077-8. Chapter 10 discusses debugging at a useful, if introductory, level, including use of the Immediate window and monitoring the Call Stack window. It continues with a good discussion of "spaghetti code" that results in hard-to-find bugs.

 Jamsa, Kris Ph.D. and Lars Klander: *1001 Visual Basic Programmer's Tips*. Jamsa Press, Las Vegas, NV, 1997. ISBN 1-884133-56-8. This well-done book is not broken into chapters but rather into "tips." Tips 546 through 553 deal with debugging issues such as breakpoints and use of the Watch window.

 Mandelbrot Set, The: *Advanced Microsoft Visual Basic*. Microsoft Press, Redmond, WA, 1997, ISBN 1-57231-414-1. This book is broken into sections done by various authors (they are not listed on the cover). Chapter 1, by Peter J. Morris, covers in-depth the subjects of error handling as well as debugging and testing, including the overlooked area of assertions (which, from my experience, is a favorite on the certification exam).

 McKinney, Bruce: *Hardcore Visual Basic, Second Edition* (which covers version 5). Microsoft Press, Redmond, WA, 1997. ISBN 1-57231-422-2. In Chapter 1, Bruce has 9 pages (pages 35 through 43) devoted to **Assert** and some advanced debugging procedures.

 Search the online books on the VB CD for "Debugging Your Code," which provides a very detailed review of the debugging process.

 Microsoft places the most current Knowledge Base on line at www.microsoft.com/support/. Enter search terms such as "debug," "Immediate window," and "Assert" to view articles detailing tips (and sometimes fixes) revolving around the issues discussed in this chapter.

There are a number of Web sites devoted to the subject of Visual Basic. Use a search engine such as Yahoo! (www.yahoo.com) or Hotbot (www.hotbot.com) with a search term such as "Visual Basic 5" (be sure to place the search term in quotes so that only pages containing the entire term as one string are returned). A well-done site with tips and sample code that I liked was the VB Palace at home.computer.net/~mheller/. Another site that was under "reconstruction" when I visited was a site hosted by Temple University at thunder.ocis.temple.edu/~shariq/vb/index.html.

14

Compiling

. . . .

Terms you'll need to understand:

√ Compile

√ Standard EXE

√ ActiveX server

√ ActiveX DLL

√ ActiveX EXE

√ ActiveX control

√ P-code and native code

√ Project

√ Group

√ Runtime engine

√ MSVBVM50.DLL

Techniques you'll need to master:

√ Compiling a standard EXE

√ Compiling ActiveX components

√ Compiling to p-code or native code

√ Using compilation optimizations

√ Creating a Visual Basic group file

√ Creating a Visual Basic ActiveX control license file

Visual Basic 1.0 took the market by storm despite everyone knowing it was a "toy" language. Strike one was the fact that it was based on the Basic language itself ("Real programmers don't use Basic"). Strike two was the fact that it was an "interpreted" language. There was no strike three, however. Instead, Microsoft evolved the language to where it is the number one development tool on the market. As to the issue of being interpreted, compilation had been the domain of "real" languages such as C (notwithstanding the fact that VB's ancestor QuickBasic was fully compiled). VB5 brings true compilation to the masses and that fact hasn't been ignored on the certification exam, where you are likely to encounter more than one question probing your understanding of the compilation process. And that is the subject of this chapter.

The P-Word Vs. The M-Word

I don't agree with those who say that a language is not "professional" if it compiles programs into *pseudo-code*. Visual C, for instance, offers that as an option. Pseudo-code is not true "machine language" (those bits and bytes that the computer and the operating system understand), but is highly tokenized code that requires the presence of a runtime helper to assist in its interpretation. These runtime engines are those VBRUNXXX.DLLs (where XXX refers to a version of Visual Basic, such as 100 for version 1.0) littering our Windows\System directories. I will discuss those in a moment.

Indeed, the loading of a runtime interpreter does make the program run somewhat slower. However, not is all as it seems on the surface. First is that even our pseudo-code (usually referred to as *p-code*) programs contain a large amount of fully compiled code. Simple arithmetic operations tend to be fully compiled, while floating-point operations tend to depend on the runtime engine. Much more significant is the fact that modern client/server programs tend to spend most of their time either "idling" while waiting for user input, or performing database operations. Regarding the former, compilation does not make the program idle any faster. Concerning the latter, the speed of database operations is almost fully dependent on the database itself and the connection engine (for instance, Microsoft Jet, the ODBC driver, and so on).

Programs that perform many CPU-intensive number calculations will benefit the most from native code. Programs that perform a lot of string manipulation or calls to the Windows API will not see much of a performance enhancement. The advantage of p-code is a smaller EXE file, but at the trade-off of slower performance. A native-code EXE still requires the Visual Basic runtime engine, MSVBVM50.DLL, but makes much fewer (and often more efficient calls) to the DLL. The archtypical "Hello World" program without a form compiles to 6 K using p-code and 6 K using native code (optimized for speed). With a form, p-code generated a 7 K file while the native code file was 9 K.

 Experienced programmers will debug their programs while compiling to p-code and do their final testing while compiling to native code, because it takes longer to compile to native code.

Still, the ability to create true executables is a much-ballyhooed development in Visual Basic 5 and *will* be on your exam so, without further ado, let's dive right in.

Compilation Basics (No Pun Intended)

The Visual Basic 5 compiler's technology is shared with that of Microsoft Visual C++ and is very efficient indeed. It is capable of producing *native code*, which is code that the computer and operating system understands without the use of an intervening runtime engine.

 Although it is true that many programs can run without the MSVBVM50.DLL runtime engine, Microsoft advises that it should still be distributed with VB applications. Even native-code applications call the DLL for various functionalities. The difference is that the DLL is then being used as a true Dynamic Link Library instead of as an engine "interpreting" the p-code.

Visual Basic supports only 32-bit executables (Windows 95/98 and Windows NT). Programs generated with Visual Basic 5 will *not* run under Windows 3.1x. This is unfortunate because there is a significant base of Windows 3.1x users. The size of that base is a matter of dispute over which I do not care to conjecture.

Projects

A Visual Basic project is a collection of modules (form, class, and standard—see Chapter 3 for more information) grouped together in what is similar to a C++ *make file*. You can group together more than one project to create your final EXE. Every project requires a startup object, but there can be only one **Sub Main**. The project name has to be unique, as it is stored in the Windows Registry as well as in the Object Browser. The project name is also used as a qualifier to describe classes within the project. The project name coupled with the class name (*project_name.class_name*) is the *programmatic ID* of that class. The name can contain no embedded spaces.

The General Tab

To set the properties of your project, select Project|*project* Properties (where *project* is the name of your project). The resulting screen looks like Figure 14.1. You set various options in the General tab. Project Type can be a Standard EXE or (Professional and Enterprise editions only) an ActiveX EXE, Dynamic Link Library (DLL), or control.

The Help file and default Help file Context ID are placed on this screen. The project description is entered as free-form text—it is not displayed anywhere. There is a checkbox that allows or disallows ActiveX controls to be upgraded for this project. If you are creating an ActiveX control, you can also check Require License Key. If you select this, the user of the control must have the control registered in his or her Registry, along with a copy of the VBL (Visual Basic License) file that is produced when the project is built. If you are creating a multithreaded application, additional choices allow you to select Unattended Operation, and to choose between either one thread or a definable number of threads per object. See Chapters 9 and 12 for more information.

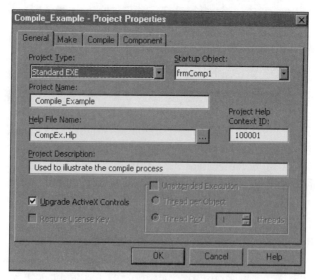

Figure 14.1   The General tab of the Project Properties dialog.

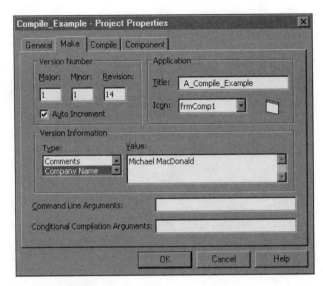

Figure 14.2   The Make tab.

The Make Tab

The Make tab of the Project Properties dialog is shown in Figure 14.2. Here you can set options that mostly reflect version information. You can set major, minor, and revision version numbers. Typically, a revision indicates bug fix releases (and possibly aesthetic changes). Minor releases are most typically functionality enhancements, whereas major releases denote releases with significant new functionality. When beta testing a project, the revision number is often used to denote the "Build" (compile) number. There is a checkbox to auto-increment this number.

You can choose the icon that represents your EXE in its minimized state, as well as within the Windows Explorer. The Make Title allows you to specify the name of the final executable file. It defaults to the project name, but you can specify a different name here. You can place text such as comments, copyright, and other legal information directly into your EXE. Finally, you can add some compilation switches, which will be discussed under "Compiling Your VB Application" later in this chapter.

The Compile Tag

The Compile tab (shown in Figure 14.3) is where you set your compilation option. It will generally be the most used page. Here you choose between compilation to p-code or native code. If you choose native code, you can fine-tune

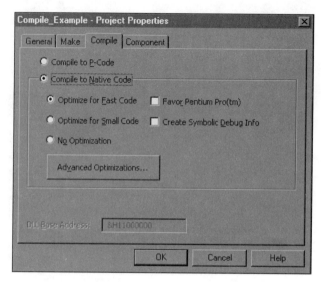

Figure 14.3 The Project Properties' Compile tab.

optimizations. For the most part, you will want to optimize for speed. You can alternatively choose to optimize for space (minimize the size of the EXE or DLL file) or choose no optimization. The compiler is able to "compact" a program by creating pointers to similar sequences of code, in a manner similar to how PKZip compacts files. This slows execution and is seldom beneficial. If your program will only be running on Pentium Pro processors, you may wish to select Favor Pentium Pros, which generates instruction sets optimized for the Pro. The Create Symbolic Debug Info checkbox allows the embedding of debugging information into the file, which can be used by many third-party debugging tools (such as Microsoft Visual C++ and Code View). If you are generating a DLL, you can specify the starting address, which the operating system will attempt to use.

The Advanced Optimizations Dialog

You can further fine-tune your compile with the Advanced Optimizations dialog, shown in Figure 14.4. Be sure you know what you are doing before selecting any of these options because program performance or reliability can be adversely affected. On the other hand, you may achieve better performance. For instance, the Remove Safe Pentium FDIV Checks option omits checks for the infamous division errors on very old Pentiums. This is overhead that is seldom needed because there are relatively few of those CPUs and the actual number of errors was not large (and the sequence needed to create the errors is not likely to appear in most business applications). These options are summarized in Table 14.1.

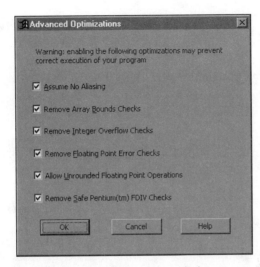

Figure 14.4   The Advanced Optimizations dialog.

Table 14.1 Advanced optimization options.	
Option	**Explanation**
Assume No Aliasing	Aliasing means referring to a variable by different name, such as when passing a variable as an argument to a procedure. You should generally leave this option off.
Remove Array Bounds Checks	VB will check that indexes are within bounds unless you turn this off. If you are certain that you have no boundary violations, set this option on.
Remove Integer Overflow Checks	Setting this option will speed up some operations by removing checks to verify that the value assigned to an integer is within range.
Remove Floating Point Error Checks	Setting this option will speed up some operations by removing checks to verify that the value assigned to **Single** and **Double** data types are within range.
Allow Unrounded Floating Point Operations	Ironically, this increases precision but it may adversely affect results, because comparisons between two numbers may fail due to mathematical errors. See Chapter 2.
Remove Safe Pentium FDIV Check	Setting this option stops VB from testing to see if inaccurate results were generated due to floating-point division problems in some older Pentiums. You should generally be able to turn this on.

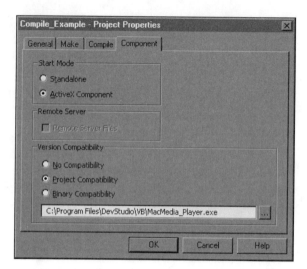

Figure 14.5 The Project Properties' Component tab.

The Component Tab

The Component tab (see Figure 14.5) is for ActiveX server applications and allows you to designate the Start Mode as standalone or as an ActiveX component. If the project is to be compiled into a standalone executable file (see "The General Tab" section earlier in this chapter), these options will be unavailable. I altered the project to be an ActiveX executable so that the options could be seen in the figure. I discuss these options in Chapter 9.

Compiling Your VB Application

Once all of your project properties are set, you can proceed with compilation. To do so, select File|Make *project*.EXE, where *project* is the name of your project. There are a number of optional arguments you can provide that are entered on the Project Build dialog. These are summarized in Table 14.2. You can also compile from the command line

```
VB5 /MAKE | MAKEDLL projectname
```

where *projectname* is the name of the project to compile to an EXE or DLL. You can specify other command line arguments as on the Project Build page and summarized in Table 14.2.

The Visual Basic Runtime Engine

If you compile to p-code, your application also needs access to the VB runtime engine (RTE), which is MSVBVM50.DLL for VB5 applications. This file needs

Table 14.2   Other native code compilation switches.

Switch	Meaning
/cmd or **/c**	Puts arguments in the Make tab. Must be the last argument.
/d *compileconst*	One or more compilation constants.
/make or **/m**	Make an EXE.
/makedll or **/l**	Make an ActiveX server DLL.
/out *filename*	Output errors to a file.
/run or **/r**	Run after compiling.

to be either in the same directory as the application or in the Windows\System directory. The file is rather large (more than 1.3 MB on my release).

Versions 1 through 3 of VB deployed only the VBRUNxxx.DLL (where xxx was 100, 200, or 300). VB4 complicated matters because it targeted both 16- and 32-bit executables. VB5 returns to some degree of simplicity in this regard.

A Word About Linking

Under MS-DOS, the process of creating an executable file included a step called *static linking*. The compiler produced a file in "object" format that included some unresolved references to calls to other libraries. The linker then attempted to find, in the supplied list of libraries, those procedures that were referenced. It assembled them and the object file into one, standalone executable.

Under Windows, there is no static link step. The executable (the program) has embedded in it call(s) to libraries to link to procedures in other libraries. Because the linkage is done at runtime, this is called *dynamic linking*. When your program makes a call to a procedure outside of your program, it supplies the name of a DLL file, which exposes some internal procedures.

 This is not always the panacea it once seemed. There are so many DLL versions running around, that conflicts can and do happen when we "upgrade" software and find that DLLs we needed have been overwritten. You can avoid this by installing your DLLs into your application's directory, even though that means there will be redundant files.

Exam Prep Questions

Question 1

> You must always set up the Project Build and Compile options before compiling your VB application.
>
> ○ a. True
>
> ○ b. False

Answer b is correct. If you don't set up the Compile options, VB will use whatever defaults you last used.

Question 2

> Visual Basic can produce a compile to what type(s) of target(s)? [Check all that apply]
>
> ❏ a. Standard EXE
>
> ❏ b. ActiveX EXE
>
> ❏ c. Standard DLL
>
> ❏ d. ActiveX DLL
>
> ❏ e. Standard control
>
> ❏ f. ActiveX control

Answers a, b, d, and f are the correct answers. Visual Basic can produce a standard EXE, as well as an ActiveX EXE, ActiveX server (DLL), and ActiveX control. Answer c is incorrect because VB cannot produce standard DLLs. Answer e is incorrect because there really is no such thing as a Standard control. (Visual Basic's intrinsic controls are actually part of an object library: VB5.OLB.)

Question 3

> How do you embed comments and legal information into a Visual Basic executable?
>
> ○ a. Insert symbolic debugging information into the file and then use any tool that can access it, such as Code View, to manipulate the EXE (or DLL) header.
>
> ○ b. Select Project|Add Header Info.
>
> ○ c. Use the Project Properties dialog.
>
> ○ d. Open the file in Notepad or another text editor and insert the comments.

Answer c is correct. You simply use the Project Properties dialog to add those comments and other info that you desire. Answer a is wrong because the symbolic debugging info is for debugging the program only. Answer b is wrong because there is no such option. Answer d is wrong because you should never edit a binary executable.

Question 4

> Aliasing refers to:
>
> ○ a. The process of compiling equivalent standalone and ActiveX executables where one runs on a remote server and the other runs on a local PC.
>
> ○ b. Adding multiple projects together into a group (each project is an alias of the group).
>
> ○ c. Passing a variable to a procedure and referring to it by another name in the procedure.
>
> ○ d. The ability of the **Variant** data type to act like another data type.

Answer c is correct because aliasing is when you refer to a variable by two or more different names. Answer a is incorrect because there is no such procedure. Answer b is incorrect because projects and groups have nothing to do with aliasing. Answer d is correct because the underlying data type of a **Variant** also has nothing to do with aliasing.

Question 5

> Assume that you have turned on the Remove Integer Overflow optimization switch. What will happen when the last loop is executed below?
>
> ```
> Dim iVar As Integer, lVar As Long
> For iVar = 1 to 150000
>     lVar = iVar
> Next
> ```
>
> O a. An overflow error will be generated
>
> O b. Nothing, because the assignment to the Long prevents an error
>
> O c. Nothing, because 150000 is a valid integer value
>
> O d. **iVar** will be some value other than 150000

Answer d is correct because the optimization prevents an overflow error, causing Visual Basic to actually "loop" the value. The maximum number that an integer can hold is 32767. On the next iteration, *iVar* wraps back to a value of 1. Answer a is wrong because no error is generated. Answer b is wrong because the assignment to a **Long** is irrelevant. Answer c is wrong because 150000 is not a valid value.

Need To Know More?

 Mandelbrot Set, The: *Advanced Microsoft Visual Basic*. Microsoft Press, Redmond, WA, 1997. ISBN 1-57231-414-1. This book is broken into sections done by various authors (they are not listed on the cover). Peter J. Morris devotes the beginning pages of Chapter 8 to an advanced discussion of compilation, optimization, switches, and so on. On page 349 is a very interesting graph showing the differences in execution speed between Visual Basic versions 4 and 5.

 McKinney, Bruce: *Hardcore Visual Basic, Second Edition* (which covers version 5). Microsoft Press, Redmond, WA, 1997. ISBN 1-57231-422-2. Bruce devotes a portion of Chapter 1 to the theory of compilation, such as the true nature of pseudo-code (as opposed to marketing hype), link libraries, and so on.

 Search the VB CD for "More About Programming" (Book 2), where you will find a number of topics detailing the compilation process. Also, search for "Designing for Performance and Compatibility," which has some more compilation related subjects.

 Microsoft places the most current Knowledge Base on line at www.microsoft.com/support. Enter search terms such as "compile" to view articles detailing tips (and sometimes fixes) revolving around the issues discussed in this chapter.

 There are a number of Web sites devoted to the subject of Visual Basic on the Internet. Use a search engine such as Yahoo! (www.yahoo.com) or Hotbot (www.hotbot.com) to search for the term "Visual Basic 5" (be sure to place the search term in quotes so that only pages containing the entire term as one string are returned). A well-done site with tips and sample code that I liked was the "VB Palace" at home.computer.net/~mheller. Another site that was under "reconstruction" when I visited was a site hosted by Temple University at thunder.ocis.temple.edu/~shariq/vb/index.html.

15

Distributing Your Visual Basic Application

. . . .

Terms you'll need to understand:

√ Setup Wizard

√ Project file

√ Dependency file

√ License file

√ Internet download

√ Digital signature

√ Scripting and initialization safety

√ Primary and secondary CAB files

√ Setup Toolkit

Techniques you'll need to master:

√ Creating a setup program

√ Determining file dependencies

√ Creating an Internet download setup

√ Linking to the Microsoft Web site for secondary CAB file downloads

√ Certifying your ActiveX components as safe

Even though our VB application has been compiled, we're not yet done with it. The last step is to package it for distribution. Distributing your program is the subject of this chapter and anywhere from four to eight of the questions that you will see on the certification exam. Visual Basic provides you with a few different ways to package your programs. As you have seen, you can generate not only standard executables (EXE), but also a variety of ActiveX projects. The Setup Wizard packages these into setup routines, which perform the necessary file installs, registry updates, and so on.

The Setup Options

There are really four different ways to distribute your VB applications. The first and most onerous is to write your own setup routine. This is not your best choice, because some of the other methods are more simple. The second option involves the purchase of a third-party utility, such as InstallShield from Stirling Technologies. Most Visual Basic developers will opt to use the Setup Wizard bundled with VB. This handles nearly all situations. Also bundled with Visual Basic is the Setup Tool for those situations where you need specialized functionality.

In the next section, I will discuss the Setup Wizard, followed by a discussion of how to customize it with the Setup Tool. Along the way, I will discuss the steps necessary to make your VB work of art function on your user's Windows 95, 98, or NT machine.

The Setup Wizard

When you are ready to create a setup for your program, run SETUP.EXE from your vb5\setupkit\kitfil32 folder. The first screen (the Select Project And Options dialog), shown in Figure 15.1, prompts you for the name of your project file. Although you will generally select a project file with an extension of .VBP, you'll need to select a *group file* with an extension of .VBG if your application has multiple projects. The Setup Wizard does not display these if you use the Browse button, forcing you to type the file name. You may select a *template file* (extension .SWT) if you have previously run the Setup Wizard for the current project. A template file contains all of the setup settings and is optionally saved when you have completely run through the Wizard.

 Visual Basic organizes related modules and classes into projects. Although most applications will consist of one project, you can make an application comprising several projects. These related projects are known as a group. I discussed this in more detail in the section titled "Projects" in Chapter 14.

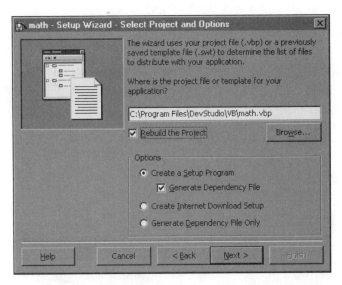

Figure 15.1   Choose output file options on the Setup Wizard's opening screen.

You should check the Rebuild The Project box if you want to force the entire project to be rebuilt. Note, though, that the project must have been built at least once prior to using this option. You will generally choose the Create A Setup Program option. However, you may also choose to generate a file to set up an application from the Internet by selecting the Create Internet Download Setup option (discussed later).

Dependency Files

If you choose to create a setup program, you can optionally choose to create a *dependency file* or you may choose to create the dependency file only (with no setup program generated at all). A dependency file is a list of files required by each DLL, OCX, ActiveX, or other component. For instance, an OCX may depend on the existence of COMDLG32.DLL in your user's windows\system directory.

If you are creating an Internet install, a What's New button appears in the Select Project And Options dialog. This allows you to link to the Microsoft Web site to check for the latest information about installing from the Internet.

When you click the Next button, the Setup Wizard scans all components attached to your project (such as ActiveX files) for dependencies. If it does not find the required dependency file (extension .DEP) for each, you are prompted

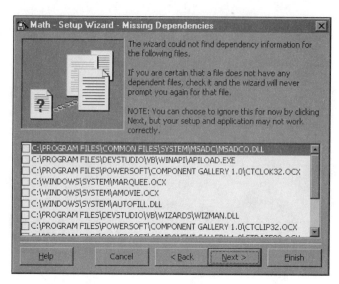

The wizard could not find dependency information for the following files.

If you are certain that a file does not have any dependent files, check it and the wizard will never prompt you again for that file.

NOTE: You can choose to ignore this for now by clicking Next, but your setup and application may not work correctly.

C:\PROGRAM FILES\COMMON FILES\SYSTEM\MSADC\MSADCO.DLL
C:\PROGRAM FILES\DEVSTUDIO\VB\WINAPI\APILOAD.EXE
C:\PROGRAM FILES\POWERSOFT\COMPONENT GALLERY 1.0\CTCLOK32.OCX
C:\WINDOWS\SYSTEM\MARQUEE.OCX
C:\WINDOWS\SYSTEM\AMOVIE.OCX
C:\WINDOWS\SYSTEM\AUTOFILL.DLL
C:\PROGRAM FILES\DEVSTUDIO\VB\WIZARDS\WIZMAN.DLL
C:\PROGRAM FILES\POWERSOFT\COMPONENT GALLERY 1.0\CTCLIP32.OCX

Help   Cancel   < Back   Next >   Finish

Figure 15.2   The Setup Wizard scans for missing dependency information.

to either supply a location or tell Visual Basic that there are no dependencies. If you have created a control that is to be included with your distribution, you should exit the Setup Wizard and rerun it to create a dependency file for your control. This is seen in Figure 15.2.

Setup Media

You are next asked to describe the type of output. If you are creating a disk-based install, you should choose one of the two floppy-disk options, otherwise you will install to the single directory option. The Setup Wizard then prompts for any required database connectivity files, as well as whether to use the Microsoft Jet or ODBC for connectivity.

Setup Components

After this, the Setup Wizard determines the ActiveX components of your project, as shown in Figure 15.3. If any required components are not listed, they should be added using the Add button. Note that the components listed by Visual Basic include those added via the Project|Component dialog within Visual Basic or references added via the Object Browser or Project|Reference dialogs. If you have inserted a reference to an OLE component, such as embedding a Microsoft Word document, this will also appear on the list. If you added any components or references that were not actually used in your project, you should remove them from your setup by unchecking them.

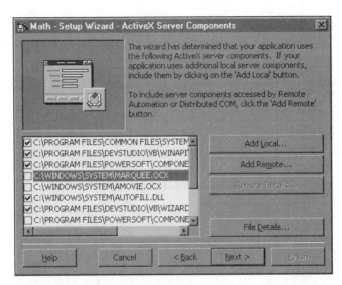

Figure 15.3   The components that are included in your setup distribution file.

After ensuring that all required components are included, Visual Basic scans each of them and builds a list of dependencies, which will also be part of your distribution file, as shown in Figure 15.4. You can add or remove files from this

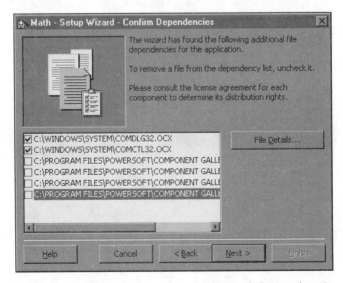

Figure 15.4   You are asked to confirm additional dependencies detected based upon the ActiveX components included in the project.

list. You need to make sure you have the proper license to distribute components, not only for legal reasons, but also because your application may not function when distributed if you do not have the proper distribution rights.

Other Distribution Files

Finally, the Setup Wizard builds a final list of files to be contained in the distribution file. You should review this carefully, not only for missing components and their dependencies, but also for icons, bitmaps, README files, Help files, and so on. You can add any missing elements at this point. Note that if you highlight any file, the Setup Wizard tells you the reason the file is required, as seen in Figure 15.5.

File Install Locations

From this same screen, you can also highlight a file and click File Details. You should do so and check where the Setup Wizard proposes to install each file. This is done via a drop-down list box, as shown in Figure 15.6.

This important step allows you to exercise a great deal of control over where components are installed, as well as the suggested default locations for your users. This is done via "wild card macros" illustrated in Table 15.1. One consideration is where to install DLL files. The traditional answer has been to install them in the \windows\system folder (windows\system32 for Windows

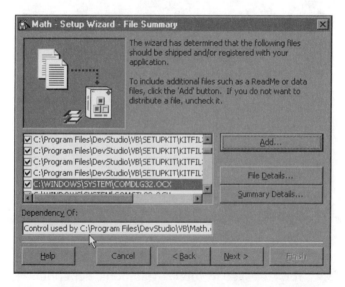

Figure 15.5 The final proposed list of files included with the distributed setup program.

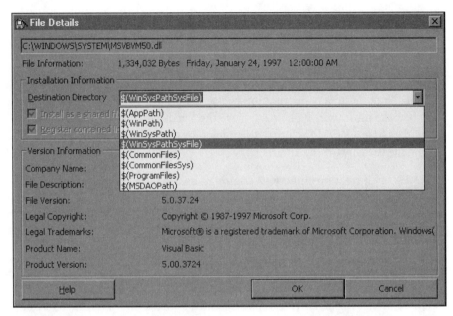

Figure 15.6   Specify the destination of each file via the directory macros dialog.

Table 15.1	Setup Wizard directory macros.
Macro	**Install Location**
$(WinSysPath)	\windows\system
$(WinSysPathSysFile)	\windows\system; not removed when app is uninstalled
$(WinPath)	\windows
$(AppPath)	Folder specified by user; set default in [SETUP] section of SETUP.LST
$(AppPath)samples	\samples folder below the application folder
C:\path	Folder identified by path; not recommended
$(CommonFiles)	Common folder (usually \Program Files\Common Files\)
$(ProgramFiles)	C:\Program Files
$(CommonFiles)\System	System folder under Common Files
Do Not Install This File	Appears if installing VB License (VBL) file; license is placed in user's Registry but file is not installed
Occache	If installing a VB License file, license is registered and file is placed in Occache folder
$(MSDAOPath)	For Data Access Objects (DAO) only; stored in user's Registry

NT) indicated via the $(WinSysPath) macro. You may opt to install them into the application directory instead to prevent accidental overwriting of user files, as well as to make uninstalls easier.

The Setup Wizard will include MSVB50VM.DLL, the Visual Basic runtime engine. Note that many distribution packages omit this file because of its size and because most users will already have the file. If you do not include it, you should include a README file explaining how the end user can obtain a copy of the file (usually off the Internet).

 If creating an ActiveX control to be used in a design environment other than VB, you must also include the property page component (MSSTKPRP.OCX) usually found in the system directory.

Setup Safety Verification

As a final step, you should verify your setup. You do this by first running a virus scanner on it, using an anti-virus package such as those from Norton, McAfee Associates, and Dr. Solomon. You should then run your setup, ensuring that it works properly, that files are installed into the correct locations, and that the installed program then works correctly.

Internet Download Setup

You can use the Setup Wizard to create Internet downloads for ActiveX controls assembled with VB5, as well as for ActiveX DLLs, EXEs, and documents. This process is done for ActiveX components that are to be hosted on Web sites. If your project creates an ActiveX component that is to be used locally, this component should be bundled in a regular setup program, as described in the prior section.

 ActiveX components are referenced in the HTML page sent to the user's browser. If the component is not installed on the user's machine, it is then downloaded.

When you create an Internet download package, the Setup Wizard creates a cabinet (CAB) file, referred to as the *primary cabinet file*, which includes your ActiveX component and an INF file. The *secondary cabinet files* contain any other needed components (such as MSVBVM50.DLL) and are downloaded separately. During the setup, you can link to the Microsoft Web site, which hosts these files digitally signed for safety by Microsoft. Alternatively, you can choose to have secondary CAB files downloaded from an alternative site, as

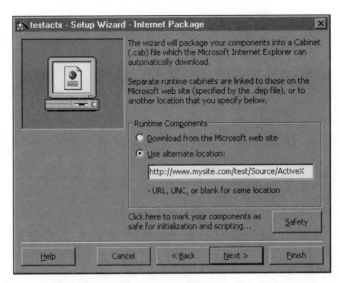

Figure 15.7   You may link to Microsoft's Web site to download secondary CAB files, or you may specify an alternate site. Note that the address shown is fictitious.

shown in Figure 15.7. On this same screen, you'll find a button that lets you digitally sign each file, certifying its safety. When you certify a component as being safe, you are signing your name to the file (digitally) and certifying that the component can *never* be disruptive to a user's computer, even if the component is used in an HTML page written by someone else.

 You will find one or two questions relating to digital certification of ActiveX components, so you should walk through the setup process and examine the options yourself. See the section "Making Your ActiveX Controls Safe" for more discussion.

Most of the remaining options are similar to those for a regular setup routine. When complete, the Setup Wizard creates an output directory containing the generated CAB file, along with a sample HTML file embedding your component. It also creates a subdirectory called "support," which includes all files that are part of the primary CAB file. You may manually rebuild the CAB file using the syntax

```
Makecab /f filename.ddf
```

where *filename* is the name of the DDF file in the support directory. You may wish to do this if you need to customize the install file (*filename*.INF). The most common reason for doing so is changing the destination directory for the

ActiveX component. Use "10" for the \windows directory, "11" for the \windows\system (windows\system32 for Windows NT), or leave it blank for the occache directory.

If any component requires a license, run LPK_TOOL.EXE found in the \lpk_tool directory of your Visual Basic 5 CD. This will create and output a LPK file for each component. See the output HTML file generated by the Setup Wizard for the Registry key that you will need to generate.

Making Your ActiveX Controls Safe

Often, when you download something from the Internet, its source is anonymous. Most PC users are aware of the risks (usually in the form of viruses) of executable programs as well as Word and Excel macros. Users are less often aware of the potential risk of ActiveX controls. It is your responsibility as a developer to ensure that the control can do no harm. Further, it is also your responsibility to ensure that the control's purpose cannot be subverted so that your seemingly benevolent control is dangerous. Ensuring the safety of your control requires verification that it is safe for "initialization" and safe for "scripting," both of which I discuss next.

Ensuring That A Control Is Safe For Initialization

Every ActiveX control has properties that are initialized when the control is instantiated. The control itself is embedded on an HTML page by the page's <OBJECT> and </OBJECT> tags. Values of the control's properties are set by the **PARAM NAME**= attributes associated with the <OBJECT> tags on the page. Any data that a web designer places in the **PARAM NAME**= attributes becomes available to the ActiveX control. Assume your control has a file filter property that you intended to be something along the idea of "*.txt" or "*.doc". The control will save a file using the file filter property. A Web designer might alter this (inadvertently or not) to "*.com", creating the potential for critical files (such as COMMAND.COM) to be overwritten. Therefore, it is your responsibility to ensure that properties cannot be initialized in a fashion such that the control exhibits potentially harmful behavior.

Ensuring That A Control Is Safe For Scripting

Much as you do not wish to have a control's properties initialized in a fashion where the control can be dangerous to a user, you also do not wish to permit a Web page developer to write script (Java or VB) that accesses properties of your control to subvert its purpose. Assume you develop a control that acts as a text editor. You do not want to allow anything outside of the control except the control's user to alter the properties of the control. For instance, your text editor control may have a filename property. If you permit the Web page developer to write script to alter the properties of the control, you need to ensure that he or she cannot change the filename to WIN.INI (causing this file to be overwritten the first time your control saves the TXT file). The control should not expose to the script on the HTML page any data, such as Registry or file information, that it reads from the disk. Nor should it perform any disk-based or API functions based on information supplied by the script.

The Setup Toolkit

There are times when you may wish to alter the behavior of the Setup Wizard. For instance, you may wish to add a "billboard" to your setup routine, to flash messages to your user as your application is installed. To do so, you should first make a backup of the setup1 directory because you will be regenerating the Setup Wizard. All of the files that you need are also in the setup1 directory. Open the VB project file SETUP1.VBP. You will need to determine manually all the project files to be installed on your user's computer, and also their dependencies.

 VB uses the **CopyFile** function to copy files to a user's computer. You should also use this function when creating your customized setup program, because it checks the date and version of files before overwriting them.

You are responsible for specifying where each file is to be located on your user's machine, as well as for compressing each. The online books on the VB CD contain detailed instructions under "Using the Setup Toolkit" in "Part 2: What Can You Do With Visual Basic?"

Exam Prep Questions

Question 1

> When distributing an ActiveX component from the Internet that includes components requiring a license, what type of file should you create?
>
> ○ a. An LIC file
>
> ○ b. A VSL file
>
> ○ c. An LPK file
>
> ○ d. A VBL file

Answer c is correct. You create an LPK file for distribution using LPK_TOOL.EXE. Answers a and b are incorrect because Visual Basic does not generate LIC or VSL files. Answer d is incorrect because a VBL file is used for standard (non-Internet) components.

Question 2

> What must you do to distribute an OCX control that you have created for use by other VB5 developers?
>
> ○ a. Run the Setup Wizard to create a CAB file for distribution.
>
> ○ b. Run the Setup Wizard to create the necessary VBL file(s).
>
> ○ c. Run the Setup Wizard to specify a setup program and the inclusion of the property page control.
>
> ○ d. Run the Setup Wizard to specify a setup program, but including the property page control is not mandatory.

Answer d is correct because the question specified that the control was to be used on other VB5 environments, which already have the property page control. Answer a is incorrect because a CAB file is used for Internet downloads. Answer b is incorrect because the creation of a VBL license file is not mandatory. Answer c is incorrect because the property page control is not mandatory.

Question 3

How can you get Microsoft to certify secondary CAB files for your ActiveX download component?

- O a. Do nothing except reference the Microsoft Web site in the Setup Wizard.

- O b. Submit an application with a sample of all components to Microsoft at www.microsoft.com/digital_safety/ application/.

- O c. Send a fee to the ActiveX development team, along with a disk containing all components and a notarized form attesting to your ownership of the contents of the disk.

- O d. Microsoft refers developers to third parties for this service.

Answer a is correct—all you need to do is reference the Microsoft Web site in the Setup Wizard. Secondary CAB files will be downloaded from there. Microsoft certifies these files automatically. Answer b is incorrect because there is no such Web site. Answer c is incorrect because no fee is required. Answer d is incorrect because Microsoft provides the service itself.

Question 4

How many dependency files are created with your setup program and what are their purposes?

- O a. You can create any number of dependency files needed to record the link between components and distribution licenses.

- O b. You can create any number of dependency files needed to record those files on which your components may be dependent, in order to execute properly.

- O c. One dependency file is created to record the dependency of the main executable (or ActiveX component) and files in the setup program.

- O d. You cannot create a dependency file.

Answer b is correct because a dependency file tells Visual Basic what files (such as a DLL) are required by different components, and you may generate as many as needed. Answer a is incorrect because a dependency file has nothing to do with licensing. Answer c is incorrect because the dependency file(s) may document more than the needs of the main EXE (or ActiveX component). Answer d is incorrect because you *can* create dependency files.

Question 5

> How do you handle the problem where a file is to be installed into $(WinSysPath) and your user has installed Windows 95 into a directory called "D:\Win95"?
>
> ○ a. You do nothing because Windows takes care of resolving the directory names.
>
> ○ b. You do nothing because the Setup Wizard resolves any directory names.
>
> ○ c. You need to run the Setup Toolkit to customize your install program.
>
> ○ d. You can't install to this directory because the directory name contains an illegal character.

Answer a is correct because $(WinSysPath) is a macro pointing to the system directory wherever Windows 95 is installed. Answer b is incorrect because the Setup Wizard cannot resolve a directory name—it does not know the names of the directories that other users might be using. Answer c is incorrect because no customization is needed. Answer d is incorrect because $(WinSysPath) is a macro indicating that the file should be installed into the system directory underneath Windows.

Need To Know More?

 Aitken, Peter: *Visual Basic 5 Programming EXplorer*. Coriolis Group Books, Scottsdale, AZ, 1997. ISBN 1-57610-065-0. Chapter 5 introduces compilation options and optimizations. Chapter 8 provides a walk-through of the Setup Wizard.

 Harrington, John, Mark Spenik, Heidi Brumbaugh, and Cliff Diamond: *Visual Basic 5 Interactive Course*. Waite Group Press, Corte Madera, CA, 1997. ISBN 1-57169-077-8. Chapter 14 provides an overview of the compilation process as well as an introduction to the Setup Wizard.

 Jamsa, Kris and Lars Klander: *1001 Visual Basic Programmer's Tips*. Jamsa Press, Las Vegas, NV, 1997. ISBN 1-884133-56-8. This well-done book is not broken into chapters but rather into "tips." Tips 897 and 905 through 918 provide a very nice discussion of the compilation process, use of the Setup Wizard, distribution media selection, and installation on client PCs.

 Mandelbrot Set, The: *Advanced Microsoft Visual Basic*. Microsoft Press, Redmond, WA, 1997. ISBN 1-57231-414-1. This book is broken into sections done by various authors (they are not listed on the cover). In Chapter 8, Peter J. Morris delves into use of the compiler to squeeze the most out of your program's performance and programmer productivity, including detailed discussion of more than you ever wanted to know about the internals of the compiler itself. I found information in this chapter that I saw nowhere else, including undocumented command line switches for the compiler.

 McKinney, Bruce: *Hardcore Visual Basic, Second Edition* (which covers version 5). Microsoft Press, Redmond, WA, 1997. ISBN 1-57231-422-2. This excellent volume does not devote any specific sections to the compilation and distribution of Visual Basic executables per se. Instead, Bruce sprinkles references to the compiler in various discussions throughout (particularly in Chapters 1 and 10) in terms of making the VB application more efficient.

Search the VB CD for the terms "Native Code Compiler Switches," which documents various optimization techniques; "Designing for Performance and Compatibility," which discusses various optimization techniques as well as the differences between p-code and machine code; and "Distributing Your Application," which discusses use and alteration of the Setup Wizard.

 Microsoft places the most current Knowledge Base online at www.microsoft.com/support/. Enter search terms such as "Setup Wizard," "compile," and so on, to view articles detailing tips (and sometimes fixes) revolving around compilation and distribution.

16

Sample Test

The sections that follow provide numerous pointers for developing a successful test-taking strategy, including how to choose proper answers, how to handle ambiguity, how to work within the Microsoft framework, how to decide what to memorize, and how to prepare for the test. This chapter also provides a number of questions that cover subject matter that's likely to appear on the Microsoft Visual Basic 5 exam. Good luck!

Questions, Questions, Questions

You should have no doubt in your mind that you're facing a test full of questions. Each exam consists of 60 questions. You'll be allotted 75 minutes to complete the exam. Remember, questions come in two basic types:

➤ Multiple choice with a single answer

➤ Multiple choice with multiple answers

Always take the time to read a question twice before selecting any answer. Also, be sure to look for an Exhibit button, which brings up a window containing longer code listings you'll need to consult in order to understand a question. (Though I have not seen it on the VB exam, some Microsoft exams have graphics exhibits. It is not out of the question that you could see one; perhaps a screen shot.)

It's easy to assume that a question demands only a single answer. However, a lot of questions require more than one answer. In fact, there may be some questions for which all answers should be marked. Read each question carefully enough to determine how many answers are needed; also, look for additional instructions when marking your answers. These instructions are usually in brackets, immediately after the question itself.

Questions that require only one answer will have radio buttons for you to click. Radio buttons are mutually exclusive—if you select one, any other that was selected will be unselected. Questions where you are expected to provide more than one answer will have checkboxes to select your answers. You can select from one to all answers.

Picking Proper Answers

Obviously, the only way to pass an exam is to select correct answers. However, the Microsoft exams are not standardized, like SAT and GRE exams—they are more diabolical and convoluted. In some cases, questions are so poorly worded that deciphering them is nearly impossible. In such cases, you may need to rely upon the process of elimination. There is almost always at least one answer out of a set of possible answers that can be eliminated because of any of the following scenarios:

➤ The answer doesn't apply to the situation.

➤ The answer describes a nonexistent issue.

➤ The answer is already eliminated by the question text.

Once obviously wrong answers are eliminated, you must rely on your retained knowledge to eliminate further incorrect answers. Look for items that sound correct but refer to actions, commands, or features that do not apply to or appear within the described situation.

After this elimination process, if you still face a blind guess for two or more answers, reread the question. Try to picture the situation in your mind's eye and visualize how each of the possible remaining answers might alter that situation.

After you can no longer eliminate incorrect answers but remain unclear about which of the remaining possible answers is correct, it's time to guess! An unanswered question scores no points, but a guess gives you some chance that the choice you make is correct. I found a good strategy to be to make your guess and mark the question for later review. (The test allows you to mark any questions that you wish to revisit later.) In this way, if you run out of time, you have at least made a guess. When all questions have been answered, use the test's review mode to look at questions that you had marked. The answer may come to you upon a second reading. In any case, you are assured that you allow enough time to answer those questions that you *do* know.

Decoding Ambiguity

Microsoft exams have a reputation for including questions that are difficult to interpret, confusing, or outright ambiguous. In my experience with numerous exams, I fully understand why this reputation is so prevalent. I'm not sure if the reason some questions are phrased so poorly is to limit the number of passing grades for those who take the tests. It may simply be that the tests are not well designed.

The only way to beat Microsoft at its own game is to be prepared. You'll discover that many exam questions test your knowledge of things that might not be directly related to the issue raised in a question. This means that the answers offered—even incorrect ones—are as much a part of the skills assessment as the question itself. If you don't know most aspects of Visual Basic development well, you might not be able to eliminate obviously wrong answers because they relate to VB topics other than the subject or subjects addressed by the question.

Questions often give away their answers, but you have to be smarter than Sherlock Holmes to find the clues. Often, subtle hints appear in the text in such a way that they seem like irrelevant information. (Sometimes, irrelevant information *is* provided in an attempt to throw you off the trail. Question 1 in Chapter 6 does this by talking about Auto Syntax Check being turned on.) You must inspect and successfully navigate each question to pass the exam.

Look for small clues that seem incidental, such as control names, Registry settings, and so on. Small details can point out the right answers; but if you miss them, you may find yourself facing a blind guess.

Another common source of difficulty in the certification exams is vocabulary. Microsoft has an uncanny ability for naming some utilities and features cogently, yet it creates completely inane or arbitrary names for others—especially for those dealing with OLE/ActiveX technology and data access. Be sure to brush up on the key terms presented in the appropriate chapters for these topics. You might also want to review the Glossary before taking the test.

Working Within The Framework

Test questions appear in random order. Many similar elements or issues repeat in multiple questions. It's not uncommon to observe that the correct answer to one question is a wrong answer for another. As you take the test, make time to read each answer, even if you find the correct one immediately. Incorrect answers can spark your memory and help on other questions.

You can revisit any question as many times as you like. If you're uncertain about the answer to a question, mark that question in the box provided, and you can return to it later. Also, mark questions you think might help you answer other questions. I find that I end up marking 25 percent or more of the questions on exams that I take. The testing software is designed to help you track your answers to every question, so use those capabilities to your advantage. Everything you want to see again should be marked; then, the test software can help you return to marked items easily.

What To Memorize

How much material you must memorize for an exam depends on your ability to remember what you've read and experienced. For the most part, the test is reasonable in not requiring you to memorize obscure syntax variations. Yet, almost out of left field, you may be tripped up by a question asking you to memorize the value of a message box constant.

Important types of information to memorize include:

➤ Compiling and distribution applications, including handling licensing and registration issues.

➤ Using the VB wizards to accomplish key tasks such as building classes.

➤ Creating and using ActiveX components.

➤ Creating a database application.

If you work your way through this book while sitting at a computer with Visual Basic loaded, you should have little or no problem interacting with most of these important items. Or, you can use The Cram Sheet that's included with this book to guide your rote memorization of key elements.

Preparing For The Test

The best way to prepare for the test—after you've studied—is to take at least one practice exam. I've included such an exam in this chapter. Give yourself 75 minutes to take the test. Also, keep yourself on the honor system and don't cheat by looking at text that appears elsewhere in the book. Once your time is up or you finish, check your answers against the answer key, which follows this chapter.

For additional practice, visit Microsoft's Training And Certification Web pages at www.microsoft.com/train_cert/ and download the Self-Assessment Practice Exam utility.

The VB5 practice test became available just as this book was being prepared for testing. In my opinion, the VB4 sample exam that I had looked at more accurately represents the types of questions that you are likely to encounter than does the sample VB5 test. For example, the sample VB5 exam had a question asking you the value returned when the user presses the NO button on a message box. You are more likely to be asked of the value in terms of a VB constant, not the actual number returned. You should nevertheless download both. Use the VB4 test to get a feel for testing conditions. Use the VB5 test to get a little more feel for the subjects that will be covered on the actual VB5 exam.

Taking The Test

Relax. Once you sit down in front of the testing computer, there's nothing more you can do to increase your knowledge or preparation. Take a deep breath, stretch, and attack the first question.

Don't rush; there's plenty of time to complete each question and to return to skipped or marked questions. If you read a question twice and remain clueless, take a guess, mark it, and move on. Easy and hard questions are dispersed throughout the test in random order. Don't cheat yourself by spending too much time on difficult questions early on that prevent you from answering easy questions positioned near the end of the test. Work your way through the entire test quickly, as a first pass. Then, before returning to marked questions, evaluate the amount of time remaining by the number of such questions. As you answer questions, remove their marks (unless you want to revisit them yet again). Continue to review all remaining marked questions until your time expires or you complete the test.

That's it for pointers. Here are 60 questions to practice on. Allow yourself 75 minutes. When you have finished, review the answers in the next chapter. For questions where you have to provide more than one response, give yourself credit only if you got all responses correct. Count up the number of correct answers and divide that number by 60. For instance, if you got 50 questions correct, divide 50 by 60 to compute your score of 83.3 percent. (Note that the test scores on a basis of 1,000 points, where 83.3 percent is a score of 833.) A passing grade is 74.5 percent (745). If you score above 80 percent, you are probably ready to take the real exam with a small cushion as a comfort factor. If you score above 90, you can probably be pretty confident of passing with no problems. A score of less than 80 percent is an indicator that you need more study or need to refine your exam-taking skills.

You may disagree with some of these answers. I have tested each line of code to ensure that the answers are accurate and I have provided reasoning for why each answer is correct or incorrect. In the unlikely (I hope) event that you do find a mistake, please drop me a line (mikemacd@tiac.net) or contact the publisher (certification@coriolis.com).

If you fail, you should have a pretty good idea of what questions snowed you. Use these as a guide for additional study and take the exam again. Whether you pass or fail, please drop me or the publisher a line and let us know.

Good luck.

Sample Test

Question 1

The following is an example of what type of declaration?

```
Dim frmCustDisplay As New frmCust
frmCustDisplay.Show
```

O a. Implicit

O b. Explicit

O c. Duplicit

O d. Omniplicit

Question 2

Consider the following code:

```
Dim sName()
ReDim sName(5)
sName(3) = "Smith"
Erase sName
```

Which of the following statements is true?

O a. All memory is released. The array **sName** needs to be declared again using **ReDim** before it can be reused.

O b. All memory is released. You can immediately reuse the array **sName** without further action.

O c. The first four elements of the array **sName** are initialized (to empty strings) but not all memory is released. You can immediately reuse the first four elements of the array but must use **ReDim** if you need to make the array larger.

O d. You will receive an error message.

Question 3

What does the **CancelUpdate** method of the **RecordSet** object do?

- ○ a. Cancels all updates to the database during the current transaction
- ○ b. Cancels all updates to the database since the last **Commit**
- ○ c. Cancels all pending updates from the **Edit** or **AddNew** operations
- ○ d. Cancels all previously committed changes to the database since the object was created (ODBCDirect only)

Question 4

You wish to download a file called EXAMCRAM.EXE from the \Public directory of the Coriolis FTP server using an InternetTransfer control called **Inet1**. Which code will accomplish this?

○ a.
```
Dim sURL As String
Dim byteBuffer() As Byte
sURL = _
"ftp://ftp.coriolis.com/PUBLIC/examcram.exe"
Inet1.OpenURL sURL
byteBufferData() = Execute "Retr", _
 "C:\examcram.exe"
```

○ b.
```
Dim sURL As String
Dim byteBuffer() As Byte
sURL = _
"ftp://ftp.coriolis.com/PUBLIC/examcram.exe"
byteBufferData() = Inet1.OpenURL _
    (sURL, icByteArray)
Open "C:\examcram.exe" For Binary As 1
Put #1, , byteBuffer()
Close 1
```

○ c.
```
Dim sURL As String
sURL = _
"ftp://ftp.coriolis.com/PUBLIC/examcram.exe"
Inet1.OpenURL(sURL, icByteArray)/SAVE _
 "C:\examcram.exe"
```

○ d.
```
Dim sURL As String
Dim Buffer As New Object
sURL = _
"ftp://ftp.coriolis.com/PUBLIC/examcram.exe"
Set BufferData() = Inet1.OpenURL _
    sURL, icByteArray)
Buffer.SaveToDisk _
    ("c:\examcram.exe")
```

Question 5

Consider the following code:

```
form1.Show
Dim newFrm As form1
UnLoad form1
```

What memory is used by the object(s) remaining in memory (do not consider the few bytes of overhead to reference the object variable)?

○ a. None. The form has been removed from memory.

○ b. None. Visual Basic will generate an error.

○ c. The memory used by **form1** is still being used.

○ d. The memory used by **newFrm** is still being used.

Question 6

You wish to force a user-defined error in your application and want to make sure that the evidence of prior errors is eliminated. How do you do this?

○ a.
```
Delete (Error)
Invoke (Error.18466)
```

○ b.
```
Err.Delete
Err.Number = 18466
```

○ c.
```
Err.Raise 18466
```

○ d.
```
Err.Clear
Err.Raise 18466
```

Question 7

Assume you have an ActiveX DLL that has not been entered into the Windows Registry. How do you correct this?

○ a. Use the ActXReg program supplied with Visual Basic.

○ b. Run RegSrv32 from the Start button's Run dialog.

○ c. Run RegEdit and locate the HKEY_LOCAL_MACHINE \Automation keys and insert the ActiveX DLL.

○ d. It is not necessary to register ActiveX DLLs.

Question 8

Consider the following code snippet.

```
Private Sub Command1_Click ()
    Dim lHandle As Long
    lHandle = Me.hWnd
End Sub
```

What is the variable **lHandle** equal to?

○ a. The handle of the Form object on which **Command1** is placed

○ b. The handle of **Command1**

○ c. The handle of the application

○ d. Zero

Question 9

Consider the following code snippet:

```
Public Sub MakeError ()
   Dim iVar As Integer
   On Error GoTo DivisionError
   iVar = 5 / 0
   Exit Sub
DivisionError:
   MsgBox Err
   Resume Next
End Sub
```

What will be displayed in the message box?

- ○ a. Nothing, the message box is never displayed
- ○ b. "Error: Type Mismatch"
- ○ c. "11"
- ○ d. "Division by zero"

Question 10

You have a Form named **form1** that includes a CommandButton named **command1**. Consider the following code snippet:

```
Private Sub Command1_Click()
   If TypeOf Me Is Form1 Then
      MsgBox "form1"
   End If
   If TypeOf Me Is Form Then
      MsgBox "form"
   End If
   If TypeOf Me Is CommandButton Then
      MsgBox "CommandButton"
   End If
```

What will be displayed in the message box(es)?[Check all correct answers]

- ❏ a. "form1"
- ❏ b. "form"
- ❏ c. "CommandButton"
- ❏ d. "User-defined Type Not Allowed"

Question 11

You wish to boldface the text on every command button on every open
form in your application. Which code snippet will accomplish this?

○ a. Visual Basic does not support this functionality

○ b.
```
Dim vButton As Variant
    For Each vButton In Controls
        If TypeOf vButton Is CommandButton _
            Then
                vButton.FontBold = True
        End If
    Next
Next
```

○ c.
```
Dim iButton As Integer
Dim iForm As Integer
For iForm = 1 to UBound (Form)
  For iButton = 1 to UBound _
    (Form.CommandButton)
    Form.CommandButtton(iButton).FontBold_
        = True
  Next
Next
```

○ d.
```
Dim vForm As Variant
Dim vButton As Variant
For Each vForm In Forms
    For Each vButton In vForm.Controls
        If TypeOf vButton = CommandButton Then
            vButton.FontBold = True
        End If
    Next
Next
```

Question 12

You have an application with the following code snippet:

```
#If Win95 Then
  MsgBox "Welcome Win95 user!"
#ElseIf Win32 Then
  MsgBox "Welcome Win32 user!"
#End If
```

The application is being run under Windows 95. Which message box will be displayed?

○ a. "Welcome Win95 user!"

○ b. "Welcome Win32 user!"

○ c. Both

○ d. Neither

Question 13

You have an application with the following code snippet:

```
Dim myVar As Integer
myVar = 3
If  myVar = 3 Then Debug.Print myVar
```

Where will the output be displayed?

○ a. On the Watch window

○ b. On the Intermediate window

○ c. On the form

○ d. None of the above

Question 14

Which of the code snippets will display the message box? (Assume the program is being run in the development environment.)

○ a.
```
Dim myVar As Integer
myVar = 1
If Debug.Assert myVar = 1 Then
    MsgBox "Assert"
End If
```

○ b.
```
Dim myVar As Integer
myVar = 1
If Debug.Assert myVar = 2 Then
    MsgBox "Assert"
End If
```

○ c.
```
Dim myVar As Integer
myVar = 1
Debug.Assert myVar = 1
MsgBox "Assert"
```

○ d.
```
Dim myVar As Integer
myVar = 1
Debug.Assert myVar = 2
MsgBox "Assert"
```

Question 15

Consider the following code snippet:

```
Dim myVar1 As Integer
Dim myVar2 As Integer
On Error GoTo Problem
myVar1 = "A"
On Error GoTo 0
myVar2 = "B"
Exit Sub
Problem:
Resume Next
```

What option would you have to set to force the program to break on the assignment to **myVar1**?

○ a. Go to the Tools|Options dialog and set Break On All Errors.

○ b. Go to the Debug|Watch dialog and set Break On All Errors.

○ c. Go to the Debug|Watch dialog and set a break expression of Not IsValid myVar1.

○ d. You would have to remove the error handling in order to force the program to break.

Question 16

Consider the following code snippet:

```
Option Explicit
Public myVar As Integer
Private Sub Command1_Click()
    Dim myVar As Integer
    myVar = 1
    myVar = Add(myVar, 4)
    MsgBox myVar
End Sub

Private Function Add(myVar As Integer, _
    b As Integer) As Integer
    myVar = 3
    Add = myVar + b
End Function
```

What will be displayed after the command button is clicked?

○ a. "4"

○ b. "5"

○ c. "7"

○ d. "Error: Ambiguous Reference"

Question 17

You want to add a menu to a form. What do you need to do?

○ a. Use Project|References and select Microsoft Menu Editor 5.0.

○ b. Use Project|Components and select Microsoft Menu Editor 5.0 to add the Menu control to the toolbox. Then, add the control to your form and customize it as required.

○ c. Select the Menu control from the toolbox, add it to the form, and customize it as required.

○ d. Select the Menu Editor from the Tools menu and customize the menu as required.

Question 18

To which of the following can you set focus? [Check all correct answers]

☐ a. Shape

☐ b. CommandButton that already has focus

☐ c. Slider

☐ d. MDIForm

Question 19

Examine the following snippet of code:

```
Dim myVar As String

myVar = "All good things"
myVar = Trim(Mid$(myVar, _
    (InStr(1, myVar, "o") + 33 / 11.5)))
MsgBox myVar
```

What is displayed?

○ a. "hings"

○ b. "ood things"

○ c. "things"

○ d. "d th"

Question 20

How can you debug an ActiveX EXE named MYTEST.EXE?

○ a. Run the ActiveX EXE project in the development environment. Open Microsoft Internet Explorer and open the MYTEST.VBD file.

○ b. Run the ActiveX EXE project in the development environment. Open a second instance of Visual Basic. Create a standard EXE to test methods of the ActiveX EXE.

○ c. Compile the ActiveX EXE. Create a new standard EXE and use Project|Components to add MYTEST.EXE to your project. Use the project to test the methods of the ActiveX EXE.

○ d. Just run the ActiveX EXE in the development environment as you would any other non-DLL project.

Question 21

Your Visual Basic application has initiated DDE communications with another application and asks the other application to send data. The VB application is known as what?

○ a. The Destination

○ b. The Source

○ c. The LocalDestinatiom

○ d. The LocalHost

Question 22

Which code snippet will return all settings from the Windows Registry related to the "Test" application's "Colors" key?

○ a.
```
Dim myVar As Variant
Dim myStr As String
For Each myVar In AllSettings
   MyStr = GetSetting (appname := "Test", _
      section := "Colors")
Next
```

○ b.
```
Dim myVar As Variant
Dim myStr As String
For Each myVar In AllSettings
   MyStr = Get (appname := "Test", _
      section := "Colors")
Next
```

○ c.
```
Dim myVar () As Variant
MyVar = GetAllSettings(appname := "Test", _
   section := "Colors")
```

○ d.
```
Dim myVar As Variant
MyVar = GetAllSettings(appname := "Test", _
   section := "Colors")
```

Question 23

You have a form with one command button named **Command1**. You enter the following code:

```
Private Sub Command1_Click()
    MsgBox 1
End Sub
Private Sub Command2_Click()
    MsgBox 2
End Sub
```

You then rename **Command1** to **Command2** and run the project. What will be displayed?

○ a. "1"

○ b. "2"

○ c. "1" then "2

○ d. "2" then "1"

Question 24

You have a form with an OLE Container control named **OLE1**. Which of the following will create an embedded object?

○ a.
```
CreateObject (OLE1, "c:\docs\mydoc.doc")
```

○ b.
```
OLE1.CreateObject (""c:\docs\mydoc.doc")
```

○ c.
```
CreateEmbed (OLE1, ""c:\docs\mydoc.doc")
```

○ d.
```
OLE1.CreateEmbed (""c:\docs\mydoc.doc")
```

Question 25

You have created a class module and are adding a property that is to be exposed for read/write access. What statement(s) will accomplish this?

○ a. **Property Get** and **Property Let**

○ b. **Property Let**

○ c. **Property Get**

○ d. **Property Let** and **Property Set**

Question 26

You are calling an API function that requires a string capable of storing 100 bytes of data. How should you declare the string to be passed?

○ a.
```
Dim myVar As String
```

○ b.
```
Dim myVar As String ()
```

○ c.
```
Dim myVar As String * 100
```

○ d.
```
Dim myVar As String * 101
```

Question 27

You have created a class module and added an event **Processing_Complete (duration As Long)**. How would this event be invoked?

○ a.
```
RaiseEvent Processing_Complete (1124)
```

○ b.
```
Event.Raise Processing_Complete 1124
```

○ c.
```
Raise Processing_Complete (1124)
```

○ d. There is no need to take special steps to invoke the event. When processing is complete, the change in value of **duration** will cause the event to be triggered automatically.

Question 28

Which of the following will add a **Node** object to a TreeView control?

○ a.
```
Dim myNode As Node
Set myNode = TreeView1.Nodes.Add _
   (,,"C:\","Root")
```

○ b.
```
Treeview1.Add ("C:\",tvwParent)
```

○ c.
```
TreeView.Node.Add ("C:\",tvwParent, _
   tvwTextOnly)
```

○ d.
```
TreeView.AddNode ("C:\", tvwParent)
```

Question 29

Which is not a property of the HScrollBar control?

○ a. **Value**

○ b. **Container**

○ c. **Picture**

○ d. **TabIndex**

Question 30

You have a TextBox control that is large enough to hold approximately 20 characters. What properties can you alter to be able to see all the text if 50 characters are placed in the control? [Check all correct answers]

❑ a. **HScroll**

❑ b. **ScrollBars**

❑ c. **Width**

❑ d. **ResizeAsRequired**

Question 31

Three command buttons on a form occupy the same location. After
the following code snippet has run, what is the order of the controls
from front to back?

```
Command1.ZOrder 1
Command2.ZOrder
Command3.Zorder 1
Command1.ZOrder 1
```

- ○ a. **Command2, Command3, Command1**
- ○ b. **Command1, Command3, Command2**
- ○ c. **Command3, Command2, Command1**
- ○ d. **Command1, Command2, Command3**

Question 32

You have a form that contains various controls used for data entry. How can you use that form to detect if the F1 key is pressed?

○ a.
```
Private Sub Form_Load()
    KeyPreview = True
End Sub
Private Sub Form_KeyDown(KeyCode As _
    Integer, Shift As Integer)
    If KeyCode = vbKeyF1 And Shift = 0 Then
        ' do something
    End If
End Sub
```

○ b.
```
Private Sub Form_Load()
    KeyPreview = True
End Sub
Private Sub Form_KeyPress(KeyAscii As _
    Integer)
    If KeyAscii = vbKeyF1 Then
        ' do something
    End If
End Sub
```

○ c.
```
Private Sub Key_Event (KeyANSI As Integer)
    If KeyANSI Is F1 Then
        ' do something
    End IF
End Sub
```

○ d.
```
Private Sub Form_Load()
    On KeyF1 GoTo Handle_F1
    Exit Sub
Handle_F1:
' do something
End Sub
```

Question 33

Assume you have three nested transactions in a Microsoft Jet **Workspace** object. You then issue the **CommitTrans** command twice followed by the **Rollback** command. What is the effect?

○ a. Changes made in the outer transaction only are rolled back.

○ b. Changes made in the inner transaction only are rolled back.

○ c. Changes made in all transactions are rolled back.

○ d. An error is generated.

Question 34

Assume you are creating an ActiveX Automation server with a property named **FontBold**. You have defined two constants, **axTrue** and **axFalse**, to manipulate the property and wish to expose these constants as data types via the table library. What Visual Basic keyword will help you accomplish this?

○ a. **Property**

○ b. **Let**

○ c. **Set**

○ d. **Enum**

Question 35

Assuming that **form1** is a valid form in your project, which of the following declarations in a class module is invalid? [Check all correct answers]

☐ a.
```
Dim WithEvents myVar As form1
```

☐ b.
```
Dim WithEvents myVar (3) As form1
```

☐ c.
```
Dim WithEvents myVar As New form1
```

☐ d.
```
Dim WithEvents myVar (3) As New form1
```

Question 36

Consider the following code snippet:

```
Dim myVar As Variant
Set myVar = Text1
Text1 = "cat"
myVar = "dog"
MsgBox TypeName(myVar)
MsgBox text1
```

What is displayed in the two message boxes?

○ a. "Variant" and "dog"

○ b. "TextBox" and "dog"

○ c. "String" and "cat"

○ d. "String" and "dog"

Question 37

You have written a database application. You have a form that allows users to update records. However, you are concerned that the user might close the form before all changes have been saved. In what event of the form could you place code to handle this?

○ a. **Deactivate**

○ b. **Terminate**

○ c. **UnLoad**

○ d. **QueryUnLoad**

Question 38

How do you add graphics to the ImageList control?

○ a. Use the **LoadPicture** function with the **Picture** property.

○ b. Use the **Add** method of the **Pictures** collection.

○ c. Use the **LoadPicture** function with the **ListImage** property.

○ d. Use the **Add** method of the **ListImages** collection.

Question 39

> You have written a procedure that accepts a variable number of
> arguments. The arguments can be of different data types. What Visual
> Basic sub procedure prototype will accomplish this?
>
> ○ a.
> ```
> Public Sub mySub (myVars ())
> ```
>
> ○ b.
> ```
> Public Sub mySub (myVars As Any)
> ```
>
> ○ c.
> ```
> Public Sub mySub (ParamArray myVars())
> ```
>
> ○ d
> ```
> Public Sub mySub (myVars As ParamArray ())
> ```

Question 40

> Assume you have a form with an array of command buttons. The com-
> mand buttons are named **CommandOK**. Which code snippet will dy-
> namically add a new command button at runtime?
>
> ○ a.
> ```
> Dim myVar As Integer
> myVar = CommandOK.UBound + 1
> Load CommandOK(myVar)
> ```
>
> ○ b.
> ```
> Dim myVar As Integer
> myVar = UBound (CommandOK) + 1
> Load CommandOK(myVar)
> ```
>
> ○ c.
> ```
> Dim myVar As Integer
> myVar = CommandOK.UBound + 1
> CreateObject (CommandOK(myVar), _
>     CommandButton)
> ```
>
> ○ d.
> ```
> Dim myVar As Integer
> myVar = UBound (CommandOK) + 1
> CreateObject (CommandOK(myVar), _
>     CommandButton)
> ```

Question 41

You have written an application and are using the Setup Wizard to create a setup program for that application. The Setup Wizard lists some controls in the Confirm Dependencies step that you did not use in your application (such as DAO objects). What can you do to ensure that extra files are not distributed with your application? [Check all correct answers]

- ❒ a. Go back to the development environment and delete any references and components from the toolbox that you are not using.

- ❒ b. Nothing. When you compile the application, the compiler will resolve all references and remove unneeded dependencies.

- ❒ c. Manually clear the checkboxes on the Check Dependencies and Data Access screens.

- ❒ d. Nothing. Visual Basic does not offer the granularity you need to remove unneeded components.

Question 42

You have created an ActiveX server to run on a remote computer. What project option causes the necessary files to be generated when the project is compiled?

- ○ a. None. Visual Basic 5 does not support the creation of remote ActiveX servers.

- ○ b. Nothing. Under DCOM, there is no difference between a local and a remote ActiveX server.

- ○ c. Remote Server Files.

- ○ d. DCOM Support.

Question 43

Which Visual Basic keyword will complete the initiation of a TCP communication session with the Winsock control?

- ○ a. **Accept**
- ○ b. **Connect**
- ○ c. **Listen**
- ○ d. **Open**

Question 44

Consider the following Visual Basic arithmetic operators:

Addition (**+**)

Division (**/**)

Exponentiation (**^**)

Modulus (**Mod**)

If a computation had all four type of operations, in which order would the operations be performed?

- ○ a. Modulus, then division, then exponentiation, then addition
- ○ b. Exponentiation, then division, then modulus, then addition
- ○ c. Addition, then exponentiation, then division, then modulus
- ○ d. The operators are evaluated in whatever left to right order they are encountered

Question 45

Suppose class A implements class B. Which of the following statements is true? [Check all correct answers]

- ❏ a. Class A cannot access the **Friend** procedures of class B.
- ❏ b. Class B cannot access the **Friend** procedures of class A.
- ❏ c. Class B must include all of the **Public** procedures of class A.
- ❏ d. Class A cannot obtain a reference to class B; there is a separate instance of class B.

Question 46

What Visual Basic statement supports using a VB procedure as a call-back procedure?

- ○ a. **CallBack**
- ○ b. **hInstance**
- ○ c. **Back**
- ○ d. **AddressOf**

Question 47

What is a **Bookmark**?

○ a. A flag you can set on the certification exam in order to return to a question.

○ b. A property that allows you to uniquely identify a record in a **RecordSet** object.

○ c. A property of the TextBox, RichTextBox, and other text-oriented controls that uniquely identifies a range of characters.

○ d. A property of the FileListBox indicating the last selected file name.

Question 48

Which Visual Basic controls have an **Index** property? [Check all correct answers]

☐ a. TextBox

☐ b. Data

☐ c. Shape

☐ d. Line

Question 49

Assume you have several controls with the same name (such as in a control array). What property can you use to differentiate them?

○ a. **AlternateName**

○ b. **Text**

○ c. **Tag**

○ d. **ID**

Question 50

Consider the following code:

```
Dim myVar As String
myVar = vbNullString
If myVar = NULL then
  MsgBox "String is null"
else
  MsgBox "String is not null"
End If
myVar = ""
If myVar = NULL then
  MsgBox "String is null"
else
  MsgBox "String is not null"
End If
```

What two messages will be displayed?

- ○ a. "String is null" and "String is null"
- ○ b. "String is not null" and "String is null"
- ○ c. "String is null" and "String is not null"
- ○ d. "String is not null" and "String is not null"

Question 51

When compiling to native code, what are valid optimization options?
[Check all correct answers]

- ❏ a. No Optimization
- ❏ b. Compile For Fast Code
- ❏ c. Allow Array Boundary Violations
- ❏ d. Create Symbolic Object File

Question 52

Which controls can be dragged? [Check all correct answers]

☐ a. Line

☐ b. CommandButton

☐ c. PictureBox

☐ d. TextBox

Question 53

Consider the following code:

```
Dim myVar1 As Variant
Dim myVar2 As Variant
Dim myVar3 As Integer
myVar1 = "1"
myVar2 = "one"
```

Which of the following statements is valid? [Check all correct answers]

○ a.
```
myVar3 = myVar1 + 4
```

○ b.
```
myVar3 = myVar1 + myVar2
```

○ c.
```
Dim myVar4 As Decimal
myVar4 = myVar1
```

○ d.
```
myVar3 = val(myVar1) + val(myVar2)
```

Question 54

You can use the keyword **Let** in assignment operations such as the following:

```
Dim myVar1 As Integer
Dim myVar2 As Integer
Let myVar1 = myVar2 * 3
```

Use of the **Let** keyword is optional and most Visual Basic developers do not use it. What is the implication of *not* using the **Let** keyword?

○ a. It is more efficient because Visual Basic does not have to parse an extra instruction each time the statement is evaluated.

○ b. It is less efficient because it causes late binding: the compiler has to build in logic to determine at runtime whether concatenation or arithmetic is being performed.

○ c. It is more efficient because Visual Basic can take advantage of an optimization technique known as Inference.

○ d. There is no difference at all.

Question 55

What does the ampersand (&) character do? [Check all correct answers]

❏ a. Type declaration character for data type **Long**

❏ b. Logical **Imp** operations on numeric data

❏ c. Concatenation

❏ d. Provides a visual cue of hot keys

Question 56

What is the result of the following computation?

```
Dim myVar As Integer
a = Int((-35 Mod 2) + 0.6)
```

○ a. 1

○ b. -1

○ c. 0

○ d. -6

Question 57

How do you find all of the fonts available to your application?

○ a. Enumerate the **Fonts** collection property of the **App** object.

○ b. Iterate the **Fonts** property of the **App** object using the **FontCount** property.

○ c. Enumerate the **Fonts** collection property of the **Screen** object.

○ d. Iterate the **Fonts** property of the **Screen** object using the **FontCount** property.

Question 58

Which of the following will find the city "Boston" in a **RecordSet** object?

○ a.
```
Seek "=", "Boston"
```

○ b.
```
Seek ("Boston", rsExact)
```

○ c.
```
Find "Boston"
```

○ d.
```
Find (rsExactMatch, "Boston")
```

Question 59

You have just opened a dynaset-type recordset. How do you determine the number of records?

○ a. Use the **RecordCount** property.

○ b. Use the **SQLCount** property.

○ c. Use the **MoveLast** method and then the **RecordCount** property.

○ d. Use the **MoveLast** method and then the **SQLCount** property.

Question 60

What control and property returns the IP address of the computer that is running the application?

○ a. InternetTransfer control and **IP** property

○ b. InternetTransfer control and **LocalIP** property

○ c. Winsock control and **IP** property

○ d. Winsock control and **LocalIP** property

Answer Key

1. a	21. a	41. a,c
2. a	22. d	42. c
3. c	23. b	43. a
4. b	24. d	44. b
5. c	25. a	45. a,c
6. d	26. d	46. d
7. b	27. a	47. b
8. a	28. a	48. a, b, c, d
9. c	29. c	49. c
10. a,b	30. b, c	50. d
11. d	31. a	51. a, b
12. b	32. a	52. b, c, d
13. d	33. c	53. a, d
14. c	34. d	54. d
15. a	35. b, c, d	55. a, c, d
16. c	36. c	56. b
17. d	37. d	57. d
18. b, c, d	38. d	58. a
19. c	39. c	59. c
20. b	40. a	58. d

Question 1

Answer a is correct. When the *New* keyword is used in a declaration, it specifies that the variable will not be created until it is first referenced. When you use *New*, you do not have to use the *Set* statement—the variable is created when first referenced. Implicit declaration actually means that the variable is allocated when it's first referenced and so, if you create a program without using the *Option Explicit* statement, Visual Basic implicitly creates variables whenever first referenced. Answer b is incorrect because explicit declaration refers to the process of creating variables when they are declared. Answers c and d are incorrect because there is no such thing as Duplicit declaration or Omniplicit declaration.

Question 2

Answer a is correct. The array *sName* is erased and all memory is released. In order to reuse the array, you need to redimension it using *ReDim*. Answer b is incorrect because you cannot immediately reuse the array without redimensioning it. Answer c is incorrect because the array is not merely reinitialized; all of the elements are deleted from memory. You cannot reuse the array at all until redimensioning it. Answer d is incorrect because you will not receive an error message.

Question 3

Answer c is correct. *CancelUpdate* cancels any changes pending as a result of an *AddNew* or *Edit* operation. Answer a is incorrect because **CancelUpdate** is not related to a transaction. Answer b is incorrect because **CancelUpdate** is not related to when the last **Commit** occurred. Answer d is incorrect because CancelUpdate does not undo saved changes to the database and the cancel operation has nothing to do with ODBCDirect.

Question 4

Answer b is correct. Using the *OpenURL* method of the InternetTransfer control, you can set the *URL* to a file within a directory on an FTP server—the file will then automatically be retrieved. The *icByteArray* argument specifies that the data will be retrieved as binary data. The data is placed into the byte array *byteBuffer*, which is then saved to disk in the last three lines of code. Answer a is incorrect. As written, the code will not run for several reasons. The OpenURL needs a variable in which to store the data retrieved. Because binary access was not specified, the method will attempt to retrieve the data as characters. The code then attempts to use an unnecessary **Execute** method with an invalid instruction—**Retr**. Answer c is incorrect because it uses an invalid argument ("/SAVE"). Answer d is incorrect because it attempts to create an object out of the result of the **OpenURL** method with the **Set** instruction and then uses a non-existent object (**Buffer**) to try to save the file to disk.

Question 5

Answer c is correct because the form is not removed from memory until it is no longer referenced by other objects. Because the variable *newFrm* still references the form, its memory space has not been reclaimed. To reclaim the memory, you have to set *newFrm* to *Nothing*. Answer a is incorrect because the memory used by the form has not been freed. Answer b is incorrect because no error will be generated. Answer d is incorrect because the object variable itself is only a reference to the form and does not take up any memory (except the four-byte pointer to the form's memory location).

Question 6

Answer d is correct. Use the *Clear* method of the *Err* object to clear out references to prior errors. Use the *Raise* method along with an error number to invoke an error. Answer a is incorrect because there is no **Error** object and no **Delete** or **Invoke** function that works on the **Err** (or **Error**) object. Answer b is incorrect because there is no **Delete** method and you can't invoke an error by altering the **Number** property of the **Err** object. Answer c is incorrect because, although it does invoke an error, it does not clear out any prior errors.

Question 7

Answer b is correct. Run RegSrv32, supplying the name of the ActiveX DLL as an argument. Answer a is incorrect because there is no ActXReg program. Answer c is incorrect because you should not attempt to manually enter the information into the Registry and there is no HKEY_LOCAL_MACHINE\ Automation key. Answer d is incorrect because you do need to register the ActiveX DLL in order to make it available to other applications.

Question 8

Answer a is correct. The *Me* keyword returns a reference to the form so the *hWnd* property is equal to the handle of the form. Answer b is incorrect because the handle of the command button is not returned. Answer c is incorrect because applications do not have handles (although they have instance pointers). Answer d is incorrect because zero is not returned.

Question 9

Answer c is correct. Division by zero creates an error causing a branch to the DivisionError label. The message box displays "11". The argument to the *MsgBox* function is *Err*. Because *Number* is the default property of the

Err object, that is what is displayed (the division by zero generates VB error number 11). Answer a is incorrect because a message box is displayed as a result of the division by zero error. Answer b is also incorrect because it implies that using **Err** as an argument in the **MsgBox** function results in a Type Mismatch error. It doesn't. Answer d is incorrect because the error text is not displayed. The default property—**Err.Number** is displayed. The trick is the question's apparent requirement that you memorize all of the VB error codes. Because this seems unreasonable, it is easy to jump to the conclusion that either answer b or d is correct. If you were not aware that VB uses the default property of an object when the object is referenced, you could jump to the conclusion that you would get a Type Mismatch error. Likewise, you might also be drawn to the "obvious" choice of answer d because that is text describing exactly what the error is. To correctly answer this question, you need to avoid jumping immediately to the "obvious" answer and instead read the question carefully and reason it out. Even though you may not know the exact error number generated by division by zero, answer c is the only answer provided that could be correct.

Question 10

Answers a and b are correct. The keyword *Me* returns a reference to the Form object and so both the first and second tests (that *TypeOf* is *Form* and *Form1*) evaluate to *True*. With the first *If* statement, the message box displays "form1". With the second *If* statement, the message box displays "form". Answer c is incorrect because **Me** does not return a reference to the command button. Answer d is incorrect because there is no error.

Question 11

Answer d is correct. The code iterates through the *Forms* collection and, for each Form, through the *Controls* collection. For each control that evaluates to a command button, the *FontBold* property is set to *True*. Answer a is incorrect because Visual Basic does support this functionality. Answer b is incorrect because only those command buttons on the currently active form would be changed. Answer c is incorrect because forms and controls are not maintained in arrays—VB maintains references to them in collections.

Question 12

Answer b is correct. The code is performing conditional compilation and examines the operating system variable. Win95 is not a valid environment constant, so the test fails. Win32 is a valid environment constant however, so the test evaluates to *True* and the message box is displayed. Answer a is incorrect because Win95 is not a valid compiler constant. Answer c is incorrect because it is not possible to perform two branches in an **If...Then...Else** construct. Answer d is incorrect because a message box is displayed.

Question 13

Answer d is correct. **The output will be to the Immediate window.** This question attempts to trick you into rushing to an obvious answer by providing option b, Intermediate window, which does not exist but is close (in spelling) to the correct answer. Don't rush through the questions! Answer a is incorrect because output is never sent to the Watch window. Answer b is incorrect because, as explained, there is no Intermediate window. Answer c is incorrect because the output of **Debug.Print** is always sent to the Immediate window—not the form.

Question 14

Answer c is correct. The *Assert* method causes execution to halt if the statement evaluates to *False*. Because the test evaluates to *True*, execution continues and the message box is displayed. Answers a and b are both incorrect because the assertion test is placed in an **If** statement, which is illegal and causes a compile error. Answer d is incorrect because the assertion test evaluates to **False**, causing program execution to halt.

Question 15

Answer a is correct. Go to the **Tools|Options** dialog and set the Break On All Errors option to force VB to break, even if an error is properly handled. Answer b is incorrect because the Watch dialog does only allows you to enter expressions to cause breaks. Answer c is incorrect because the expression is invalid. Answer d is incorrect because you do not have to remove error handling.

Question 16

Answer c is correct. Because *myVar* is defined as a local variable in both procedures, there is no error. The function *Add* ignores the first variable that is passed by making its own assignment. It adds the number 3 to the value of 4 passed from the *Command1_Click* procedure to return a result of 7. Answer a is incorrect because the value of **myVar** from **Command1_Click** is ignored. Answer d is incorrect because there is no variable naming conflict.

Question 17

Answer d is correct. Choose the Menu Editor from the Tools menu. Answers a and b are both incorrect because there is no such thing as the Microsoft Menu Editor 5.0. Answer c is incorrect because there is no Menu control.

Question 18

Answers b, c, and d are correct. Answer b is correct because you can set focus to a control even if it already has focus. Answer c is correct because you can set focus to a Slider control. Answer d is correct because the MDIForm object can receive focus. Answer a is incorrect because you cannot set focus to the Shape control.

Question 19

Answer c is correct. The interactions of the nested functions need to be reasoned to solve this. The code using the *Mid$* function finds a portion of the string. The second argument specifies that the first character of the sub-string is the position defined by the *Instr* function. This initially returns "6" ("o" is the sixth character in the larger string). Then, you are asked to add to it the result of 33/11.5, which returns 2.869. Add 6 + 2.869 and the result is 8.869. This gets rounded to 8 and so the sub-string starts at position 9 (the space between "good" and "things"). Because the optional length argument was omitted from the *Mid$* function, the calculation returns the rest of the string beginning at position 10. Then, the outer function (*Trim*) acts to remove any leading and trailing spaces, which gives the final result of "things". Answer a is incorrect because it miscomputes the result of the mathematical operations. Answer b is incorrect because it does not take into account the modification to the beginning position. Answer d is incorrect because it assumes the math operation will be rounded down.

Question 20

Answer b is correct. Because the ActiveX EXE is an out-of-process server, you need to create a second instance of Visual Basic to test it. Answer a is incorrect because you use Internet Explorer for ActiveX Document EXEs, not ActiveX EXEs. Answer c is incorrect because the ActiveX EXE is not a control that can be added via Project|Components. Answer d is incorrect because you need another application to test the ActiveX EXE, which is an automation server component.

Question 21

Answer a is correct. The requester of data in a DDE conversation is known as the Destination. Answer b is incorrect because the Source is the end of the DDE conversation that fulfills the requested data. Answer c is wrong because there is no such thing as a LocalDestination. Answer d is incorrect because LocalHost is a term used in TCP and UDP communications.

Question 22

Answer d is correct. Declare a variable of type *Variant* and then use the *GetAllSettings* function as shown to return all the Registry values for the given application and section. Answer a is incorrect because settings aren't maintained in a collection and it uses an invalid function (**Get**). Answer b is incorrect because settings aren't maintained in a collection. Answer c is incorrect because you should not declare the variable as an array.

Question 23

Answer b is correct. When you rename your control, the code in *Command2_Click* will run. Answer a is incorrect because the code in Command1_Click is ignored. Answers c and d are incorrect because there is no way for both message boxes to display.

Question 24

Answer d is correct. *CreateEmbed* is a method of the OLE Container control that creates an object from the specified file. Answers a and b are incorrect because they use the **CreateObject** function incorrectly. Answer c is incorrect because **CreateEmbed** is not a VB function, it is a method of the OLE Container control.

Question 25

Answer a is correct. You need to provide a *Property Get* to allow read access and then a *Property Let* statement to allow write access. Answer b is incorrect because you cannot use a **Property Let** statement alone. Answer c is incorrect because **Property Get** only allows read access. Answer d is incorrect because **Let** is used for data type variables and **Set** is used for object type variables. You cannot mix both of them for the same variable.

Question 26

Answer d is correct. You need to create a string at least one byte longer than is needed to allow for the null termination character. Answer a is incorrect because the string needs to be pre-allocated to the correct size. Answer b is incorrect because you cannot pass a string array when it is not expected by the calling function. Answer c is incorrect because it does not allow for the null character at the end of the string. This question could be a little tricky to answer because of its wording. One might reasonably assume that if the requirement were for a string long enough to hold 100 bytes, this would include the null termination character. However, the question specifies that the string is long enough to hold 100 bytes of data. It is not reasonable to assume that the termination character would be part of the data.

Question 27

Answer a is correct. Use the *RaiseEvent* function to invoke the event. Answer b is incorrect because **Event** is not an object and does not have a **Raise** method. Answer c is incorrect because **Raise** is used to invoke an error, not raise an event. Answer d is just plain wrong.

Question 28

Answer a is correct. A variable of type *Node* is created and then the *Add* method of the *Nodes* collection is used to add the node to the TreeView control. Answer b is incorrect because the TreeView control does not have an **Add** method. Answer c is incorrect because **Node** is not a property or method of the TreeView control. The control has a **Nodes** collection property. Answer d is incorrect because the control does not have an **AddNode** method.

Question 29

Answer c is correct. There is no *Picture* property for the HScrollBar control. Answer a is incorrect because **Value** reflects the current position of the scrollbar. Answer b is correct because **Container** returns a reference to the Container control. Answer d is correct because **TabIndex** reflects where in the tab order the control is.

Question 30

Answers b and c are correct. You can set the *ScrollBars* property to allow the control to scroll or set the *Width* property to make the control wide enough for the text. Answers a and d are incorrect because there is no **HScroll** or ResizeAsRequired property.

Question 31

Answer a is correct. A ZOrder of 0 (zero) places a control in front. If no ZOrder is specified, it is assumed to be zero. A ZOrder of 1 places a control in the back. After the first instruction, Command1 is in back. After the second instruction, Command2 is in front. After the third instruction, Command3 is moved to the back (Command2 remains in front). After the fourth instruction, Command1 is in back and Command2 remains in front. Answer b is incorrect because it assumes that a ZOrder of 1 places a control in front. Answer c is incorrect because there is no way for that configuration to occur. Answer d is also incorrect because the code does not execute in a manner to place the controls in that order.

Question 32

Answer a is correct. In order to process keys at the form level, you need to set the *KeyPreview* property to *True*. Then, you can detect non-ANSI keys (such as the F1 key) with the *KeyDown* event. Answer b is incorrect because the **KeyPress** event does not handle non-ANSI keys. Answer c is incorrect because there is no **Key_Event** event. Answer d is incorrect because you cannot handle key presses with an **On** condition construct.

Question 33

Answer c is correct. Any *CommitWork* or *Rollback* affects all transactions, even those already committed or rolled back, until all transactions have ended. Answer a and b are incorrect because the **Rollback** affects more than the one transaction. Answer d is incorrect because no error is generated.

Question 34

Answer d is correct. Use *Enum* to create an enumerated variable type. It will be added to the table library file and thus be available to other applications. Answer a is incorrect. You can use the **Property** statement (with **Get**) to expose properties in a class module to other applications, but they will not be added to the table library. Answers b and c are also incorrect because **Let** and **Set** act in concert with **Property** to allow updates to class variables—not what we are looking for.

Question 35

Answers b, c, and d are correct. Answer b is correct because Visual Basic does not permit the declaration of arrays with the *WithEvents* clause. Answer c is correct because use of the *New* keyword with the *WithEvents* clause is illegal. Answer d is correct because it attempts to declare an array and use the *New* keyword in conjunction with the *WithEvents* clause, both of which are illegal. Answer a is incorrect because the statement is valid.

Question 36

The correct answer is c. The *Variant* is originally a TextBox, but is then changed by the assignment in the fourth line. The prior line of code had changed the *Text* property of *Text1* by addressing the default property, which is what you would expect in the next line. But *myVar* is a *Variant* and its underlying data type changes in an unexpected manner in the fourth line. We see that in line 5 when the message box displays "String". The next message box displays "cat" because line 4 did not change the text box—it merely changed the underlying data type of the variable. Answer a is incorrect because **TypeName** never displays "Variant". It always displays the underlying data type. Answer b is incorrect because the underlying data type has been altered and is no longer "TextBox". Answer d is incorrect because the text box does not contain "dog."

Question 37

The correct answer is d. The *QueryUnLoad* is the last event before the *UnLoad* event and gives you the opportunity to cancel the close, prompt the user to save the changes, and so on. Answer a is incorrect because **Deactivate** happens right before a form loses focus (is no longer active). Answer b is incorrect because **Terminate** is not an event of the Form object. Answer c is incorrect because **UnLoad** is not a proper place to attempt to cancel a form close. For instance, if the user closes Windows, the **QueryUnLoad** event can be used to cancel that. You can't cancel that with the **UnLoad** event.

Question 38

The correct answer is d. *ListImages* is a collection that is a property of the ImageList control. Use the *Add* method to add graphics to the collection. Answers a and b are incorrect because there is no **Picture** property. Answer c is incorrect because the **LoadPicture** function does not work with the **ListImage** object.

Question 39

The correct answer is c. To declare a variable number of arguments, use *ParamArray*. Answer a could work in some circumstances (with some ingenuity) except that the function prototype does not list the data type. Answer b is incorrect because it will only accept one argument. Answer d is incorrect because the data type is **ParamArray**, which is invalid.

Question 40

The correct answer is a. The second line uses the *UBound* property of the control to determine the highest index number in the control array. That number is incremented. In the third line, the *Load* statement is used to create a new instance of the control. Note that the control is not visible when created—you need to set its *Visible* property to *True*. Answer b is incorrect because it uses the UBound function to determine the upper index of the number, which is invalid with arrays. Answer c is incorrect because it attempts to use the CreateObject statement to create the control, which is invalid. Answer d is wrong because it incorrectly attempts to use both the **UBound** and the CreateObject functions.

Question 41

The correct answers are a and c. When you create a Visual Basic project, VB adds some references and controls such as DAO objects. You may not use them. Answer a is correct because you can go back to the development environment and choose Project|References and Project|Components from the VB menu and clear any items that you are not using. Recompile the application and run the Setup Wizard again. Answer c is correct because you could instead manually clear the references from the Check Dependencies and Data Access screens. VB will then remove references to those files. Answer b is incorrect because you have already compiled the program (you cannot run the Setup Wizard if you have not already compiled your project). Answer d is incorrect because VB does offer you some granularity concerning the files that you distribute.

Question 42

The correct answer is c. Select Project|Properties, click the Components tag, and select Remote Server Files to produce an ActiveX server that can be run on a remote server. Answer a is incorrect because VB5 does support the creation of remote servers. Answer b is incorrect because you do not create additional files to support remote servers. Answer d is incorrect because there is no DCOM Support option.

Question 43

The correct answer is a. *Accept* is the statement used to accept an incoming connection request. Answer b is incorrect because **Connect** is the event that occurs when the communication session has been accepted. Answer c is incorrect because **Listen** is the method of the Winsock control that causes it to listen for communication requests—it does not complete a connection. Answer d is incorrect because **Open** is not supported in the Winsock control.

Question 44

The correct answer is b. Visual Basic has a predefined set of rules to determine the order of operations. Computations in parenthesis are performed first. Then, any exponentiation operations are performed followed by negation, division and multiplication, integer division, modulus, and addition and subtraction. If there is a "tie," operations are done from left to right. Answers a and c are both incorrect because they list operations in an incorrect order and would produce an inaccurate result. Answer d is incorrect because certain operations take precedence over others and are resolved in a left-to-right manner only if there is more than one operation of the same priority (such as two multiplication operations in the same computation).

Question 45

The correct answers are a and c. The controller of a class cannot see the *Friend* procedures of that class. When a class implements another class, it must include all *Public* procedures of the implemented class and those procedures become methods of the implementing class. Answer b is incorrect because class A can access the **Friend** procedures of class B. Answer d is incorrect because the implemented class can obtain a reference to the implementing class.

Question 46

The correct answer is d. You can use the *AddressOf* statement to pass the address of a VB procedure to an API function, which then uses the address to make a callback to that procedure. Answer a is incorrect because there is no such VB statement. Answer b is incorrect because **hInstance** returns the address of the application and is a method of the **App** object. Answer c is incorrect because there is no such VB keyword.

Question 47

The correct answer is b. You can use the *Bookmark* property to uniquely identify a record so that you can later scroll back to it or perform other operations on it. Answer a is incorrect because, although you can flag questions on the exam, it is not a Visual Basic function. Answer c is incorrect because there is no such property associated with text-oriented controls. Answer d is incorrect because you use the **FileName** property to return the selected file name.

Question 48

The correct answers are a, b, c, and d. All Visual Basic controls can be part of a control array. Control arrays are keyed by the *Index* property. The trick is to read the question slowly and understand it. The answers list two types of controls—the TextBox and Data controls can receive focus, the Shape and Line controls cannot. This can create confusion about the meaning of the question. Don't read something into the question that isn't there.

Question 49

The correct answer is c. The *Tag* property of a control can be used for any purpose that the developer sees fit. For example, the string can be used to differentiate controls. Answer a is incorrect because there is no **AlternateName** property. Answer b is incorrect because the **Text** property of controls is usually subject to modification by the user and many controls do not have a **Text** property. Answer d is incorrect because there is no **ID** property.

Question 50

The correct answer is d. Both *If* tests fail for a number of reasons. The first test fails because *Null* is a value that is really only applicable to data type *Variant*. To test a null string, use the constant *vbNullString*. Second, any comparison to null always returns false, even when the item being compared is null. That is why you need to use the *IsNull* function. The second test fails because the string is no longer a null string—it is an empty string. Answer a is incorrect because the two tests fail. Answer b is incorrect because the first test fails. Answer c is incorrect because the third test fails.

Question 51

The correct answers are a and b. No Optimization specifies compilation will take place with no optimizations such as Fast Code or Small Code. Compile For Fast Code specifies that compilation will optimize for speed at the expense of program size. Answer c is incorrect because there is no such option. However, there is an option called Remove Array Bounds Check. Answer d is incorrect because it is not a valid option even though there is an option to Create Symbolic Debug Info.

Question 52

The correct answers are b, c, and d because the CommandButton, PictureBox, and TextBox controls can all be dragged. Answer a is incorrect because the Line control cannot be dragged.

Question 53

The correct answers are a and d. Answer a is correct because the addition operation checks to see if the first *Variant* has a recognizable number format and, if so, adds it to the second number. Answer d is correct because it adds the value of the two variables together. The result of the first *Val* function is 1 and the result of the second is 0. Answer b is incorrect because VB looks at the first variable for a recognizable number format and, not finding one, attempts to concatenate the strings. However, the result is assigned to a numeric variable, which is illegal. Answer c is also incorrect because it attempts to declare a variable of type **Decimal**, which VB5 does not support. To create a decimal, you must use a variable of type **Variant** and use the **CDec** function to covert the number.

Question 54

The correct answer is d, there is no difference at all. The compiler examines the statement and the variable types and creates the same machine language or p-code instructions whether *Let* is used or not. Answer a is incorrect because the extra instruction is not actually part of the compiled executable. Answer b is incorrect because late binding refers to object resolution. Further, there is nothing inherent in the **Let** keyword that says the following operation is numeric and not concatenation. Answer c is incorrect—there is no optimization technique known as "Inference." The tricky part of this question is that most VB developers only vaguely know that **Let** can be used and have no idea of the impact of its use. I tried this question on four different accomplished developers and all "wanted" to select answer d but became intimidated. Three of the four opted for answer b.

Question 55

The answers a, c, and d are correct. Answer a is correct because the ampersand declares that a variable is of type *Long*. Answer c is correct because the ampersand acts as a concatenation operator. Answer d is correct because typing an ampersand followed by a character causes the character to be underlined, providing a visual cue that Alt plus the underlined character is a control's hot key. Answer b is wrong because the ampersand is not the **Imp** operator.

Question 56

The answer is b. The *Mod* operation returns -1 (the remainder after dividing -35 by 2). Adding .6 yields an intermediate computation of -.4. Using the *Int* function then converts the result to -1 because, with negative numbers, *Int* returns the first negative number less than or equal to -.4. Answer a is incorrect because the **Mod** operation returns a negative number. Answer c is incorrect because the **Int** operation rounds down. Answer d is incorrect because **Mod** returns the remainder portion of the operation.

Question 57

The correct answer is d. The *Fonts* property of the *Screen* object is an array of available fonts. The *FontCount* property of the *Screen* object returns the number of fonts in the array. Answers a and b are incorrect because **Fonts** is not a property of the **App** object. Answer c is incorrect because **Fonts** is not a collection.

Question 58

The correct answer is a. Use the *Seek* method of the *RecordSet* object followed by the search comparison argument and the value argument. Answer b is incorrect because the value being searched for is out of order and because there is no **rsExact** constant. Answers c and d are incorrect because there is no **Find** method.

Question 59

The correct answer is c. When you open a dynaset-type recordset, the *RecordCount* property does not contain a record count until all records have been accessed. You can accomplish this by using the *MoveLast* method to move to the last record. Answer a is incorrect because **RecordCount** is not accurate until all records have been accessed. Answers b and d are incorrect because there is no **SQLCount** property.

Question 60

The correct answer is d. Use the Winsock control's *LocalIP* property to return the IP address. Answers a and b are wrong because the InternetTransfer control does not have a property for the IP address. Answer c is incorrect because there is no **IP** property of the Winsock control.

Glossary

Accept—A method used by the Winsock control to accept a TCP communication.

Active client—A client capable of performing dynamic processing on the Internet within the Web browser via VBScript or ActiveX controls.

Active server—A server capable of performing server side processing on the Internet via ActiveX components.

ActiveX automation—Automation implemented via ActiveX technology. See also *automation*.

ActiveX component—An ActiveX EXE or ActiveX DLL. See also *ActiveX automation* and *ActiveX server*.

ActiveX control—Sometimes known as an OCX file or as an OLE control. ActiveX controls encapsulate functionality into objects that can be reused in development environments, Web pages, and so on. The CommonDialog control, for instance, is an ActiveX control.

ActiveX DLL—An ActiveX component implemented as a DLL. ActiveX DLLs are in-process servers and have a class object that exposes functionality of the ActiveX component. To use an ActiveX DLL, other applications create a reference to the class object and use its methods and properties to implement the services of the ActiveX DLL. See also *ActiveX component* and *ActiveX server*.

ActiveX Document DLL—An ActiveX DLL that includes user documents (but does not allow forms). See also *UserDocument*.

ActiveX Document EXE—An ActiveX EXE that also includes user documents (but does not allow forms). See also *UserDocument*.

ActiveX EXE—An ActiveX component implemented as an EXE. ActiveX EXEs are out-of-process servers and have a class object that exposes functions of the component. To use an ActiveX EXE, other applications create a reference to the class object and use its methods and properties to implement the services of the ActiveX EXE. See also *ActiveX component* and *ActiveX server*.

ActiveX server—An automation server implemented via ActiveX technology. See also *Automation*.

AddressOf—A Visual Basic operator that computes the memory address of a procedure. This is usually used when passing the address of a procedure in an API call, particularly in callback operations.

Alias—A keyword used in Visual Basic **Declare** statements to provide the real name of an API function when the name is illegal in VB or otherwise inconvenient to use. See also *Declare*.

ANSI—The character set defined by the American National Standards Institute. Defines a 256 character set in which each character is comprised of 8 bits.

Any—A keyword used in various declarations (**Declare, Function,** and **Sub**) in place of the data type where an argument can be of any data type. This forces VB not to perform type checking on the data type.

API (Application Programming Interface)—A library implemented via "exported" functions in a DLL that expose the library's services to other applications. Typical examples include the Windows API, the ODBC API, and others.

Append—In a VB **Open** statement, this command causes any updates to a file opened in sequential mode to be added to the end of the file.

arrays—(1) A method of declaring a Visual Basic variable to be part of a "list" that allows access to any of the elements via the array's subscript. Arrays may be multidimensional and may be either fixed (containing a fixed number of elements) or dynamic (containing a variable number of elements). (2) A Visual Basic function that creates an array by providing a comma separated list of values to a variable. X = **Array (8, 2, 1)** creates a one-dimensional array of variable X with three elements.

Assert—A debugging tool. VB provides **Assert** as a method of the **Debug** object, which tests that an argument is true and, if so, halts program execution.

asynchronous—A type of communication in which an object can send a request to another object and continue processing, without waiting for the first request to be completed. See also *synchronous*.

automation—A technology in which an application can expose its internal behaviors to another application. This is accomplished by allowing the "client" application to create objects or instances of the "server" application. ActiveX components provide automation services.

binary—(1) Consisting of two possible values, zero or one. Computers perform binary operations in which a bit is either on (one) or off (zero). (2) A VB keyword used in file open operations specifying that the file is opened in binary mode instead of text mode (sequential access).

bind—A method of the Winsock control to initiate UDP communications by binding the control to a local port. (Also see *early binding* and *late binding*, which refer to compiler operations.)

buddy control—A control that is paired with the UpDown control. The buddy control reflects the **Value** property of the UpDown control. For example, a TextBox control would display a number as the user clicks on the UpDown control. See also *BuddyControl* and *UpDown* control.

BuddyControl—A property of the UpDown control determining which control is the buddy control paired with the UpDown control. See also *buddy control* and *UpDown* control.

ByRef—Dictates that a variable being passed to procedure is passed by reference. In other words, the actual address of the variable is passed, allowing the procedure to alter the value of the variable. See also *ByVal*.

ByVal—Dictates that a variable being passed to procedure is passed by value, i.e., a copy of the variable is passed and not the actual address. The procedure cannot alter the value of the variable. See also *ByRef*.

CAB file—A file with the extension .CAB that includes compressed files. Use the Extract program to extract any files within the CAB file. See also *primary CAB file* and *secondary CAB file*.

Call Stack—In debugging, Visual Basic provides this method to view the call stack, which is a list of the procedures that have been called but not completed. Available from the View menu.

checkbox—(1) A box on a window or form with two possible values: checked (on or **True**) or unchecked (off or **False**). (2) On the certification exam, questions with only one correct answer provide checkboxes. (3) A Visual Basic control that provides a method for the user to choose one of two possible values: checked or unchecked.

child—(1) Depending on the context used, an object or process that is subservient to the parent or master. (2) A property of the **Node** object returning the first child node on a TreeView control. (3) Visual Basic refers to MDIForm objects as parents, and forms with the **MDIChild** property set to **True** as children. (4) Controls on a **UserControl** object are referred to as child controls.

class events—Events in a class module. Classes have only two built-in events: **Initialize** and **Terminate**. You can add events to your custom classes and invoke them with the **Raise** method.

class modules—A code module that encapsulates functionality and data so it can be reused. Other modules that wish to use the functionality of the class module must declare a reference to the class and then access the class' publicly exposed methods and properties. The class module includes all of the procedures and declarations within the class. A class module is saved with the extension .CLS.

Clear—(1) A method of the **Err** object that resets all of the properties of the object. (2) A method of the MSFlexGrid control to clear the contents of all cells.

Close—(1) A method used by the Winsock control to terminate TCP communications. (2) An event of the Winsock control invoked when TCP communications have ended. (3) A method of the Animation control that ends an AVI file that's in the process of being played. (4) A VB statement that closes the file number specified. If no file is specified, all open files are closed.

Collection class—A special Visual Basic class that allows like objects to be grouped together. Collections allow grouped items to be indexed and enumerated via keys. Unlike an array, collections shrink and grow as necessary. VB has a number of built-in collections such as the **Forms** collection and the **Controls** collection.

COM (Component Object Model)—(1) Microsoft's technology proposal to allow component-based development. See also *DCOM*. (2) Sometimes communications (serial) ports are referred to as COM ports (i.e., COM1, COM2, etc.)

Commit—An SQL command that forces the database to permanently save all updates made to the database since the last **Commit** or **Rollback**. Terminates a transaction.

Common Dialog control—An ActiveX control that provides a variety of dialogs such as File Open and File Save As.

compile—The process of creating an executable file.

component—An object that can be reused in development.

conditional compilation—A method of producing different executables based upon the environment. In Visual Basic, tests are done in code and preceded by a pound sign (#) to determine whether statements are included in the final executable.

Connect—(1) An event of the Winsock control that occurs when a communications link has been established. (2) An event of the **rdoConnection** object that occurs when a connection to the database has been established. (3) A property of DAO (Data Access Object) and RDO (Remote Data Object) specifying parameters to connect to a database.

Container—(1) A DAO object defining documents that describe the current state of databases, tables, and relations. (2) A Frame or PictureBox control. (3) A property of Visual Basic controls that describes the container control.

containment—This describes the process and hierarchy of objects and containers with DAO and RDO objects.

context-sensitive help—Help that is supplied by the application, and is pertinent to an action currently being performed by the user.

control—A Visual Basic object that can be placed on a form or MDIForm to perform various operations. Examples include the TextBox and CommandButton controls.

Controls collection—Every form object has a **Controls** collection, which defines the controls placed on the form. Visual Basic maintains these collections automatically. **Controls** is a property of the form object.

CreateObject—A Visual Basic function that creates and returns a reference to an ActiveX object, such as a Microsoft Word document.

DAO (Data Access Objects)—A collection of objects, properties, methods, and events that allows you to access and manipulate databases.

data bound controls—Controls that are bound to one or more columns in a database displaying the data from those column(s). Typically, the control is bound via a Data control.

Data control—A Visual Basic control that connects to a database and supports methods to scroll through a record set as well as to update, delete, insert, and so on.

DBCS (Double Byte Character Set)— A method of representing characters using 16 bits,

DBEngine—A DAO object, the **DBEngine** (database engine) object controls all other objects in the DAO hierarchy. There can be only one **DBEngine** object in an application.

DCOM (Distributed Component Object Model)—Microsoft's proposed standard for object interoperability. Under DCOM, any object can communicate with any other object regardless of the second object's location on the network.

DDE (Dynamic Data Exchange)— A method of communication between two objects, it was the original fulfillment of Microsoft's "document-centric" philosophy. This allowed users to manipulate documents without needing to know which application created the data on the document. DDE is accomplished by opening links between a DDE client and a DDE server.

debug—The action of testing a program to ensure proper performance and accurate results.

Declare—A Visual Basic statement used to declare a reference to a procedure in an external dynamic link library (DLL), such as those contained in the Windows API.

delegation—A methodology to achieve reuse in an application. In Visual Basic, classes can be combined so that the methods, properties, and events of one class can be used by another. This process is known as delegation.

DeleteSetting—A Visual Basic statement to remove a key from the Windows Registry.

dependency file—A required file that allows another file to operate correctly. Applications often require the functionality provided by dynamic link libraries. The DLLs are thus dependency files of the application.

Description—(1) A DAO and RDO property that returns a string describing a database error. (2) A property of the **ButtonObject** in a toolbar that sets the button's displayed text. (3) A property of the **Err** object that returns a string describing the most recent application error.

digital signature—An electronic "signature" attached to an ActiveX control packaged for distribution certifying that the control is safe to use.

Dim—A Visual Basic statement to declare a variable and allocate memory to the variable. It is short for "dimension."

dynamic arrays—An array that is not of fixed size. It can grow as needed and can be resized. See also *arrays*.

dynaset—A type of **RecordSet** object representing a dynamic collection of records from a database defined by a query or a table. If the data source is ODBCDirect, a dynaset represents an SQL cursor.

early binding—The process of creating a reference to an object in such a way that the compiler can pre-allocate space and resolve references to the object. Early binding represents a more efficient way to access an object, at the expense of the object being "fixed" (that is, the allocation is specific). See also *late binding*.

Empty—A VB keyword indicating that a variable of type **Variant** contains uninitialized data.

encapsulation—The process of placing data and functionality inside of an object, "hidden" from other objects. Other objects can only access the data and functionality via the object's exposed methods. Visual Basic implements encapsulation via class modules.

Enum—A Visual Basic keyword to create an enumerated variable. Enumerated variables can only be declared at the module level and their values cannot change. Other variables can be declared as the enumerated variable's type.

enumeration—(1) The process of iterating through a collection. (2) The process of creating enumerated variables. See also *Enum*.

Err—A Visual Basic object containing properties and methods to handle runtime errors.

event-driven programming—A method of application development in which the program reacts to events, usually initiated by the user. Code is placed in event procedures, which are defined by user-driven events such as **Click**ing on a command button.

Exam Preparation Guide—A guide available from the Microsoft Web site that gives exam-takers some idea of the specific subjects covered by the certification exam.

exam study guide—A study guide, such as this book, to help those who wish to take a certification exam. A study guide is meant to supplement, not replace, real-world experience and to steer the test taker to those topics most likely to appear on the exam.

Execute—(1) A DAO or RDO method that executes a SQL query for a **Connection** or **Database** object. (2) A method of the InternetTransfer control that performs an action such as retrieving a file from an FTP server.

exhibit—On the certification exam, a table or other display that is presented as background for a question. For the Visual Basic exam, this is most typically a block of code.

expose—To make visible to other objects. An object makes its methods and properties visible to other objects by making them public.

extender—A property of the UserControl that returns a reference to an **Extender** object. The **Extender** object holds those properties of the UserControl that are maintained by the container control (i.e., Form, MDIForm, and PictureBox) on which the UserControl is placed. Examples of these properties are **Top** and **Left**.

form modules—The procedures contained within a form, including the event procedures of all of the form's controls and any general procedures within the form. Also includes all declarations within the form. A form module is saved with the extension .FRM.

Forms collection—A collection of all Form objects within an application, maintained automatically by Visual Basic.

Friend—A type of declaration within a class module that makes the procedure declared visible (callable) by other modules within the project. **Friend** procedures cannot be called by controllers of the class (i.e., other class objects that have implemented the class).

FTP (File Transfer Protocol)—A protocol or "language" that two computers use to communicate between a client and an FTP server. FTP servers are typically organized by directories and allow files to be uploaded and downloaded.

functions—A type of procedure that returns a value to the caller.

GDI—Graphical Device Interface. A portion of the Windows API that controls graphical operations such as printing and drawing to the screen.

Get—(1) A Visual Basic statement to retrieve data from a file opened in binary or random access mode. (2) A qualifier to class procedures that exposes properties of class objects to other modules.

GetAllSettings—A Visual Basic function to retrieve all keys and settings for a given application from the Windows registry.

GetData—(1) A command that returns a graphic from clipboard. (2) A method of the Winsock control that retrieves data from the input buffer during TCP or UDP communications.

GetObject—This function assigns a reference to an ActiveX object from a file, such as a Microsoft Word document, to a variable.

GetSetting—A function to retrieve the value of a key for an application in the Windows registry.

GotFocus—An event that signifies a Visual Basic control received focus.

Group—A Visual Basic file that contains multiple projects, its file extension is .GRP. Sometimes called a *project group*.

Group by—An SQL statement to summarize data.

Having—An SQL statement to restrict the result set of an SQL query, based upon summarized computations.

hDC—(1) A handle to a graphical device context. (2) A property of a Form object, and several other Visual Basic objects and controls, that returns the handle to the object's or control's graphical device context.

HelpContext—The property of most VB controls that sets or returns the Help Context ID for the control.

Help Context ID—A string that acts as an index to a specific help topic within a Help file.

HelpFile—A property of most VB controls that defines which Help file to display when the user presses the F1 key.

hInstance—(1) A handle (pointer) to the address of an application. (2) Property of the **App** object that returns a handle to the application.

HTML (Hypertext Markup Language)—A standard cross-platform language to set up Web pages. HTML listings consist of tags, text, objects, and applets. The Web browser interprets the tags to display the Web page.

HTML tag—A tag within a Web page to control formatting or other aspects of the page's behavior. All tags are paired, which means that one tag defines the beginning of a block and the other tag defines the end of a block. Tags are enclosed in brackets. The tags <**B**> and </**B**> define that all text between them is to be boldfaced.

HTTP (Hypertext Transfer Protocol)—A protocol for communications on the Word Wide Web.

hWnd—(1) A handle to an object in Windows. (2) A property of the Form object and most Visual Basic controls that returns a handle to the object.

hyperlink—(1) A standard for navigating between documents on the World Wide Web. The object of the hyperlink is expressed as a URL (Uniform Resource Locator). (2) A Visual Basic object, with a **NavigateTo** method, to jump to a given URL. (3) A property of ActiveX controls, the **UserControl** object, and the **UserDocument** object, which returns a reference to the **Hyperlink** object.

Image—A Visual Basic control to display various graphical files such as bitmaps. This is not as functional as the PictureBox control but is more efficient.

ImageList—A Visual Basic control used in association with other controls to manage graphic files based on an index. Most typically associated with the TreeView and ListView controls.

Immediate window—A window available while debugging in the VB development environment that allows the display of data and the execution of procedures. The output of the **Debug.Print** statement is the Immediate window.

Implements—A Visual Basic statement that allows a class to implement the properties and methods of another class.

inheritance—A method of reuse allowing an object to derive all of the attributes of the class from which it is inherited. Visual Basic does not support inheritance.

in-process server—A server that runs in the same memory space as its client. See also *ActiveX EXE*.

Input—(1) A function that reads from files opened in binary or input modes. (2) A qualifier to the **Open** statement specifying that a sequential file is opened for read access only.

instancing—A property of classes in ActiveX EXEs and ActiveX DLLs that defines the availability of class objects to other applications.

instantiation—The process of creating an object from a class definition.

Internet download—A file or document downloaded from a server via the Internet or the process of downloading a file or document from a server on the Internet to a client computer.

Internet Transfer—A Visual Basic control that supports connections to FTP and HTTP servers. See also *FTP*, *HTTP*, and *Winsock*.

Kernel—A portion of the Windows API that provides Windows services such as File I/O.

KeyDown—An event that detects when a key is pressed. The event occurs before the key has been released. Applies to any VB control that can receive focus, as well as the Form object.

KeyPress—An event that detects when a key with an ANSI value is pressed. Any control that can receive focus can receive this event, but the Form object can receive it only if there are no visible controls on the form.

KeyPreview—A property of the Form, PropertyPage, UserControl, and UserDocument objects that dictates whether keyboard events for the object are invoked before keyboard events for the controls.

KeyUp—An event that detects the releasing of a pressed key. Applies to any VB control that can receive focus as well as the Form object.

LastDLLError—A property of the **Err** object that returns a system error code produced by a call to a dynamic link library.

late binding—The process in which an object reference cannot be resolved at compilation, forcing the compiler to add extra logic to resolve the reference at runtime. For instance, the following statement creates an object variable: **Dim myObject As Object**. Because the variable may later be assigned to any type of object (such as a control), the assignment will be done using late binding. However, the statement **Dim myObject As CommandButton** explicitly assigns the object variable, allowing the compiler to do early biding. Late biding is less efficient than early binding, but it allows for more flexibility in object assignment. See also *early binding*.

Let—(1) A Visual Basic keyword to assign a value to a variable, as in **Let A = 3**. Visual Basic does not require the use of **Let** in assignments. (2) A qualifier to property procedures within class objects that allows other modules to alter the value of a property.

license file—A VBL file distributed with ActiveX controls that allows the control to be used at runtime. If generated out of the setup process, the setup program will register the control in the Windows registry.

Listen—A method used by the Winsock control to listen for TCP communication requests.

ListImage—A member of the **ListImages** collection. A bitmap that can be used by other controls. See also *ListImages* and *ImageList*.

ListImages—(1) A collection of **ListImage** objects. (2) A property of the **ImageList** control that returns a reference to the associated **ListImages** collection. See also *ImageList*.

ListItem—A member of the **ListItems** collection consisting of text and, optionally, a graphic. Used in conjunction with the ListView control. See also *ListItems* and *ListView*.

ListItems—(1) A collection of **ListItem** objects. (2) A property of the ListView control that returns a reference to the associated **ListItems** collection.

ListView—An ActiveX control that displays items in one of four presentation formats similar to Windows Explorer: Large Icons, Small Icons, List, and Report. See also *View*.

LoadPicture—A function that loads a graphic into the **Picture** property of an Image control, PictureBox control, or Form object.

LocalPort—This property of the Winsock control sets the port that the computer will use to communicate.

Locals window—A window provided while stepping through code in Visual Basic to monitor all variables that currently have scope.

LostFocus—An event of most Visual Basic controls that occurs when the control no longer has focus.

MDI—Multiple Document Interface. See also *MDIForm* and *MDIChild*.

MDIChild—A property of the Form object specifying that the form is a child of the MDIForm object.

MDIForm—A Visual Basic object that contains all Form objects whose **MDIChild** property is set to **True**. These forms are said to be children of the MDIForm. When an MDIForm closes, all of the child forms also close. There can be only one MDIForm per project.

Microsoft Jet—An access method of the **RecordSet** object. Microsoft Jet is an engine that permits connections to relational databases, as well as to non-relational databases via ISAM (Indexed Sequential Access Method).

modal—A presentation format for forms. When a form is presented modally, nothing else can occur in the application until the form is closed.

modeless—A presentation format for forms. When a form is opened modelessly, other forms in the application can also be accessed.

MSComm—An ActiveX control that allows use of the serial or COM port to build communications applications.

MSVBVM50.DLL—The Microsoft Visual Basic runtime engine. Visual Basic applications require this DLL, although applications compiled to native code access it much less often than those compiled to p-code.

multiple-choice question format—Questions on the certification exam in which more than one answer can be chosen. You should check all correct answers. It is unclear whether partial credit is given if you do not select all of the correct answers. The certification exam will usually specify how many answers to choose.

named arguments—A convention for supplying arguments to procedures by explicitly naming them. This allows for using arguments out of order. To use named arguments, supply the argument name followed by a colon and equal sign, and then the value as in: **myFunction (fontface: = "bold", fontsize: = 12)**.

native code—A compilation option. Visual basic generates "native code" (machine executable instructions) rather than p-code, which requires a runtime interpreter.

Node—(1) A member of the **Nodes** collection. (2) An object on a TreeView control that can contain text and graphics. See also *Nodes* and *TreeView*.

Nodes—A collection of **Node** objects. See also *Node* and *TreeView*.

Nothing—A Visual Basic keyword to disassociate an object variable from an object. For example: **Set myObj = Nothing**.

Null—(1) The absence of data. (2) A Visual Basic keyword indicating that a variable of type **Variant** has a value equal to null—it contains no valid data. This is different than **Empty**. See also *Empty*. (3) A null string is not an empty string. It is a string with a value of zero. To pass a null string to a DLL function, use the constant **vbNullString**.

Number—(1) A property of the **Err** object indicating the current error number. (2) A property of the DAO and RDO objects indicating the current error number.

number types—The type of variable used for numeric data. The variable type determines the efficiency and accuracy of a number (these are reviewed in Chapter 2). Valid types are: **Integer, Long, Single, Double, Currency,** and **Decimal**. Although they are not used in numeric computations, the **Boolean, Byte,** and **Date** data types are numeric also.

Object—(1) A Visual Basic data type indicating the variable is of type **Object**, which can then be used to reference any other object such as a control or a class. (2) An instantiated item derived from a class definition. Objects include controls, forms, classes, and so on. See also *CreateObject* and *GetObject*.

Object Browser—A Visual Basic design time tool allowing the developer to browse type libraries for objects and definitions.

<OBJECT>—An HTML tag that denotes an embedded object such as an ActiveX control. See also *HTML* and *ActiveX control*.

ODBC—Open Database Connectivity. A widely adopted Microsoft standard that allows access to different databases in a common manner using SQL.

ODBCDirect—An access method of the **RecordSet** object that allows connection to a database using ODBC rather than Microsoft Jet. See also *Microsoft Jet*, *ODBC*, and *RecordSet*.

OLE—Object Linking and Embedding. An advancement of DDE that allows communication between objects. Now called ActiveX. See also *DDE*, *ActiveX*, and *Automation*.

OLE automation—A method of automating services of an OLE object to a requesting application. Now termed ActiveX automation. See also *ActiveX*, *DDE*, *ActiveX automation*, and *Automation*.

OLE container control—A Visual Basic control that allows you to add objects into a form. Using the OLE container control, you can, for example, embed a Microsoft Word document directly into a Visual Basic application.

OLE server—An object providing OLE Automation. Now called an ActiveX server. See also *ActiveX server*.

On Error—A Visual Basic statement to turn on or turn off error handling in an application.

Open— Visual Basic statement to open a file.

OpenURL—A method used by the InternetTransfer control to connect to a given URL (Uniform Resource Locator). See also *Internet Transfer*.

Order by—An SQL clause that sorts a result set by one or more columns.

order of operations—Defines in what order mathematical operations will occur in a compound expression. In general, computations within parentheses are performed first. Multiplication and division operations take precedence over addition and subtraction. After that, operations are performed from left to right.

Out-of-process server—A server that runs in its own memory space. An ActiveX EXE is an out-of-process server.

Output—(1) Specifies that a sequential file is opened for write operations. (2) A property of the MSComm control that sends a stream of data to the communications port.

overloaded function—A function that behaves differently based on the number of arguments and/or data types of the arguments it receives.

Panel object—A member of the **Panels** collection. A **Panel** object is part of a StatusBar control and can display various pieces of information such as the time or date. See also *Panels* and *Panels collection*.

Panels—A property of the StatusBar control that returns a reference to the associated **Panels** collection. See also *Panels collection*.

Panels collection—A collection of objects of type **Panel**.

<PARAM NAME=>—An HTML tag that can supply values used by an associated object.

ParamArray—Indicates that an argument is an optional array of type **Variant** and is comprised of an arbitrary number of values. Used with Visual Basic declarations.

parent—(1) A property of most Visual Basic objects that returns a reference to the form, container, object, or collection that contains the object. (2) In an MDI application, refers to the MDIForm object.

password—(1) A property of the InternetTransfer control indicating the password of a user when connecting to an HTTP or FTP server. (2) A property of DAO and RDO objects used when connecting to a database.

p-code (pseudo-code)—A compile time option that specifies what type of instructions will be generated. P-code requires a runtime interpreter for the application to run; native code does not.

PictureBox—A control used to display various graphics formats such as bitmaps. It is not as efficient as the Image control but has greater capabilities. The PictureBox control can also act as a container for other controls.

polymorphism—An object-oriented term indicating that an action can be used to communicate with different objects in a common manner to accomplish a common task. For instance, if an application wants to send the output of an object to a printer, polymorphic behavior dictates that the application can use the **Print** command without knowing or caring how the object accomplishes the task. Thus, an application can specify **Word.Document.Print** or **Excel.Worksheet.Print** and allow the object to handle the chore of sending the output to the printer.

primary CAB file—In the setup process for Internet packages, the primary CAB file contains all the components needed to distribute an ActiveX DLL, ActiveX EXE, or an ActiveX control, including the INF file, any licenses, and any files not contained in other CAB files. Also includes a reference to any secondary CAB files. See also *CAB file* and *secondary CAB file*.

Print—(1) A Visual Basic statement to send output to a form. (2) A method of the **Debug** object to send output to the Immediate window.

Private—A declaration object specifying the visibility of a procedure or variable.

process of elimination—The technique of making intelligent guesses to correctly answer an exam question. Often, if you are not sure of the correct answer, you can eliminate patently incorrect responses by looking for non-existent keywords, odd looking syntax, non-existent menu options, and so on. Usually, you can quickly eliminate two out of four responses, increasing your odds to 50-50.

project—A collection of modules, controls, and so on, comprising a Visual Basic application.

Project file—A file with the extension .VBP containing the definition of a project. See also *project*.

Property procedures—Procedures in a class module allowing the manipulation of class properties. There are three types: **Get, Let,** and **Set.**

PropertyBag—An object supplied by the container of an ActiveX control that allows behavior states to be saved between invocations of the object.

PropertyPage—The base object of an ActiveX control's property pages. You can use property pages to expose the properties of the control at design time.

Public—A declaration specifying that the procedure or variable is public (global) in scope.

QueryDef—A member of the **QueryDefs** DAO collection that defines a query via its **SQL** property.

radio button—(1) Known in Visual Basic as an option button. Provides mutually exclusive choices. (2) On the certification exam, questions with only one correct answer will be presented as radio buttons.

Raise—A method of the **Err** object to create an error condition.

Randomize—A function to seed the random number generator so that it does not generate repeating values. Also see *Rnd*.

RDO—Remote Data Objects. A collection of objects to manipulate remote ODBC data sources, as well as Oracle and Microsoft SQL Server databases.

RecordCount—A property of the **RecordSet** and **TableDef** objects that returns the number of rows in the result set.

RecordSet—A DAO and RDO object used to manipulate data in a database at the record level. There are several different types of **RecordSet** objects including table-type, dynaset-type, snapshot-type, forward-only-type, and dynamic-type. Also, a member of the **RecordSets** collection.

RecordSetType—Defines the type of **RecordSet** object. See also *RecordSet*.

ReDim—Resizes a dynamic array. Can also be used declaratively, but this is not recommended as it can lead to hard-to-find bugs.

RemoteHost—A property of the Winsock control that defines the name of the computer acting as the remote host (TCP and UDP communications) or the IP address of the computer acting as the remote host for TCP (TCP only).

RemotePort—A property of the Winsock control that defines the port on which the remote host listens for data.

Resume—A VB statement controlling how a Visual Basic application should proceed after an error condition has been handled.

reuse—An object-oriented technique to reuse previously written and tested objects to make code more efficient. Inheritance is the most powerful reuse technique, but Visual Basic does not support inheritance. VB does support a more indirect method known as delegation. See also *delegation* and *inheritance*.

Rnd—A Visual Basic function to generate a random number. See also *Randomize*.

Rollback—A SQL statement that discards all changes made to a database since the last **Commit** or **Rollback**. See also *Commit*.

runtime engine—The MSVBM50.DLL file that provides support functions for applications and runtime interpretation functionality for programs compiled to p-code.

SaveSetting—A function to save a key value in the Windows Registry.

Screen object—A VB object representing the monitor screen. It provides a number of methods to change the mouse pointer, and so on.

scripting and initialization safety—Ensuring that properties of an ActiveX control embedded in a Web page can't inadvertently or maliciously be altered to cause damage to a client computer.

SDI (Single Document Interface)—An application in which all forms are opened independent of one another. If one form closes, other forms remain open. See also *MDI*.

secondary CAB files—In an Internet setup package, a CAB file that contains components required to make the files packaged in the primary CAB file functional. The secondary files are provided and digitally certified by Microsoft. Typical components include the runtime engine: MSVBM50.DLL. See also *CAB files* and *primary CAB files*.

Select—(1) Part of a **Select Case** conditional VB statement to branch according to the value of a variable. (2) A SQL statement to retrieve data from the database.

SendData—A method of the Winsock control to send data to a remote computer.

Set—(1) An assignment operator for object variables. Assigns an object to a variable. (2) A qualification for a class procedure declaration that allows a variable of type **Object** to be assigned. See also *Let* and *Get*.

SetFocus—A method that allows a control to set focus to itself.

Setup Toolkit—A Visual Basic-supplied toolkit that helps you develop a setup program to distribute VB projects.

Setup Wizard—A VB-supplied aid to assist in the use of the Setup Toolkit.

Slider—An ActiveX control that can be used to set or monitor a value.

snapshot—A type of **RecordSet** object used for static data. It is more efficient than the dynaset but typically does not allow rows to be altered (some ODBCDirect drivers allow a snapshot to be updated). It is most often used to provide lookup values for reports.

Source—A property of the DAO **Err** object that returns the source of the most recent error.

Space$—A function to pad a string with spaces.

SQL (Structured Query Language)—Used to access and manipulate relational databases.

standard EXE—A Visual Basic project type that generates a standard executable file.

standard modules—A file with the extension .BAS that contains declarations and procedures.

StateChanged—An event in the InternetTransfer control that occurs whenever there is a change in the state of communications, such as when a link has been established.

static—A declaration for variables and procedures. When used to declare a procedure, all variables within the procedure retain their values between invocations of the procedure. When used to declare a variable (valid only with procedures), causes the variable to retain its value between invocations of the procedure.

StatusBar—An ActiveX control that provides panels to display information such as date and time.

Subs—A declaration for a sub procedure. Sub procedures do not return values.

synchronous—A method of communication that requires the caller or client to wait until the request has been completed before continuing execution. See also *asynchronous*.

TabIndex—Sets or returns the tab order for controls on a form or user control.

table-type recordsets—A type of **RecordSet** object that manipulates rows from a single table.

TCP—Transfer Control Protocol. The "language" by which computers communicate across the Internet.

ToolTip—A short phrase that indicates what an object does. It is displayed at runtime when the user pauses the mouse pointer over a control whose **ToolTipText** property has been set.

Transaction—(1) A logical unit of work (LUW) in a database. A series of actions that can be rolled back or committed with the **Commit** or **Rollback** command. See also *Commit* and *Rollback*. (2) A property of RDO objects that defines whether a database supports transactions.

TreeView—An ActiveX control used to display graphics and text hierarchically using **Node** objects. See also *Node* and *Nodes*.

type library—A file containing automation descriptions of objects, such as enumerated variables, as well as the objects' properties, events, and methods. Type library files have an extension of .TLB. Object libraries, ending with an extension of .OLB, contain multiple type libraries.

UDP—A protocol that does not require two computers to be continuously connected in order to communicate. Supported by the Winsock control. See also *TCP* and *Winsock*.

Unicode—Sometimes called wide character, a character set format comprised of 16 bits, native to Windows NT and used internally by Visual Basic 5.

UpDown—An ActiveX control to "spin" through a series of values by clicking on up or down arrows. The UpDown control is paired with another buddy control to display the current value. See also *buddy control* and *BuddyControl*.

URL ()—An address of a computer on the Internet.

User—A DAO object representing a user profile describing a set of permissions to the database.

UserDocument—An object, similar to a form, used by ActiveX Document EXEs and ActiveX Document DLLs to present a user interface inside of a Web browser.

UserName—(1) A property of the InternetTransfer control that sets the user ID when accessing a Web server or an FTP server. (2) A property of the **Workspace** object that sets or returns the name of a user or group of users in DAO operations. (3) A property of the RDO **rdoEnvironment** object that defines the user name to the database.

variable accuracy—The ability of a variable to maintain numeric accuracy across computations. Generally, the larger the data type, the more accurate the result, but at the expense of performance.

variable defaults—The default value of variables when they are initialized. For numeric data types, the value is zero. For strings, it is an empty string. For booleans, the default is **False**.

variable precision—The capability of a variable to maintain decimal accuracy (i.e., the number of decimal places that can be accurately represented).

variable promotion—Refers to the process by which Visual Basic increases the size of a temporary variable as needed during computations. Visual Basic will use the smallest data type possible.

variable scope—Refers to the visibility of a variable through a project as defined when the variable was declared.

variables—A named memory location where Visual Basic stores values. Variables have different data types that dictate what types of information they can hold.

Variant—A special type of variable with a data type is **Variant,** but it can have any underlying data type. The data type **Variant** is Visual Basic's default for an undeclared variable type.

Variant arrays—An array of type **Variant.**

VBScript—A scripting language similar to Visual Basic for Applications (VBA), used in Web pages to create applets that run on a client computer.

View—A property of the ListView control that determines how items will be displayed. See also *ListView.*

Visual Basic data types—Visual Basic variables have data types that dictate what type of data they can store. This includes **String** for character data, **Variant** for varying data types, and a number of different numeric data types. See also *Number types, variables,* and *Variant.*

Visual Basic operators—Symbols or actions that perform operations on variables, such as addition, which is represented by the plus sign, and concatenation, which is represented by the ampersand character.

watch expressions—Expressions defined in the Visual Basic debugging environment. You can constantly monitor the values of variables or expressions when stepping through code, or instruct Visual Basic to break when an expression evaluates to true.

Watch window—The window used to monitor variables.

What's This Help—A method of providing short (usually a sentence or two) snippets of context-sensitive help. See also *WhatsThisMode.*

WhatsThisMode—A method of the Form and MDIForm object that invokes What's This Help. The mouse pointer turns into a question mark and the user can click on an object to view a short snippet of help text.

Where—A clause of the SQL **Select** statement restricting the result set by specifying filter conditions.

wide character set—See *Unicode*.

Winsock—An ActiveX control that provides TCP and UDP services to a Visual Basic application. See also *TCP*, *UDP*, and *InternetTransfer*.

Workspace—A DAO object that defines a database session including whether the source will be ODBCDirect or Microsoft Jet. The object contains the **Connections**, **Databases**, **Groups**, and **Users** collections.

WWW (World Wide Web)— A portion of the Internet that presents a graphical interface to display documents with a Web browser. WWW documents typically support point-and-click navigation via hyperlinks. Web servers are known as *HTTP servers*. See also *HTTP*, *InternetTransfer*, *TCP*, *UDP*, and *Winsock*.

ZOrder—A method of VB objects that specifies the order in which objects appear from front to back. If a **ZOrder** of 1 is specified, the object is placed at the back of all other objects. If 0 is used, then the object is placed in front.

Index